EXPECT A MIRACLE
MY LIFE
AND MINISTRY
ORAL ROBERTS
AN AUTOBIOGRAPHY

OLIVER
NELSON

THOMAS NELSON PUBLISHERS

Nashville • Atlanta • London • Vancouver

Published in Nashville, Tennessee, by Thomas Nelson, Inc., Publishers, and distributed in Canada by Word Communications, Ltd., Richmond, British Columbia.

The Bible version used in this publication is The King James Version of the Holy Bible.

The photographs that appear in this book are the property of Oral Roberts, Oral Roberts University, and Oral Roberts Evangelistic Association and are used with permission.

Library of Congress Cataloging-in-Publication Data

Roberts, Oral.
    Expect a miracle / Oral Roberts.
      p.   cm.
    ISBN 0-7852-7752-8
    1. Roberts, Oral. 2. Evangelists—United States—Biography. 3. Healers—United States—Biography. I. Title.
    BV3785.R58A3 1995
    269'.2'092—dc20
    [B]   95-2787
                                                              CIP

Printed in the United States of America.

3 4 5 6 — 00 99 98 97

CONTENTS

PART 4: ORAL ROBERTS UNIVERSITY

PART 5: OUR CHILDREN—THEIR TRAGEDIES AND TRIUMPHS

PART 6: NOT SO WILD A DREAM

INTRODUCTION

TO EMBARK on a life of ministry is no easy task, I have found—particularly having a healing ministry and building a university. So why did I do it? Simply because God told me to do it.

If there's a major conviction in my life that sums up how I've accomplished what I have, it is this: God speaks to those who will listen, and when we hear and obey His voice, He in effect becomes the Head Partner with us in the endeavor.

I have also discovered that when someone believes that God does speak to people, and then makes a decision not only to listen but also to obey His voice, some type of divine calling inevitably comes with that commitment.

This conviction that God speaks to me, and that I have no choice but to obey when He does, has led me into a life of controversy. But had I not had this conviction, I don't believe I could ever have scaled the mountain of my calling. *Hope* was not enough by itself. *Compassion* to see others healed and delivered was not enough. *Drive*, *ambition*, and *education* were not enough. I had to know beyond a shadow of a doubt that I heard Him speak and none other. Then the dream became possible of fulfillment.

I think of a particular story as I reflect on my calling from God to take His healing power to my generation. Years and years ago during the old Morse code days, there was a job open for people who knew the dots-and-dashes system. Many had come to apply for the job, and all were waiting in the outer office to hear if they had gotten it. After a while, a young man came in, and as he entered the door, he stopped and listened, for he heard the dots and dashes. He looked around at the other applicants, and they were all talking. So he walked right across the room and through a door into the next office. After a few minutes, he came out and said, "You can all go home. I've got the job."

They said, "What do you mean? You just got here. We've been waiting all morning."

He said, "Didn't you hear the dots and dashes saying, 'Do you read me? Do you read me? If you can read this, come in. You have the job'? Well, I knew the dots and dashes. I was prepared, I was listening, and I went in. I now have the job. You can go home."

You might say that Oral Roberts got the job because I was listening! All my life I've tried to listen to a higher call. At first I didn't associate it with God. I vividly recall the time, early in my life, when my own dream for myself failed. That's when I turned my full attention to listen to what God Himself was saying to me, and it was confirmed through others. That was the beginning of a stirring new life for me.

I have lived seventy-seven years at this writing, more than a third of the history of this nation (which began with the inauguration of our first president, George Washington, in 1789). I have lived under fifteen different presidents. My healing ministry of forty-eight continuous years spans nearly one-fifth of the life of this country. I have conducted approximately three hundred healing crusades, given thousands of sermons and speeches, prayed for the healing of the sick in person in forty-six states in the U.S. and in seventy nations in all continents, and built a university and a medical center. I have known and felt America, as well as the world, as few have.

And after preaching face-to-face to many millions, and praying for more than 1.5 million sick people individually by the laying on of hands, I can testify that every person is sick, in one way or another, and that person won't be made whole without good medical science plus a miracle from God. God's healing streams are to flow together.

Something has to give in this real world we live in. In my experience, I had to give up my way. I had to come to the end of myself. I had to look to a Higher Power, Who at first seemed a billion miles away, if He existed at all.

Once I never had a thought about miracles. I thought success in life depended totally on me, what friends I could get, what dreams and opportunities I could make for myself, and how I could use my energy and my abilities to achieve my dreams.

Papa was a preacher and my mother prayed for the sick when called upon, but I saw nothing in the supernatural realm that I could relate to for my life and destiny. Few young men had more ambition or higher goals than I had, or with more limited opportunity to lift myself by my own bootstraps.

I lived my life by going my way until the dreaded disease of tuberculosis struck me down before the discovery of antibiotics, and before I knew there was a possibility of a miracle of healing. The idea of miracles had never crossed my mind.

Had anyone told me by far-reaching sight that I would become a helpless young man, confined to a bed for 163 desperate days with the terminal illness of my mother's people, the Cherokee Indians of Oklahoma, and that I would be raised up by a miracle and given a call from God, I would have laughed in his face.

But my family not only believed in doctors, but also believed in miracles. I've never grown weary of thanking God for my family— my parents, my two brothers and two sisters (three of whom are still living)—who played a large part in my miraculous healing and recovery to preach the gospel and to obey the Voice that spoke to me:

"You are to take My healing power to your generation; and someday, you are to build Me a university based on My authority and on the Holy Spirit."

The most important thing God wanted me to learn was to so sharply put Jesus into my focus that He would truly be the center of all my thoughts, my dreams, my plans, my accomplishments, my destiny, and any legacy I might leave behind.

I discovered God is a *Now* God to me. I learned He is never far away or shrouded in the mist of indefiniteness. He was and always is here with me. I sought to reach people for Christ and to get sick people to see the same thing, to feel His "nowness."

And that's what my life and my healing ministry have been all about the past exciting forty-eight years. I may say things in my autobiography you have not heard before, things you have not read or seen in the media, things that haven't registered in your thoughts yet. You may wonder at first at some of the slogans concerning miracles I've come up with. Until you read my whole story, you may think I've gone off the deep end.

What you are about to read may be as strange and as controversial a story as you have read in your lifetime. You could also find the miracle you've always wanted whether, like me, you've ever realized it or not.

I have never felt myself perfect in what I came to know was God's calling on my life and ministry. I identify with what the apostle Paul wrote: "For now we see through a glass, darkly; but then face to face: now I know in part; but then shall I know even as also I am known" (1 Cor. 13:12).

I can't save or heal or be a perfect example to anyone. I am a mortal man. I make mistakes and have many shortcomings. But I also know that after God deals with me long enough concerning doing something for Him, and I have tested it out, then I am to undertake doing it in His Name. I will not let opportunity slip. I believe we've got to think ten years ahead and work backward. That's the way I've lived my life.

To be strong, to be a leader, to obey God with all of your understanding and ability, you need a considerable ego. I discovered I could not afford to lose my sense of self-worth, to get into self-pity, or to be whining and complaining all the time. I had to let my ego function.

Of course, there are times I am assailed by doubts, but I made up my mind a long time ago to cultivate the ability to *doubt my doubts and believe my beliefs*. In fact, I made that one of my vows to God.

The road of life is strewn with the lives of men and women who let their doubts defeat their faith. God said, "The just shall live by faith" (Heb. 10:38).

Live by their faith, not by their doubts.

Yet faith begins with doubt. That is, you can't just accept something the first time it comes around. You have to doubt it until your spirit and mind can check it out according to God's Word and the leading of the Holy Spirit, and you have to seek evidence—proof in the world you live in—that you have a firm base of reality to stand on. Then, and then only, can you doubt your doubt and go into faith that is an *inner knowing* that God is in it. It is something God Himself has willed for you to be and to do.

All my life I have felt there is so much yet for me to do and much of it so daring that it seemed the mountain was too high to climb. Once when I was a young pastor—just twenty-three years old—a lady in our church came to Evelyn and me and told us of a dream she'd had. In the dream, all of us in the church were climbing a mountain. As we would grow tired, there would be a resting place. Everybody would sit down to rest, except me.

Each time I started to sit down, the group said to me, "Oh, no, Brother Roberts, you can't sit down. You have to keep climbing." She said that I looked so tired, but no one would let me rest. I had to keep climbing.

We climbed and climbed. Finally, when we were nearing the top of the mountain, even though the rest of them were stopping to rest, they still wouldn't let me stop. They said, "Brother Roberts, you've got to go on until you reach the top."

When we left that church to pastor in another city, in bidding us good-bye, this lady said, "Remember the dream God gave me, Brother Roberts. In all the years ahead of you, you'll come to understand it's very real for your life and ministry. You can never stop."

There has not been a year since then that I have failed to think of that dream or that Evelyn has not reminded me of it, particularly when the climbing got rough and even dangerous. Every time I wanted to slack off or to sit down and rest and let the world go by, I would hear in my spirit: "The people will not let you stop. *They* can stop and rest, but that's not for you. You've got to keep on climbing, no matter how tired or weary you become or how hard the climb becomes. You must scale the mountain."

Whether I have done that is for others to decide. All I can say is the mountain-climbing spirit has driven me on . . . and on . . . and on.

Maybe someday I'll reach the top of the mountain. Then I can rest. But I suspect that will be on the other side.

With that, I now want to tell you the full story of my life and ministry, one filled with controversy, attempts on my life, family tragedies, healings and miracles, mistakes, failures, and triumphs. I also want to set the record straight.

It all began with Mama.

PART 1

"WE'LL CALL HIM ORAL"

CHAPTER 1

"WE'LL CALL HIM ORAL"

MAMA WAS only five feet tall, but she was Indian and had eyes of steel that could look right through you and drive her words into your memory forever. The most direct impression she made on me was one day after we had moved to Ada, Oklahoma, near where I was born, to live for a few months while Papa was building a church there. While I was at school, a gang of little boys had closed in on me and heckled me to talk so they could get a good laugh. I had been born a stutterer, and they loved to hear me stammer my words. I burst through them and ran home with them at my heels, yelling and taunting me.

Mama heard and saw us coming, and she ran out to the gate to meet us. After shaming the boys and sending them away, she took me into the house, set me on her lap, and for the first time told me the story that she would recall to me over and over in the years to come.

She told me how one fateful evening, she was called to pray for a neighbor's child. Back then in Pontotoc County, Oklahoma, your closest neighbor could be three or four miles away so they sent a runner for her. When he arrived, he said, "The doctor says little Francis Engles won't live through the night with this pneumonia. Sister Roberts, you must come and pray for him."

Mama told me she knew she had to get there in a hurry, but she was pregnant with me at that time, so she cut through the fields. On her way, a storm came up with loud thunder and terrible lightning. The rain started to fall, and it drenched her. She didn't know whether to turn back or go on. As she hesitated there in the woods, the storm suddenly was over, and to her surprise, it grew quiet all around her. Soon she discovered she was standing near a barbed wire fence. In those days, the fence had to be strong enough and the barbs had to be sharp enough to keep the cattle and horses of the Oklahoma ranches and farms in their proper boundaries. Not only could an animal that tried to force its way through be cut to pieces, but the barbs could cut and bloody a person as well.

Although heavy in body from carrying me, Mama lifted the strand of one of the wires, pressed her foot down on the one just below it, and literally began crawling through, regardless of how easy it was to get dangerously entangled in the sharp barbs.

After she crawled through, something stopped her, and she felt the presence of God. I'll never forget the words she told me she said to God that evening: "Oh, God, the child I'm carrying in my body will be my last. My other children have black eyes, but I'm asking that You will give me a son with blue eyes and black hair. And if You'll heal my neighbor's child tonight when I pray for him, I'll give You my son when he's born. I vow this, Lord, if You only hear me."

While I was sitting on her lap that day as she was telling me this story, she spoke softly, and gentle tears ran down her cheeks. Her mind and heart were back at that place.

She looked at me and said, "Oral, God answered my prayer for little Francis and for you. Soon after that, you were born." Then Mama told me how Papa's niece, Minnie Lewis, had been there to help her at the time of birth of all five of her children. When I was born, Mama told her she could name me. Instantly, she said, "We'll name him Granville Oral, and we'll call him Oral."

At the time, Mama didn't have the slightest idea that *oral* meant "spoken word," but she told me that day that I would preach the gospel someday and have a special ministry for suffering people. "But, Mama," I said, "I stutter. I can't even talk."

Pulling me to her, she kissed me and said, "You will, son. Someday God will heal your tongue and loose it, and you will talk and speak to multitudes."

As chills went down my backbone, a spark of hope was lit in me as she told me this without a shadow of a doubt in her spirit or voice.

Mama and I were bound together by more than blood. Her vow to dedicate me to God if He healed her neighbor's little son made a deep and lasting impression on me. In addition, we were drawn close by her love of books, which she read incessantly when she could get them. She was always seeking to buy or borrow books to put in my hands. I devoured them, and I could never get enough of them. Her other children did not seem to have the thirst to learn like I did.

Mama was the one who talked up going to school at a time when schools in our part of Pontotoc County were many miles apart and there were no school buses. Regardless of weather or how far we had to walk to school, she always insisted that we go. Walking in the winter, we often had to wade through a foot or two of snow and face the howling Oklahoma winds. Our thin clothes provided little protection against such weather, and we sometimes went barefooted until Papa could get enough money for our shoes.

Poverty made it hard to pursue an education or to see over the wall it created or to dream dreams with the conviction that I could truly realize those dreams. But I inherited many of Mama's desires for a better life. Although she seldom lived in towns or cities before her marriage because of the nomadic ways of the Indians, she had a tremendous thirst for knowledge. She never fought the white man's ways in her spirit. She married a white man, and she soon saw that the day of the Indians' "old ways" would not survive. Her people would have to learn new ways and live in the now, or they would be left behind in the fast-growing nation of the United States.

It was in the wildest part of this new nation, Indian Territory, now Oklahoma, that Mama and Papa met and married. And that in itself was a miracle!

Married by a Miracle

Once a man said to me, "I don't believe in miracles." I said, "You will when you need one."

Since then, I've often said that I breathe by a miracle. I talk by a miracle. I live by a miracle. Take miracles out of Oral Roberts's life, and I'd be dead.

Some people believe in miracles; some don't. But I think it is more than a coincidence that my father, whose family came from

Wales, and my mother, whose Indian family roamed this land, met and married in an area far from their origination. The far-reaching hand of God was directing a sovereign meeting and marriage beyond human understanding. Let me tell you this unbelievable story.

The Roberts clan had been very close in Wales, and they came to America in the 1800's in one group. My father's grandfather, John Roberts, was only a young boy when the family settled in Tuscaloosa, Alabama.

John Roberts fathered a large family but with only three sons, Amos Pleasant, Jim, and Ed. Amos Pleasant, the oldest child, was called Pleas.

As a twenty-year-old young man, Amos Pleasant Roberts was exempted from the Civil War because he was the overseer of one hundred slave families. Slavery of black people was a way of life in the South until President Abraham Lincoln and the bloody Civil War, in which more men were killed than in any war in history, made them a free people. I remember my grandfather telling us children that the Civil War freed the slaves physically, but that was about all.

While watching the carnage of a war between "brothers" of the North and the South and carrying out his "duty" over one hundred black families, Pleas became sickened and disillusioned with the whole sorry affair. In 1871, at the age of twenty-six, he organized a twenty-wagon team of families and headed west. It took them three months to make the trip to central Arkansas. He settled the group in a place they built, named Robertsville, which is still there. There my father, Ellis Melvin, was born in 1881.

At about the same time, Frank Irwin, a white man, had fallen in love with an Indian girl, Demaris Holton, whose forebears had been among the Cherokee who were forcibly and cruelly marched from the East. The march was made by the five civilized tribes— Cherokee, Choctaw, Chickasaw, Seminole, and Creek—who were driven from their ancestral homes in the southeastern states, giving way to the white man's desire for these lands, to an area west of the Mississippi River consisting of millions of acres. The land was divided into five nations, each sovereign and not a part of the United States. In the drive west, the Cherokee suffered the most. Being moved in the winter caused thousands of them to die on the trail, for there were few roads. This event in American history came to be known as the Trail of Tears.

Just four years after my father was born in Robertsville, Arkansas, a few miles away, my mother, Claudius Priscilla Irwin, was born. The Priscilla part of her name came from the famous Pilgrim, Priscilla, who married John Alden in Massachusetts in colonial times.

In 1890, both families migrated to Texas, near Sherman, close to the border of Indian Territory. Neither family knew of the other. The stay of both families in northern Texas was short, for by 1891, they had migrated a third time, this time to Pontotoc County, a part of the Chickasaw Nation of the original five civilized tribes. Miraculously, Pleas Roberts and Frank Irwin had once again settled their families close to each other without knowing each other.

The migration of my father's people from Arkansas to Texas and then to Indian Territory was to get a new start. The migration of the Holtons and Irwins was for an entirely different reason. My people on my mother's side, in spite of her mother's marriage to a white man, were still nomadic. They were almost constantly on the move, living mainly on the rivers where fish and game were plentiful.

The Robertses worked the land, built towns, and became judges. The Holtons and Irwins followed the life of the Indians, staying mostly with the "old ways." That makes it even more fascinating that they lived near each other when in 1901, Ellis Roberts, at age nineteen, met and married Claudius, at age fifteen. There, a family from across the sea in Wales and a family driven from the ancestral lands in Georgia in the new nation of America were joined together despite the hatred of intermarriage of whites and Indians.

Jesus Is a Person!

From the union of Ellis and Claudius Roberts, I, Oral Roberts, was born on January 24, 1918. My birth date was a time of upheaval on the earth. The First World War was coming to its bloody end in Europe, while in America a flu epidemic was wiping out even larger numbers of Americans than were killed in all of World War I.

Families died like flies all around my people, but the flu did not strike our little home. The two-room log cabin with a small lean-to room built onto it was located in the country twelve miles northwest of Ada, Oklahoma.

Papa had built a new church in Ada and a three-room parsonage beside it. There I remember first being aware that Jesus is a person and that He is real to people in this life. I was about five years old. The walls of that twelve-by-thirty-six-foot shotgun house were so thin that when Papa and Mama awakened each morning around five o'clock and talked before getting up, my brother, Vaden, and I could hear them. They would pray and talk to Jesus as if He was there beside them.

One particular morning I awakened at the same time my parents did, and sure enough they were talking to Jesus: "Jesus, we love You. Jesus, remember us and our family, and all those we are praying for. Remember Vaden and Oral, that they will know You and Your plan for their lives and follow it."

Before I realized what I was saying, I punched Vaden and said, "Vaden, Jesus is in our house."

"No, He's not," Vaden said and went back to sleep. Vaden was very sleepyheaded, but I would awaken at the smallest sound.

I punched him again and said, "Yes, He is. Papa and Mama are talking to Him. Don't you hear them?"

Of course, I eventually learned Jesus was not there in the flesh, but as far as my parents were concerned, His reality to them and their being on intimate terms with Him made it seem to me that He was there in person.

I know this: An indelible impression was made upon my mind as a child that you could be so close to Jesus that you could talk to Him. I shudder to think what might have happened to me if I had not been birthed and raised by the parents God gave me.

CHAPTER 2

MAMA AND PAPA

D R. BURNS delivered me at 11:00 A.M., for the princely sum of twenty dollars. I know that because Papa never let me forget how much I cost him. "T-w-e-n-t-y d-o-l-l-a-r-s," he would say. That was a lot of money in those days. Dr. Burns was the only doctor in our part of Pontotoc County, and he had to come seven miles by buggy to assist my mother at my birth.

My parents were very close to their children, and especially tender toward me, the baby of the family, because of my stuttering. I loved my parents deeply.

Papa, with his limited education and background, overcame many obstacles in his burning desire to preach the gospel, win souls, and build churches. Although he was not formally educated, he was intelligent, memorizing a large portion of the King James Version of the Bible. His unusual natural speaking ability and a strong prayer life and anointing made him a powerful preacher who was much in demand. Like Grandfather Roberts, Papa had a strong voice, easy to listen to, and what he lacked in education, he had in practical experience through the rough-and-tumble of life.

He loved the Bible as I had never seen anyone love it. With his concordance, his Bible dictionary, and several volumes of a commentary, he would spend hours a day studying. Then after he had read himself full, he would preach it out that night to the people who had come from miles to hear him.

Although my papa was strong in his preaching, his faith for healing was not as strong as Mama's. Papa believed in healing through prayer and faith, and he preached it. But Mama had the faith. I never knew her to doubt God could and would heal people if they would only pray and believe.

When Papa finished preaching, he would ask Mama to take over the final part of the service. Sinners would flock to the mourner's bench, and Mama would start rejoicing and pray them through to salvation and the baptism of the Holy Spirit. Then those who were sick would come to the same altar bench, and she would lay hands on them, praying and believing God to heal their sick bodies.

In those days in Pontotoc County, few Christians believed in praying for people who were sick to be healed or for miraculous things to happen. Looking back, I know that is why many of our neighbors called Mama to come and pray when there were serious sicknesses in their families.

Even now I can remember specific nights when Mama prayed for desperately ill people and the supernatural power of God brought a change in them. Although Mama believed in medicine, her greater belief was in the power of prayer, whereas Papa was a strong believer in doctors and medicine. Their individual strengths cooperated beautifully in the integration of God's healing streams.

I grew up making no difference in our home between the doctor coming to give treatment or being prayed for, for healing. Later I came to realize that had made a strong impression on my belief and acceptance that God uses both medicine and prayer in healing people—God being the Source of both. I thank my parents for this priceless balance I learned. Several times it has saved my life.

─────── *Brush Arbors*

On the Oklahoma frontier, not long after it had become a state in 1907, there were few church buildings, and they were mainly Methodist, Baptist, Presbyterian, and Catholic. In many ways it was virgin territory for the gospel, particularly for the Pentecostal out-pouring of the Holy Spirit with speaking in tongues, divine healing, and other miraculous manifestations that later came through the Pentecostal Holiness, Assemblies of God, and Church of God churches.

Since there were few church buildings, Papa and other volunteers would build brush arbors. They cut down saplings and trimmed them for poles, which they sank into the ground at various distances, then laid a lattice of tree branches over them for a roof. From the lumberyard they would rent two-by-twelve-foot pieces of lumber for seating, and they would hang up coal oil lamps to see by. By nightfall, they were ready to preach.

When enough people were converted and filled with the Holy Spirit, Papa would lead them in cutting down trees for lumber to build a forty-by-sixty-foot building. He would then organize a church, secure a young pastor, and move on to the next place. It was simple but effective.

I was accustomed to this type of tabernacle at my parents' revivals, as was my brother Vaden. We were raised like twins, although he was two years older than I. I was tall and thin; he was three inches shorter and chunky. Elmer and Jewel, my older brother and sister, were married and gone. My other sister, Velma, had tragically died at nineteen from pneumonia coupled with epileptic seizures. Vaden and I were left to grow up together. I loved him dearly.

We had to go to church, including Papa's brush arbor meetings, especially if they were close enough to wherever we lived at the time. Papa didn't have a car until we were grown. Walking two or three miles to preach was not unusual, and until Vaden and I were old enough to walk the distance with Papa and Mama, Papa would carry one or both of us on his back. How well I remember falling asleep and waking up at home after he had carried me the several miles back after the service.

In those days, preachers' children were thought of as mean little boys. Vaden always said if we were, we took after the deacons' children.

One night in a brush arbor revival, while Papa was preaching away, Vaden and I were on a quilt that Mama had spread on the ground near her. That quilt was our territory, and woe unto any other boy who touched it. That particular night, in the midst of Papa's sermon, a little boy sneaked off his own quilt and began yanking on ours.

"You better quit that," Vaden whispered.

Soon he did it again.

"I'll cut your ear off if you touch our quilt again," Vaden hissed.

The little boy laughed. He didn't know Vaden like I did.

The third time the little boy tried to pull our quilt out from under us, Vaden grabbed him in a choke hold, and with his little knife, he started cutting on the little boy's right ear! (Of course, I wasn't doing a thing. I was just holding the little boy.) That was when Papa heard a new sound under the brush arbor. The little boy saw the blood, and he let out a big yell.

Papa took one look and paused in his sermon. Looking straight at us, he said, "Boys, when I get you home, I'll take care of you!"

He believed in the stars and stripes. He put on the stripes, and we boys saw the stars!

There is another incident with Vaden that I will never forget. Papa had cut down a big tree in our backyard, leaving a big stump. Vaden was handy with tools. I remember walking around the house and finding him driving nails into that stump. I asked, "Whatcha doing?"

"Can't you see? I'm driving nails."

"Let me drive one."

"Now, Oral, get away. I've just started."

Putting my right hand on the stump, I said, "If you don't let me drive some, then I won't let you drive any."

"Get your hand off that stump."

"I won't do it."

"Oral, I'll nail your hand to this stump."

"You haven't got the nerve."

He promptly drove a nail through my hand to the stump.

I let out a yell.

When Vaden saw what he had done, he began yelling and jumping up and down. When I saw what he had done, I began jumping up and down and yelling louder.

When Mama came to the back door, she saw her two little sons jumping up and down and yelling, so she began to holler. She saw her baby boy was nailed to a stump, and she ran out to us and soon freed me. Vaden was a good boy, though!

The Pentecostal preachers in the early days were often derisively called Holy Rollers. At school, Vaden and I were sometimes called that, too, and the name infuriated us.

There's one in every crowd who takes the lead, especially if he's bigger. One day a six-foot boy began hollering, "Vaden and

Oral are Holy Rollers," and soon the whole gang was chanting it with him.

Vaden was a fighter with his fists, much better than I was. Papa, as a preacher opposed to fistfighting, warned us, "If you get in a fistfight, you'll also get a whipping when you get home." Papa meant to keep the peace. But it was tough on us boys as his sons.

Vaden called me off to the side. "Oral, we can take that big bully."

"What?" I said. "He's at least five years older and a foot taller."

"Never mind. Just do as I say."

"What am I to do?"

"I'll go straight up to him and call him out. He'll leap at the chance. When we get outside the ring of boys and he and I square off, you come up behind and swing a haymaker on his blind side."

"Then what?"

"Your blow will catch him off guard, he'll turn to see what hit him, and I'll smash his jaw and down he'll go."

When Vaden called the bigmouthed kid out, the other boys formed a ring around them but paid no attention to me. I was a little taller than Vaden, very slim, and rather frail looking, but I did have long arms.

The boy said to the others, "I'll finish this Holy Roller off real quick." About that time, I had come through behind him, and I took a mighty swing to the side of his head. He yelled and jerked his head around to see who hit him. Vaden waded in with his hard little fist and instantly knocked the boy to the ground.

We both leaped on him and flailed away. All the while he was yelling, "Get 'em off me! Get 'em off me!"

The other boys were so startled they stayed still. We kept on pounding him. Suddenly, he yelled, "I give up! I'll never call you a Holy Roller again."

"You really promise?" Vaden asked.

"Oh, yes, cross my heart and hope to die."

When you said, "Cross your heart and hope to die," those were big words and everybody knew you meant business.

We let him up and looked around to see if there were any other challengers. When there weren't, we nonchalantly put our hands in our back pockets and walked away as kings of the hill.

News of the fight never got to Papa, but after that, we were respectfully called Vaden and Oral. Vaden was my hero.

——— *God Will Take Care of Us!*

Papa was known as a good man, honest to a fault, and one who would never buy anything on time. He paid for it, or we did without. He hated debt.

While farming, which he did on the side during a number of my growing-up years, he literally despised going to the bank to borrow money to put in the next year's crop. When the cotton came up and separated into those big bolls, the whole family pitched in to pick it. As soon as we finished, Papa loaded up the wagon, with Vaden and me on top of it, and drove twelve miles to the cotton gin in Ada. He got his money, rushed to the bank, and paid off his debt.

Using what was left, he bought our winter clothes and our winter food staples. He always carried a twenty-dollar bill in his pocket. He hated to be poor so much that I guess the twenty-dollar bill gave him hope that someday his ministry would be appreciated and the people he won to Christ would support him. He could then quit farming and give his whole life to the ministry.

Papa conducted some revivals that were too far for Mama and us boys to walk, so he'd have to leave us at home. He often preached a revival for two weeks at a time. It was on a freewill offering basis where there was no will and it was only free from Papa's standpoint. Often he would receive less than five dollars and walk home at the end of the revival, saving it all for us.

One evening while he was gone on a revival, Mama called Vaden and me in: "Boys, your daddy hasn't gotten home yet with any money. We're out of groceries, and I'm sorry but we'll have no supper tonight."

Vaden didn't take that very well. He kept asking Mama why we couldn't have a daddy like other children. Why did Papa have to preach? We hardly ever had enough to eat.

Mama didn't say anything, but I could tell she was hit hard. Later that evening, she took us to visit our neighbors, the Campbells, a widow and her children. As we walked onto the porch, Mrs. Campbell met us. "Oh, Sister Roberts, you're just in time for supper. Come on in and eat with us."

Mama said, "Thank you, but we're not hungry. We just came to visit."

Vaden growled, "Well, I'm hungry. She ought to ask me."

Mama shushed him, and we went in, watched them eat, and then visited. When it was time to leave, Mama and Sister Campbell knelt and started praying and thanking God for being so good to us.

Vaden jabbed me in the ribs and said, "God ain't been very good to me." I told him not to let Mama hear him say that. All of a sudden these words came rushing up from inside me: "Besides, God will take care of us." I had no idea how I came to say that.

When we reached our little house, Mama told Vaden to open the door. He turned the knob and pushed, but the door wouldn't budge. So I came to help. We pushed and got it open about a foot. "There's something behind the door," Vaden said. Mama pushed with us, and we got the door open and turned on the light.

There on the floor in a cardboard box was a bunch of groceries. Mama never hesitated. "Put it on the kitchen table, boys."

We set it all out there on the table: a country ham, a sack of flour, ten pounds of lard, ten pounds of sugar, a sack of potatoes, and lots of other good things.

Meanwhile, Mama was putting on her apron. "Stand back, boys, and I'll cook supper."

An hour later, we sat down to a feast. With my mouth full of biscuits, country ham, and mashed potatoes, I turned to Vaden and said, "I told you God would take care of us."

"Yeah, He sure will, won't He?" Vaden asked.

Many years later, as I was wrestling with all that God has called me to do, my words of that night came back to me over and over: "God will take care of us."

I've discovered that most of us never try to reach higher than about 50 percent of our faith capacity or our God-given ability and dreams. We stop short when the going gets a little tough, then tougher, and we settle down to a mediocre life. It seems the majority of the human race operates on that percentage. But not my mama.

From the time I was a boy, I heard Mama tell of her dreams. I saw how she inspired my father, who was not trained for the ministry, to reach out, forgetting his past and believing God that He could move mountains. She was always burning up inside with the Spirit of the Lord. Mama was an original "go ye" person.

Papa had a habit of preaching a few revivals, getting us on our feet financially, then staying around home resting for two or three months. Mama would let him get by with staying around the house just so long, then she would tell him it was time to go for another revival or to start a new church, and to believe God for money to feed our family. And Papa would go.

As we grew older, Vaden and I agreed Papa would have been satisfied to live that mediocre kind of life. But Mama kept urging Papa to climb another mountain.

Mama was industrious, always keeping our little house clean as a pin. She hated houses with dirt floors, and she rejoiced when we moved into one with wood and linoleum floors. She would "pretty" the house with curtains in the windows, keep the place aired out, and see to it that however crowded we were, Vaden and I always had a bed to ourselves.

She would wash Vaden and me around our ears and necks with a washcloth until she was sure there wasn't a speck of dirt left on us. I was the darkest of the children, showing my Indian blood the most, and I would cry, "Mama, that's not dirt. That's the color of my skin." Only then would she turn me loose. We were two clean little boys.

She loved her family, and she was Papa's strongest ally. She had a burning ambition to get ahead and simply would not stop pushing us on.

Often she would talk to me alone. It hurt her that I stammered so badly and that my body was frail, unlike Vaden's and Jewel's and Elmer's. I think she had a secret fear that the disease of tuberculosis, so rampant in her Indian people, would settle on me and would take me as it did her father at fifty years of age and her two older sisters in their teens.

She would say things like, "Oral, your body is frail, but no matter what happens, you're going to make it." Or "Oral, God is going to heal your stuttering and you'll talk." Or "Here, read these books, learn all you can, remember all you learn, and never settle for anything but your best."

I would try to do all that she said. As I watched her, I didn't know how to say it, but down deep I knew Mama was a great lady.

As I was growing up, whenever I went beyond the ordinary in some endeavor, Elmer or Jewel or Vaden—and even Papa—would say, "That's Mama in him."

I've always said I believed women are the most beautiful creatures God ever made. Although eventually I ran away from her and my family, vowing to make it on my own and to do it my way, Mama and her zest for the best, her dreams ever alive in her, were seldom far from my mind.

Papa's solid goodness meant a lot to me, also. His hatred of debt, his word as his bond, his unswerving integrity, and his love for God and the Bible had a more important place in my mind than I realized.

Unfortunately, I had to run away from them before I could truly understand and appreciate who they were and what they stood for. But it took a long time for that to happen.

CHAPTER 3

THE RUNAWAY

AS A TEENAGER fighting my way through life with my stammering and the poverty of my family, I got the idea that if I could get away from the people who knew me, I could start over. Then maybe, just maybe, I would lose my stuttering and be able to really reach my dreams.

In spite of how close I was to my parents, especially to my mother, I decided to leave home at sixteen years of age. I had already attended ten different schools by the time I was a sophomore in high school. I knew there was something better for me.

I was like a runaway horse, strong-willed and determined to get away as fast as possible, no matter who I hurt along the way. I *had* to get to a new place, which was, for me, a new life. I had determined to let nothing but nothing hold back my dreams of being a lawyer and later governor of Oklahoma. Although I moved from school to school, sometimes two or three times during one school term, I never remember making any grade less than A for the term, and that had to be a miracle.

The only days I got a bad grade were when we kids were called upon to recite *orally*. Regardless of how well I knew the lesson, the words stuck in my mouth, my tongue froze, and my insides felt paralyzed. My fear was such that I simply couldn't talk or recite publicly.

Sometimes the teacher sent me out of the classroom to get a drink of water, but it didn't help. I needed more than water. I needed something or somebody to shore me up inside, to give me a knowing in my belly area that I could talk. As young as I was, I knew that my stuttering was more than physical—something inside was making me afraid, tormenting me with fear that I would never be able to talk like other children.

Coach Herman Hamilton, under whom I played basketball, was leaving Ada for Atoka, which is in southern Oklahoma, to teach and coach in the high school there. Because I was tall and gifted athletically, he asked me if I would like to go with him.

I had never been out of my county. Going so many miles to a strange place seemed to be at the end of the world.

My stuttering didn't bother my coach, I suppose, because I was his best player—at least his highest-scoring player. As long as I could score, he was happy with me. I made up my mind to go.

My father got wind of my decision and pulled me aside the day before I was to leave. "Oral, I won't let you leave home. If you persist, I will have the highway patrol stop the car and return you home."

Our clash of wills was suddenly like two swords striking. As we looked at each other, I knew what was going through his mind. Mama's vow of giving me to God when I was born and her prophecy that someday my speech would be healed and I would do the dearest thing in the world to him—preach the gospel.

To him, it was madness for me to leave their loving, protective care and go off with my coach where they might never see me again. It was breaking his heart. But all I could think of at that moment was missing the first six weeks of school to pick cotton, moving from one school to another, and living in what I considered then an overly religious atmosphere, one in which I hadn't the slightest hope I would ever amount to anything, let alone realize my dream and carry out my vision.

I wanted to get away as far as possible from the poverty that engulfed us since the moment I was born. There was never a more decisive young man than I when the moment came to leave. I'd had it with poverty. Had I accepted it, my life would never have had a chance to amount to a hill of beans.

"I'm going, Papa!" I declared.

His shoulders sagged, some of the light went out of his eyes, and he said no more.

Mama had been listening. She knew I had her drive, and I had gone too far to back out. Even though I was six feet one and one-half inches tall, the tallest of her five children, she pulled me down to her five-foot frame so that my face touched hers. "Oral, I made a vow to God concerning your life. I dedicated you to Him. Son, every night you are gone, I will rise from my bed and pray for God to bring you home." Then she branded me with her tears. All the months I was away I never forgot those tears or her vow.

Atoka was full of Indians, and I felt right at home. One group I could get along with was Indians. My Indian blood showed, although I am only one-eighth Indian. It was evident I was a person of color, and I've always been proud of it. I've never understood people resenting their race or the color of their skin. We are all of one blood, the Bible says, regardless of our skin color (see Acts 17:26).

I decided that when I left home with my coach, I would never return to my parents or to the church. I never wanted to hear my mother tell me again about God's plan for my life. But there was one thing I could not shake off. It was a troubling in my spirit. I felt God had His hand on me and would not take it off. In spite of efforts to seek to remove all thought of being God-conscious, I felt a sensitivity that I had in me the very thing I had heard my father say: "In every human being there is a God-shaped blank that only He can fill."

Coach Hamilton was not a churchgoing man. I saw the kind of life he lived, and I allowed it to take hold of me and lead me far afield from my moral and spiritual upbringing. During those first weeks away from home, I broke loose to do my own thing, following my dream, refusing all corrections from others, and being totally the Oral Roberts I wanted to be.

But it wasn't easy. I discovered I couldn't get my mother's vow concerning my life, which she had made while climbing through that barbed wire fence, out of my mind. Things I had heard my father say to his audiences in his sermons, and to me as his son, had stuck and rose up in me. I couldn't keep them from bothering me.

I became friends with some kids who went to the First Methodist Church in Atoka, and they prevailed upon me to go. It was a friendly church, and I, as a stranger in their midst, was welcomed heartily. I began to run around with some of the kids from that church who had good values. However, the bottom line was that my desire to go my own way was too set in concrete.

Still, God would not let me alone. I remember like it was yesterday when my swirling thoughts awakened me out of a sound sleep. It was like God and I were having it out once and for all. I remember crying out, "God, leave me alone. Take Your hands off my life, off my dreams, off my way. Don't deal with me anymore. I'm not returning home. I'm going to live my own life and fulfill my own dreams. Just get out of my life and leave me alone!"

The strangest feeling came over me. I heard no voice, but it was like He said, "All right, I will get out of your life. I will stop dealing with you." It scared me like I had never been scared before. I thought, *What if this happens, and I am out in the world alone, away from God?*

Then I stubbornly said to myself, "Good. It's over. Now I can go my own way." And I did with a vengeance.

It was like I was being driven by an inside force stronger than I, like a hammer driving a nail, blow by blow, and I let it take me where I had always dreamed of, far away from my raising.

Although I had joined the Methodist church around the age of ten, and had grown up under my father's ministry and in the church, I had not made a profession of faith in Jesus Christ as my Savior; yet hearing the gospel had had an effect on my life. I knew what sin was, and I knew when I was determined to play life my way that somehow it was wrong. Committing sexual indiscretions during the months I was away from home, learning to drink alcoholic beverages, using obscene language, feeling lust for power, leaving my parents out of my life, not being respectful to the church, not ever praying—all those and more meant I was sinning and I needed to repent and change my life God's way.

I worked myself into a problem that was more than a few sins. I was soon making sin—having my own way regardless of the long haul or the consequences in this life and in eternity—a way of life. In short, I was becoming a sinner.

It was like mixing concrete and pouring it while it can be shaped before it sets in its permanent mold. I was losing my innocence. I grew hardened to the extent the concrete was no longer shapable; it was set. I was a sinner, and the only way I could be changed was to do what you have to do to change concrete that has set—you break it.

I still stuttered but not as much. It felt good to talk a little better. I was elected president of my high school class. Being a good basketball player didn't hurt any, either. As the tallest player on the team and as a center, I managed to score 40 percent of the total scores of the team. That gave me a big push, increased my confidence in life, and also helped me secure jobs on the side to fully support myself without help from my parents—help that they didn't have to give anyway. I had a false sense of security. That's when I made a fatal error.

To make it on my own, I worked for the *Ada Evening News*, which I introduced to Atoka. I also had a job in the large home of the widow of the late district judge, Judge Linebaugh, where I had to rise each day at 4:00 A.M. and build the fires in the kitchen and the rooms where the men slept. I got free room and board for this chore. My coach and many of the other teachers roomed and boarded there. Then on Saturday, I worked ten hours in a grocery market.

In addition to my studying, my jobs, and my basketball playing, I did some courting, and I often stayed out late at night. With no parents to watch over me and my health, I usually didn't get to bed before midnight. That gave me four hours of sleep a night.

I had come from a family on my mother's side where tuberculosis was rampant. Physically, I was never as strong as my two older brothers, Vaden and Elmer, or my sister, Jewel. The relentless pushing of my body caught up with me six months later. Our basketball team was playing in the district tournament, and the other team members and I were winning. Our next stop was going to be the University of Oklahoma at Norman for the state tournament. The crowd was cheering and yelling. I had the ball and was making a driving layup when I lost consciousness and hit the floor, blood running out of my nostrils. I didn't know it, but something far worse than stuttering had hold of me: tuberculosis, which would soon be diagnosed as being in both lungs.

Coach Hamilton ran out on the floor, picked me up, and said, "Son, I'm taking you home." Home to me was back to poverty, back to religious faith that found no place in me, back to dreaming with no way out.

He drove me home and knocked on the door. When Papa answered, Coach Hamilton told him his boy was lying in the backseat of the car, and he asked Papa to help carry me in the house. I was barely conscious, and hemorrhaging from both lungs, when they put me to bed.

The first one I saw was Mama. She came from the kitchen with her apron on and sat down on the side of my bed. With her face buried in her apron, I heard her mumbling.

"What are you saying, Mama?" I asked.

"Oh, Oral, every night you were gone I arose after midnight, walked the floor, and prayed to God to bring you home."

Her face flooded with tears. She fell across my body that was burning with fever and said, "I asked God to bring you home at any cost. But I didn't know the cost would be so great."

Years later, I would understand what Mama meant. Although God was not the author of my disease, He used it to bring me home. Countless times throughout my life I have seen God take what the devil intended for bad and turn it for our good. God was working in my behalf without the slightest awareness on my part.

When Vaden got the news of my illness, he left his job and rushed to the house. He fell across my body as he cried out, "Oh, Lord, put this on me. I've always been stronger in my body than Oral."

I pushed him off my body and quickly fell unconscious again. I don't remember getting through the night, except I remember the hard coughing and the spitting up of blood.

Papa called Dr. Craig and Dr. King, both friends of our family. When they finished with their examinations and conferred with my parents and left, I knew something bad was wrong with me.

I hated every moment of being back home. I scarcely heard the doctors say, "Give him milk with eggs beaten up in it, and that will keep his strength up." Soon the doctors sent bitter-tasting medicines for me to take.

Papa and Mama would come in my room, each unable to hold back the tears, and just stand there looking at me and praying.

I finally demanded to know, "What's the matter with me?" They simply shook their heads. Then Mama said, "Son, you'll be all right."

I wondered why Mama and Papa were crying if I was going to be all right. And why did my lungs feel like knives were cutting them? Why was I coughing up blood? Why was I so hot all over my body?

Papa said, "Oral, you've got tuberculosis, and the doctors think it's in the final stages."

I cried out to Mama, "Didn't your father and your two oldest sisters die with TB?"

"Yes," she said.

I began to think of all the Indians I had seen with tuberculosis, of those I had seen die as I accompanied Papa on his preaching tours among the Indian people.

I asked Papa, "Are there any medicines that will cure me of TB?"

"None that the doctors know of, son."

"Then why should I have to take these things? If I'm going to die, I'll just die." In fierce anger I swept the medicines off the windowsill, and the bottles broke on the floor.

Mama was weeping as she took me in her arms, "Son, I prayed for you all the time you were gone. God hears and answers prayer. I've seen Him heal people as bad off as you are. Son, don't give up hope." She cried and cried, but she never gave any sign of giving up.

My father kept bringing new doctors to see me. I hated to see them shake their heads, yet give Papa prescriptions for medicines that didn't work. The power of the medicines of that day to cure tuberculosis was as far from a cure as it is around the earth and farther. The doctors knew it but were doing what they knew to do.

For days I lay there, dreading the nights of sweating, the coughing spells, the hemorrhages, then being unable to eat the next day.

It was no-man's-land and I was in the middle of it.

I couldn't even think of my dreams of being a lawyer or of the vision of someday being governor of Oklahoma, both of which had been driving forces in my young life. I thought only of blasted hopes, a life cut short, and death riding my chest.

I had taken myself in hand, left home, expecting to go on with my life my way. Stuttering had hindered me, but tuberculosis had floored me. What good were my plans now? How real were my high-sounding dreams? What hope did I have not to die before my time? Such unanswerable questions raged in my mind, while my body hurt like the pangs of hell, and the end was drawing near.

Days became weeks, weeks became months, and finally, I lost the power to walk. My weight slipped from 165 pounds to 120, leaving me looking almost like a skeleton.

Meanwhile, Papa moved us seventeen miles west to Stratford, Oklahoma, where he established another church. During those months, friends and neighbors came to visit and pray for me. They all wanted me to become a believer in Jesus Christ as my Savior. They were sincere people, but they echoed the ways they had been taught to get someone like me to "give in" to God.

They would tell me that God had tracked me down when I ran away from home and the church. He had my number, and He had put TB on me to teach me a lesson.

Truthfully, I wanted to spit on them!

Some days, different people would say, "Oral, God *can* heal you of tuberculosis." As I thought on this, they would say, "But of course, it might not be His *will* to heal you."

What did God have to do with my being brought down with a death-dealing disease? I had never done anything to God. I didn't even know of Him except through my parents since I had no personal relationship with Him. I was not a praying person. I was a dreamer, a visionary, one who wanted to make his own way.

The pastor of the Methodist church of which I was a member heard of my condition and came to visit me. I was impressed by him until he said, "Son, you'll just have to be patient with this disease. If it's God's will, He can spare your life."

The thought flashed through my mind: If I'm *patient*, I'll *die*!

I'll never forget the day my mother put an end to all that theological garbage from otherwise good Christian people. As they continued to confuse my mind with their traditions and ideas about God putting TB on me, questioning whether it was His will to heal or not, I saw my mother's eyes flashing. She was a little thing then, maybe weighing a hundred pounds, but she was one ardent child of God and full of faith as I had never known any other person to be.

She stood up, looked over Job's miserable comforters, and said in terms they could understand that she loved all of them and appreciated their coming to visit her son in his illness. But she made it clear that if they believed what they had been saying about God putting TB on me and that it may not be God's will to heal me, she wanted them to leave our house and not come back until they could lift my faith and not tear it down.

How I loved Mama in that hour! What spunk, what true grit, what protectiveness!

I wanted to shout for joy. I thought, *If God is really real, there's no way He can be like He has been represented to me lying here on this bed. If He put the TB on me as a punishment, how long will it be before He stops punishing me? And if He can heal, why is it His will to heal some and not others?*

Day after day I continued to lie on that bed coughing and hemorrhaging my life away. First, I blamed my mother's people for the germ they had in them to pass on to me. Also, almost in my subconscious I had a feeling Satan had had a part in my situation, but I certainly had no defined sense of scriptural understanding. I had enough sense not to associate evil with the Creator, although He was not my personal Savior.

I was not quite aware of it, but I was listening and looking for some sign of God's goodness. In hearing my father preach from a child up, I had one particular Scripture stick in my mind. It often came to me while I was away from home, and it came to me again as I lay there counting my days: "The goodness of God leadeth thee to repentance" (Rom. 2:4).

There is no way, according to the Word of God, that tuberculosis was sent to me from a good God. If God was bad like Satan, yes. Then He would have robbed me of my health, sought to kill my body, and removed all the good of my life from the earth. But Jesus said of Satan and of Himself, "The thief [Satan] cometh not, but for to steal, and to kill, and to destroy: I am come that they might have life, and that they might have it more abundantly" (John 10:10).

Of course, I wasn't able to state this then as plainly as I do now, but I did have at least a small inner understanding that God was good and the devil was bad. I even had knowledge, as I think all people do, that ultimately each of us has to deal with God.

Shakespeare wrote

> There is a tide in the affairs of men
> Which, taken at the flood, leads on to fortune;
> Omitted, all the voyage of their life
> Is bound in shallows and in miseries
> (*Julius Caesar* 4. 3. 218–21).

My way of saying that is there is always a turning point in a person's life with God. If you take it, you can succeed according to His purpose for your life. If you refuse it, you will fail. It's a turning point of His purpose for you, also your destiny. Mine was about to be decided, and my sister, Jewel, was God's instrument to bring me to that point with seven simple words, without which I wouldn't be alive today.

CHAPTER 4

SEVEN SIMPLE WORDS

M Y CHILDHOOD memory of my sister, Jewel, is limited because she is seven years older than I and she left home at an early age.

My most predominant memory is what happened one day when Jewel was fifteen. We were all picking cotton close to my birthplace in Pontotoc County. In those days, the cash crop was cotton, and the whole family picked it during the fall. I noticed that as Jewel was picking the fleecy cotton from the bolls on the cotton stalks and putting it in her sack, which she was dragging behind her, she kept looking toward the road.

About midafternoon, I saw her drop her cotton sack and slip quietly toward a car that had parked in the road across from us. Before Papa knew it, the car door slammed, the car roared away, and Jewel was gone!

A brash, good-looking young man had come into our area and, unknown to my parents, centered his attention on the preacher's daughter, Jewel. She was tired of the cotton fields, weary with constant poverty, and was feeling the first flush of womanhood in her veins. It was so easy for the man, an escaped convict from a Kansas prison, to sweep her off her feet and lure her away.

Just weeks after they married and she was pregnant, she learned the truth about the man with whom she had eloped. The officers of the law located him, put the handcuffs on, and drove him back to prison. Crushed, Jewel had only one place to go: back to her family. When the baby, Billie June, was born, my parents virtually adopted her so Jewel could live out her life and have a decent chance for a future.

Two years later, Jewel married a man of character and stability, and he gladly took little Billie June into his heart. His name was Leo Faust. He and Jewel had two children of their own: Gloria and Gale.

It was long after that when tuberculosis struck me down. One hundred and sixty-three days passed with me flat on my back. The district judge of Ada, our county seat, had signed the papers to place me in the state sanitarium in the mountains of eastern Oklahoma, in the Indian-named town of Talihina.

When Judge McKeown signed the papers, he told my father, "Ellis, I hate to do this. Putting anyone in the sanitarium in Talihina usually means he comes out dead. Oral deserves better than that."

When his words were reported to me, cold chills went down my spine, and I turned my face toward the wall near my bed and sobbed until I thought my body would break.

Jewel knew of Mama's vow when I was born and felt in her spirit that God didn't want her baby brother to die before he had a chance to live. Somewhere, as she was growing up as the daughter of Ellis and Claudius Roberts, the spark of God's healing power had been ignited and lay smoldering in her heart. One day it came flowing up inside her like a river that God not only *could* but *was* going to heal her baby brother. A *knowing* came into her spirit that she was to come to where I was, hovering at the edge of death, to tell me what God had spoken in her spirit.

Although she had a tender spirit and a loving heart, Jewel was not one who always expressed her thoughts. When that knowing hit her, she turned to her husband and said, "Leo, I've got to go tell Oral the words God has given me. If I don't, I won't be able to live with myself. May I have the car?"

When she arrived, she came straight to my bed. With shining eyes and fire in her words, she said seven simple words that changed my life: "Oral, God is going to heal you!"

Instantly, I asked, "Jewel, is He?"

"Yes, Oral, God is going to heal you."

How can I explain what I felt inside me? I felt that Jewel knew that all the healing I had heard about was going to come to me. To me!

Prior to that time, I had reached a place in my thinking that I later discovered millions of people reach in their illness: *I am not going to get well.* But Jewel replaced those seven words of death with seven words of life, and hope was birthed in my soul.

The thought of God healing me, restoring my life, and giving me another chance never left me. I had been on the wrong path, but suddenly, the light shone all the way from heaven to my wasting body on that bed—and God in that moment became powerful, real, and alive to me.

Although there was no specific time set for my healing to take place, Jewel had delivered the good news. For the first time in my life, all doubt in my heart about God having a plan for my life left me, and I knew that I knew it was true!

That opened me up to the reality of God and gave me the first feeling that I wanted Him in my life. I saw it as clearly as the noonday sun: If God was going to heal me and restore my life, I realized I had made a terrible mistake to tell Him to get out of my life.

Now, with my experiences of dealing with thousands to whom sickness and other bad things have happened, I know that too many people associate God with bad and not with anything good. Bad events in nature that are recorded in our government's official documents are referred to as acts of God. Most people have a belief that God has it in for them or He is far removed. How in the world would He ever think of them in their hard knocks of life? Many people think, *Who am I to be so brazen to think that God, with all the mighty things He has to do, has time to come to my aid?* To others, it's actually sacrilegious in their belief to call on God to help them individually. Among those who do ask God for help, they ask Him to help others, but not themselves, as if they are not as important to God as anyone else.

The following night after Jewel said those life-changing words to me, my father came in my room and announced, "Oral, I'm going to kneel beside your bed and pray and not stop until you give your heart to God and get saved."

Mama and the nurse, who was helping with me, knelt with him. As Papa continued praying, they finished and sat up in their chairs. Papa didn't stop. If ever a father talked to God about his son and his true condition, Papa told God about me. He told the Lord he couldn't stand to see me lose my soul. This disease taking me was bad enough, but for me to go into eternity unsaved was more than he could bear.

I raised my head from the pillow, looked across my body at him kneeling at the foot of my bed, and saw the big tears rolling down his face. He was in agony about my soul.

While I looked at him, Papa's countenance changed in my sight. A bright light seemed to envelop him, and suddenly, the likeness of Jesus appeared in his face! From the depths of my soul I called on the name of Jesus for the first time ever to save my soul and my life!

I felt God's presence go through my whole being. My spirit, mind, and body felt like they were suffused with God's presence. I felt strength enter my body that had not been there for months. The glory of the almighty God was permeating every cell of my body, and for a few moments I didn't feel like a boy who was dying with tuberculosis in both lungs, with a body wasting away.

Faith had leaped in my heart to turn my defeated life over to Jesus to be born again. He had forgiven me of all my sins and, more important, of the rejection of God in my life. I had such deep dissatisfaction with the status quo that had surrounded me in poverty and in religion, so I had turned from the very One who could bring me to greater fulfillment and accomplishment of life.

I discovered I could avoid the status quo, starting with repentance toward God, only by turning my life and ways over to Him. I was ready for the next step God had for the plan of my life. Something powerful and full of destiny was on the way to Oral Roberts!

—————— *"You Foul Tormenting Disease"*

At the same time all that was happening in my life, God had providentially sent a healing evangelist to Pontotoc County, which had never been visited by an outpouring of God's healing power in that way.

Reverend George Moncey didn't conduct his revival in a church building. He stretched a tent in Ada, and hundreds were filling it nightly. Many people reportedly were being healed by the prayer of faith as he laid hands on them (see Mark 16:18; James 5:14–15).

My older brother, Elmer, and his wife, Ora, had been attending the revival. Elmer was fourteen years older than I, and we were not close. He was a hard worker, ambitious to get ahead, and he became a building contractor. He had always thought that Papa and Mama had been too soft with me when they let me leave home. Not knowing the fierce burning in my heart to rise above my background, he had often said to me, "Oral, you're not worth the salt that goes in your bread," and he didn't smile when he said it. There was a distance between us that nothing had been able to bridge.

Little did I know God was changing my brother's feelings toward me as he and his wife sat in that tent and watched people they knew get healed through the prayers of a man of God. He knew his baby brother was home dying with terminal illness. He was hearing that "still small voice," like the prophet Elijah had heard in Bible times (1 Kings 19:12).

Once he knew what to do, Elmer was a man of action. "Ora," he said, "I'm going to get Oral and bring him here for prayer." Ora was a believer, and through her tears, she said, "You do that, Elmer."

Only days after Jewel's visit and witness that God was going to heal me, and I had received Christ as my personal Savior, Elmer drove up to our house, rushed in, and grabbed me by the hand. He said, "Get up, Oral. There's a man praying for the sick in Ada, and I've come to take you there."

We had never known Elmer to have a religious feeling before. All I could do was explain to him that I was too weak to get up.

That wasn't going to stop him. He decided that he would carry me on the mattress I was lying on and put it in the backseat of his car.

At that moment, Mama and Papa came in the room. Elmer explained to them how he had seen some of his friends healed in the revival, and he had come to take me to be prayed for. Elmer had never had much to do with Mama and Papa's ministry after he had gotten married and left home. It was hard for him to believe God could come close enough to people to heal them. Seeing such a demonstration of God's personal and loving touch on people's lives had broken him up. He was now ready to believe his own brother could be healed of a deadly disease by God's power.

Immediately, Mama had a knowing inside her spirit that it was my time for healing. She told us the story of how recently she had gone to the grocery store and was thinking about me and couldn't keep the tears back. The man tending the store saw her and asked her if Oral was dead. She said to him, "No, I'm crying because I know that God is going to heal Oral and he will live."

There was an anticipation in us all as Elmer dressed me in my one and only suit that swallowed my thin body, put me on the little mattress, carried it out to the car, and placed it on the backseat. Papa and Mama sat in the front seat with Elmer, and we drove the seventeen miles to Ada that evening.

Lying there on that mattress, my body hurting at every bump in the dirt road, I listened to Elmer say that the preaching of the healing evangelist was different. He had a boldness and an ability to make the Bible come alive, and Elmer and Ora just couldn't stay away from the meetings each night.

As he talked, my thoughts took over, and I ceased to hear any more of what Elmer was saying. I remembered a time when my mother had urged me to pray, and I had said, "Mama, I don't know how to pray."

Her answer came back to me there lying on that mattress: "Oral, you don't have to know how to pray. Just talk to God as if He was in front of you and tell Him you want Him to help you, then believe He will do it."

In retrospect, I've never heard a better explanation of how to pray.

Lying there, I grew very quiet inside. It was as if I was totally alone. Then I heard that Voice I've heard many times since:

> *"Son, I am going to heal you and you are to take My healing power to your generation. You are to build Me a university and build it on My authority and the Holy Spirit."*

That it was God's voice, I had no doubt. By the time Elmer drove up to the tent, I *knew* I would be healed.

Once inside, they placed me in a rocking chair with pillows at my back and sides because my body was so sore. Sitting there, I listened to the evangelist preach, and I saw people coming forward to accept Christ as their Savior. Then as he began praying for sick people, he came over to me and whispered an encouragement: "An Indian boy was healed here a few nights ago." I suppose someone had told him I had Indian blood.

Up till that time when someone visited me to pray or to talk about healing, it was all so traditional. The man's words were totally different. There was no dillydallying around about God's will and desire to heal. *He was waiting on the people to believe God for His healing power and miraculous operations in the same way they believed for their personal salvation.* He stated unequivocally that both salvation and healing are in Jesus' atonement on the cross, and also are in the Holy Spirit with His supernatural gifts, such as the gift of faith, the gift of healing, and the working of miracles (see 1 Cor. 12). He gave Scriptures for everything and told of miracles being done down through the centuries. He also stated that God is a God who changes not; what He did in Bible times He does today, and as far as the evangelist was concerned, the matter was settled.

It was a long service, lasting until 11:00 P.M., and I was the last one prayed for. The evangelist's wife touched my head with olive oil on her finger to anoint me for her husband's prayer.

When he finally came over to pray for me, my parents stood me up, one on either side holding me. I had never had anybody pray for my healing with any degree of authority or healing faith. However, as I grew up, I was accustomed to seeing other people prayed for to receive various blessings from God. Usually, those who prayed had a lead-in-type prayer, like they were warming up. Then they would launch into a longer prayer, ending with, "Lord, if it's Your will, please bless [or heal] this one in Jesus' name. Amen."

The evangelist's prayer had no opening. He didn't begin with the idea of getting himself worked up. With boldness, he laid his hands on my head and literally spoke to the disease binding me: "You foul tormenting disease, I command you in the name of Jesus Christ of Nazareth, come out of this boy! Loose him and let him go free."

As he stepped back, I felt something like an electrical shock go through my whole being. Then a strong warming sensation flowed into me. I felt my lungs open like a flower, and the most exhilarating energy swept over me.

The next thing I remember I was breathing from my lungs all the way down, with no coughing, no sharp shooting pains, no weakness. I actually yelled, "I'm healed! I'm healed!" Then I cried, laughed, and praised God. The entire audience leaped to their feet to praise the Lord, and together we gave glory to God.

Reverend Moncey said, "Son, tell what the Lord has done for you."

To my utter amazement and joy, the words no longer stuck in my throat. All fear that I could not talk without stammering was gone, and the words flowed from my lips like a spring gushing up from the earth.

One moment I had been standing there between Papa and Mama, my body trembling with weakness, my lungs feeling as if they would burst, fearing I might have to talk. Now with one sweep of His eternal power, Jesus Christ of Nazareth had touched me as He did the sick when He walked this earth (see Matt. 4:23).

Anyone who has experienced the healing power of Jesus knows something about God that most others do not know. Of course, the greatest miracle of all is the saving of the soul. However, one can have the greatest of all miracles and still become so sick that the medical help at that time cannot bring a cure, and then the only thing that can possibly deliver him is Jesus Christ of Nazareth—healing him directly or through one of His believing believers.

The next day there was great rejoicing at the Robertses' home. Life was coming back into my being. I was walking; I was eating; I was in awe of the wondrous change in me.

However, I was soon to learn one of the greatest lessons of my life. My strength, although it had come quickly in my healing, did not increase as fast as I naturally expected. The truth was that I was still weak in my body, even though I no longer felt the TB or the fear of stuttering.

My mother probably saved my healing. One day when she found me in the yard depressed, she asked me what was the matter.

I explained to her that I couldn't understand why, if I really had been healed, I was still so weak in my body.

Mama reminded me that I was bedridden for many weeks and I had even lost the power to walk. She explained it was just going to take some time to recover my full strength.

As I was thinking that over, she instructed me that when I would take a little rest in the afternoons, I was *not* to get into my pajamas and go to bed. I was to lie across the bed in my clothes.

Mama knew that would change my sickness attitude and sickness posture. It was a signal to my spirit and mind that I was really healed, and I was lying down a little for the sole purpose of regaining my strength. She also made me walk more and do some light work, letting my body readjust to life.

She was right. It took almost a full year to become strong in my body again, but it happened exactly as my mother's wise advice foretold.

Mama was determined to hang on to her faith for my healing. She had lost her oldest child, and she wasn't going to lose her youngest. She kept rehearsing an earlier scene about my sister, Velma, who became epileptic at age five and died at nineteen with pneumonia. I was only two years old when Velma died.

Mama told me how they called on Rev. Bill Dryden, a local preacher who was known for his great faith, to pray during one of Velma's seizures. As Reverend Dryden prayed over Velma, the violent seizure immediately stopped. She jumped up from the ground and began to sing. (Mama said Velma could sing like a mockingbird until the day she became epileptic.) She told me that they all began to cry and praise God, for they thought Velma was healed. After Bill left, the sickness came back on Velma and stayed until she died.

Mama had always believed Velma almost had a healing, and she was sorrowful that they had quit praying too soon. They were too new in the baptism of the Holy Spirit, having just received the experience a short time earlier, and didn't know the power of the Lord could bind that disease and keep it from returning. That was a key to my own healing.

The next thing we did was ask Dr. Shi, our doctor in Stratford who had become a close friend, to examine me at different times. He did that and was pleased with my progress.

He recommended that my blood be sent off to the Oklahoma Medical Center in Oklahoma City for testing, and also that we should go to the Sugg Clinic in Ada and have my lungs fluoroscoped, which we did.

Dr. Morey of the Sugg Clinic did the fluoroscope, and his face lit up with a big smile. "You're okay, Oral," he said. "Just forget you ever had tuberculosis."

The chief thrill we received was hearing the results of my blood test: no tuberculosis found!

Those things worked positively to convince me in faith, mind, and spirit that all I had to do was to keep regaining my strength and get on with my life. The healing touch of Jesus Christ of Nazareth had been instantaneous, but my recovery had taken many months. I learned a valuable lesson: "They shall lay hands on the sick, and they shall recover" (Mark 16:18).

Bigger than my healing was my call. God had spoken in my spirit words I had heard audibly:

"You are to take My healing power to your generation. You are to build Me a university and build it on My authority and the Holy Spirit."

It was impossible for me to fully understand this awesome call, but I am grateful that I believed every word and that a *knowing* came into my consciousness that I would be able to obey God and do those things.

About eight months later when the time had come for me to preach my first little sermon, I went into the woods alone to practice, talking to the birds and animals. I walked among the trees, with my new Bible in my hands, looking up at the trees and saying the words I felt in my heart until I was sure of myself. Then I knelt and prayed and declared by faith that I would preach without stuttering, I would have the strength to do it, and God would anoint me and be with me.

When I finally preached that twelve-minute sermon, a man and his wife accepted Jesus as their personal Savior—the greatest miracle that could have happened!

My twin calls burned in me, but at eighteen years of age, I had almost everything to learn. There was no other way to learn them than to plunge my life into furthering my education at the university level, pastoring little churches, studying God's Word, reading books about God and His world by the hundreds, traveling to preach in other churches, and always feeling the sense of waiting on the Lord's time to fulfill His greater calling on my life.

I have said earlier, I must have inherited my thirst for knowledge and the love of books from my dear mother. In the back of my little blue Chevrolet coupe, which I was able to buy with the money I earned, I carried one hundred books that I studied at every opportunity.

This part of my life and ministry prepared me for what was to come when God's time came. But first there was a very important person who had to come into my life to help me and be by my side as no one else ever had or ever would.

PART 2

BEGINNING TO PREACH GOD'S WORD

CHAPTER 5

MY DARLING WIFE, EVELYN

Who can find a virtuous woman?
for her price is far above rubies.
—Proverbs 31:10

I FIRST MET Evelyn Lutman, a young schoolteacher, in August 1936. We both were attending the annual camp meeting of the Pentecostal Holiness church of which our fathers were both ordained ministers. A camp meeting in those days meant that all the families lived in small tents during the ten days the services were held. Evelyn (whom I had not met yet) and I both played guitars in the orchestra in the opening part of each night's services.

One evening I was running late, and I rushed to my regular seat. The young woman at my right was already seated and was tuning up her instrument. I was in such a rush I hadn't had time to check my hair.

Turning to her, I asked, "Is my hair combed?"

Very sensitively, she said, "Oh, yes. You look very nice."

I thanked her, and as the service began, I played my instrument with no further comment or interest in the girl sitting beside me. I was just entering full-time ministry and was to be ordained during the conference held near the end of the camp meeting. My thoughts and intents were so singularly on the Lord and my preparation to obey His call on my life that I paid no real attention to the attractive and talented young woman.

I learned later that after the service, Evelyn went to her tent and wrote in her diary, "I met my future husband tonight." She said she wanted a tall, dark, black-haired young man to marry, one who loved the Lord, and one of whom she could be proud. She

39

showed the diary to her mother and sister, and they had a big laugh.

Evelyn's mother said to her, "Evelyn, have you seen his mother?"

"No, but why?"

"She's an Indian."

Evelyn said, "Mama, I'm not going to marry his mother."

At this camp meeting, the East Oklahoma Conference conducted its business, the ministers and churches gave their reports, and then the leaders made pastoral assignments for the coming year.

During the conference, my father was assigned to pastor the church in Westville, Oklahoma, on the eastern edge of Oklahoma only seventy-five miles from where he was born in Robertsville, Arkansas. That was the home church of the family of Evelyn Lutman.

My, how God has such a personal touch in directing our lives! He loves us too much to leave life to chance, and He has given us the beautiful and practical teaching of His Holy Word, the infilling of His Holy Spirit, and signs along the way for us to observe and absorb and follow with the keenness of our minds and the whole-heartedness of our hearts and efforts.

I began to realize that as a young minister of the gospel, I should be married. I courted several girls, but I had no serious relationship.

Considering the immoral life I had lived when I ran away from home, my new purpose in life was a miracle. From the day of my conversion and healing, I never thought of girls in an immoral way again. I was living proof that "if any man be in Christ, he is a new creature" (2 Cor. 5:17).

I discovered that when a person, at any age, is genuinely and soundly converted, his physical desires are under control, although they remain normal. There is an inner strength to wait for holy matrimony, then to remain holy in that marriage: "He is able to keep that which I have committed unto him against that day" (2 Tim. 1:12).

Several young men and women who have heard me refer to this Scripture have said, "Yes, we know God is able, but are we able as normal human beings?" My answer has been: "God said to you in His Word that He is able to keep that which *you* have committed to Him."

No commitment *cancels* God's ability. Commitment *connects* with His ability. God would never have said He is able to keep us when we make the commitment unless it were so. It is a tremendously encouraging word to everyone.

Ten Qualifications I Wanted in My Wife

After my parents moved to Westville, although I was traveling in my evangelistic work, I stayed with them between revivals.

One year prior to our moving to Westville, Evelyn had gone to Texas to teach in a school south of Corpus Christi. Baffin Bay School, grades one to eight, was only a few miles from the Gulf of Mexico.

There was a man in Westville whose family attended the church where Evelyn's parents attended and my father pastored. He owned a trucking line, and he asked me to take trips with him when I was home. God seemed to have brought Frank Moss across my path at a critical time in my life.

One day as we were driving with a big load in his truck, he turned to me and said, "Oral, it's time for you to get married."

I said that I knew he was right, but the problem was twofold: One, I hadn't found a girl I loved, and two, I had laid out the qualifications for her, and they were outrageously high.

"Anybody in mind?" he asked.

"Not a one."

"Well, let me tell you who she is."

"How do you know who she is?"

"Because I know Evelyn Lutman and have for several years."

Vague memories came to me: Could this be the girl I sat by in the orchestra at the camp meeting? I thought that was her name.

"Does she live here?"

"She did, but she's teaching school in Texas. She's the girl for you."

"How do you know that?"

"I know her and have admired her for many years. She's everything you'll ever want in a wife."

"As a man and as a young preacher?"

"Yes, in every way."

He saw my eyes focused on him. I was looking at him, measuring his words, but also looking through him to a young woman he had described. I could see her, for I knew exactly what I wanted in a wife.

"Frank, do you know what I want in a wife?"

"Oral, I've gotten to know you. I've watched you. Yes, I believe I know the kind of wife you want. And I know Evelyn Lutman is the woman for you."

That was pretty strong medicine. I hadn't asked for it. Yet I knew Frank was my friend; he was not a meddler or overly talkative.

"Frank, here's what I want in a wife, and not necessarily in this order, but every part totally important. I have each of these stored in my mind."

Then I proceeded to list them for Frank. Although at that time I may not have articulated them as well as I have written them here, these were the ones I had in my heart. In fact, these are the qualifications I'd recommend to anyone choosing a mate.

"First, she must love the Lord and have some of the same background as mine.

"Second, she must be intelligent and be up-to-date on two worlds: God's and this world we live in on earth.

"Third, she must understand in her heart of hearts what my calling from God is, and not fight me on it, but cooperate with it as a part of her own commitment to the Lord."

Frank drove on, but he was really listening. Every now and then I'd see he was in deep thought, and then he would break into a smile.

"Fourth, she must have a good figure, be attractive, but not a raving beauty—just a man's woman who has the ability and desire to be a full wife physically."

I looked again at Frank real closely. He wasn't bothered yet.

"Fifth, she must love children and want a family of our own.

"Sixth, she must be industrious, not lazy, a good housekeeper, and one who loves order in her home.

"Seventh, she must be calm in her demeanor, not given to fits of rage or jealousy or impatience. [I knew life with me would put demands on her for a calm spirit. Because I'm part Cherokee, sometimes I would want to talk, and other times I would go for days without talking to anybody. My mother used to say I was moody. In this, my wife had to be my opposite.]

"Eighth, she must be a good conversationalist. I want her to be able to talk with me, to be a sounding board for things I believe God has called me to do.

"Ninth, she must have backbone, be willing to stand up to me when I'm wrong or my temper gets out of hand, yet in a way I know that she cares about me and the things I'm feeling inside.

"Tenth, she must love me and marry me for life. I want her to be my helpmate, and I want to be her husband for life. When I marry her, it must be a done deal."

"Are you finished?" Frank asked.

"Well, that's the heart of it. As you can see, I've been thinking about this for a long time. I'm deadly sincere in everything I've said."

Frank hit me on the knee. A smile filled his face from ear to ear.

"That's Evelyn," he said, "all the way."

"Are you sure?"

"As sure as you and I are sitting in the cab of this truck."

"How can I see her?"

"I'll get you the address and you can drive down to Texas in that new blue Chevrolet coupe you just bought and see her for yourself."

"How do you know she'll want to see me? If it's the girl I remember at camp meeting, I really don't know her."

"She knows you."

"How could that be?"

"Boy," Frank said, putting his hand on his heart, "she knows you right in here."

"How would you know that?"

He didn't reply, but he smiled and drove on.

I knew if Evelyn and I got together, it was going to have to be God bringing us together. I believe God is the Author of all good, and He is ever seeking to make us aware that good is knocking at our door: "Behold, I stand at the door, and knock: if any man hear my voice, and open the door, I will come in to him, and will sup with him, and he with me" (Rev. 3:20).

Someone said, "The knob on the door is on our side. We've got to open the door, then God will reveal His treasures to us."

One thing I knew about Frank Moss: He was a good judge of people, he cared about me, and I trusted him.

I promptly wrote a letter to Evelyn. I enclosed a little booklet I had written, *Salvation by the Blood,* and stated I looked forward to meeting her sometime. Back came a letter in which she thanked me for the booklet and said she also looked forward to meeting me. With only the vaguest memories of how she looked, something turned a flip-flop inside me. Suddenly, a knowing came in me that she was the one.

We began to write each other, and through our letters, I knew I was falling in love. I wrote her that I would like to drive down and visit her in September. She said she would be delighted. Again I felt something turn over inside me.

When my mother learned I was going to drive six hundred miles to south Texas to visit a girl, she knew I was serious. "I'm going with you," she said.

"Going with me?"

Mothers don't ordinarily accompany their sons on six-hundred-mile courting trips, but my mother was not an ordinary mother. Claudius Priscilla Roberts, in climbing through that barbed wire fence some twenty-one years before, knew the child she was carrying inside her body would be dark, black-haired, and blue-eyed and would preach the gospel.

I wasn't about to say no to Mama Roberts. I remembered how many times she had made the difference in my life. I felt it was right for her to go, so we got ready and left.

When I drove up to Evelyn's school, it was recess time. The little children cried, "Miss Evelyn, your boyfriend is here," and began clapping their hands.

A very attractive brown-haired young woman walked toward me. I introduced my mother to her, and she gave no hint of how she felt about my mother being with me.

I was dressed in a pearl gray gabardine suit, white shirt and tie, and well-shined black shoes. I had bought that suit on sale for fifteen dollars, quite a price in those days.

About that time the school bell rang, and Evelyn invited us to sit in her class. It was a class in English, and that was the day of the week she read a story to the children.

Whether she was nervous or not, she had it under control, and she read with the best modulated voice I had ever heard. She and the class were one, with every eye on her and everyone scarcely breathing. Even I got caught up in the story.

At the dismissal of the school day, she invited us to stay in the boarding house where she lived with other teachers. She didn't breathe a word about her feelings concerning me that she had written in her diary a year before. As for me, I had my eye on her.

That first night after coming from her school, I had forgotten to ask if she played the piano. It was such a little thing, but it was serious to me. We drove back to the school after dark and felt our way into a room where there was a piano, and she sat down and played beautifully. If God was having me come six hundred miles to see a girl I might marry, even this qualification played its part.

That weekend, she invited Mama and me to go with her to visit her grandparents, the Wingates, who were growers of oranges and grapefruit in the Rio Grande Valley at San Benito.

Evelyn's father, Edgar Lutman, had been a merchant in Warsaw, Missouri, when he married Edna Wingate. After Evelyn and her sister, Ruth, were born, he began to drink. He soon contracted tuberculosis and went to Arizona to see if that climate would cure him.

Soon afterward, Evelyn's mother and he divorced. She remarried a year later to Ira Fahnestock, who later became a minister. Edna had to go to work, and the two girls were raised mostly by their grandparents until they were in their teens. Mr. Wingate had loaned Evelyn three hundred dollars during her time at college to get through.

Evelyn loved the Wingates, and they her, and it showed when we arrived. They welcomed my mother and me and showed us to our rooms.

Mrs. Wingate whispered to Evelyn, "He's so thin."

On my six-foot-one-and-a-half-inch frame, I carried 150 pounds.

"Is he a mama's boy?" she asked Evelyn.

"Grandmother, he *is* thin and I don't know about his mother, but what's strange about a boy loving his mother?"

Mr. Wingate took me with him all over his farm and showed me the Rio Grande Valley covered with lush citrus groves. I had never seen such black, rich soil. When I mentioned to him that I thought anything could be grown in that soil, he asked me if I had grown up on a farm.

I explained I had, until I was fourteen, in between our family's moves when my father accepted preaching assignments. I had learned to plow, to plant cotton and corn, and to pick cotton and gather corn. In fact, I had worked all my life.

Later Evelyn told me he said, "That young man will do. He's been a farm boy."

On Saturday, Evelyn and I decided to go fishing nearby in the Gulf of Mexico. We fished all day, and all we caught was each other. All the things I had told Frank I wanted in a wife, I believed I was seeing in her. She was easy to be with, she was highly intelligent, and she was not intimidated by me. We talked about the Lord and my ministry in a perfectly natural way. I talked of my plans, and she of hers. We discovered there was absolutely nothing separating us; it was like we had been together every weekend for months.

When a person begins to believe God for something important in his life, there must be a knowing inside him, both of the natural and of the spiritual, which is not easy to explain. As someone said, "It's better felt than 'telt.'" I felt Evelyn, as a person, a woman, a believer, a gracious hostess, was one I wanted to hold near me and never let go.

Back in my car, parked on the hard sandy shore, I knew it was time to propose. But first, the humorous side of me came out. As a boy, I had learned a special proposal, and for fun, I tried it out on Evelyn.

"Evelyn, my huge, happy, hilarious heart is throbbing tumultuously, tremendously, triumphantly with a lingering, lasting, long-lived love for you. As I gaze in your bewildering, beauteous, bounteous, beaming eyes, I am literally lonesomely lost in a dazzling, daring, delightful dream in which your fair, felicitous, fanciful face is ever present like a colossal, comprehensive constellation. Will you be my sweet, smiling, soulful, satisfied spouse?"

She took me seriously. "Listen here, Oral Roberts, if you're trying to propose to me, do it in the English language."

I then proposed to Evelyn with words that were simple and few: "Evelyn, will you marry me?"

Teary eyed, she said, "Yes, I will marry you," as if she had said it before in her mind.

We sealed it with a kiss and a brief word of prayer, and we drove off to tell her grandparents and Mama.

Mr. Wingate was delighted to hear it. Mrs. Wingate, a very proper woman, wasn't so sure at first. She said, "That's nice." Evelyn told me later that her grandmother was terribly upset. She told Evelyn that she was making a big mistake. She felt Evelyn was a well-educated young woman with a great future. She should marry someone like a school principal or a businessman or a lawyer. If she married a preacher, she'd end up with nothing but a houseful of kids.

But Evelyn explained to her grandmother that she loved me. She knew I was the one for her.

By the next day, her grandmother had thawed out. She cooked a Sunday bridal dinner for us, and by that time, she was patting me on the back and saying, "Evelyn couldn't have done better."

Mama had one comment that she said to me alone, "Son, your father will love this girl just as I do. You've made the right choice. I knew it before I ever met her."

Sure enough, months later at our wedding, Papa met and loved Evelyn immediately. He was a man of God. He knew when he was in the presence of a lady, especially one who was a woman of God.

Originally, Evelyn and I were to wait until June of the next year to get married due to her commitment to finish her teaching contract in Texas. However, I decided I wanted to move it up to December.

It took some doing to get Evelyn's school administrators to let her off long enough to get married, but we finally received the word of approval. After our wedding, she was to return to finish out the school term.

The time was set for 3:00 P.M. on Christmas Day, 1938, in the church Papa pastored in Westville and to which Evelyn's family belonged. We were to be married by my dearest friend, Rev. Oscar Moore, pastor in Okmulgee, Oklahoma, who was only eight years older than I. Oscar is still my dear friend. Our friendship began when I was eighteen years old and continues today. Oscar was my first choice to be a member of the Board of Trustees when I incorporated my ministry in 1948 in Tulsa, and he is still on the board.

As Christmas drew near, it dawned on me that I didn't have the money to get married. The feeling in those days in many of the churches in which I preached seemed to be, "God, You keep Oral humble, and we'll keep him poor." They had succeeded.

In my favor, I had my blue Chevrolet coupe, which I bought by saving every nickel and dime I could over a period of a year. I bought it brand-new for $620, 10 percent off for being a minister. I had decent clothes, but buying gasoline and keeping up the car for my travels kept me low on money, particularly when I often received no more than $10 to $20 for preaching a two-week revival.

I love Dr. Pepper, which cost five cents a bottle back then. I rationed myself to three bottles a week, with one of them given to the pastor for whom I would be preaching.

It came down to my needing to borrow $20 at the bank to get married. The banker wouldn't let me have it without a cosigner. Sheepishly, as I was learning high finance, I asked Rev. Oscar Moore to sign with me. (I've never asked for a personal cosigner since!)

Oscar laughed and went with me and signed. But not before the banker took out $2 for interest in advance. I needed $20. The banker took out $2, leaving me $18. It didn't seem right to my inexperienced financial mind, but the man with the money was in charge. It was a lesson I was never to forget.

Oscar drove two hundred miles round trip to marry us, and I gave him $5 of my $18. I paid $5 for the marriage license and spent $3 for flowers. As someone said later, "Oral just threw the rest of his $18 away." It wasn't funny to me.

Evelyn was earning $80 a month teaching school, and I about $40 a month preaching. I told her she wasn't a very good businesswoman to give that up and marry a man making half as much. She just smiled.

I had her wedding present in layaway, and it cost $10. I didn't have the money so she said, "Oral, you can borrow it from me." I was so embarrassed that I wanted to die right there.

I said, "Evelyn, I will pay you back not only for this but the $300 you owe your grandfather." I was sure her grandfather thought he would never be repaid.

I had integrity. I was poor and embarrassed to call on Evelyn to help me, but I would overcome it, given time.

I will never forget the day I paid her grandfather in full, then saw him so moved by my honesty he made a decision to accept Christ as his personal Savior. He became one of the best friends and supporters, along with his wife, I ever had.

Right after the marriage, I became ill with the measles. Somehow I was able to drive Evelyn back to Texas to finish out the school spring semester. My measles were refusing to break out. Mrs. Wingate bundled me up, put me to bed, and gave me the first drink of hard liquor I'd ever had, which was also the last. "Drink this," she said. "It will break the measles out."

She was right. Soon I was up, and Evelyn and I resumed what was left of the few days of our honeymoon.

I returned to Oklahoma to continue my revivals while Evelyn stayed in Texas to continue teaching. I felt we were hardly married. I didn't see her except one weekend in those final four months of her school term. I drove down, and that weekend our first child, Rebecca Ann, was conceived.

Nine months later when Dr. Giesen delivered her in my parents' house, I stood by and watched. She was dark as I was and had a full head of curly black hair. She looked like a little Indian.

Some people believe that most marriages never become totally complete until the birth of the first child. I knew it made a difference to me. Evelyn was a mother, I was a father, we were parents, and life stretched out ahead of us, it seemed to me, into infinity.

I Can Count on Her

I know that when I married Evelyn Lutman, I received a gift from a Higher Power. She is a woman of German descent who fits me like a hand in a glove. She is not only warm, protective, and close like a glove; she has been my wife, my lover, the mother of my four children, my adviser, my partner, and my darling for fifty-six years.

Evelyn is not a weak woman who takes everything I say as gospel or lets me boss her around. I would never have wanted a woman like that to be my wife.

No two have been more different in temperament. This difference has caused some very rough moments in our marriage, but we always returned to our faith in God, which brought us together in the beginning.

For example, during the first year of marriage when I would get moody and not speak for three days, Evelyn would wonder what she had done wrong. My mother, learning of it, explained to Evelyn that all her people were like that, and I showed the Indian traits more than any of her children. She advised her just to ignore it, and as I got used to living with Evelyn, I would come out of that.

Evelyn said that took a load off her mind. She learned to ignore my "Indian spells," as she called them, and in time I was able to change.

In our home, Evelyn is orderly, disciplined, and clean as a pin. It took me quite some time to even approach her orderliness around the house or in the care of my clothes. She has given me a pretty tough time in this area.

I am orderly in my ministry, disciplined in my relationship with God, and punctual. I am true to my word, and whatever I have bought I have tried never to get the family in debt.

Evelyn and I have always been close in our love and marriage. Yes, we've had our ups and downs, our disagreements and hurts, but over the years, we found ourselves growing even closer in our prayers, our hard work, our seed sowing, and our expectation of miracles. We literally had to do this to survive!

No matter how much obedience I have to God, how strongly I preach the Word of God, how much I use my faith to help others, or how strong is my character and honest are my dealings with one and all, I have realized more and more the truth of God's Word: "Whoso findeth a wife findeth a good thing, and obtaineth favour of the LORD" (Prov. 18:22).

I have found myself leaning on my wife in times of stress, in times when I'm attacked as I carry out God's call on my life, and in times of just being a man subject to mistakes and shortcomings. To feel her arms around me, to have her say, "Oral, let's look at this from the standpoint of God's Word," or to know she is often in her prayer closet or is doing little things for me so that would not take away time from my studies, my writings, my preaching and praying, and my doing the things in our ministry that only I as the founder can do has been a real comfort to me.

I know when it is time for God to hand out whatever rewards He has for Evelyn and me, hers will exceed mine. For I know we're rewarded not just for the things that people can see and praise or criticize. Those things often done behind closed doors, in the name of the Lord and for His glory, bring God's highest rewards both on this earth and in eternity.

Without question, Evelyn has been the most respected and popular person on the Oral Roberts University campus and in this total ministry. I take that as a great honor to me. I had the wisdom to listen to my discerning friend, Frank Moss, who shared the beauty and qualities of Evelyn Lutman with me at the perfect time in my life. I had the ability to recognize Evelyn as the one for me and the good sense to wait until I was ready to get married.

In all the years, no matter what God spoke in my heart and I sought to obey, she has never once tried to hinder me. She has questioned me, as she ought, until she felt in her own spirit I had, indeed, heard God speaking more of His plan to me.

She has prayed alongside me, both day and night; she has wept with me when the going was complex and hard and the opposition seemed too much to bear. She has hated it when people and certain church leaders misunderstood that I was not acting on my own when I did what God called me to do (knowing I have many shortcomings as a human being and ordinary man). She has hung in there through good times and bad, and she has never faltered in supporting and loving me as her husband. I owe all that to God.

I trust my wife. She is my best friend. She will not desert me. I can count on her.

I cannot even try to estimate the number of people who have told me, "Oral, without Evelyn you never could have accomplished what you have." I couldn't agree more.

I was about to learn this firsthand as we were embarking on a journey of experiences harder, yet more glorious, than either of us could ever have imagined. During the next few years, my growing dissatisfaction with the status quo of my ministry would cause our home to be uprooted and changed many times. I was searching for an avenue to fulfill God's call on my life and hitting dead ends everywhere I turned. Something somewhere had to break, but what, where, and how?

CHAPTER 6

MY SPIRITUAL VOLCANO

THE BEST way I can describe myself from the time I heard God's call on my life until the day I actually began taking His healing power to my generation is with three words—*a spiritual volcano*! A volcano seems peaceful on the outside, but underneath it can be experiencing a tremendous amount of pressure to bring about a change. Finally after the pressure has built up enough, it erupts and flows out everywhere, effecting a change on the surface of the land forever.

I knew pressure was building inside my spirit to fulfill God's call on my life—to take His mighty healing power to hurting people. The spiritual eruption had to happen, or I could never truly be used to bring God's miraculous deliverance to defeat sin, sickness, demons, fear, and lack in the lives of others. I also knew once the spiritual eruption of God's power and anointing took place, it would flow out on others, change the direction of the church far more toward the miraculous power of God, and give multimillions hope who did not have it. What I didn't know was how painful that eruption would be. As with any volcanic eruption, some old things have to die to make room for the new. But it was going to take twelve years of hard work and growing dissatisfaction in my life before even the smoldering of change could be seen.

When Evelyn and I and little Rebecca began traveling as I preached revivals in churches in many states, we encountered the real, cold world—literally. I had joined the Pentecostal Holiness

Church, which had ordained me through Bishop Dan T. Muse, a man who became my friend for life.

That first revival after Rebecca's birth was in January 1940, in Byars, Oklahoma, and it was bitterly cold: four below zero, and much lower with the chill factor when the Oklahoma winds blew. We really had to bundle up.

During the three-week revival, we stayed in a home of a member of the church. The house was rather open, with plank walls that let the wind through. Only in the kitchen and the living room, where the woodstoves were kept going day and night, was there warmth in the house.

In our bedroom, Evelyn would say, "Please, Oral, get in bed first and warm my side."

I did and then rolled over to my side of the bed, and we placed little Rebecca between us. Soon her body was like a heating stove. We had to be careful that she wouldn't be smothered.

When Evelyn would awaken to nurse Rebecca and change her diaper, with the subzero winds seeping through the house, she really got cold. It didn't take long, however, to get warm again when she put Rebecca between us. Her little body kept the bed warm.

The best thing after getting up in the morning and dressing on the cold wood floors was to go into the warm kitchen where a breakfast of hot biscuits, country ham, and either cream gravy or eggs was waiting. We would sit there and eat and talk together with the family about the Lord.

There was no indoor plumbing. Going to that outhouse at four below zero and using an old Sears catalog for toilet paper was an experience. The first time we stayed in a home where there was indoor plumbing we thought we had died and gone to heaven!

Both Evelyn and I had just turned twenty-three years old. We never thought any of that was a hardship; we were just happy somebody wanted my ministry.

At the revival each night in the little small-town church, we had a full house. The pastor said, "They came to see and hear that young Roberts boy who'd been healed of tuberculosis and was called to preach."

Evelyn played the piano for the little choir. Rebecca was in her bassinet, which was placed where she could see her mother or she would let out a yell. Later, when we pastored a little church,

Evelyn had to put Rebecca's bed close enough to her hand that she could hold Evelyn's finger or she wouldn't go to sleep.

In that revival in Byars, the people kept coming every night despite the cold. A big woodstove in the middle of the little thirty-by-forty-foot building was kept red hot all through the services.

I couldn't hold out to preach more than fifteen to twenty minutes, but the people said I took them with me through whatever area of the Bible I was preaching. One older lady said to me one night at the close of the service, "Hold in there, son. You keep preaching like this, and you'll be a preacher one of these days."

That upset Evelyn a little bit. She said to me later, "You can preach *now!*"

——— *The Thirst for Knowledge Continues*

In 1942, I left the evangelistic field for several years to pastor a church in Shawnee, Oklahoma. Also at that time, I felt a sharp need for more education, so I enrolled at Oklahoma Baptist University in Shawnee. Once again, God was beginning the preparation for the part of my calling that I didn't completely understand yet:

"Build Me a university and build it on My authority and the Holy Spirit."

I threw myself into my studies and into the church. The church prospered, the Sunday school tripled in size, and there were many conversions. But even with every ounce of energy being drained from me, I could not escape the insatiable drive that God had put inside me to bring healing to the people. I felt closed in and limited everywhere I turned. The church's means were not broad enough or dramatic enough to allow me to capture and portray God's call on my life. After a few years, I resigned the church to go back on the evangelistic field, but was soon pastoring again in Toccoa, Georgia.

Everywhere I looked, I saw very little, if any, miracle signs and wonders happening in my denomination's church services. For that matter, I didn't see it happening in *any* denomination's church services. Something was missing that was there in the New Testament when Jesus and the apostles walked this earth—and it was the power of God! To the depths of my being, I ached to see this power demonstrated in my life.

One of the Greatest Secrets I've Learned

I knew what God had called me to do, but I felt no consistent and long-lasting anointing or power to accomplish it, although a few miracles occurred here and there. One of these miracles happened when I was pastoring a Pentecostal Holiness church in Toccoa, Georgia, shortly after I had resigned from the Shawnee church.

One of our deacons, Clyde Lawson, had a terrible accident in which he dropped a car motor on his foot. Another deacon of the church, Bill Lee, immediately drove out to Clyde's house with me when I was called to pray with him.

When we got there, Clyde was on the ground, holding his right foot in his hands, absolutely in excruciating pain. The toes of his foot had been crushed, and blood was running out of his shoe. Clyde was screaming at the top of his voice. All he could do was point at his crushed foot, trying desperately to get us to pray.

As I looked down at him holding his foot, a sudden compassion came over me. Without thinking, I knelt down and touched the end of his shoe with my hand. I said a few words of earnest prayer and straightened up. The moment I straightened up, Clyde quit screaming. He tried to move his toes in the shoe and found that he could do so. The pain was gone. Jumping to his feet, he stomped his foot on the floor and said, "Brother Roberts, what did you do to me?"

I said, "Clyde, I didn't do a thing."

He said, "Yes, you did. The pain is gone. My foot is healed."

I was amazed. While I watched him, he stooped down, took off his shoe, and showed us his foot. It was perfectly normal. I could not deny that a miracle had been wrought.

When we left, Bill Lee said, "Brother Roberts, do you have that kind of power all the time?"

I said, "Bill, I wish I did."

He said, "If you had that kind of power all the time, you could bring a revival to this world."

I thought a lot about what Bill said. Yes, if I had that kind of power all the time, I could bring a revival to this world. When the power of the Lord comes upon a man to deliver the people, he brings a revival to mankind. I would never forget that.

I began to *expect* to receive ideas for the call I had to take God's healing power to my generation and later to build Him a university. I knew it would take millions of dollars to do all the things necessary to get God's healing message across America and into the world containing my generation. I had no money to speak of, just a call from God, but not the slightest idea how to do it on a global scale. I had no idea how to have an impact on preachers and churches or people outside the kingdom of God. No one had ever done it before on the scale of the call with which my spirit was erupting.

Fifty-Five Dollars a Week

Not long after that, I left Toccoa, Georgia, and returned to Oklahoma where I reentered Oklahoma Baptist University in Shawnee. By that time, we had our second child, Ronald David. It was just too much to take Evelyn and the children to the revivals I was preaching, and we were without a car, so I would thumb my way to and from the local revivals—no matter what the weather. Sometimes I would make it home just in time to go to my university classes the next day.

Thank God, that didn't last long. In the fall of 1946, at twenty-eight years of age, I accepted the invitation to be pastor of the Pentecostal Holiness church in Enid, Oklahoma, and I immediately enrolled in Phillips University in Enid. Enid was a beautiful little town of thirty thousand people. I felt like I might remain there for life.

The little church I was pastoring was growing stronger. Quite a number of young couples, who were the age of Evelyn and me, had been converted under my ministry and joined the church. I often met with the young men to plan for greater things in the future.

I loved the people of that church, which had some German-speaking families, but they could understand English pretty well. Evelyn, being German, was their prize, and she loved them as much as they loved her. It seemed they eagerly awaited my sermons, and it was a joy to minister both in the church and in the community. The church was excited about us, and we were excited about the opportunity before us.

Although the future looked bright, we were having struggles with the present. I was pastoring full-time, carrying sixteen semester hours at Phillips University, and trying to provide for my family with two children—all that on a salary of fifty-five dollars a week. Another struggle was that nobody in authority in the church seemed to have the slightest concern about where we were to live.

When I came as the new pastor, the house the church had been renting for the pastor was no longer available. One of the men in the church invited us to bring our two children and live with his family until another house could be located.

He and his wife had four children, we had two, and the house had five rooms—two were bedrooms and one a bathroom. At first, things went fine. A few weeks, however, were enough for the new to wear off. The children got into little fights, and the crowded conditions of that house set on the nerves of all, especially the two mothers who had their own responsibilities to their families.

Nothing was happening in securing a place for us to live. The church board didn't feel the church had the money, nor could they get it, to buy or build a parsonage. That was when things came to a head.

Evelyn is a patient, hardworking, and loving woman. But when she saw the church was stalling and I was not pressing the issue as a pastoral leader should, she called me aside to give me the most uncharacteristic news of our marriage.

"Oral, I'm going to my mother's. I'm taking the children with me and staying until you find us a house."

"You what?"

"Oral, I love you, and I appreciate this family opening their home to us, but everybody is getting miserable and soon things will blow up. It's not right. *Either you lead the church, or it leads you.* Meanwhile I have a responsibility to our children."

I knew she had reached the end of her rope, and I knew she would do exactly what she said.

"All right," I said. "Honey, just give me a couple of weeks and let's see what can be done."

I went right to work with the members of the church board. They gave me a good hearing but took no action. The two weeks I had asked Evelyn to wait were swiftly passing.

My entire thought was, *What will the church board do?* I discovered they were doing nothing. Meanwhile, the Lord had been dealing with me concerning a pretty drastic action on my part. He was impressing me deeply:

"Let it begin with you!"

I didn't dare tell Evelyn what I was thinking. Our fifty-five-dollar salary each week was seemingly smaller and smaller and the bills bigger and bigger, and there was no parsonage or any kind of house to move to.

Over and over I felt the Spirit's impression:

"Stand up before the people, not the board, and give your whole week's salary to start a fund to buy a parsonage."

The idea seemed so foolish when that salary was getting us further behind every week.

Strange are the ways of the Lord! He said in His Word, "For my thoughts are not your thoughts, neither are your ways my ways, saith the LORD" (Isa. 55:8). He also said, "If ye be willing and obedient, ye shall eat the good of the land" (Isa. 1:19).

My mind said, *If I do this, Evelyn will not understand, the church people will think I am out of my mind, and worst of all, my fifty-five dollars will go down the drain. When Evelyn leaves with the children, I may have to leave with her!*

I literally had to pray it through until my spirit took over my mind and got me in harmony with the deep impression of the Lord and found peace about sowing this as a seed for a harvest of a home (although at the time I didn't understand seeds of faith as I did soon after).

The Parsonage Challenge

Following my sermon during a Wednesday night prayer meeting of the church when only a handful of people were there, I called the church treasurer forward and handed him my week's uncashed salary check. I said to the people, "I am giving this as a seed out of our need for a new parsonage. If anyone feels what I feel, that the Lord wants us to have a place to live and serve the church better, and you feel you should give—even sacrificially—I, as your pastor, invite you to do so."

A quietness came over the people that I could feel. Outwardly, I felt like I was on the edge of a cliff in the midst of a hurricane, but I had peace in my spirit. I knew I was being obedient, and God had promised in His Word that we would eat the good of the land.

Almost as an afterthought, these words came out of my mouth: "Remember, the greater the sacrifice, the greater the blessing. Give God your best, then expect His best."

Suddenly, it was like a dam broke. A German man stood up and said in broken English, "This is our pastor. He didn't ask to come here. We asked him. We all know of the living conditions of two families in one small house. Brother Roberts spoke of a seed. Well, I planted my wheat seed, and now my harvest is here, which I am selling for a good price. I give five hundred dollars to help with a down payment, and I do it unto the Lord."

He sat down. The quiet remained. A young couple stood and haltingly said they would give twenty-five dollars. A widow pledged one hundred dollars, and it shook the place up.

Over to my left, sitting in a chair against the wall, was the largest building contractor in the church.

I saw him getting up and heard him call my name. "What would happen if I gave one thousand dollars?" he asked.

"Brother, we accept your one thousand dollars in the name of the Lord. We praise God because you are so successful in our city as a builder, and we believe your large gift will ignite the fire in the whole church to move forward in securing a church parsonage, not only for me as your present pastor, but for those who will follow."

He didn't sit down. He *fell* down in his chair. He was speechless. I went on with the meeting while others made their gifts and pledges. I prayed over all and then dismissed them.

On the way out, that brother stopped me. "Brother Oral, did you realize I was only asking a question?"

"No," I said. "I thought the Lord was giving you one of the greatest opportunities of your life to learn the joy of giving and receiving God's blessings of return to you."

He looked around at the people watching. "Very well. I'll have the check to you by Sunday."

When I reached the house that evening and recited the happenings at the church, Evelyn sensed I was holding something back. Innocentlike, she said, "And what did you give from us?"

"Our whole week's salary," I blurted out.

"Oh, Oral, you didn't. We've already paid our tithes, and I'm all for that. I know 10 percent of our income is the Lord's. But He doesn't expect you to give everything. How will I buy groceries Saturday? How will we get through the week?"

When she looked at me, I must have looked happy because then she said, "You may be happy tonight, but when we have no food to put on the table, you may not be so happy."

"But, Evelyn, God dealt with me. I could obey or disobey. What would you have done?"

"Oh, Oral, I'm not mad at you. I'm just hurt because I carry so much of the responsibility for the children, and this seems like it's going too far."

Finally, we went to bed. About 4:00 A.M., a loud knock on the front door awakened me. It was a cold night, and it was snowing. I opened the door and saw Art Newfield, a large wheat farmer who had previously left the church but had returned under my ministry.

He said, "Oral, I hope you will pardon me for coming at this hour of the night. After the service tonight in which you gave your entire week's salary, I went home but couldn't sleep. About two hours ago, I rose up from bed under what I believe was a direct leading of the Lord, went out into the yard, and dug up this." He handed me four one-hundred-dollar bills. "As a farmer I know I have to sow seed first before I can expect a harvest. The Lord said to give these to you as seed money."

I looked around, and Evelyn had on her robe and was peering around the bedroom door. As Art left, I walked over to her, waved the money in front of her eyes, and said, "See, I told you God dealt with me about giving our fifty-five-dollar-a-week salary."

She burst into tears. "Oral, it wasn't that I was losing faith in the Lord when I said I was leaving for my mother's house. As your wife and a mother, I had to do something. And I wasn't mad at you for giving our salary, but it was such a surprise, such a blow. I couldn't see any future."

"I know that, Evelyn, because I know you. I also know you want me to obey God."

Then I said, "Here, you hold these four one-hundred-dollar bills and compare them with the fifty-five dollars I gave to the Lord tonight. I didn't know God was going to send them, but I knew if I obeyed and gave first, God would do something out of the ordinary. This proves it."

The struggle to get a parsonage was over. But there were more struggles to come.

────── *A Physical Machine and a Spiritual Moment*

Shortly after that, I drove home one evening from making house calls on different members of the church, and I pulled up in front of our house, which was the new parsonage, in my now old beat-up Chevrolet. A car was parked directly in front of me, and when I put on the brakes to stop, they didn't work very well, and I smashed into the back of it!

I was emotionally crushed. We had very little money, and I'd hit a car and damaged the back end of it.

It was just like the devil to whisper, "The owner of this car will never know you did this. Don't say anything about it." No wonder Jesus calls Satan "the tempter" (Matt. 4:3)!

I knocked on the door of the house next to ours, and a man answered the door. "Sir, my name is Oral Roberts. I'm your next-door neighbor. Is that car out there yours?"

"Sure is," he said.

I proceeded to tell him that I had just run into the back of his car. I told him if he would get an estimate on the cost for repairs, I would pay it.

He came out of his house and looked at his car and said, "Why did you tell me? I never would have known who did it."

"But I would have known it, and it's right that I pay," I replied.

"My name is Gustavus," he said. "Just call me Mr. Gus." He shook my hand. "Young man," he said, "you just forget you hit my car. I'll take care of it."

When I started to tell him I was responsible to do it, he seemed embarrassed and went in his house.

I was mowing my lawn in the backyard late one afternoon when Mr. Gus leaned over the fence and said, "Mowing your lawn, huh?"

"Yes, I've been neglecting it." The truth was, Evelyn had lit a fire under me to get it done.

Mr. Gus said, "That *is* your car out in front, isn't it?"

"Yes, sir, it is."

"It's not much, is it?"

"No, I guess not."

"Well, you come down to my office in the morning. I want to talk to you about it." And he gave me the address.

When I arrived at his office the next morning and was seated, Mr. Gus said, "Young man, I am not a member of your church, I am not even a Christian, but something tells me you are about to do something unusual in this world."

I did not say anything, but I was thinking of the strong urge I was feeling concerning my calling.

Mr. Gus continued, "What you're going to do is too big for this town. It will take you to the world."

I could scarcely believe what he was saying.

"I have felt ever since you came to my door and told me of hitting my car and offered to pay for repairing it that I should take that old worn-out car off your hands."

I was too stunned to reply.

"I am the Buick dealer, you know," he said.

I did not know.

"You drive your old car to my car lot tomorrow. I'll take it and sell it for the highest price and get you a new Buick at my cost. I'll even arrange any financing you need."

He did not know I had grown up loving the Buick automobile. To me, it was the best. I could scarcely believe I was about to own one, a brand-new one.

"Well, what do you say?"

"Are you sure you want to do this? My old car is not much."

"Oh, yes, I want to do it. As a matter of fact, I won't be happy until I do it."

"All right, then," and I started breathing normally again.

Later to my further surprise, Mr. Gus said he got quite a high price for my car and the difference between that and the new

Buick at his cost was only a few hundred dollars. He had the papers ready for me to sign.

Evelyn was overwhelmed. I reminded her of that fifty-five dollars I had given, which was over and above our tithes, and how that seed had gotten the church started in getting a parsonage. We had received about seven times more than we had given through God dealing with Art Newfield, besides becoming spiritually closer to the Lord. "Now," I said, "look what a larger harvest God is giving us on that seed: a new Buick!"

After we went to pick up the new car and were driving it home, Evelyn suddenly said, "Oral, stop the car!"

"What's the matter?"

"Just stop the car and get out with me."

She put her hands on the car and asked me to put mine on, too. She said, "Oral, this is more than just a new Buick. It represents what God will do when we obey and take Him at His Word. Let's just praise the Lord."

As the cars whizzed by, it must have looked strange to see a young man and woman with their hands on a car, praising the Lord.

It was a *physical* machine, but it was a *spiritual* moment! It seemed our faith took wings, and the call to take God's healing power to this generation and someday to build Him a university didn't seem so impossible after all.

CHAPTER 7

THE STIRRING OF MY NEST

T HINGS WERE going pretty well in Enid. I had even selected a potential site on which to build a university when God's time came.

However, as I neared my twenty-ninth birthday, tremendous dissatisfaction seized my spirit and mind. No longer was the beautiful little town of Enid a delight to me.

I began to feel deep within me God's time had come to begin carrying out His call to take His healing power to my generation. Every breath that I took, I knew I could take it only because the Lord had healed my lungs twelve years before. The call became certain in me to begin praying for the sick.

Someone once said, "Coming events cast their shadows before them." There were shadows all right.

I became terribly aware that I knew of no healings in the Enid church since I had been pastor. I had preached on healing, giving examples from the Bible, especially concerning Jesus and the believers in the early church. I had given the history of healings documented through the centuries, including my own. But like the parsonage situation, there was no response that I could see or feel. Yet I was burning inside to get on with the call that I had carried since the evening of my healing. My nest was being stirred.

Get Off the Briar and Get on the Wing!

The best way I know to describe what it was like during that time is to compare it to a mother eagle teaching her babies how to fly. She stirs their nest to get them off the briar of the nest and onto her wing so she can show them how it feels to fly. God talks about this in Deuteronomy 32:11–12:

> As an eagle stirreth up her nest,
> fluttereth over her young,
> spreadeth abroad her wings, taketh them,
> beareth them on her wings:
> So the LORD alone did lead him,
> and there was no strange god with him.

The first thing the mother eagle does is to build her nest in a high place, usually some inaccessible area. There in the loneliness of the heights, she gathers all kinds of materials such as briars and sticks to build the nest. Then she covers it with her own soft down feathers. She makes it comfortable, snug, and secure.

She lays her eggs, and then she hatches her young ones. There they spend the early part of their lives while she flies far and near to get food for them. The mother's warm body hovers over and near them, protecting them. While they watch, she flies and soars into the sky—into that great unknown to them. They are content to remain in the beautiful soft nest.

The day comes when it is time for the baby eagles to leave the nest and to learn to fly. But the nest is so comfortable.

Built into the mother eagle's nature is a way to get her little ones out of the nest. If she doesn't, they will forfeit their rights to be eagles and never become all that God intends them to be. So the mother eagle begins to remove the soft covering and let the little eagles down on the sharp briars where they begin to stir uneasily. They wonder why the world is treating them like this. They become frightened and begin to scream.

When the little eagles see that soft wing, that powerful wing there on the side of the nest, while they are stirring around uneasily on those sharp briars, they start climbing out of the nest and getting on the wing. The moment they have fastened their talons on the big broad strong wing of the mother eagle, she begins to fly, and they hang on for dear life.

There she goes—up and up, mile after mile—soaring, flying, drifting, winging her way across the sky. The little eagles forget about everything else from the sheer ecstasy of that flight. Up over the hills and into the deep blue of the sky, up and around and down they fly.

Then she brings them back, and she puts her wing down. They jump off and get back into the nest only to find that they are right back on the sharp briars. She puts her wing back down, and immediately, they climb off the briars, get on her wing, and up she goes again. She comes back and dumps them off. Again they get back on, and up she goes. She keeps on until their fear is taken away.

Then one day, with them on her wing, as she is soaring high above the earth, all of a sudden she lurches and they fall off into space. The little eagles begin to scream and plummet toward earth like rocks, beating their wings and screaming at the top of their voices. Before they can hit the ground, the big mother eagle speeds downward with superb accuracy. Spreading out her wings under them, she catches them, and up she goes again, high into the sky. She shakes them off and then catches them up again until they stretch out their wings and find that they, too, can fly. There they go, side by side, flying, soaring, and gliding.

That was how God was dealing with me. I felt like the rug had been pulled out from under me. I no longer felt at home in Enid. I felt like I would smother. When I would try to share my feelings with the bishops of my denomination, seeking counsel, they would send me home, telling me I should be satisfied and thankful that I was pastoring one of our most successful churches at such a young age.

I recalled how, shortly after I had begun preaching, my dad and I were sitting in chairs leaning back against the outside of the house. We had been reading our Bibles together and sharing our thoughts.

"Papa, do you believe that a return to the miracles of the early church after the day of Pentecost, as told in the book of Acts, will come again?" I asked.

"I not only believe it," he replied, "I know it. And you have got to know that is the very reason God raised you up and told you His plan for your life and ministry."

"What do you think I should do?"

"Keep on learning the Word, keep listening to the Holy Spirit, who is in you, and continue to preach as you are now until God's time comes. And it will come. I may not be alive when it comes upon you and upon many, many others, but when I die, I'll know those great miracle days are coming to deliver people all over the world."

Mama had walked near, and looking at me, she affirmed Papa's word. "It will come, son. Just remember to obey God and stay small in your own eyes, and God will bless the world through you." I have tried to live by those very words.

Forced Out of the Nest

One day, when I was sitting in my sociology class at the university I was attending at that time, the professor began talking about God and creation. He seemed to have no trouble with God creating man. But when he reached the place where the Bible says, "And the LORD God caused a deep sleep to fall upon Adam, and he slept: and he took one of his ribs, and closed up the flesh instead thereof; and the rib, which the LORD God had taken from man, made he a woman, and brought her unto the man" (Gen. 2:21–22), he stated, "It is a scientific impossibility for God to have made woman from a man's rib."

He paused.

Although it was a church-related university, no student said a word. I was not a member of that church and had determined that because of the privilege given me to pursue my education there, even when I disagreed, I would not provoke controversy. I remained quiet, but inside I was seething.

Suddenly, I heard God speak to me as clearly as He had on the evening I lay in the backseat of Elmer's car on the way to the healing evangelist in Ada:

"Son, don't be like other men. Don't be like any denomination. Be like Jesus, and heal the people as He did."

Raising my hand, I asked the professor if I could be excused. I went to my car and drove straight home. On the way home God continued speaking to me. I asked Him how I could know how to be like Jesus and heal the people in the ways He did. He told me to

read through the four Gospels of Matthew, Mark, Luke, and John
and the book of Acts three times consecutively during the next
thirty days and do it on my knees, and He would show me Jesus
and His healing ways.

Evelyn was surprised to see me home so early. When I told
her what God had said, she asked, "What can I do to help?"

I knew what I had to do. I replied, "Don't cook for me until I
tell you. I'll fast as Paul did. You remember he said, I fast often
[2 Cor. 11:27], and like him, I am not led to fast long periods at a
time but one meal or two meals or five meals or ten—whatever. I
will tell you in advance when to cook for me." I thought of how
honored I was with the wife God gave me.

As I began to regiment my life, it wasn't easy—so many demands! But I could not be distracted. My entire being cried out for
the Lord's power. I wanted it more than anything else in the world,
and I refused to let anyone or anything get in the way of what God
was trying to do in my life.

Through that time of fasting and prayer, my weakness as a
man was indelibly imprinted on my spirit. I soon understood the
apostle Paul's hard-learned lesson that God's strength shall be
made perfect in our weakness (see 2 Cor. 12:9).

I also learned it is not the fast itself that helps a person, but the
change in attitude that transforms him. If that doesn't happen, the
fast becomes a mere physical sacrifice. Through my fasting, I
gained great inner strength, a strength that would be needed to
fulfill all that God called me to.

My View of Jesus Changed Forever

Nothing else had ever come close to the importance in my life
and ministry of reading the four Gospels and Acts in the way God instructed me—getting the right view of Jesus and actually experiencing Him until He became part and parcel of my whole existence.
After all, the original information about Jesus is in these five books.

I think the Greeks who sought out Philip to get him to introduce them to Jesus expressed it well. They said, "Sir, we would see
Jesus" (John 12:21), and see Him they did!

I've often wondered at the different approaches Christians
take in their Christian experiences. To me, the greater majority

I've known or observed do not have the person of Jesus and the life He brings uppermost in their minds.

Unfortunately, more often they major on something about Jesus—His philosophy and theology, His sayings, or His doctrine—rather than His person. What is wrong with that approach? Nothing in itself. In my opinion, what is lacking is knowing about Jesus Himself and building a doctrine exclusively on Him in spite of denominational ties or in spite of being from an independent church. Above all, real Christianity is not a thing; it is a life, and life is a person—Jesus Christ of Nazareth!

There is no way I can count or name the major books I've studied of the different religions of the world: their philosophies and promises and practices. Nor can I count or number the times and places in the many, many nations in which I've ministered or the more noted leaders of these religions to whom I've been introduced.

To me, it is true that much of what they teach is not much different from Jesus' teachings. Truth is truth wherever you find it. What I failed to see and feel and grasp was this: Where is the life in their religions? In fact, where is the life in Christianity? To me, our focus is to be on the crucified, risen, ascended Jesus and on the blessed Holy Spirit, who inspired men to write the infallible Word of God so that in it we have a living, risen Savior and Deliverer Himself before us. The old spiritual, "Take the whole world but give me Jesus," expresses it well.

True, every truth has power to bring change. Whole truth, however, is a man, Jesus Christ of Nazareth. Jesus Himself said it: "I am the way, the truth, and the life" (John 14:6). He didn't come to talk about life; He is life!

My first discovery of this began when my sister said to me, "Oral, God is going to heal you." It was accentuated when Rev. George Moncey laid his hands on my sick body and without hesitation or doubt said, "You foul tormenting disease, I command you in the name of Jesus Christ of Nazareth, come out of this boy! Loose him and let him go free." Life, glorious life, flowed into my bleeding lungs, my stuttering tongue, my innermost being—and I became alive! I had health again! His life became my life!

This is where, I believe, the so-called purists miss it. They think if they believe the fundamental, evangelical things about

Jesus and build them into a precise doctrine, they have it all. I believe they fall short of the mark of God and His high calling, and that is a serious thing.

What is that shortfall? It is too often failing to allow themselves to see Jesus as more than fundamentals and evangelical truths and doctrinal imperatives. In so doing, they say the Word is everything, nothing less, nothing more. However, I believe without the Holy Spirit giving revelational knowledge through the gifts of the Spirit, the written Word of God becomes as mere paper and ink in the Bibles we buy. The Holy Spirit inspired men to write the Bible, and the Holy Spirit gives it life in the "now" as we depend on Him to bring it alive in our hearts.

My father told me when he first began studying the Bible, as a man who was not born again by the Spirit of God, he became so confused that he threw it on the floor. My older sister with epilepsy, not knowing any better, tore it up.

He said, however, when he heard anointed preaching of the Word, the Holy Spirit convicted his mind of sin and of righteousness and of judgment to come (as Jesus said in John 5:25–29), and he was instantly born again. He was filled with the Holy Spirit, feeling and experiencing the miraculous life of Jesus flooding his whole being and making him a new creature in Christ (see 2 Cor. 5:17). From that time, the Bible became a living book of God Himself to him.

While my father, Ellis, was responding to the preaching of the Word, my mother was responding to the singing of the hymns of the church by anointed singers. When she did, she threw up her hands and surrendered her life to God. She was soundly converted, feeling and experiencing the supernatural life of Jesus Christ of Nazareth.

Originally, the Pentecostals stood on believing all that the Bible said—all of it—including being baptized with the Holy Spirit, with speaking in tongues and miracles. They connected with Jesus, who said of the Holy Spirit, "He shall testify of me" (John 15:26). The Holy Spirit brought them life, miraculous life. They have tried to hold to the principal thing: the life of the Savior through the indwelling Holy Spirit and His gifts. That made them different from many of the old-line historic denominations.

I was after that miraculous life in Enid as I began reading the four Gospels and Acts to see how God would show me Jesus of

Nazareth, His ways of healing the sick, and the whole of His life, ministry, and doctrine.

I read how Jesus made the lame to walk, the mute to talk, the deaf to hear, the blind to see, the leper to be cleansed, and the dead to be raised to life. He came against demons, sin, disease, fear, and lack. He was a man of compassion, action, and power! He spoke of Himself as coming to give men life and give it to them more abundantly (see John 10:10).

As all that soaked into my spirit, I felt my mind expand and my spirit explode! I understood what God meant when He told me not to be like other men or like any denomination, but to be like Jesus and heal the people as He did.

I realized I had been unwittingly preaching to please the church people instead of burning inside to see the sick, hurting, and lost people be delivered and established in the life of Jesus. I had inadvertently become a mere echo of my denomination. I came to feel it must have been a stench in the nostrils of God. I became fed up with myself.

Third John 2

During this focused time in my life, God began to bust my "theology" wide open. I was discovering there was so much more to Jesus and His ways and principles and actions than I had ever fathomed.

Not only was I reading the four Gospels and Acts at special times, but I was also reading other parts of the Bible during my regular morning devotions. One particular morning, I was in a rush, and my Bible fell open to the little book of 3 John. When I came to the second verse and read it, my thinking about God's desires for our lives was changed abruptly and completely.

The words seemed to knock me off my feet. I almost could not believe my eyes when I read: *"Beloved, I wish above all things that thou mayest prosper and be in health, even as thy soul prospereth."*

I read the entire one-chapter book, and as I did, the second verse kept pulling at me. As I read it over and over, it was like dawn breaking after a dark night; it was like experiencing the goodness of God being poured out all over me. I was His beloved, and He wanted me to *prosper* in every area of my life. My soul was set free, and my spirit soared with ecstasy! God had revealed His character, His very nature and, most of all, His greatest desire for our lives to me. That one simple little verse made it all come alive in the flash of a second.

I couldn't contain myself. I called to Evelyn in the kitchen. When she came in, I handed her my Bible and asked her to read 3 John 2 out loud. As she read, I tingled all over with the presence of God. Her first reaction was the same as almost everyone's is to this day when I share that Scripture.

"Oral, is this verse in the Bible?"

"Sure it is. You just read it."

"Did you know it was there before this morning?"

"No, I didn't."

"Oral, do you mean to say you have read the Bible all these years and the past few months practically day and night, and yet you didn't know this verse was in the Bible?"

"That's right. I have read it many times, but I just didn't see this verse."

We stood there talking about this wonderful verse for several minutes. I asked Evelyn to read it just one more time. She read, "Beloved, I wish above all things that thou mayest prosper and be in health, even as thy soul prospereth."

I asked, "Evelyn, can you explain what God means by that verse?"

She said, "Well, I guess it means what it says."

I sat there examining this verse as if I had it under a microscope. The verse begins with "beloved." It is a word a man uses for his wife, his mother, his child, or his dear friend. It contains the wish of God. What is that wish? His wish is that we prosper, that we have health even as the soul prospers.

True prosperity begins in the soul and springs out into the physical from there. As the soul is strong and healthy, so God wishes the body to be strong and healthy. As our souls and bodies are strong by God's power, so He wants us to prosper in our daily lives. That includes financial prosperity but much more: the whole of our lives in Christ.

That was a revelation to my soul. I had heard one of our greatest preachers say that he wanted to be poor so he could be like

Jesus. I had heard countless Christian people say that they believed that God had put sickness on them so they would be better Christians.

I had never believed it, and the Word of God substantiated what I believed. I found that there was a true scriptural basis for believing that God wants man to be happy, healthy, strong, and prosperous. I saw that mankind can be delivered in soul, mind, and body.

Third John 2 became a battering ram that began to tear down the walls for a new theology! It was exactly what I needed to complete my struggle for the power of God. It closed the door to the past and opened another through which I saw the hand of Jesus of Nazareth beckoning me to enter.

The Dream God Gave Me

At that point, God began to deal with me by giving me the same dream night after night. In my dream, God let me see people as He sees them and hear them as He hears them. For the first time in my life, I saw that everybody is sick or in trouble in some way. To see people with the eyes of my spirit by the Holy Spirit and then hear their inward (and often outward) groans, sighs, and cryings almost took my breath away.

Night after night I would awaken, having dreamed of the individuals and families of the human race in our generation. I saw them in all kinds of clothes, housing, transportation, work, play, and other activities. The high and the low, the average and the genius—every one of them, without exception, has a problem, is a problem, or lives with one. More than that, however, they have learned to camouflage their feelings, their hurts, their heartaches, their losses, their sicknesses and diseases, and their attacks from the devil. That is what God sees and hears every moment of every day, and He let me see and hear it.

Once again, I was changed abruptly and, I believe, completely. The encounter grew so intense that as I dreamed, I began walking in my sleep—something I had never done before.

When Evelyn discovered what was happening, one night she touched me, awakened me, and said, "Oral, what's the matter? You've been doing this several nights now, and I want to know why."

I told her about the recurring dream. "My time has come," I said to her with tears. "The healing ministry God said I was to have is here. What is happening to me now is a part of it, although I can't explain it all."

"I knew it," she said.

"How did you know it?"

"Don't you know God speaks to me, too?"

I was really shaken up. The following Sunday as I preached, people in my church looked different under the Sunday-go-to-meeting clothes they wore. There were sicknesses of all kinds, and their cries were going up to God, even when my ears could not hear them.

I began preaching differently, not so much by sermon outlines, but more extemporaneously out of my heart, out of compassion, and out of a growing faith that great healings were coming—and God would make me the instrument for many of them to happen throughout America and the world.

CHAPTER 8

"FROM THIS HOUR..."

THE THIRTY DAYS were up, and I had finished reading the four Gospels and Acts three times consecutively on my knees. What I had read was deep inside me. It was only then that I understood what God meant when He said,

> *"Son, don't be like other men. Don't be like any denomination. Be like Jesus, and heal the people as He did."*

I knew also that Jesus is in the "now," and that "now" was inside me. I would have to begin doing what He commanded me to do *somehow*.

I remember what was going on inside me—a driving force, hammering at my very soul. Finally, it came to me what to do next. I drove to my little church, entered the small pastor's study, picked up my Bible, and slowly turned the pages of Matthew, Mark, Luke, John, and Acts. It seemed everything I had seen Jesus be and do filled the screen of my vision.

God said if I would read those five books in the way He told me, He would show me Jesus. He kept His word. The whole man and the whole story were before me. Tears slipped down my cheeks. The thirst in me to drink of the Living Water, to touch the hem of His garment, to give my life in following His example—in letter and in spirit—was overwhelming.

I fell to the floor, stretching out my long, lanky body. Lying there, I said, "Lord, I am not going to get up until You reveal

Yourself to me as I have seen You in the Gospels and the Acts," and He knew I meant it.

Filled to the brim with the revelational knowledge of Jesus and the dynamite of His character, His purpose, His teachings, His compassion and desire to heal, I was at last in a position to get to the heart of the Christian faith that had brought salvation and healing to my wretched life and given me God's call on my life— forever. I was alone with God in every sense of the word. That was where I was supposed to be. His Word, with Him at the center, had brought me there. I was determined not to get up until I had crossed over from all I had missed in Christianity to all there was for me and what I could take to others.

Time didn't matter. I lost track of it. Lying there, I felt like a tiny speck in the universe. I was holding on to the little end of the greatest thing of all: Jesus, the same yesterday, today, and forever (see Heb. 13:8). I wanted the whole Jesus in the "now" of my life, to know how to do the three things He did: to teach, preach, and heal (see Matt. 4:23–24). Not that I thought, for a minute, I could ever be Jesus or do His works remotely as well. But I could be Oral Roberts losing myself in Him and yet being me as He enlightened and empowered me to take His healing power to my generation.

I sought Him with everything in me. Soon the tears were such that I had my face in them on the floor.

I testify to you that during those crucial hours, the panorama of the living Christ spread out before me. It was like I was there with Him, hearing His words, seeing His healing hands, knowing beyond all knowing He was all I wanted and the only One I wanted to try to be like.

I had been the recipient of personal salvation, I had been baptized with the Holy Spirit and had spoken in tongues, and I had spent twelve years studying, teaching, and preaching but with only a healing or two confirming my ministry. I felt exhilarated to be there, yet crushed that I had not gotten hold of Jesus enough to be like Him. It hurt. I was in anguish.

Finally, after I had poured myself out before Him as water from a vessel, I was emptied out. I was alone. I couldn't pray anymore. I simply lay there as time passed—minutes, hours—I never checked to see.

How much later, I do not know, I heard His voice:

"Stand on your feet!"

I rose up.

"Go get in your car!"

I walked out of the little study, through the sanctuary, out the door, and got in my car.

"Drive one block east, and turn right!"

I started the motor and drove as directed, turning right at the corner. Then I heard these words:

"From this hour you shall have My power to heal the sick and to cast out demons."

When I heard Him say that, I wasn't crying anymore; I was hollering. I knew that I knew my hour had come and God had finally gotten me in the position in which He could direct me.

When I reached the parsonage, I jumped out of the car and ran inside. I hollered, "Evelyn, Evelyn!"

She said, "What is it, Oral?"

I said, "Cook me a meal, honey, I've heard from God!"

A big smile flashed on her face. We hugged and kissed, and I danced her around the room.

My weight had dropped from 212 to 172, from a size 46 suit to a 38, and none of my clothes fit. "Yes, cook for me, honey. Then I'm going to buy me a suit that will fit. I'll never get as big as I was before. I've got to be near this weight the rest of my life for the job I have to do for the Lord."

Evelyn had ridden the river with me through it all. She really loved the Lord, and she loved me and believed in me.

As we ate, I began to tell her what I felt led by God to do next. I knew it was serious business, and I couldn't afford to make a mistake.

I was to put out three fleeces, similar to what Gideon did in Bible days (see Judg. 6:36–40). There could be no doubt in my spirit and mind that God had called me. I felt that if God answered the three fleeces I was going to bring before Him, I would never look back; I would never wonder whether I had done the right thing. That would give me confidence and give other people confidence that it is not me doing this; I am acting under divine orders. Only then would my healing ministry work; only then would it last; only then would it make its mark for God.

The Three Fleeces

My fleeces were a prayer.

I prayed for God to bring 1,000 people to my first citywide healing service, which I was going to hold in the educational building in downtown Enid. Going from about 175 in Sunday church to more than 1,000 in one service was a huge jump for an unknown young minister like me. That was fleece number one.

I prayed that when the offering was received for the rental of the auditorium, the $160 rent would be given by the people without pulling or begging. That was fleece number two.

I prayed that God would heal at least one person who would know it for sure and that the crowd would know it and I would know it. There had to be evidence that we could see and feel and know a miracle of healing had happened. That was fleece number three.

I was so committed to the Lord answering all three fleeces, I said, "Lord, if these three things don't happen, then I know it's time for me to give up my ministry." Then I went the fatal step: "And to stop being a Christian."

What I meant was—and I know the Lord understood—if He healed only me (as great as that was to my life) but was not going to use me as the vessel to whom He had spoken and commanded to take His healing power to my generation, then I was not willing to live the rest of my life with the status quo of denominational church life as I knew it.

I am a serious person who acts on his convictions, however they appear to other people. I am responsible to God, and to myself, for my actions. No one had to tell me how dangerous it was to put out the three fleeces, especially if they weren't answered by the Lord. *I would be checking out with my soul.*

One side of me was frightened beyond description, scared that I was doing the most foolish thing I could do, and that if it did not work, I would hurt the small group of believers around me. Thankfully, I was not well known. Most of the dealings of the Lord had been between Him and me, and the only other person to know most of the details was Evelyn. Though she was quivering inside for her man, as any good wife would, she knew that I was not prone to do foolish things. I would take a step into the unknown of such magnitude only because I was absolutely serious before God, and I really wanted reality as it was in the church in the book of Acts and the entire Word of God. She never doubted my integrity of heart.

The other side of me was hilarious. I was bubbling over inside with the joy of the Lord that at last I had crossed over the line and was willing to go all out as I struck a blow for deliverance for people who were sick and without Christ as I had been. In my spirit I could feel and see the miracles coming, and many of them would be coming from the living Christ through me.

I saw the clouds lifting and the dawn breaking for a new day in the lives of believers in the body of Christ itself. I saw an impact made in all the future upon lost and suffering people worldwide. I had been one of those lost and suffering persons. I knew the darkness of soul, the pain and tragedy of a terminal illness, and what it was like to be put upon by sincere Christians who didn't know whether it was God's will to heal.

Through all these years, as I have tried to do what Jesus did in healing the people as He did, I have tried to do it with the picture in my mind that He felt what we felt and He sat where we sat. And as part of His trial and death on the cross, He suffered the stripes on His back for our healing. The same blood that poured through the nail prints and the spear hole in His side at Calvary was the same blood that flowed from the deep and cruel stripes on His back for our healing.

Years later the apostle Peter, who was there at Calvary, wrote, "Who his own self bare our sins in his own body on the tree, that we, being dead to sins, should live unto righteousness: by whose stripes ye were healed" (1 Pet. 2:24).

By revelation through the Word of God, by Jesus' own words, and by the deed of the blood-bringing whipping of Jesus of Nazareth, Peter saw that a full healing had been achieved. Healing is there as an eternal and direct result of what Jesus suffered and what God identified as "His stripes," being laid on and carried by His dear Son as a deliverance from our sicknesses. And if healing is for one, it is for all!

So I did not believe I was going off the deep end through laying out the three fleeces that, when answered, would further shape my life as a Christian believer and as one called to *teach*, *preach*, and *heal* as Jesus did. Laying out fleeces before the Lord may not be for anyone else. That's between God and him or her. I knew it was for me.

The service was set for a Sunday at 2:00 P.M. I preached in the morning service at the church I was pastoring in Enid. I announced the healing service and asked all who felt it to agree with me with their prayers and faith. In spite of what appeared to be a risk too great, the possible loss to the church of their young pastor, the potentially bad influence it might leave behind if I had to walk away, I felt a certain inner fire in their spirits.

They had not been a church of healing, but they knew it was in the Word of God. They had heard many sermons on how Jesus and His followers in the early church in the first century had healed the sick and performed many miracles. They were part of the outgrowth of the great Pentecostal outpouring that had fallen in the early 1900s. They knew what healing was, even if they had not been experiencing it in a personal way.

When the church service was over, no one went home for Sunday dinner. We all stayed in the church sanctuary, both cautious and expectant, until it was time to go to the educational building auditorium for that all-important leap of faith.

I've often thought, *What must have been going on in heaven that day? What was Jesus doing? What were the angels doing? How did God the Father look on it, and what was the action of the Holy Spirit? What were the people of the Enid area, who knew of this healing test, thinking that day?*

The Enid newspaper had carried the notice but had not commented editorially. Had the editors not taken the event seriously? Had they any inkling concerning the storm of controversy the media would later involve me in because of my healing ministry and the things I would feel led to build that actually challenged the power structures of this nation and of the body of Christ? Did they have any idea of how the little seed that I was sowing that day would grow into a world harvest of souls saved, sick people healed, and powerful changes brought in the theology of the church world as well as in the thinking of millions outside the church? If they had only known. . . .

When Evelyn and I and my church deacon board arrived at the auditorium, we were told to enter by a side door. As we did so, the caretaker of the building was there. "Which one of you is Oral Roberts?" he asked.

"I am, sir."

"I understand you wanted one thousand people to be present for this service."

"That's right."

"Would you like to know how many are here?"

"Yes, I would."

"Well, I have already personally counted twelve hundred!"

I felt a churning inside, and my associates began to quietly praise the Lord.

Fleece number one was fully answered.

The pastors of all the Pentecostal, or what was more popularly known as Full Gospel, denomination churches in that area and pastors of several other churches had been invited. Some twenty were seated on the stage when I was directed to my seat with them.

The song service began right on time. The crowd sat hushed and had to be urged a little by the leader to join in as songs we all knew were being sung.

The pastor with the largest membership was of the First Assembly of God. He was asked to present the need of the $160 to pay for the building rental. There were no other expenses.

He made a sincere explanation of the service, of the hopes God would meet with us today, and he asked all who felt in their hearts that they wanted to give an offering to do so. Then the ushers passed the offering plates among the people.

I had asked that the service be stopped until the offering was counted, then announced publicly. The second fleece was more important than the $160 it cost to rent the building.

A week prior to the service, a brother in the Lord had come through the town to hold healing services in a local church. Many of us pastors had cooperated with his conducting the healing services, and we were impressed with his genuine healing gifts and his efforts to preach and pray for the healing of the people. But we had been *sickened*—and that's the word for it—when no matter what the amount of the first offering taken near the beginning of the service, he always took another at the end of the service, and he used up to an hour in taking up that offering.

After he was gone, I was raising all kinds of questions with the Lord about the sickening feeling I had and of the bad taste left in the mouths of so many of us who had lent our influence to the man's ministry in our city.

As clear as a bell, I remembered God's words to me:

"You are not to touch the gold or the glory."

I also vividly recalled my vow to God not to do so.

Around that time, I had an experience with someone who had the wrong attitude about money and ministry, and I wasn't about to let it be a part of me.

One day a man from the church, who was very close to me and is close to me today, had a big change in his life. It seemed like the devil influenced him overnight. He walked in my little study there in the church and said to me, "I want in on this racket."

I asked, "What racket?"

"You know, this healing thing that you're going into."

I said, "I don't know what you mean."

"Well," he said, "you know, the money."

I was confused and reminded him, "You're a member of my church, which pays me fifty-five dollars a week. You mean you want part of my fifty-five dollars a week?"

"No," he said, "I'm talking about the *big* money out there."

I couldn't believe what I was hearing. I just hoped it would pass and he'd drop it, but it didn't and he didn't. Everywhere I went it seemed he was there, trying to get to me.

Finally, I went home one day and told Evelyn, "Honey, I'm going to quit before I start. I'm an honest man. I've really never had anything in my life. And I'm not going to have a healing ministry. If this is the way that I'm going to be accepted, that all I want is people's money, then I'm not going to do it."

My wife—you know how a wife can be when she really loves you and gets under the anointing—said, "Oral, this is a trick of the devil to stop you from obeying God. God has to have somebody out there praying for the sick people. I know you, you're my husband, the father of our children, and I know you've got integrity. What the man said is not in your heart. That is the devil trying to stop you."

"Well," I asked, "what are we going to do? We can't stop him." Then it came to my mind what I'd heard as a young Christian about binding as explained in the Bible (see Matt. 18:18). I had never done anything like that. But I remembered my father had talked about how people of God could bind those who came against them to stop the flow of God in their calling.

"All right," I said to Evelyn. "Will you come into agreement with me? We're going to bind this man in the name of Jesus. We're not going to say one word to him. We're just going to talk to God."

We held hands, and we spoke in the name of Jesus to that man as though he were in front of us. We said, "We bind you in the name of Jesus Christ that you will not touch God's anointed and you will do God's prophet no harm." And it was over with. As far as I was concerned, he didn't exist anymore. I went about my work as though he had never been born. I saw him, and he saw me. It made no difference. I had turned it loose. I had obeyed God.

Later, after I had left Enid, I was preaching in Tulsa one night. When I gave the invitation to the unsaved, I looked down and saw a man coming who was jerking and almost falling down, shaking from head to foot, and I realized it was this brother. As I left the platform to meet him, he threw his arms around my legs and said, "Oral, if you don't loose me, I'm going to die. I have had no rest. I have slept, but it gave me no rest. I have eaten, but it did not digest." He said, "I am nearly dead. If you don't help unbind me, I'm going to die."

I said, "If you will truly repent, not to Oral Roberts, but if you will repent toward God and you will vow you will never touch God's anointed servants again, I will release you." He made the vow, and I released him in the name of Jesus. He became one of the greatest friends of my ministry. Gib Bond and I are very close today. I count him as one of my dearest and trusted friends.

Now you can see why I was very sensitive to how the offering was handled in my first citywide healing service. The careful handling of the money in God's work has always been of utmost importance to me.

That day, we all sat silently while the offering was taken and then counted. The slip of paper on which the amount was written was handed to me and then to the pastor who received the offering.

He stepped to the microphone and announced, "The offering is $163.03." Turning to me with a smile, he said, "It's $3.03 above what you asked God for."

Fleece number two was fully answered.

I was not free yet. The healing—the third fleece—had not happened, and without that, the first parts of the service were no more than had happened at most local churches. The big one was still to come.

When I was presented to preach, I spoke on the topic "If You Need Healing, Do These Things!" It later became the title and content of my first book on healing.

As I got into my message, I was speaking from my heart without notes. Before, I had always preached from an outline, the points of which I could glance at when I felt it necessary. But I was more caught up in the people's need to be healed as I had been healed, and of the fact that healing usually comes through us as individuals and groups of believers doing the things Jesus taught and demonstrated for us to do. Not very often does healing come sovereignly (when God chooses to heal someone regardless of circumstances).

I felt the people were hanging on every word I was saying when suddenly, without warning, the power of the Lord came upon me. I felt it surge through every fiber of my being. The next thing I knew, I had leaped off the platform onto the floor of the auditorium. As I did so, without a word from me, the audience rose up like a covey of quail. I found myself going down the left aisle. I saw a woman reaching out to me with her left hand. I stopped. She showed me her right hand, gnarled, crippled, and stiff. I touched her hand and said, "In Jesus' name, be healed!"

The woman began opening and closing her right hand. When she saw it was loosed, she screamed at the top of her voice, "I'm healed! I'm healed!" She came from the large German settlement near Enid so she spoke in broken English, and we all felt her sincerity.

Pandemonium broke loose. Different ones began pulling at me, and I began praying for everything that moved. Someone seized the back of my coat and whirled me around. It was the husband of a woman who was a member of the church I pastored. On either side of him were six other husbands of wives in the church. All seven of them were unsaved, and I had striven to win them to Christ with no results.

The man holding my coat said, "Oral, all seven of us see that it is the power of God working through you to heal these people. We want to receive the Lord into our hearts."

There had been no moment like that in my memory that I had seen anywhere. It came to me in unmistakable terms that it was somewhat like the way it had happened when Jesus taught, preached, and healed. It broke through the hard outer layer of people's resistance to Him as the Lord and made their hearts tender to the gospel.

In fleece number three, I had prayed somebody would be healed so that the person would know it, I would know it, and the crowd would know it. The healing of the woman's hand, which had been stiff for thirty-eight long years, was an answer to that fleece—we all knew it. Nothing had to be pumped up, no one had to be sold on it, the healing was real—something only God Himself could do miraculously!

That healing was another fulfillment of Mark 16:20: "And they went forth, and preached every where, the Lord working with them, and confirming the word with signs following. Amen." I went forth in Jesus' name, I preached His Word, I prayed for the healing of people, and the woman's healing—seen by all there—was the Lord confirming His Word with signs following.

With that confirmation those seven grown men, all now bawling like babies over their sins and wanting me to lead them to Christ, surrounded me. Prior to that, when I preached on Sunday morning and evening in the church, I had begged God to save at least one soul each Sunday. It did not happen often. That day when

I preached, then prayed, and a genuine healing happened in the presence of all, those unsaved men, who seldom came to church with their wives, actually held on to my clothes and, in effect, demanded me to pray with them to receive Christ as their personal Savior.

I prayed until 6:00 P.M. for everyone who wanted me to. As I finished, there was not a dry thread in my clothes. In fact, later my wife had to help me pull my clothes off because they stuck to my body. I am not relating this about my wet clothes because I think it's something outstanding. I just want to show how intense that first service was when three fleeces were put before the Lord by a twenty-nine-year-old preacher and university student who meant business with God.

And that was to be the story of my life; not an ending but a beginning of what was to come.

CHAPTER 9

THE BRUSH OF DEATH AND THE POWER OF GOD

I KNEW BY THEN that God was ready for me to take the message of His healing power to my generation. I resigned the pastorate in Enid and moved to Tulsa. I chose Tulsa because it is centrally located in the United States and has excellent air travel facilities. Also, as a native Oklahoman, I wanted to set up my headquarters in my home state. I think Tulsa is one of the most beautiful cities I have ever seen. It is a wonderful place to live.

Our main difficulty was that I had very little money with which to locate in Tulsa. Evelyn and I searched for a house to rent, but none was to be found within our financial ability.

Oscar Moore, the man who had married us and who had been called by the Enid church to take my place as pastor, lived in Tulsa at that time. Upon his invitation, we stayed overnight in his home, and he tried to help us secure a place to live. The following day he told us that he had sold his house to a man who was coming that evening at six o'clock to close the deal. Suddenly, I had the feeling that it was our house. Then I thought how absurd that feeling was, since he had already sold it.

After a few minutes I went into the bedroom to pray, but it seemed that I was unable to pray through on the problem. I told Oscar that I wanted to drive through a certain section of the city again looking for a house and that I would be back soon. A few minutes later I parked my car near one of the city parks and sat there trying to work things out in my mind. Things were growing serious. I gave up the Enid pastorate with whatever security it had for my family, and I launched upon a ministry that had many un-knowns. The amount of money I had was very small—twenty-five dollars to be exact. Still, I felt each step I had taken had been or-dered by the Lord.

As I sat there behind the steering wheel, things looked pretty dark. I felt stranded. There was no human source to which I could turn for help. With an uncontrollable urge to cry out to God, I bowed my head over the steering wheel and told Him of my predicament. I told Him of the needs of my family and of His call upon my life. I said that if I were to begin in this ministry, I must have help immediately.

When I had prayed myself out, I became quiet before God. It was then that I felt the Holy Spirit come upon me. The words of an old church hymn, one I had known since early childhood, came into my mind:

> O the joy of sins forgiv'n!
> O the bliss the blood-washed know!
> O the peace akin to Heav'n,
> Where the healing waters flow!

The thought came to me: *Why am I worrying? My sins are for-given. I am washed in the blood of Christ, and the peace akin to heaven is in my heart.* I felt everything was going to be all right. I drove back and arrived in time for dinner.

The man who had agreed to buy Oscar's home did not arrive at the appointed time. By 7:30, he still had not appeared.

We had all planned to attend a revival meeting under Rev. Steve Pringle's big tent that night. Oscar urged us to go on, and he would wait for the man a little longer. That night Steve Pringle asked me to conduct my first Tulsa crusade under his tent. I agreed to preach for one week.

The next morning as we sat around the breakfast table, Oscar said that he would give his friend until eight o'clock that morning to come and close the deal on the house. A little after eight o'clock a strange look came across his face. Turning to me, he said, "Oral, would you and Evelyn like to have this house?"

I smiled and said, "Oh, I don't know."

He said, "It's a nice house."

He told me how much he would take for it, and I replied that it was too much. He asked me how much I would give, and I told him. When he said he would accept my offer, I said, "Sold."

I looked over at Evelyn, who did not know of the prayer the day before or of the confidence I now possessed. What she did know was that her husband had only twenty-five dollars and had just agreed to buy a house!

While Oscar was gone to the bank to arrange for the transfer of the ownership papers, I told Evelyn that everything would work out all right.

When Oscar returned, he told me how much the down payment would be. The amount almost took my breath away, but I nodded my head.

While we were going through the papers, he paused and said, "Oral, Anna and I really have no need for the down payment at this time. If it is agreeable, you and Evelyn can take up the monthly payments beginning the first of the month, and you can give us the down payment later, say, half in six months and the other half in twelve months."

I caught my breath and said, "Oh, just as you say."

Later, in our room, Evelyn and I shed tears of joy because we knew we had witnessed the loving hand of God intervening in our behalf.

Oscar did not know until a year later that I had bought his home with only twenty-five dollars in my pocket.

The first service of my Tulsa crusade under Steve Pringle's tent opened in a driving rain to a small crowd. But from the moment I opened my mouth, I was conscious of the anointing of the Holy Spirit. I was able to preach with the fire and the power of God upon me.

A few sick people were present, and we had a prayer line for them. Some of them felt that they had been definitely and miraculously healed. Several others were converted to Christ.

It seemed that within hours the news spread like fire over Tulsa. Three nights later, the tent was packed. On Sunday, the place was filled, and hundreds were standing around the edges of the one-thousand-seat tent. Steve said, "Oral, you can't close this meeting. God is with you, and you must stay another week." We continued the revival for nine straight weeks, with standing room only for the people.

I was beginning to see what the ministry could do to bring people together. It blotted out denominational barriers, color lines, and disunity. In a flash, I saw when we people get hungry enough, we'll be happy to sit at the table with anyone. As I stood up each evening to preach, I felt the greatest anointing I had ever known. I preached for an hour and a half in each service, and the people from different churches and no churches at all responded like hungry children. God opened the Scriptures of deliverance to me when I preached of His goodness and His power. I threw my old sermon outlines away.

It was in this, my first healing crusade, that I had my first brush with death as an evangelist of God. One night I was preaching, and a man, whom none of us knew, stood on the outside of the tent. He stood there a few minutes, pulled out a revolver, pointed it at me, and pulled the trigger. The bullet plowed through the canvas about eighteen inches above my head. The next day I saw the bullet hole. Standing there, I wondered what was ahead of me in my ministry, and I asked God to give me courage and divine protection until I had finished my work.

The news services headlined the shooting, and overnight I was labeled a controversial evangelist. Something else happened. The news media played up the story, and in twenty-four hours my name was known nationwide as a man praying for the sick. It was a pretty scary way to have my name known.

Little did I know the healing part of my ministry would stir up one of the greatest spiritual controversies that had been manifested yet in the U.S. of A. But it was about to explode onto the scene of the nation and the world. Pastors out of state, upon hearing the news of a man praying for the sick and of the shot taken at me, began flying in to see what God was doing. I received invitations to come to their cities as soon as possible. The man who shot at me didn't know how he helped spread a brand-new healing ministry where masses of sick people would come to see that healing is, as Jesus said, "the children's bread."

The Point of Contact

Shortly after finishing the nine-week crusade in Tulsa, I was asked to conduct a one-night service in Nowata, Oklahoma, fifty miles to the north. That spring night would be one of the most important nights in my life and in the life of a little deaf boy.

After I had preached to an overflow crowd of three hundred in the small church sanctuary, there was such a great spirit of expectancy and excitement, I made the appeal to the unsaved. So many came forward, they did not have enough room at the front of the building to stand. Right where they were, I prayed with them to accept Jesus Christ of Nazareth as their Lord and Savior, and then I began the healing line. As always, I was going to lay hands on those who came forward for prayer.

A mother brought her little boy, who was deaf, in the prayer line. As I stood there looking at the mother, then at the little boy, who appeared to be about eight years old, that Voice I had heard before, as if God were standing behind me, spoke inside me:

"Son, you have been faithful to this hour, and now you will feel My presence in your right hand. Through My presence, you will be able to detect the presence of demons. You will know their number and name, and will have My power to cast them out."

Because the Voice was so clear, the words so distinct, and the presence of God began coming immediately in my right hand, I placed the first finger of each hand into the little boy's ears. I felt nothing of God's presence in my left hand—it was merely flesh on flesh. My right hand, however, was feeling God's presence in ways I still find difficult to explain: like a strong warmth, like an electrical charge, only it did not sting or hurt, but more like a vibration I could feel surging from my elbow clear through my hand. I held my hands up and looked at my right hand, then my left hand. They looked exactly the same.

I put the finger of my right hand in one ear at a time of the little boy, and I said, "In the name of Jesus Christ of Nazareth, you tormenting spirit of deafness, come out! Come out!"

Instantly, the little fellow looked around. He put his hands over his ears, and he began to cry and look at his mother.

I said to her, "He is apparently hearing noise and voices for the first time, and it scares him."

Then I asked her to speak to her little son. She called his name, and he answered. I asked her to get behind him, where he couldn't see her lips, and talk to him in a normal voice, which she did.

Each time he whirled around to her while he said her words back to her as best he could talk (evidently, he had been able to talk somewhat, but not hear).

By that time, the audience and I were in a sense of awe. They had read of such things in the Bible, and they had believed some-day they would happen again. They were truly excited they were seeing it happen. I was feeling the same way.

I wanted to yell at the top of my voice, "God is healing people again." Instead I contained myself, but I felt an inner knowing that it was the genuine thing of God's healing presence, almost like Jesus Himself having touched the boy's ears.

Someone picked up a woman who had trouble walking. She had brought her kitchen chair she had used to scoot around on during the past eight years to do her housework. My right hand flew to her forehead. Again I felt the presence of God race down my elbow into my hand and into her being. She leaped up, raised her legs up and down a few times, looked around, and took off running through the crowd, praising God and crying.

The people in that Assembly of God church had a Pentecostal shout, some danced in the Spirit, some fell under the power, and others spoke to God in tongues. We were all raised into the same state of divine ecstasy, knowing no one but God and His presence could do such miracles of healing that we had just witnessed.

I was astonished, to say the least, for it was totally unlike any-thing I had ever felt of the presence of God. I had often felt His presence flow through my whole being. It was something we had been accustomed to calling feeling the power of God, which was a tangible feeling, an overpowering sense of God's personal pres-ence, and which took us out of our humanness for that time into God's own self.

Every Holy Spirit–baptized believer I knew had felt this anoint-ing to some degree. It became what we all expected when we came together to pray and hear the Word preached and worship together and win souls. The main difference was, that time God was telling me how I would feel His presence directly in my right hand and what He would accomplish through it.

The word to me concerning detecting the presence of demons did not begin to establish itself in my mind until sometime later. I heard what the Lord said, but I did not understand it until a little later in my ministry. I learned it had to do directly with confronting demonic spirits that were some of the very same ones Jesus and His disciples had cast out, but were still on earth today tormenting and possessing people. They were part of the one-third of the angels who had fallen with Lucifer in his rebellion against God in heaven and who with those spirits had been cast down to earth (see Rev. 12:7, 9).

Having lost their celestial bodies, they could satisfy their hatred against God and their lusts only by entering human beings, making them what they were as they oppressed them with the same spirit of rebellion that had caused God to cast them out of heaven. I had seen people possessed with evil spirits, and I knew they often violently destroyed those people's lives and disrupted the lives of others through their satanic actions.

Eventually, I would be able to detect a demonic spirit, or the number of them, in a person by three different ways. One was the smell of the breath, and another was the unusual look in the eyes. The third was through the presence God said I would feel in my right hand. At the moment, all I could understand was what I was hearing God say to me about having been faithful to that hour, and henceforth I would experience His presence in my right hand.

Not once did it occur to me then, or later, that it was some *personal power* of my own. I knew better than that theologically. In fact, if I had thought that is what I heard, I would have rejected it immediately.

Among Pentecostals, our belief and experience were that although we had to do something to meet God's conditions in His Word, *His power* of the Holy Spirit coming upon us did His works as mighty acts of God. Claiming personal spiritual power to heal was blasphemous.

A few days after the Nowata service, I was invited to conduct services in Tulsa's noted Faith Tabernacle, pastored by W. F. Garvin, a former leading Presbyterian minister in Tulsa who had received the baptism of the Holy Spirit under Raymond T. Richey's Tulsa crusade years before. Again there were an overflowing crowd and great expectancy.

Irma Morris and her sister, Eve, had come for healing. Evelyn and I had known them for several years, and we were close friends. Irma had been in and out of the sanitarium for tuberculosis, and she had not been able to get well from the same disease of which I had been healed.

Eve brought Irma in the healing line after I had preached and given the altar call to the unsaved. I had not said anything about feeling God's presence in my right hand, not even to Evelyn. It had become more overwhelming—and mysterious—to me almost hour by hour. I did not feel it all the time. I could not make it come. When it happened, it was just there. That night I noticed that during my sermon, God's presence had come in my right hand again, and it was still there when I approached Irma.

She was burning up with fever, and the TB smell was on her body. I could smell it because it was exactly like I had smelled it on myself when I had TB. I couldn't stand to see Irma being destroyed by disease, particularly tuberculosis, which I hated with a passion.

My right hand shot out to her forehead as I began to command the TB to loose her body and let her go free in the name of Jesus of Nazareth.

Her body almost jumped, and she asked, "Oh, Oral, what did you do to me?"

"What do you mean, Irma?" I asked.

"Your right hand. It felt on fire when it touched me." Then as tears rolled down her cheeks, she said, "Something in your right hand is causing a warmth to go through my lungs. My lungs are opening up. I believe I am being healed!"

I looked at my right hand. No outward change. It looked the same as always. She was right, however, for God's presence was charging through my right hand, and it did so during the rest of the healing service.

Back home, Evelyn and I had a big discussion about this new thing that was a phenomenon to me. Evelyn has always been extremely levelheaded and practical in every way. Yet she is a deeply spiritual woman, hungry for God to move, and she was deeply appreciative to Him for beginning to use me to heal the sick and do other miracles in His name.

"Do you suppose if you put your hand on my head, Oral, I could feel it?" she quizzed.

"I don't know, Evelyn. It comes when it comes. So far it's come only as I have preached and as I have touched some of the sick people."

"Touch me, please," she said.

I touched her and did not feel a thing. Neither did she.

"Maybe if you prayed for this thing in my body I have been suffering with, it would come."

"Evelyn, I didn't know you were suffering with anything."

"Well, I have been for several weeks."

Without my understanding of it whatsoever, I began feeling the presence of God run down my elbow and right arm and into my hand. Suddenly, Evelyn was not like she was my wife, she was someone in the healing line, coming to be healed. When I laid my right hand on her, the vibration was going through it, and she cried, "Oh, Oral, you are right. It is in your right hand. It is God!"

"But what about the pain you mentioned. Is it still there?" I asked.

"Oh, no," she said, weeping. "It is totally gone."

She began praying, "Dear Lord, we know this is not something Oral has of himself. I know him too well for him to claim it is his own power. It's Your presence, Lord Jesus. Help us to hold it precious and to give You praise for it."

Evelyn was a great blessing to me that night. A unity of the Holy Spirit came into us greater than we had known before. From that day to this she has never doubted it when the presence of God has come in my right hand.

How Do You Explain It?

I was soon to realize there was much about the way God healed I would never understand. At first, when I felt God's presence in my right hand, I really thought everybody I touched would be healed. It didn't happen, and that surprised me.

I noticed that when I felt the presence of God in my right hand, the person I was praying for would usually feel it, too. Many such persons would be healed or start to mend from that moment.

For sure, God's presence coming in my right hand was a sign to great numbers of sick people that there is a God and it is His nature to heal. For some who felt the warmth in my right hand, but healing did not come, they would cling to having felt God's presence with the hope they would be drawn closer to God. They couldn't deny what they felt, but they were sometimes perplexed as to why their healing did not happen.

I did not understand it much better than they. It was totally new to me. *Perhaps,* I thought, *it's a sovereign act of God. I can't make it come, and I usually have no inner notice it is coming.* I had to live with the most powerful spiritual force for miracles I had ever experienced, yet I did not have all the answers. It tested my faith, but I knew it was real. I could not deny it and be honest.

There was much speculation about it. When it came, it was unmistakable. I mean, *it was there*! When it was not there, I was so ordinary, everyone knew it was not there. I had to live with that, also.

That was where faith came in. I believed it was God and nothing of myself—except that He had said I had been faithful and that from that hour I would feel His presence in my right hand. I chose to believe Him rather than allow myself to become confused with the new spiritual phenomenon in my right hand. *There simply was no human explanation.*

As for the skeptics, they had no understanding of how such a thing could happen. They took a cynical attitude. It offended many ministers, and it created apprehension in some who had believed I was called into the healing ministry.

One outstanding pastor in Tulsa, who felt he could talk to me man to man about it, said, "Oral, with God having you feel His presence in your right hand, and the tremendous response of the sick to it, where does that leave the rest of us ministers?"

I had not thought about it. I said, "I really don't know. I had nothing to do with God saying I would experience His presence in that way. All I can say is, it came after God said I had been faithful. I suppose all I can say to you is to seek God concerning His way of working through you and let Him deal with you as He wills. I realize that He doesn't deal with us all alike. While our goals for the Lord are the same to deliver the people, our methods are different. Anyway, I really believe in you, and I value your anointed ministry highly. In no way could I equal your results as a pastor of a great church. Just pray for me that I will honor the Lord with this new impartation of His grace and gifts to me."

He put his arms around me and said, "I understand it better now." We remained close friends until his homegoing thirty years later.

The Race Is On!

Prior to that time, I had been like a racehorse waiting in the gate raring and ready to burst forth with all the force and power its muscles would allow and then some. I became like the horse on the racetrack, going full speed ahead with one thing in mind: to get to the finish line and God's winner's circle. The apostle Paul wrote, "Know ye not that they which run in a race run all, but one receiveth the prize? So run, that ye may obtain" (1 Cor. 9:24).

As I began having larger crusades, not many auditoriums in the cities at that time could handle the crowds. It came in my heart to get a big tent. I had been healed in one twelve years before at Ada, Oklahoma. My first healing campaign was under Steve Pringle's tent in Tulsa.

God showed me the vision of the big new tent and gave me the full details. He told me to get the biggest tent I could and carry it to the metropolitan areas. In that manner, I could reach the masses of lost and suffering humanity who would come from everywhere to see and hear the wonderful works of God. I ordered our first big tent, which seated three thousand, and two trucks and semitrailers to carry it, along with the folding chairs, piano, organ, and other equipment for the crusade sites.

I used it for the first time in June 1948 in Durham, North Carolina. It was jammed. We raised the tent flaps so thousands more could stand five and ten deep outside all around the tent and see the healing service. By the last night of the crusade, twenty-one days later, the police estimated the crowd inside and out numbered nine thousand. That figure was astonishing to me. I knew God had a greater purpose for my healing ministry than had dawned on me before.

In Durham, my feeling God's presence in my right hand created the first national controversy. In the healing lines I prayed for whoever came, and I prayed for people who could not walk in a specially reserved place behind the platform. None were preselected. I let "whosoever will" come into the healing line.

Soon I noticed that six or seven deaf children were brought into the healing line. I was so expectant with my faith that I plunged right in by laying my right hand on each of them and calling on God to open their ears and restore their speech.

It was the most marvelous thing I had yet seen when one by one the children, without hearing and speech, felt their ears pop open. We taught them to say words, such as *mother*, *daddy*, *Jesus*, *I can hear*, and *I can speak*. It electrified the crowd—and me most of all.

Each night among the hundreds in the healing line there would be another group of deaf children, some nights as many as twelve. I found out later they were all from a school for the deaf. I must have prayed for fifty to sixty of those children during the crusade. Not everyone received the same measure of healing, but everyone received some hearing and speech, and quite a number appeared to have received the beginning of a whole healing.

Our portable stage was four feet high and open underneath. After a few nights, some unbelievers got under the platform and looked for electrical wires coming up to be attached to my body. They really thought my right hand was hooked up to a physical electrical current.

Word spread about what they were doing, and the local press carried a story on it. When I woke up one morning and read about it, I felt a shock to my spirit.

"Lord," I said, "if physical electric wires attached to me or to anyone else could restore hearing and speech, then the authorities should be having it done."

Of course, it was the natural mind of man spreading such a rumor because the people could not understand that God still heals today or that a mortal man such as Oral Roberts could actually feel His presence in my right hand. I couldn't understand it, either, but it was happening. Those little boys and girls, upon feeling that vibrating warmth suddenly enter them, believed with all their hearts God was healing them. I don't know if I would have had the boldness to pray for so many children from a school for the deaf had not the presence of God come so strongly in my right hand.

It was a point of contact for my faith. As I felt the warmth running through my hand, my faith for healing seemed to leap out of my heart and up to God. It helped me to understand the absolute necessity to release my faith and to inspire the people to release their faith to God, also. That was a new way of expressing it at that time in the history of the church, but it soon caught on. In fact, the rallying cry since then in my ministry has been: Turn your faith loose! Release your faith to God! Let it go up and out of you to God.

I had been previously taught faith was something you had to get, and if you were prayed for, be sure you had faith in your heart. I began to learn that faith is not passive or static, and if it is not released out of your heart to God, your chance of miracles happening to you is slim.

I discovered Romans 12:3, which became one of the early foundation Scriptures of my ministry. In it we are told, "God hath dealt to every man the measure of faith." That stopped me in my tracks from praying or, rather, *begging*: "God, give me faith." This Scripture, and others I discovered throughout the Word of God, showed me: *Faith is not something you get; it's something you already have!*

Faith is like oil in the ground that has been there all the time waiting for oil men to take their powerful drill bits and drill down to it, to release it to begin flowing upward. I had grown up among the oil fields of Pontotoc County—the Benedum and Tree field, Fitz field, and others. Papa, upon entering the ministry four years before I was born, had sold his 160-acre farm the year before oil was struck in our area and so we had never received oil money. His father, my grandfather Roberts, and his older brothers, Willis and John, struck oil on their land and became wealthy according to the standards of those days. Papa remained a preacher who was poor.

In my ministry, that was really what I was doing: being a faith releaser. By my preaching and my praying for the sick, I could encourage people to become God-conscious, then faith-conscious, then learn to turn their faith loose to the Lord and see what the Lord would do. My touching the people with the presence of God pulsating through my right hand became the point of contact for their faith *and* my faith to be loosed to God for their healing.

The anointing I felt in my right hand, which I now believe is really God's presence felt in a tangible way, began to develop much larger than manifesting itself mainly in my right arm and down into my hand. I don't mean to indicate I felt God's presence all the time, although I knew I was filled with the Holy Spirit and His presence was in me at all times. I don't believe any mortal could feel God's presence twenty-four hours a day and live in physical flesh. It's too powerful. However, to claim to have Christ but never feel God's presence is something I don't understand at all.

If you can't feel God's presence in you at times, how will you know He dwells in you, or how will you know He has left you when you turn back to sin? By the Word only? I think it's not only what the Word says, but also the deeper knowing and feeling you have inside you by the Holy Spirit. At least, that is my experience and the experience of those I deal with in my ministry.

Frankly, I feel the hullabaloo over my crusades was totally unnecessary and pointless. Either God heals, or He does not. Either He is the same today as He has always been—a healing God—or He is not.

What I had begun to see concerning God's presence focused in my right hand became all-important to me as I stood before the great audiences with their sick among them. I was soon to be put to the big test of whether I would and could live by this.

PART 3

MY HEALING MINISTRY

CHAPTER 10

THE ANOINTING

BY JULY 1950, some three years after I had begun the healing ministry, I knew beyond all doubt that facing thousands of people in my crusades as the mere man I was, without having the anointing, would cause me to fall on my face and, worst of all, would cause serious harm to one of the greatest moves of God in our generation. Upon feeling God's anointing, I felt I could carry out God's call on me as I stood before the people. God placed me before the types of people of which few men of God had faced in such increasingly large numbers, and with such diverse diseases and sins, since the days of Jesus and His early disciples during the first century.

I had to fight against an overwhelming sense of being engulfed by the enormity and seriousness of it all and quitting and returning home. I had seen how the "sign" in my right hand could activate my faith and the faith of the people, including those who were sick or at the point of death as I had been.

To deal so closely with people's lives was awesome to me. People's disappointments with a man of God who could not produce in a creditable way could lead to despair or perhaps worse. The constant sense of my humanness with my shortcomings, and my inexperience in preaching to and praying for thousands in a single crusade service, was upon me. By that time, the three-thousand-seat tent had been replaced by the largest tent ever constructed at that time, one seating twelve thousand. I wish I could describe to you the feelings that swept over me when

I stood before the crowds, knowing that after I preached and extended the invitation for the unsaved to receive Christ, hundreds of very sick people were going to come before me, one by one, as I took on all their sicknesses with my faith in the living Christ.

Eventually, I developed a resting and prayer time, beginning at 3:00 P.M. until time for me to go to the crusade services each evening. I discovered that if I hung on expectantly, the presence of God would start coming into my right hand for a few minutes before I went to minister and would cause my faith to become active inside me. Those minutes of experiencing God's presence coming into my right hand—which was the most powerful stimulus I had ever felt—helped prepare me and made me bold to preach the healing gospel to hurting people. It was no small thing to face thousands of needy and desperately ill people, many of whom were given no more hope by medical science.

I had read in the Bible of the mighty right hand of God—how He stretched it out and made the earth out of nothing, created man from nothing but dust, and raised His Son Jesus from the dead. I had seen in the book of Acts how God stretched out His hand to heal and how the disciples asked Him to stretch forth His hand and do mighty miracles (see Acts 4:30).

The people in my crusades were interested only in hearing a man preach and in receiving his prayers, a man who they felt was in direct contact with God, one who would refuse to be intimidated by any and all opposition and controversy concerning something like feeling God's presence in his right hand.

The turning point came during my first crusade in Philadelphia. We were scheduled in the great old Metropolitan Auditorium in the City of Brotherly Love. I was having my special time before God, and it was down to a half hour before I was to be picked up at my hotel and driven to the Met. I had finished studying and preparing my sermon, and I had pretty well finished my preservice prayers when it dawned on me that the presence of God had not come in my right hand.

I had vowed to God I would attempt nothing for Him without first knowing this sign was working in me. That evening in my room, however, it would not come. During all my preparation from 3:00 P.M. on, I had not felt it.

At first I panicked with the thought: *What if it doesn't come before my driver comes? If it doesn't come, what about my vow? If it doesn't come, how can I face not only the general audience but also the ones I feel for the most: the really sick and hurting ones, including many brought by ambulances?*

"Dear God," I prayed, "I have not been in this spot before. Please, will You help me?"

My stomach was churning. I knew I would keep my vow. If God's presence didn't come, I would not go to the auditorium that evening. I knew there would be many people who had driven great distances in addition to people from Philadelphia. Great pains had been taken to get very sick people there, some as a last hope. I knew what that felt like. I had been through every step of it myself. It was no substitute experience for me. I was one of them in every fear they had, every pain they suffered, every hope that had been blasted.

In a period of thirty minutes I felt I was being split apart. One side of me was saying, *Oh, what difference does it make? I have my sermon prepared from the Word. The Holy Spirit is in me. I feel the call.* The other side was saying, *But God said you would feel His presence in your right hand.*

True, while I ministered to those in the healing line, I did not always know when I would feel the power in my right hand. It would come and go when God decided, and I had to live with that. But it had become something I depended on as part and parcel of my getting ready to face the people in the crusade services.

When I heard my driver's knock on the door, I still felt nothing. The test had come.

Suddenly, the real inner me rose to the surface. I decided I would obey God and not leave for the service until His presence came.

I stepped to the door and asked the man to wait. He said, "But you'll be late."

I nodded. "Just wait," I said.

Later I learned he walked the hall, upset because he thought he might lose his job. He did not understand at all.

"Okay, God," I said, "I am Your property. You told me I was to take Your healing power to my generation. You know it was not my idea, and I did not call myself. I cannot go without absolutely knowing the anointing, Your presence, has come upon me."

I put my Bible down, took off my coat, and sat down, my hands folded in my lap. "I am going to sit here until You let me feel Your presence," I said. When I did that, I felt my vow go into gear as never before.

The same thing occurred a few times later, but that was the first and I did the only thing I knew to do: *Wait on the Lord and not rush out in my own strength.*

Ten minutes passed . . . twenty . . . I still sat there.

I knew Bob DeWeese, my associate evangelist, was a spiritual man, a discerning man, a strong man, and we were very close in every way. He would do what he had to do.

As I was thinking of that, the presence of God seized my right hand and began throbbing through it. I let out a yell, grabbed my Bible and coat, ran out of the room, and hollered at my driver, "Let's go. God's presence is with me!"

As the car slowed at the side door of the auditorium, I flung open the car door, jumped out, rushed in, and headed for the platform. To my astonishment, the crowd saw me enter, leaped to their feet, and burst into tears and praise.

It has always impressed me to see how a crowd is like one person: It can sense things as a body of people at the same time and most often in the same way. It happened to that crowd.

I hit the platform as Bob began his introduction, "Now, ladies and gentleman . . ."

My usual way of following his introduction was to step to the microphone, lift my hands as a signal to the audience to rise as I sang a little hymn, "Where the Healing Waters Flow," then read my Bible text and begin preaching.

That night, I did not wait for Bob's complete introduction (later we could laugh about it). The people were already on their feet, sensing something powerful was about to happen from God. If stars fall at such times, they fell that night.

The currently world-renowned R. W. Shambach, a mighty evangelist of our time, was there at the service as a twenty-year-old, seeking God for his life.

The Cardone family of Philadelphia was there. The Pentecostal family, headed by Michael Cardone, Sr., and his four brothers, had founded the new business of rebuilding carburetors and other worn auto parts for General Motors, Ford, and Chrysler. They met

God in a new way in the crusade, and they received such a new infusion of the Holy Spirit that soon they had outgrown the basement where they began their business. They began building what is today the largest and most prestigious company for rebuilding used auto parts in the United States. Two of the brothers, Michael, Sr., and Nick, later became founding members of the Board of Regents of Oral Roberts University when it was chartered in November 1963. Michael, Sr.'s son, Michael, Jr., an ORU graduate and currently owner of the company, now fills a position on the ORU Board of Regents, and he is one of the most godly and successful young businessmen in America.

After the Philadelphia crusade, we tried to compile a list of people who were in that service and who became widely used of God. It was quite a list!

As for the miracles, I saw many get their healing. Not all were healed, but there were many more than in any previous service.

The impact on me reached deep into my soul. My vow had held. I had not foolishly ignored it and gone on anyway just because it was the customary time to go. I think I learned as never before that God has His own timetable, and if you belong to Him and if you hold to your obedience, He will more than make up for any time that may, at first, appear to have been lost.

I saw, too, it boiled down to who was in charge: God or me. I still remember virtually every moment and every emotion of that time in my hotel room and my belated arrival at the auditorium. Not only was nothing lost, but thousands of people came into a new realization that when God is in charge, He moves forward with His mighty gospel!

─────── *The Anointing*

I have been asked many times what the anointing is. I searched the Scriptures for every instance when individuals or groups felt God's anointing. I saw that by experiencing the presence of God, they were able to do mighty exploits for the Lord. I saw, too, that when the anointing of God's Spirit did not rise up in them, they were as ordinary in themselves and in their works as any of us are today. There was no halo around them. They were not supermen or superwomen. They were believers but still flesh and blood.

I focused on Luke 4:18. Jesus said to the people in the syna-gogue in Nazareth, where He had grown up:

The Spirit of the Lord is upon me,
because he hath anointed me to preach the gospel to the poor;
he hath sent me to heal the broken-hearted,
to preach deliverance to the captives,
and recovering of sight to the blind,
to set at liberty them that are bruised.

The revelation came to me that *the anointing is a time when God separates you from yourself and fills you with His glory so that when you speak it's like God speaking, and when you act it's like God acting.* You are yourself, but you are not yourself. I mean, you have not taken leave of your senses. Still, you are keenly aware that another Self—the Spirit of God Himself—has taken over and is, at that time, in full charge of you, and you are acting under His divine unction or guidance and power from above.

The glory of the Lord that comes upon you at the time of anointing removes all fear, fills you with a holy boldness, and gives you revelational knowledge of how and what to do. It is an incomparable experience. God who is in you is now flowing up by His Spirit from your belly area (your inner being) and giving you a covering that Satan cannot penetrate (see John 7:38–39).

The difficulty I have had with the anointing when it comes in my right hand is twofold. One, the presence of God is so forceful in my hand that if I am not extremely careful, I touch the person I'm praying for too hard. In the heat of this experience I have an insatiable desire to literally drive the sickness or disease or demon or fear or poverty or any other destructive power out of the person. I confess it is a driving force possessing me far beyond any powers of my own. My normal compassion appears to be multiplied a thousand times. My urgency to rid the person of the tormenting power of Satan almost consumes me.

Many times I have had to ask the people after I prayed for them to forgive me for touching them too hard. Usually, the people are so caught up in the power of the living God to heal or deliver them and they are so thrilled to be set free that they couldn't care less how soft or hard I touched them. They came to get results,

and when the miracle delivers them, their gratitude to God over-
flows their hearts.

Two, I have no control over when the presence of God comes
in my right hand. Nor do I have control over when the anointing
stops. For example, I can be praying for people coming single file,
or praying for an entire audience by using the word of knowledge
(see 1 Cor. 12:8), and the anointing may stop. It does not mean I
have any less of God in me or the people have less faith. It's simply
that the overflowing anointing—the tangible presence of God—is
not mine. It belongs to God.

The prophet Elijah said, "Let [God] be God" (1 Kings 18:24).
That is exactly what I had to learn to do. At first, when the anointing in my right hand abruptly stopped, I did not know what to do
except continue laying hands on the sick and praying. However, it
was soon apparent to me, and to most others, I was back on my
own spiritual level. That meant a few would be healed, but the
healing of a higher percentage and of more serious diseases seemingly did not happen.

I could be praying for a huge number of people with
terrible diseases, some even demon-possessed, and the anointing
in my right hand would stop. I found that the best thing to do was
to stop abruptly and ask the audience to stand for the benediction.

The point I am trying to make is that Jesus Himself had to feel
the anointing when He was doing His preaching, teaching, and
healing. Who am I and who is any other believer to think we can
do anything in the area of the miraculous unless the presence of
God is upon us? I do not mean to suggest that anyone else's anointing must be like what God manifests in me at times. God alone de-
cides *how* He manifests a gift of the Spirit, and for what period of
time, on a given occasion.

The apostle Paul said that God's ways are past finding out (see
Rom. 11:33). I, for one, believe it. I also believe that is where faith
and trust come in. Either you believe God is and trust Him, or you
don't. It is not merely attending church services, as important as
that is. It is going with the flow of God's Spirit. It was extremely
important to me that I go with the flow of God's anointing not only
in my prayers for people but also in my sermons. I abhorred the
thought of spending a few minutes preaching a "nice" sermon that
wouldn't move the people, let alone set them free with the Word of

God. I had had enough of such sermons in my earlier preaching. No more.

The Drama of My Sermons

My way of preaching now is not much different from that of the years of my tent ministry. My guidance was that after I got the facts and themes of the sermon together, I was to make it into story form as much as possible. It wasn't just a story I told. It was a story I lived in my spirit so that as I preached in story form, I would take the listeners with me and they could see and feel what I was talking about.

I was never a preacher who used many adjectives. I laced my messages with verbs and adverbs. I think I did that because as I paid attention to the Bible and read and studied it, I saw that it's not so much a description as it is taking the reader on a trip with God. You can see and feel and touch and be touched by the supernatural power of God. The Bible puts you there. I know that it got hold of me, filling my senses, making me come alive spiritually, and causing my inner man to stand up inside. The Bible account had a powerful effect on me.

That may be why when my healing ministry began at age twenty-nine, I developed sermons such as "The Fourth Man," "Samson and Delilah—Battle of Champions," "You Can't Go Under for Going Over," "Deliverance from Demon Possession," "A Man's Life," "Holding the Rope," "The Point of Contact," "Expect a Miracle," "The Miracle of Seed-Faith," "Running Faster than You Can Run," "David and Bathsheba," "The Drama of the End Time," and many others.

In my healing crusades, many people came for more than the healing lines or the prospect of getting healed. I'd been able to build my sermons so that each one was almost a drama in itself. A crowd of ten thousand or twenty thousand immediately got with me because I had no lead-ins to tell to relax the people. From the first word out of my mouth, it was "go"—and the people knew we were going to take a journey that night until we reached the climax that often had the people on the edge of their seats.

For example, one night in 1951 during my first Los Angeles crusade, my sermon was "Samson and Delilah—Battle of Champions."

I came to the place where the blinded Samson, now repentant and restored from his backsliding, had been led by his enemies from prison into the heathen temple of Dagon where they set him between two pillars. With three thousand lords and ladies of the Philistines there, mocking and jeering at Samson and his God, they dared him to pull the temple down. They were not aware that after Samson's repentance, God had restored his supernatural strength. But Samson knew. He could feel it surging through every fiber of his being.

At that point in the service, I became Samson, and I placed my arms around one of the tent quarter poles that was on the platform to help support the big tent. I told of Samson praying these words in the midst of the mocking crowd: "O Lord God, remember me. Remember me just this once. Let me pull the temple of my enemies down."

I told of how the jeering stopped, and a hush came over that great gathering of the Philistine leaders. They heard the desperate cry of Samson and felt something sweeping toward them. The mighty power of God had entered the sightless Samson, now God's champion again. Putting his arms around the two columns that supported the weight of the huge temple of Dagon, the false god, Samson made a move of his shoulders and the columns began to move. With my arms wrapped around the tent pole, I shook it. A pastor seated nearby cried out, "Look out everybody, he's going to pull this tent down!"

It snapped the people's attention from the temple of Dagon to the tent of Oral Roberts, and suddenly, a nervous laugh broke out. It took me several minutes to refocus the attention of the people on the point I was trying to make: Can a human being who has fallen come back to God again?

People later said they could almost feel the tent being pulled down as Samson was pulling the temple down three thousand years before. In the final minutes of the sermon, I told of Samson pulling the temple down. The roof sagged, the columns crumpled, and down came the huge building on the screaming lords and ladies. I acted out pulling the stones off Samson, and I leaned down with my microphone close enough to carry a whisper. I had Samson saying, "My soul has seen the glory of the Lord," and then I recited the words in the Bible account: "So the dead which he

slew at his death were more than they which he slew in his life"
(Judg. 16:30).

That sermon, with the anointing all over me, never failed to
cause hundreds of the unsaved to leap up from their chairs and
rush forward for me to lead them to repeat the sinner's prayer and
to believe on the Lord Jesus and be restored to God and the right
path of life.

In those beginning years, I was laying the groundwork to
make every service, no matter what area of the Bible I covered, become a living story, one that took the listeners there so they would
come face-to-face with the God of the "now." And only the anointing of the Holy Spirit upon me could enable that to occur.

Can the ordinary Christian experience God's anointing? Yes!
No one is more ordinary than I am. I believe every one of us can
experience the special portion of His anointing that God has for us
if we understand it is for us, if we want it and believe for it, and if
we always remember it is God who anoints. God does the mighty
work, and He will not share His glory with any person.

It would scare me spitless if I thought for one moment that
any miracle of healing or any other miraculous deed came because I have something in myself. I know that I do not. I must do
my part and always trust God, but He alone does the miracle deed.
And what mighty miracles He does! There are so many that I
would like to share—enough to fill this book many times. God
showed His mighty power again and again in our healing tent and
auditorium crusades, and He still does today through this ministry.
Let me share with you one of the greatest miracles that happened
in the midst of the greatest unbelief, and one of the most unlikely
miracles ever to happen.

CHAPTER 11

THE MIRACLES OF LITTLE DOUGLASS AND UNCLE LUTE

I REMEMBER THIS miracle as if it happened yesterday. The setting for it could not have been more difficult. The faith of a little boy, Douglass Sutton—in the midst of the heaviest unbelief I'd ever encountered in a large audience—shone through like a sunrise.

We had rented the biggest facility in the area, a B-29 hangar, in which we could seat nearly ten thousand and have room for several thousand more to stand. A healing crusade had never come to Goldsboro, a tobacco city in eastern North Carolina. When the newspapers announced I was coming for a sixteen-day crusade, the news spread like wildfire.

News stories planted doubt about healing being possible today as it was reported occurring in the days of Jesus and the early Christians. They say ignorance is bliss. Fortunately, I was ignorant of those reports before I arrived. I had been informed, however, that fewer than ten local and area pastors dared to sponsor the crusade and risk their reputation with the public.

In spite of all those happenings, when the doors opened the first night and I was driven up to the building, thousands of cars were parked around the hangar and at least a half mile down the runways.

I've always loved a full house. I never saw an empty seat converted or healed. I was excited when I walked in and saw every seat filled. There was a balconylike platform behind and high above the platform from where I preached, and I saw that it was jammed.

"This is going to be a great crusade," I whispered to the chairman of the crusade, Pastor W. W. Thomas of the Assemblies of God. "Yes," he said, "excitement has been building. I've never known such interest in healing or a crowd this size coming together like this."

The sponsoring committee and I met behind stage, joined hands, and prayed. Then I heard myself being introduced, and I rushed up the steps to greet the people.

I did the greeting; they did the staring. "What is Oral Roberts like?" had been the talk of the area.

I knew instinctively I was in hostile territory. It was instantly clear to my spirit the battle lines had been drawn. There were thousands of them, but only one of me along with my crusade team of seven and a few local pastors who dared to stand up for what Jesus was and what He did while He was on earth and what He would do again today if He could find faith in enough people.

When I hit the stage and stood before the microphone, I felt those thousands become as one powerful doubting person. I knew it would take a miracle of undeniable reality that all could see to have even a chance of turning the tide.

Much of the hope for that miracle, and others, depended solely on my preaching the Word of God. The Word of God flowing through the words of my mouth had to take the people out of their present spiritual setting, that of hostility and unbelief, into the very heart of the living Christ. Whatever I read to them from the Bible had to be made familiar to them, so they could feel it was meant for their time, for the "now" of their existence on this earth.

I couldn't just tell stories out of the Bible I held in my hands. I had to paint a picture from it that they could see and feel and smell. There in the Bible Belt of the South I knew God had given every one of them "the measure of faith" (Rom. 12:3). But their faith had to be ignited by the Word of God: "How shall they believe in him of whom they have not heard? and how shall they hear without a preacher? . . . Faith cometh by hearing, and hearing by the word of God" (Rom. 10:14, 17).

At that moment before them, all I had to stand on was the Word of God, the call of God upon my life, and the anointing. I knew, however, in the deepest part of me that if I had the courage to preach to them, my Savior would work through me to win souls and heal the sick as Mark said, "And they went forth, and preached every where, the Lord working with them, and confirming the word with signs following" (Mark 16:20). The Word would be confirmed *if* I preached it that first evening, no matter the present attitude of that great audience.

Usually when a preacher preaches, he can feel a response or a reaction from the people. On that night, I saw people sitting with their arms crossed and a look of "show me" on their faces.

The fact of facts is that faith comes by hearing, and hearing comes as the gospel is preached by one anointed by the Holy Spirit, who expects the Word of God he preaches to be confirmed with signs following—miracles of healing and other acts of human deliverance from sin, disease, demons, fear, financial need, frustrations, and inner conflicts.

The promise in the Bible is that when the Word, that is, the *full* Word, is preached, God will confirm or reveal it with signs that follow. A miracle, or a healing by faith, is one of these confirmational signs.

I believed the Word of God implicitly. I had no doubt of it whatsoever. Already during the first two and a half years of my healing ministry I had seen thousands of those miraculous signs of confirmation of His Word preached by me. His presence coming in my hand, as He had spoken to me, was as real as my very being.

At Goldsboro, I did not give up. I sincerely and boldly preached with everything I had in me, praying that something would break, one way or another, before long.

Nothing broke until the fifth night. As the people in the healing line moved slowly toward me while I sat in a chair on the platform, I was praying with all my compassion and faith for each one. The sweat was pouring off me, even though it was December and very little heat was in the building other than that of the bodies of several thousand people. Over and over it came to me that my Savior knew about sweat, even to the point that His sweat became mixed with His blood in the Garden of Gethsemane.

I looked to my left to the people coming in the healing line. About ten people away were a mother and her son, who looked to be eleven or twelve years old. He was on crutches, with one leg lifted and supported in a brace that was strapped to his shoulder.

As Luke said of the Virgin Mary when her cousin Elizabeth's "baby leaped in her womb," faith leaped in my spirit that the confirmation of the Word I had preached was about to happen. I could scarcely wait to pray for the little fellow. I didn't know what was wrong, but my faith was saying Jesus of Nazareth was about to make it right. A mighty healing was about to happen.

When they stood before me, I noticed both were beaming, an expectation in them that bonded with me. When I looked at the prayer card, giving the name of the boy, the address, the church connection, and a description of what was wrong, I saw by the number on the card the mother had been there with him since the third night.

They were totally unaffected by the seeming hostility of the crowd, the wait-and-see attitude. Nor did they pay any attention to the sweat rolling off me. They had heard the Word preached, and their faith had come up inside them. Nothing else mattered.

Since that night, I've seen thousands of situations where the faith of a person was not negatively affected by any kind of circumstances or attitude of others. There's something about faith that comes up through the Word of God being preached—the hearing of it in the inner self—that is the master key to deliverance.

Real faith is not timid.

Real faith is not intimidated.

Real faith doesn't take no for an answer.

Real faith breaks through all barriers and touches the heart of the Savior Himself.

The little boy was named Douglass Sutton. His mother told me he had had Perthes' disease since he was quite young. (This is a flattening of the hip bone.) The doctors hoped that by having the leg supported in a brace so that it would not touch the ground, the leg would have a chance to grow out over enough time.

I had seen one other case like this healed in an earlier crusade. I knew it could be done.

I also know that God is a good God; however, He doesn't run around healing everybody indiscriminately. With God, healing is not an end in itself. It is a divine means to a greater end. It really means "to be continued." It is to show God's original desire that people be as He created them—whole. God wants to heal the whole person.

"Jesus, heal!" I prayed as I touched the little boy. Something was in my voice that had not been there before in that crusade. I had been swimming against the current. Every sermon I delivered seemed to hit a wall and fly back in my face. By faith, obedience, and dogged determination, I had been preaching as if each message was my last and the last that crowd would ever hear. I felt so many lives hanging in the balance. If only one visible miracle of healing could happen as a confirmation of the preaching, everything could change.

Newspaper people were everywhere in the building. They seemed to sense something was about to happen.

When I prayed, "Jesus, heal!" I felt the presence of God run down my arm into my right hand and flow into that little boy's flat hip bone. Inwardly, I knew God was working His healing power in the boy's entire body.

I looked up at the mother. "Do you believe God has touched your son?" Without any hesitation she said, "Oral Roberts, I know He has!"

I said, "You mean right now?"

She said, "Oh, yes, right now."

Looking at her son, I said, "How about you, Douglass? Do you feel any of God's healing power going through you?"

"Yes, sir!"

"What do you want him to do?" I asked the mother.

For an answer she leaned down, unstrapped her boy's leg, and took his crutches. He put his foot to the floor.

That was the fateful moment.

I heard a sound from the crowd. People were getting up to see, great wonderment filling their hearts.

"What do you want to do, son?" I asked.

"I want to run!"

He looked at his mother. She nodded, and he took off from the lower platform on which he stood in front of me. In a split second he was racing down one of the long aisles.

Like a cloudburst, the voices of the people roared. I felt something pulling me to my feet, and as I looked, men and women were jumping, running down the aisles, shouting at the tops of their voices, and crying. Oh, how the tears were flowing, including mine!

The boy ran back to his mother and me, and he began jumping up and down. She grabbed him and hugged him. When she put her hand on his previously flat hip bone and saw that a miraculous recovery had happened, she took off down an aisle praising God, with Douglass right after her.

The explosion of the audience could not be stopped. When I said, "Will you be seated, please," it was like a voice into the wind. For a full fifteen minutes, there were rejoicing and praising God as I had never seen them before.

Later, my friend, Lee Braxton, said, "Oral, that's the first time I've ever seen you lose control over your crowd."

I said, "Lee, God was in that, and a hurricane couldn't have stopped those people as long as they knew they had witnessed a miracle of God's healing power."

Finally, and I mean *finally*, people had praised God until they were finished of their own accord and sat down. If you've ever been in a hot, sweltering place and a strong cool breeze suddenly blew in, and you sighed and said, "Ah, that feels so good!" you know what I felt about the sudden change in the attitude of that huge crowd.

God had confirmed His Word by the faith of the mother and son that came up in them and they released back to Him. I felt it was also because I wouldn't give up, I wouldn't quit. I was willing to obey God and do what He had called me to do, no matter what.

The rest of the crusade was totally unlike its beginning. Extra crowds broke through the lines the fire marshal had erected. Joy swept over the people and over eastern North Carolina. The boy's healing and the healings that came so often every night until the end of the crusade were the talk on radio, on television, in newspapers, in factories, in warehouses, on the streets—everywhere. People discovered which hotel room was mine, and a squadron of volunteer men had to be put around it at night after the services so I could sleep.

The final Sunday afternoon, the crowd had filled and overflowed the B-29 hangar. They stood on the runway completely around the building. I was told over twenty-five thousand had gathered for the final service. By some miraculous touch of God on my being, I was able to personally touch and pray for approximately

Oral as a baby, 2 months

Oral and his brother, Vaden (l)

Ellis Roberts, Oral's father, with the Bible and folding organ he used in revival services

Evelyn, just before going to Texas to become a schoolteacher in 1936

*Oral, Evelyn, and Oral's mother,
Claudius, in Rio Grande Valley,
Texas in 1938*

*Oral and Evelyn during their first
weekend of courting, at the Gulf of
Mexico in 1938*

*Oral and Evelyn on their wedding
day, December 25, 1938*

*Oral and Evelyn at a TV taping in the
ORU studio*

...e church at Enid, Oklahoma, where Oral ...stored just before entering the healing ministry ... 1947

Oral and Evelyn's first home in Tulsa, Oklahoma, purchased for $6,000

A Florence, South Carolina, tent crusade

...ob DeWeese, Oral's co-evangelist and ...ight-hand man for thirty-eight years

The big tent (220' x 470'), which seated 12,000

Oral preaching the gospel in a tent crusade

Prominent North Carolina businessman Lee Braxton, who joined Oral's team in 1949 and remained for 33 years as a-dollar-a-year man

The big tent after the storm hit in Amarillo, Texas in September 1950

Breaking new ground by bringing TV cameras into the tent meeting in 1954

The healing line in Oral's tent preaching days

Oral praying for healing

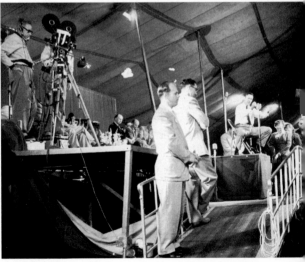

Cameras shooting the healing line in the tent days

Ruth Rooks, Oral's one and only secretary since 1947

Workers typing Oral's answers to Partners of the ministry

Oral doing a radio program in 1948

Oral Roberts Evangelistic Association trustees breaking ground for Oral Roberts University in 1962

Oral and Billy Graham at ORU dedication, April 1967

Oral's response to news of accreditation in 1971

ORU students going from chapel to class

Oral and James Winslow, M.D., who was in charge of all ORU medical activities

The controversial ORU Prayer Tower, which receives one million telephone calls a year

The City of Faith medical complex—2,200,000 square feet

The Learning Resources Center at ORU—over 600,000 square feet

An aerial view of ORU

Pat Robertson and Oral, just after the ORU Board of Regents voted to transfer the ORU Law School to CBN University, now Regent University

ten thousand sick people that afternoon after I preached and gave an invitation to the unsaved.

The miracles confirming the preaching of the Word on that fifth night had broken the souls of the people open to a sense of their own unbelief and need of God. Several thousand came to Christ.

Pastors who had held back at first were heard saying they wished they had been official sponsors to begin with. Every financial need of the crusade was met with a balance to be given to the sponsoring pastors.

The miracle at Goldsboro lives in me today.

One thing for sure, a miracle settles the issue. I suppose that's one reason I keep saying, "Expect a miracle!" I have truly had to live by those words. I've seen God take great disasters that should have made me quit the ministry altogether and turn them into a great miracle by the touch of His mighty hand.

The Miracle of Uncle Lute

I must tell of one more incident from 1949 that stands out among the others. My crusade in Bakersfield, California, was the first time I had stretched the big tent on the West Coast. One evening I had preached, had given the invitation to the unsaved, and had prayed backstage for the people who could not walk. I was sitting in my chair on the platform praying for the sick who were able to walk before me. About an hour into the healing service I looked up and saw a man, perhaps seventy years old, who looked familiar.

"What is your name, sir?" I asked.

"Lute Irwin."

"Mr. Lute Irwin of my mother's family?"

"Yes, I am your mother's brother."

Instantly, I remembered what I had always been told about his feud with Jody Robertson. My mama's oldest brother, Lute, had hidden out in the notorious Cookson Hills in eastern Oklahoma during World War I as a desperado. The law dared not enter those hills. Desperadoes from all over the country hid out there, for they knew they would be safe. That continued until Judge Parker, the famed "hanging judge" of Fort Smith, Arkansas, was appointed by the U.S. government to clean up the wild lands of Oklahoma.

Uncle Lute received a pardon in 1930, mostly because he was an Indian. Even when he left the Cookson Hills and had his pardon, he always carried a gun. The youngest son of Mama's family had been accidentally killed by Jody Robertson in Pontotoc County, and Lute sought to kill Jody on sight. It was a long feud.

As he stood before me, I asked, "Do you have your gun on you?"

"I do."

"Then if you want me to pray for your healing, Uncle Lute, you'll have to take your gun out and lay it here on the platform."

Without a word, he did it.

Thousands in the audience, as they heard us talking over the public address system, stood up to see the gun.

"What brought you here, Uncle Lute?"

"I heard Claudius's son, Oral, was praying for the sick here. I live in California now, and I'm here to be healed."

"A complete healing?"

"A complete healing, yes."

I told the audience of the death of the youngest brother, the feud between Lute and Jody Robertson, and the hiding out in the Cookson Hills during World War I. I told them that was my first meeting with my uncle.

I knew Uncle Lute knew what I meant when I asked if he wanted a complete healing—meaning soul and body and all past wrongs, wrongs from him and wrongs he did to others, and any vengeance he still felt in his heart.

"Are you willing to forgive Jody Robertson?" I asked.

He didn't say anything. I knew he wasn't refusing to answer. People with lots of Indian blood usually don't talk quickly. You have to wait them out.

I could feel the crowd was hanging on to every word. Finally, he said, "Yes, I forgive Jody Robertson."

"Once and for all?"

"Yes."

"Never to try to kill him?"

"Never."

I led him in the sinner's prayer. He repented, asking God's forgiveness and believing on the Lord Jesus Christ as his personal Savior. A huge smile came over his face as big tears trickled down to the floor.

"Uncle Lute, will you take this microphone and turn to the crowd and tell them what Jesus has done for you?"

Once his tongue got loose, the words poured out, some of them very beautiful and tender, as he gave a clear public confession of faith in Jesus Christ as his personal Savior.

I couldn't wait to phone my mother back in Oklahoma that night and tell her she wouldn't have to pray anymore that Uncle Lute wouldn't kill Jody Robertson. I've learned never to underestimate the power of a miracle.

CHAPTER 12

TWO GREAT DISASTERS TURNED INTO TWO GREAT MIRACLES

I T WAS SEPTEMBER 1950, and we had pitched our crusade tent in Amarillo, Texas. The tent was the third one I had purchased, and it seated seven thousand folding chairs we carried in our big semitrailers, with plenty of space for overflow crowds when the tent flaps were up.

One evening while the service was in progress, a terrible storm came over the city. I was in the healing line, praying for the people as they came by me, when I heard a mighty roar. Within seconds, it seemed, the winds had swept in off the Texas Panhandle and hit the tent.

The next thing I knew, I was standing up urging everyone to be calm and telling the men who were seated near the big tent poles to try to hold them down. I said that we should all trust God.

Suddenly, as if by a miracle, the wind lifted me off the platform and laid me down on the ground ten feet away, like a mother putting her child to bed. I was not hurt, but I could have been broken to pieces.

I vaguely remember the great audience starting to sing. While lying there on my back, I saw the huge canvas lift like a balloon, leaving the people exposed to pounding rain.

I rose up, climbed back on the platform, grabbed the microphone, which was amazingly still on, and told the people to slowly and carefully make their way to their cars. I remember that there was no hysteria, no loud cries, and the people carried out my instructions almost as if there was no storm at all.

By that time, I was wondering where Evelyn and Richard were. He was two years old at the time and had come with Evelyn to the crusade. Someone ran up to the platform and grabbed me and said, "Your wife and child are under the platform. They're safe." Quickly, I found them, and we stood holding each other, crying and thanking God our lives had been saved with no harm. Meanwhile, I left them in the care of my brother, Vaden. Vaden had been traveling with us in the ministry, handling the big equipment and coordinating setting up the tent.

I went outside the tent among the people as they were going to their cars. I laid my hands on hundreds, praying for them not to be hurt, and I gave encouragement to as many others as I could during the next hour. People were hugging each other, others were still singing, and I returned to the platform in awe of the God who was stronger than that storm.

About that time someone saw me and pointed at a man in a wheelchair who had been pushed out of the area where I prayed for invalids. His voice carried above the wind and rain, "Oral Roberts, help me get out of this wheelchair!"

At a time like that, you don't think or doubt; you just *act*. I rushed over and put my right hand on his rain-soaked head and said, "In the name of Jesus Christ of Nazareth, rise up and walk!"

Out of that wheelchair he came, his legs receiving new life and coordination returning to his body. He took off running, and that was the last I saw of him.

When all the people left, we were driven to our hotel, where I talked to the Amarillo press and called Lee Braxton. Lee was a businessman (in fact, a millionaire) and prominent Christian living in North Carolina, who had come on staff virtually as a full-time volunteer. He had been traveling with my team as a dollar-a-year man (literally for a dollar a year). In addition to owning twenty-two corporations, Lee was a motivational speaker. He had spoken on the same platform with Dale Carnegie, who wrote *How to Win Friends and Influence People*; with Frank Bettger, whose book *How I Raised Myself from Failure to Success in Selling* has influenced thousands; with Napoleon Hill, known for his book *Think and Grow Rich*; and with several other best-selling authors and speakers.

When I called Lee, I told him of the storm. "I'll catch the next plane," he told me, "and be at your side sometime tomorrow."

The next morning the headlines of the Amarillo newspaper read, "Saving of 7,000 Called Miracle." They described how the fire department had come to the scene, looking for hundreds to be injured or killed. They discovered only three people with injuries and called ambulances to rush them to the hospital. Only one of the three was injured seriously enough to remain in the hospital.

The article, filling almost the full front page, reported interviews with several people who had been at the tent during the storm. They stated how remarkable it was that there was no panic and how the people sang hymns during the exit after the tent blew down and left them exposed to the wild elements. During all the years of my healing ministry, there has never been a more honest and objective piece of writing than the Amarillo newspaper reporters did.

The following day, I went to the hospital and prayed for the injured person who was still hospitalized. He was released soon afterward. On the one hand, I was praising God for saving the lives of seven thousand people, while on the other hand, my faith was pretty well strained to believe such a mighty miracle had come at the height of a storm so powerful it could have destroyed us all.

When Lee Braxton arrived, we drove out to the tent site. The parts of the canvas that remained over the chairs had been cut in pieces by the firemen who were looking for injured or dead people. As I talked with them, man after man said, "Preacher, it's really not possible, but yet it happened. It's a miracle!"

Someone drove up with a bunch of telegrams from ministers and others across America, telling me they had read the news or heard it on the radio and gave thanks to God for our deliverance.

One telegram in particular lifted my spirits. It was from a family in Colorado who had been won to Christ in another crusade. They had enjoyed my sermons, especially one about a storm on the Sea of Galilee in which Jesus was riding in a boat. Their telegram said, "Dear Oral, you can't go under for going over!" That was the subject of the sermon they had heard me preach on the great storm that struck the little boat of Jesus and His disciples and yet they had been able to survive and go over to the other side unharmed.

As Lee read the telegram, he said, "They're right. The miracle here means this ministry can't go under for going over. God is not

through with you yet. I'll begin a search of tent-making companies, and we'll have a tent made that seats ten thousand and is
built to withstand storms like this."

Lee had rightly discerned my state of mind: I was wondering
whether I should continue. That telegram that repeated the title of
my sermon to me and Lee's well-earned reputation for getting
things done heartened me. "Go to it," I told him. "Let's have one
built to withstand a hundred-mile-an-hour wind."

Employees of a company in Chicago that made the big tents
for the Ringling Brothers Circus put their heads together, and although no tent had been made in America seating ten thousand,
they figured they could do it and build one that would be safe
enough.

God had turned the Amarillo disaster into a miracle of saving
seven thousand people from physical harm and helped us get a
larger tent, seating ten thousand, then one that seated twelve thousand. The tents withstood winds and hailstorms without any ap-
preciable damage.

When we left Amarillo, the budget of the crusade had not been
raised, and we had very little money to pay our workers. Evelyn
and I emptied our little savings and added that to the offerings that
were taken prior to the storm hitting, and we made the payroll. It
also paid for cleaning up the lot and for stacking the seven thousand folding chairs and other portable equipment and loading it all
in the semitrailers, which remarkably had not been damaged. No
bill was left unpaid in Amarillo, and the news people mentioned
that in a favorable way.

That was not the first time Evelyn and I had emptied out our
savings for the sake of the ministry—nor would it be the last. As
my ministry had begun to expand, I had become increasingly
aware that I needed to be scrupulously responsible with my personal finances as well as the ministry's. If there was any hint of
taking personal advantage of people in need, it would be a big
black mark on my work as well as my conscience. I believed that
the best way to do that was to organize the ministry so that others
would share in the financial decisions.

In July of 1948, I had felt it best to incorporate into a nonprofit
religious organization. We called it Oral Roberts Evangelistic
Association, Inc. Evelyn and I had several hundred dollars in a

savings account—the first we had ever had. We drew it out and gave it to the attorneys, and it became the nucleus for the ministry to be established financially.

Absolute and final authority over all financial matters was put into the hands of a board of seven trustees, only two of which were Robertses, Evelyn and I. They were dedicated Christian business-men and women who had an effective Christian witness and good business sense as well.

——— Can We Go On?

Evelyn and I were not all back together in our thinking after the Amarillo happening. It had been more than a jolt—it was greater than anything we had faced in the first two and a half years of our healing ministry. We had no tent, yet we had a year's sched-ule of meetings ahead of us. Our funds were exhausted, and we simply did not know what to do.

Lee Braxton never faltered. He encouraged us as only a busi-nessman, who had known large difficulties, could. "This is not the end," he told us over and over. "Oral, you're only thirty-two years old. The anointing is still on you. You can make it a seed that will produce an equivalent benefit."

Lee and I had begun to discuss the Bible principles of every-thing being a seed. Jesus was the seed of David, and Jesus Himself compared our faith to a seed that we sow, and after we do, we can expect a harvest (see Matt. 17:20).

Somewhere Lee had gotten hold of the truth that in every loss, there is a way out. If you will sow a seed—give or do something that costs you and is your best—and do it in the midst of a loss you've suffered, you can expect to receive a benefit as great as or greater than the loss. He called this sowing a seed of an equivalent benefit, and it came right out of the Word of God.

Through Jesus' death on the cross, God had planted Him as a seed to ensure the harvest of the Resurrection that followed. This principle can be applied to any kind of loss we suffer.

Years later the revelation I called miracle of seed-faith began to take shape and form in my spirit. That teaching was to become one of the foundations of my entire ministry, and it became the hope of millions to whom I would teach it in person and in my writings.

Bob DeWeese said my introduction of seed-faith to the people would be the single greatest thing I would leave after I am gone. "Planting a seed" has become a household phrase in churches and homes as millions have caught on to the Bible principle of seed-faith. It gives people hope and expectation that seed sown to God will be multiplied back in every area of life. It is a powerful principle. I never attempt or do anything without first planting a seed of my faith to God and getting into expectation to receive from His bountiful harvest.

─────── *Meeting Billy Graham*

Upon arriving home from Amarillo, I had a call from Tacoma, Washington, where we had conducted a crusade the year before. Friends, upon hearing of the loss of our tent and of the interruption of my ministry, called to invite us to come for a few days and rest and get back on our feet.

They helped us financially with our airfare, and Evelyn and I, after arranging for the care of our children, left for Tacoma. We were received with open arms. They took us fishing in Puget Sound where we caught many large salmon. "See," our friends said, "you can still catch fish in the natural world. Soon you'll be catching fish as Jesus said in winning souls and healing the sick."

We began to feel the Holy Spirit moving in us, the gloom began to leave, and we soon became aware of a quickening in our spirits that it wasn't over yet.

I have always believed, since becoming a believer and then a minister of the gospel, that God works from the inside out, that is, He begins in the inner man before the outer man can know what to do.

As we were preparing to leave Tacoma, friends of ours in Portland, Oregon, called us and said that Portland had erected a big wooden tabernacle seating ten thousand. Billy Graham was packing it each night.

In Billy's tent crusade in Los Angeles in 1949, the great Hearst newspaper organization had given him positive coverage. That, along with the powerful call on Billy's life, his inherent ability, and his dependence on God, had been the catalyst for his Los Angeles crusade to catch fire and grow until it was carried by the news media everywhere.

Many great talents of Hollywood, such as Stuart Hamblen, who later wrote the great song "It Is No Secret What God Can Do," were converted in that crusade. Seemingly overnight, Billy Graham was a sensation for God known to millions. No one was more thrilled than I.

Evelyn and I decided to go to Portland and attend his meeting. As we were walking out of the hotel that night to get a taxi, Billy was also leaving for the crusade.

He grabbed our hands and said how delighted he was that we were there. He explained that a cab was waiting to take him to the tabernacle and asked if we would go with him. We didn't want to impose, but he insisted, so we rode with him and Ruth.

On the way, he said, "Oral, I want you to lead in prayer tonight."

My response was genuine. "Billy, you can't be serious. I don't want to cause a problem for you by being on the platform and giving the prayer. You know my ministry is very controversial."

He knew I was referring to the fact that although our ministries were much alike in that we were preachers and soul winners, there was a wide difference of belief between the evangelicals who sponsored Billy's crusades and the Pentecostals who sponsored mine. One difference was the baptism of the Holy Spirit with speaking in tongues, and another was healing as a confirmation of the Word when preached.

When Billy announced I was on the platform that night and asked me to pray before he preached, I heard a stir in the audience. I don't remember what I said in my prayer, but I did pour my heart out to God in behalf of the services and the results to follow.

From the beginning of my knowledge of Billy Graham, and later my acquaintance with him, I have felt—as millions of others have felt—he is the number one evangelist in this generation.

I have heard men of God who can preach as well as Billy, although he is powerful in his preaching. But something else about him puts him in his own class. I think it is his spirit, his graciousness, his openness to all believers—including the Pentecostals and charismatics—and his absolute focus on Jesus without whose anointing he believes he would be nothing.

Billy has tremendous organizational ability and the dedication of his team to organize prayer groups a year in advance in each city to which he goes. He has powerful choirs from all churches organized under the direction of Cliff Barrows, the premier song leader of our time.

Another difference in Billy is the way he has found a way into the hearts of not only the common people but also the elite of the world. Presidents of the United States from Truman to Clinton have been good friends to him. The media took a liking to Billy and have seldom put him in a bad light.

All of these things are important and well deserved. But as Billy so often says, "The Holy Spirit alone keeps me going." No man in the gospel has been more cordial and open to me or to my ministry.

Two most providential things happened after Billy's service that night that involved me. I had just taken Evelyn by the hand to get a cab back to the hotel when I was stopped by a woman and her husband. She had cancer and said she had been praying the Lord would send me to pray for her healing. She asked if I would pray right there.

We were under the edge of the tabernacle in an area where I felt the sponsors of Billy Graham would not want me praying for the sick. I have an innate courtesy and respect not to engage in healing prayer when I am with people who sincerely do not understand or believe in it. I certainly was not going to do anything that might bring embarrassment to Billy's crusade.

I explained that to the woman and told her I was sorry, but I did not feel it was appropriate for me, not being a member of the sponsoring groups, to pray for her there as the service was closing.

Her husband pointed his finger at me. "Oral Roberts," he said, "my wife is dying with cancer. God has called you to pray for the sick. If you refuse to pray for her, God will hold you accountable at the judgment."

His words hit me like a ton of bricks. I knew he was right. I also knew I was right in not praying for healing when I had been invited to a crusade where healing was not part of the program.

"I will pray for her on one condition," I said. "Come out into the street away from the tabernacle."

"That's fine with us," he replied.

Standing in the middle of the street, I laid hands on the suffering woman and prayed in the name of Jesus Christ of Nazareth for the foul, tormenting disease to come out of her body, to loose her and to let her go free. It was a powerful moment. I felt it and she felt it. I committed her to God and started to walk away.

"Brother Roberts," a voice nearby spoke.

"Yes," I said, turning toward the voice.

It was Dr. Harold Jeffreys, one of Billy's sponsoring pastors and the pastor of the very large local body of the International Church of the Foursquare Gospel.

"I watched you tonight," he said. "I felt the fervency of your prayer when Billy asked you to pray. And I just saw the way you handled this touchy situation of being asked to pray for this woman's healing."

"Oh?" I said.

"Yes, you're everything in anointing, in integrity, and in compassion for the sick that I heard you were. I'm asking you to allow me to bring a group of sponsoring pastors together and make arrangements for you to bring your big tent to Portland this time next year."

"But, Dr. Jeffreys, I lost my tent."

"Yes, I heard. I also heard you've ordered a new one seating ten thousand. Will you come?"

After accepting and initiating the details, I thanked him, and we returned to the hotel. As we entered the hotel's coffee shop, we bumped into Billy and Ruth, who were already there. They asked us to join them, which we did.

I complimented him on the service that evening, with special appreciation for the large number of decisions for Christ.

He thanked me, then surprised me by saying, "Two years ago when you first brought your tent to Florida, Cliff Barrows and I came to your services. We sat in the back and listened to you preach, saw you invite sinners to Christ, then began praying for God to heal the sick. We were deeply touched."

"You really did that?" I asked. "You believe in healing then."

"Oh, I certainly do. God has not called me to pray for the sick, but He has given you the gift."

In the fifteen or twenty times Billy and I have met, during the times I've been in his crusades and conferences, and when he was a guest on my TV program and also dedicated Oral Roberts University in 1967, there has been nothing but friendship and mutual appreciation between us. He and Ruth are very dear to Evelyn and me.

The next time I heard from Billy was in 1957. He sent me a telegram from Australia during his great crusade there. It came after God had turned another great disaster into a great miracle.

————— *"Oral Roberts, Get Out of Australia!"*

The year prior to Billy's Australia crusade, 1956, my ten-thousand-seat tent and equipment were shipped to Australia for crusades in Sydney and Melbourne, the two largest cities.

The Sydney crusade went off well with overflowing crowds, large numbers saved and healed. We even filmed it to show on our TV program back home.

Melbourne was a different situation. A longshoremen's strike was going on. Communists were among them, and the government was gravely concerned. Violence on the docks and in other places was becoming common.

However, the first night in Melbourne the tent was packed, and we were off to one of the finest efforts in the gospel of my entire ministry. Nothing could have been more perfect as to attendance and response to my preaching, success with the salvation of souls, and healings of the people. The hunger among them was very strong. No healing crusade of that magnitude had ever come to the land "down under." I never met a lovelier people.

On our second night the tent was filled, and several thousand were standing around the edges. When I stepped on the platform to preach, there was a sudden wild and loud intrusion of the service by several hundred men from the longshoremen's strike. They filled the aisles, shouting obscenities, and several rushed on the stage and slapped me around. Policemen, who had been stationed in various places in and around the tent, stood with hands folded, handicapped by the lack of a law to bring order back into the service.

We did not know that the constitution of Australia had no law giving protection to churches. Rowdies could enter any church and cause disturbances without breaking any law.

Somehow we got through the service.

The third night was even worse. The tent was only half full, and again a gang rushed us, cursing the people and making fun of them, and coming on stage to spit on me and hit me in the face and chest and shoulders.

Sponsoring pastors tried to restore order but failed. Once when they hustled me off stage, they handed me a glass of water, only to find that beer had been poured into it.

Bob DeWeese, who had been an Olympic swimmer as a youth, and who was about six feet three inches tall, doubled up his fists and said, "Here I am. Come and get me, you low-down, stinking cowards."

No one took his dare.

Meanwhile, the media were carrying the news of the invasion of the crusade by the hooligans and did so in a way to aid and abet them. The pastors gave names and addresses of people genuinely healed to the press, but the media refused to accept the people's testimonies.

I had heard of yellow journalism, but I became its victim. Never had I been harassed like this by the newspapers and by radio announcers, been called such names, or been mocked for being a fraud. The point they aimed at was *not* my preaching, *not* my invitations for people to make decisions for Christ (which a thousand did on the very first night), and *not* the careful way the chairman of the crusade received offerings for expenses. *They criticized the healing line.*

Had I not prayed for the healing of the people, I'm convinced there would have been no violent onslaughts on us. But neither would it have been the real me who had come with the same call of God as I had in the United States and in other nations.

"Oral Roberts, get out of Australia" and such slogans filled the airways and newspapers. At first, my mind was flooded with grief. Over and over the Scriptures came to me, reminding me that violence most often came to Jesus and later to His followers after His ascension when they prayed for the sick and did mighty healing miracles.

Finally, on the fourth night, in an attempt to stop all the attacks on us, the sponsoring pastors asked one of the highest-ranking leaders of Melbourne, respected by all, to interrogate me publicly on the platform before I preached. The tent was nearly full, despite threats of further violence.

The man was gracious but firm in questioning me before the audience as to my education, my station in life in America, my acceptance in other nations, and in particular the validity of healing as part of the Christian faith. He appeared most satisfied with my answers, but he was somewhat taken aback with my reply concerning healing as an integral part of Christianity.

I gave chapter and verse of Christ's healing ministry and of His command for all His disciples to go into all the world and preach the gospel to every creature and these signs would follow them who believe: Demons would be cast out of people, the sick would be healed, and as His Word was preached, He would confirm it with signs (miracles)!

The man turned to the crowd, much like Pilate did after interrogating Jesus before the cross, and practically echoed Pilate's words when he said of Jesus, "I find no fault in this man." He stated that he felt I was in Australia to do good and that all violence should cease.

The moment he finished saying that, the gang that had been waiting rushed the stage and spit on him, shaking him to the roots of his composure. Then they broke up the service.

I was quickly led out to the car to be taken to the private residence where Evelyn and I were staying. Suddenly, I was stopped and rushed in another direction. I asked, "What's wrong?"

They had seen the car in which I was to ride, and a part of the gang was rocking it for the final time to turn it over, thinking I was in it. I broke loose to get there, for I knew Evelyn was in that car. "No! No!" the pastors said. "When they see your wife in the car, they won't turn it over to injure or kill her. But if you get in, we don't know what they will do to you."

They slipped me into another car, which sped away. Soon after I arrived at the residence of our friend, Evelyn came, white as a sheet, but with determination in her eyes. "Oh, Oral," she said, "I was scared to death they were going to turn the car over. They saw you were not in the car and left. Honey, this can't go on any longer."

We heard voices all around outside the house. Our friend, with whom we were staying, went out to check. The media had several reporters mixed in with some of the gang from the tent, who were going to remain there all night to get to me. He yelled to them, "Listen to me, men. I survived as a captain in World War II. I was almost killed several times during the war. I am not afraid of any or all of you. This is the first time in my life I am ashamed to be called an Australian. Now get off my property and let this man of God sleep."

All noises stopped as they left.

Unknown to me, our insurance company was withdrawing the insurance on the big tent. The U.S. embassy sent word it was not safe for me to remain, and the U.S. government could not protect me. My team, upon hearing this, did not awaken me. They got help to take down the tent and load it, along with the folding chairs and other equipment, into the eight semitrailers we used. They loaded everything on the ship, secured tickets on the airlines for Evelyn and me to leave on the earliest flight for America, and waited for daybreak.

One other thing my team and the sponsoring pastors did as we were flying home was to take out ads in the newspapers to explain what had gone on and why I had been forced to leave—a lack of law to protect religious freedom in Australia. A storm of controversy arose. Most churches did not know there was no such law. Most of the violence had been in the despised little Pentecostal churches, the leaders of which had been my sponsors. I loved them dearly.

The leading voice for religion in Australia, a prominent Presbyterian pastor, challenged the media on his daily broadcasts. A change began to come over the attitude of the people, and soon a new protection law was passed.

That made Billy Graham's telegram to me a year later all the more appreciated. He was filling an eighty-thousand-seat soccer stadium nightly, with perfect freedom with or without healing. His telegram read something like this: "Oral, I know that you had a rather difficult time here, yet for your encouragement I have met many people who were blessed through your God-anointed ministry."

When our plane reached American territory in Honolulu, the man at customs, having read of our troubles in Australia, put out his hand to shake ours. "Welcome home!" he said.

I confess his welcome felt mighty good.

My mother made it even more worthwhile, however. When a Tulsa reporter interviewed her concerning her feelings about my experience in Australia, she replied, "There's only one in the world like him and I birthed him."

The next twelve months—1957—as I ministered in the big tent in many American cities, we had our largest crowds in any year—over two million people—and the largest number of conversions and the largest number of healings.

Best of all, a seed of faith had been sown in the great nation of Australia. Shortly afterward, the Holy Spirit began a very large work throughout the nation. Today, many anointed evangelists from America, including Kenneth and Gloria Copeland, Oral Roberts University alumni, have been conducting great crusades there unabated. Kenneth's solid integrity and powerful faith message, coupled with Gloria's amazing gift to preach and pray for the sick, have really helped Australia up to the ministry of the miraculous. In addition, several Australian pastors, some who were converts from my aborted crusade there and others through Billy Graham's tremendous crusades in Sydney and Adelaide, have burst forth with an evangelistic zeal never known before in Australia. Churches are flourishing, the Pentecostals/Charismatics are leading the pack, I'm told, and I rejoice.

My son, Richard, was invited for a healing crusade there several years ago, and it was a happy surprise that the Australian media followed his endeavors in a most positive way, reporting the crowds and the miracles with acclaim. They even followed him on one of the outstanding golf courses of Australia, reporting what a great golfer he was!

Faithfulness to God changes things.

The Australian disaster had resulted in religious protection for churches and evangelistic crusades and growing churches in the future. And it was one of the seeds of future revival and growth. I was willing to be an instrument God used, despite the persecution it brought.

I was becoming no stranger to persecution.

CHAPTER 13

THE INCREASE OF PERSECUTION AND PRESSURE

EVERYBODY WHO has something of value must be tested in the forge of the fire. The blacksmith's anvil on which he bent iron into the shape of useful tools while using heat and pressure still has its place today. My pressures and persecutions were beginning to increase!

Prior to the Australia incident, there were death threats on my life during several of the crusades. One such threat came as a result of our stand against racial prejudice.

Wherever we conducted crusades—in forty-six states and in seventy nations eventually—we allowed people of all races to sit wherever they found an empty chair. We really never gave any thought to it or made announcements about it. We just did it because that was us.

I grew up with parents who were without racial prejudice. Papa had no greater delight as a pastor than to exchange pulpits with pastors of black churches. And he spent much of his ministry with the Indian people in Oklahoma. He simply thought of people as people who needed the gospel. He was a true example of what he preached.

In Ada, he built a second church directly across the street from the segregated area of black people. Vaden and I played with the children, and during garden season, we went to their homes to sell fresh vegetables. I could always outsell Vaden.

Vaden dressed nicer and was better looking. He was very outgoing and blessed with a good personality. I went barefooted, and because of my stuttering, I had a hard time getting the words out of my mouth about the green beans, English peas, onions, lettuce, radishes, and tomatoes I carried in my basket.

The black mothers knew what hardship was. They didn't buy much from Vaden, but they bought everything I had—everything. "We like that little stuttering boy," they told each other. Selling produce to them was a big morale booster to me.

Later in my life when I began my ministry, black people were always attracted to it. Their spirits seemed to connect with mine.

When we took our crusades to the South, we had no difficulty in letting "first come" be "first served" and permitting all races to sit wherever seats were available. My healing line always had black people in it, and the invitation to be converted brought forth blacks with whites and others. I believe the services had a richness because of that, and there was an increase of the anointing and power of God to deliver.

That is where my mind was: to deliver the people. To me, people are people—period.

In a particular city where one of the death threats came, we seemed to be going along just great. Blacks and whites intermingled freely. Apparently, people attracted to my crusades felt pretty much as I did: People are people, and all of us are created by God and are of one blood (see Acts 17:26).

Unexpectedly at the end of an evening service, Bob DeWeese brought me a message someone had given him. It said, "You must segregate your audience. The blacks must be told to sit in one section of the tent. Further, you must not have so many blacks in the healing line. Disregard this message at your own peril."

Bob asked, "You want to reply?"

I shook my head and went on to my hotel room, thinking no more about it. We would carry on God's work as we had since I began.

A few nights later, Bob and some of the sponsoring pastors got a special visit from a certain group. "You tell the preacher, tomorrow night is his deadline. A rifle will take care of him if he doesn't carry out our tradition and our order," they said.

When I saw the faces of my associates, I knew it was a scary time. "We know where you stand, Oral, and we stand with you. But don't take this threat idly. They mean business."

I thought of the saying, "It's a good time to die." But instead I said, "We will carry on as usual. We are in God's service, and we must act like it."

The next night, no announcement was made to segregate the audience. As I ministered, the death threat came to my mind several times. Each time, however, the anointing pushed it out of my mind.

I was experienced enough to know there was mortal danger. But what is a man's life worth anyway—even the life of a leader? Jesus said, "Take heed, and beware of covetousness: for a man's life consisteth not in the abundance of the things which he possesseth" (Luke 12:15). Say it's a preacher. What is his life or her life worth if he or she obtains the approval of those people who deny human rights to people who happened to be born with skin of a different color? Do they possess their lives in that approval?

Jesus said NO!

I said NO, also!

Something did happen that evening. Some black people were roughed up during the service, and a few were pulled to the ground from their chairs. A commotion like that occurred three or four times as I ministered. I glanced at Bob, whose countenance was calm. Sponsoring pastors fidgeted some, but none left. I kept preaching, then dealt with the hundreds of blacks and whites, and I conducted the healing line with members of both races. The angels must have been surrounding me because no one shot at me.

I believe the healing ministry, with its compassion to touch the pain and the heart, had a lot to do with our integrating and staying that way through the U.S. Supreme Court decisions that began to integrate the country. We didn't think of being ahead of our time. Nothing was preplanned. We were simply who we were.

My calling was to be myself in my treatment of all people, and it has been my joy to do it. I live for the day when people will look at people and see other human beings, persons, creations of God, and act the way Jesus would: with love and acceptance.

I felt I had to continue my healing ministry as I began it. I knew if healing were taken from my life, I wouldn't still be alive and well on this earth today. If healing is taken from the gospel, you have the verbal part of teaching and preaching but not what Jesus called signs and wonders, which confirm the Word of God when it is scripturally taught and preached.

Signs and Wonders Bring Pressure and Persecution

It was soon evident that God was moving at a time in history when something miraculous had to be taught and preached, then confirmed with signs and wonders. I was not the only one who had begun to pray for the sick, although I was the only one who did it the way I have described. Others like William Branham began a year before I did under the leadership of Gordon Lindsay. Gordon Lindsay was a man of vision and deep feeling for people. Later he organized scores of healing ministers into an International Fellowship, founded Christ for the Nations Bible School in Dallas, and was a prolific writer. His wife, Freda, took over Christ for the Nations, International (CFNI) after his death and is doing a magnificent job. At the time, I knew few of these men, and none intimately, as I was following God's specific instructions to me. However, I appreciated them mightily.

I was unprepared for the pressures that were going to come down on me because I was so different from anyone seen before by the leaders of denominations—from the smallest ones to the largest ones. As they saw it, the great old denominational churches were doing God's great work through the centuries when men such as I were only a thought in God's mind.

I had nothing of a personal nature to say against any denomination. I knew each had a piece of the truth of God, just as I had a piece. It just so happened that my call was what was missing: the healing ministry of Jesus returning to the people.

From the beginning when my miracle healing ministry was launched and the power of God began to flow through me, I discovered that people generally understood my heart, my message, and my prayers better than the entrenched hierarchy of the powerful denominations. Even the chambers of commerce in various cities worked with local pastors who had begun to invite me for crusades because they knew that large crowds would flood their cities while I was ministering there and a temporary financial boom would occur.

I have discovered people and institutions do things for their own reasons, and they are not always open to anything new. I know it put pressure on me I had never known, and I had to learn to live with it or go home!

I was tested in what I had learned from the Bible and what God had said to me audibly in revelational knowledge by the Holy Spirit who lived in me.

I was tested to see if what God said to me lined up with the written Word of God so that it became a *rhema* (God's spoken word) to me.

Never had I experienced so many intelligent people attacking the truths and the positions I held in the healing ministry of Jesus that became my lifestyle.

For that reason, as my audience grew toward ten thousand and more each service, it was soon evident that they came not only to see the miracles but to hear me teach and preach the foundational Scriptures and revelational knowledge I was receiving from the Holy Spirit. My crusades were more than healing crusades alone.

I learned the people during those times wanted not a glib fifteen-minute talk but a solid hour-and-a-half sermon put together with the Scriptures from Genesis to Revelation. They wanted the material organized point by point, and inspired with some stories, personal examples, and references to certain of those miracle healings I could prove were still existing month after month as my ministry continued. They wanted the meat of the gospel, the reality of the "now" Christ. I began to discover a new strength, a broader understanding, and a greater ability to survive and take what was dished out to me, making me more balanced, more caring, and more enduring as the pressures continued to mount and never go away.

Back then, in addition to the pressures from denominational hierarchies, the power structure of a city, and the media in general, there was the constant need to raise the funds to build, to pay bills, and to make payrolls. Evelyn and I started with a part-time secretary, but over the years the ministry grew to many hundreds of full-time workers. I had to keep my senses under all conditions, good and bad. Today, these same pressures—and more—exist.

Although I didn't want them, I needed the pressures. I still need them. An honest person feels the pressures but knows without them there is no other way to develop as Jesus did: "And the child grew, and waxed strong in spirit, and was in the deserts till the day of his shewing unto Israel" (Luke 1:80).

I learned that when the pressures stopped, I had let something slip from my calling. I quickly went back to my beginnings to find when I had failed and corrected it so that the power of God could come upon me in the way I had to have it.

For a Bible man or woman of God, there is no substitute for the power of God—for having the life of Jesus, for doing His healing works, and for living a supernatural life in a natural world. That is just the way God works, and He will never change: "For I am the LORD, I change not" (Mal. 3:6).

There is no question in my mind that God changes methods as the times change, but He never changes His principles. What He is, He is forever. That is why we must develop absolutes, yet our methods can change to meet the changing needs of people. There is no discrepancy in doing that; rather, it reflects good common sense and steady obedience to God in His eternal existence and character. I determined that in spite of the persecution and pressures, I was going to change methods as God led me, for the sake of getting His message and ministry to the people.

CHAPTER 14

EXPLORING UNKNOWN TERRITORY

T O REACH THE crowds of people with the saving and healing power of God, I started with a big tent. I started with one that seated 3,000 and the crowds grew into one seating 12,000, which, with the flaps of the outside pulled up, thousands more could stand five to ten people deep around the tent. It was 470′ long and 220′ wide and it stretched a quarter of a mile in its outside perimeter and as big as 3 football fields.

But there were times I used auditoriums and stadiums instead of a tent. When I was overseas, I used public areas where the people could sit on the ground, often numbering from 50,000 to 100,000 a service. In South Korea, I used the huge Olympic stadium with my beloved friend and brother, David Yonggi Cho, who pastors the largest church in the world with over 600,000 members.

In 1954, we made a major change in the method of getting the healing message to the people who did not attend the crusades. In spite of being told by the media experts that it could not be done, we began filming the services live and aired them on prime-time black-and-white television each week.

Credit must be given to my able friend, Rex Humbard, whose oldest son was healed of tuberculosis in my Mobile, Alabama, crusade in 1949. He inspired me to believe we should film the crusades for all America. He had the vision and I caught it.

It caused a sensation! People had never had a live healing crusade service coming right into their front rooms via TV. Millions of people in America and Canada had a front-row seat to see and hear a man, who despite all his faults and shortcomings, was really called of God. They could see the expressions on our faces, hear distinctly every word of my preaching and teaching, and literally see the healings. Hearing and seeing what was happening sharply divided the nation between those who believed and those who did not.

Thousands of letters came to my headquarters in Tulsa from people telling me that when they had seen a particular healing for the first time in their lives, they had given their hearts to God. Many fell to their knees or threw their hands up in the air and turned themselves toward the Lord while watching the services on TV.

In some cities, whole churches were built from such conversions. At one time, because the crusades were so strong, more than one thousand pastors asked me to form a new denomination. I declined on the grounds that God had not called me to do that. Besides we had more than enough denominations and the fellowship between them was almost nonexistent, which in my opinion was a travesty in the Lord's eyes.

What I wanted them to do, I said, was to take the Word in their hands and go down on their knees with it before the Lord, reread it with fresh new eyes, and let God show them Jesus. They needed to see that the three things He did were done equally: *teach, preach, and heal, with the healings confirming His Word preached.* Then I encouraged them to take the best of what they heard and saw me do, as it lined up with the Word of God and the way Jesus healed the people, and adapt it to their own ministries.

Hundreds of them did, and over the years thousands have done it in America and in nations throughout the world. Just now I am thinking of scores of leading pastors and evangelists, teachers, apostles, and prophets who have personally shared with me how the healing ministry, which I've carried on the very best I know how, helped them to become powers for God in their cities and positions and outreaches.

A Mail Ministry Like None Other

By 1957, we were receiving some one thousand pieces of mail a day. Nearly every one came from a desperate person or family. I saw, as I had in my dream in Enid, how people were hurting. I realized that people looked good, but when they opened up, you knew they were sick or hurting in ways you had never perceived. Letters coming to me proved that far more than I had seen in my crusades.

In my first healing revival, I had received eight urgent letters from people who wanted me to pray and write back to them. When Evelyn and I bought the little five-room house from Oscar Moore, I also paid him twelve dollars for a small desk. There in the corner of our little dining room, I wrote to those several people. That was really the beginning of my determination to answer the mail I received as personally as possible. Each week the number of letters grew, and I felt I nearly wore my right hand out as I endeavored to answer each one.

Three young women attending that Tulsa crusade were secretaries at a large oil company. They spoke to Evelyn and offered to come to our house directly after getting off from their jobs at 4:30 each day and help with the mail. They wanted to donate their time. They would type my answers until time for the healing service, then they would stop and go to the evening services. They had never seen people healed before, and their hearts were really with us. Their names were Ruth Hanson, Eloise Rowland, and Erlene Hanover.

When I closed at the end of nine weeks that summer in 1947, letters had poured in from coast to coast, and the mail was filling up our dining room. Soon the three volunteer secretaries were not enough to answer it all, so we turned our garage into an office. Eventually, the whole house became the office, and we moved to a larger house since our family had grown.

Ruth Hanson stayed with us, quitting her job. She said, "I feel it's the highest honor of my life to type your answers to people who are really sick and feel they have no place or way to turn." Ruth was seventeen, but mature and a hard worker. She pounded the typewriter eight hours a day without a complaint.

We hired Ruth as my first secretary, and for forty-eight years she has been the only secretary I've ever had. Loyal, able, and compassionate, she has stayed with us from the little house on North Main to our present office on the ORU campus.

We soon outgrew one typist and one typewriter to answer the hurting people who were writing us, some who were saying, "Oral Roberts, your prayers are my last hope. Please answer me."

Instead of feeling overwhelmed, I saw each letter as a person, and I felt that anointing running down my arm into my right hand. I would grab up a stack, hold them to my heart, and stand there crying like a baby and praying my heart out for the people who had been knocked down, and nearly out, in the battle of life—like me when I lay 163 days with tuberculosis.

The letters continued to increase. Soon we left the home that had been turned into an office and moved into a $40,000 one-story office building, then shortly after that into a three-story office building. In 1959, we built a beautiful seven-story white office building in downtown Tulsa as our international headquarters. (That was not to be the last office building. Eventually, we built one unique to the functions of my ministry; it was on the campus of Oral Roberts University.)

As the computer age began to emerge, and our mail continued to run into astronomical numbers, we realized we had touched the very soul of the nation and many people in other countries. We had enough daily mail to know about nearly everything noteworthy happening in America, and knowing it soon. In addition to the people telling us in their letters what was happening in their areas, we had the Abundant Life Prayer Group.

In 1959, we organized the Abundant Life Prayer Group and put the members on duty twenty-four hours a day, seven days a week, on eight-hour shifts to serve the people calling by the tens of thousands for prayer and counseling. If an earthquake hit, or there was a flood, a big political change, an outbreak of disease, or really anything of major importance, our phones rang off the wall with people calling and asking for prayer. This information was passed on to me wherever I was, at home or in a crusade.

Our communication lines were open. Although I was just one man and therefore had normal limitations, we as an organization were so united, so in touch with hurting people, and so caring that I felt we ranked next to the national media in knowing what was happening. In some ways we knew it even more intimately than they knew it.

I hired and trained both men and women from the churches of Tulsa to work eight-hour shifts to help me get out my letters as I felt each answer from God to each person who wrote to me. I worked with the employee-associates to help them grasp what each letter meant, to see how delicate were the problems of the people. Every letter had to be read, categorized according to need, and then answered with the laying-on-of-hands compassion and anointing I felt. I could not abide a printed or form letter sent as the answer. I wanted answers personalized.

We had something like three hundred typists, yet we couldn't keep up with the amount of mail I was receiving. When I returned from a crusade and saw piles of my answers waiting to be typed, it broke me up. I believe the healing ministry caused me to think not in parts but in wholes. I wanted to serve the people in every way they had need that we, with God's anointing, could try to meet.

My office manager at that time, Manford Engel, and his assistant, Al Bush, caught the spirit of what I was trying to do, and so did most of the people we hired in this area. Al had a technical mind, so I said, "Al, how can we be more personal in our answers? How can we speed up our answers going back into the mail? How can we help the people feel what we feel for them? Isn't there a better way?"

A few days later, Manford and Al came to my office. Manford said, "Oral, I think you ought to send Al to IBM in New York and let him explain our problem. I would go, but Al is better qualified to talk with the engineers on their turf."

IBM was just turning out the new 1400 computers. When Al arrived in New York and sat down with IBM's engineers and explained our need, he saw at once the 1400 could be adapted to do everything I wanted. When my Partners (supporters in prayers and finances for my ministry) received my answers, I wanted them to feel we knew them by name, by need, and by the same feeling I felt when I laid hands on the sick and prayed for them as the presence of God was in my right hand.

Because the IBM engineers had no experience with our particular needs, Al had to physically show them how to break down the 1400 computer and build one for us. They got excited in this joint effort with us, and they and Al did the job. The 1400 was finally shipped to us, so that for the first time words by this new computer could be put in both upper and lower case. It was a tremendous advance in the existing technology.

Al took me in hand and tried to show me how the 1400 worked.

"You're wasting your time, Al. I'm not mechanically minded," I said.

"Well, say it's you back there lying bedfast with tuberculosis and you wrote us a letter for prayer. What kind of letter would you want to get back?" he asked.

"Oh, I would want you to address me by name: 'Dear Oral Roberts.' Then I would want to read something about what I had said in my letter so I would know you had read it. I would want some scriptural references showing me how Jesus healed people like me and how He gave this power to His disciples. Finally, I would want you to pray for me by name, by the disease or need I had, and send the letter with an encouragement that I could be healed, and that you really believed it."

"And that's what you want *your* answers to do for those who write to you?" Al asked.

"Absolutely."

"You've got it."

"In this IBM 1400 computer?"

"Yes."

"How did you get it done?"

"You told me to go to IBM's main plant and not to come back to Tulsa until I had shown them your heart, your determination, and your goal to take the very latest thing beyond the typewriter so you could answer person to person."

"You saw that it will work?" I asked.

He said, "Go in there, write out your answer, and let's see what this computer does with it."

When they ran my answer through the computer in seconds and handed it back, I read it and wept. "At last," I said, "we're on the right road. Now we'll have to adapt this so that I can say every personal thing I want to say and gear it to insert a special category of need."

"That's right. I was told by IBM's engineers that it's never been done before, and they're anxiously waiting for the news that you feel it will work."

By sending my answers through the 1400, we could handle the mail with far fewer people and save the ministry thousands of dollars a week. How anxiously I waited to see if the people I wrote would be able to tell any difference as they read my letters! Soon people began writing back, thanking me as though I had done every part of the letter by hand, for they said it was so personal, so warm, so anointed, it was almost as if I were there laying hands on them.

I called in Manford, Al, and the letter helpers and I read the openings of the apostle Paul's letters to Timothy and to those in Corinth, Thessalonica, Philippi, Colosse, Rome, Galatia, and Ephesus.

"Now," I said, "do you feel Paul wrote these words to you?"

"Oh, yes," they said in unison.

"Yet these letters were written two thousand years ago. The words I'm reading are in ink and on paper in a book called the Bible. Still, you feel it's totally personal to you?"

"Yes," they said, "we'd never thought of that before."

"The reason is that this man of God, Paul, wrote letters only when he was inspired of God. Each word was laden with the Holy Spirit. Distance between him and those for whom the letters were intended didn't matter. God's Spirit was in Paul, and his heart was in his letters. Those who helped Paul write the letters were also moved upon by the Spirit.

"Therefore, if you and I will work as a team, never growing careless or hardened or matter-of-fact, but allow God to work His compassion and His faith through us, our letters will meet needs— not like the Word of God itself can do—but as close to it as possible."

There was a release. There were tears. There was new excitement, expectation, and a spirit of working together. I could feel all of that.

New machines have replaced the 1400 as it had done the typewriter, so that today we answer even better and quicker. When you use machines simply as instruments, and not in the place of your spirit, your compassion, and your personal faith, it seems to me it is a way to do the very best job possible to help people at the point of their need, even by a letter.

It's fair to say that when some people learned we were no longer using typewriters but computers, they thought there was no way my answer could be personal. I would have felt the same way if I had not been part of the magnificent improvement that the computer is over the typewriter. Simply put, due to the 1400 and its far better successors, my answers can be even more personal, really carrying my heart with them, and we can answer letters days earlier (which often can make the difference in the miracle of deliverance being wrought).

Manford and Al worked together to carry out the assignment that I felt an urgency to begin. Manford stayed with me as the head man of the office for over twelve years. He left only because his wife felt they should move to Phoenix for health reasons, but his heart, in many ways, stayed with us.

In all the years of this ministry only a few men have served in managing the office. Bill Lee, who was an administrator at Le Tourneau Industries in Toccoa, Georgia, served as our first manager beginning in 1947. Then followed Manford Engel, and after him, Al Bush.

Al, with his second-in-command, the very able George Stovall, continued to come up with new ideas and equipment to help me make all our efforts of writing and receiving phone calls through the Abundant Life Prayer Group more completely person-centered as we sought to bring God's healing power to the people, no matter the distance between us. George was our fourth manager, the fifth was Ron Smith, and the sixth is Jeane Alcott, an ORU graduate. This means in 48 years, we've had only six managers of our ministry.

I owe much of the success of my office and the crusades to the teams God called to be by my side.

How My Evangelistic Team Worked Together with Me

Bob DeWeese had been chairman of my 1949 Tacoma, Washington, crusade. Pastor of a thriving Tacoma church, Bob was the most effervescent man of God I'd ever known. He really had the joy of the Lord, and it flowed out of him like his breath.

At the same time, he was as steady as a rock, and as loyal to me and to this ministry as a mother is to her newborn baby. He was unshakable in his faith that God is in the "now," God heals today, healing is at the heart of tendering people's hearts toward God and a major force that Jesus said would confirm His Word.

We hit it off like long-lost brothers. His lovely Charlotte and my Evelyn became closer than blood sisters. We became a team welded together by heaven.

In thirty years of working side by side, we never had a cross word. We anticipated each other's actions and responses and flowed together in the Lord.

Bob set up the crusades with the sponsoring pastors in America and overseas, directed the services, and presented me with never-failing exuberance. He stood by me as I preached the gospel, won souls, prayed for the sick, and did "the work of an evangelist" (2 Tim. 4:5). He also conducted the afternoon services for the thousands who came daily to receive prayer cards. He preached his own message and explained in detail how each person was to respond in receiving my healing prayer. To me, Bob was the indispensable man, the perfect coevangelist and manager of the crusades.

My dear friends, Reg Hanson and Dr. O. E. Sproul, who had preceded Bob, paved the way for him to enter right into the interworkings of the crusades, of understanding me, and of seeing how he could by his own preaching in the afternoon services reach more people in a few months than he could in a lifetime of preaching on his own (which is something he reveled in).

Because of Bob's efforts, my job was made much easier. My call was to take God's healing power to my generation, not to be involved in the myriad details that would take away from my ministry and sap my energy.

Bob worked closely with Collins Steele, formerly a young executive with the Aluminum Corporation of America in Mobile, Alabama. Collins was manager of our mobile equipment: the tent, thousands of folding chairs, supplies, and the fleet of trucks and semitrailers to haul it all from city to city. He also was the head usher, and he arranged the sick into lines so they could come in an orderly way individually before me for the laying on of hands and the release of my faith for their healing.

Bob was close to Lee Braxton, our one-dollar-a-year businessman who gave himself to all of us unstintingly, particularly to business and professional people attending the crusades. Lee helped them understand how the ministry worked.

Bob also worked with Dr. Myron Sackett, who joined us with his Hebrew Bible ministry. Dr. Sackett helped us print and place more than one hundred thousand copies of the entire Bible in the Hebrew language throughout Israel and other nations where

Jewish people were interested in having both Old and New Testaments.

Each of these four able men of God, two of them ministers, two of them laymen, had personal access to me when necessary. But Bob DeWeese was the catalyst through whom I felt most comfortable in the oversight of the total crusade ministry. He never let me or the people down. Audiences everywhere we went greatly loved him, and I was proud that God had raised up such a co-laborer to stand by my side. His final position was as chairman of the Board of Regents of ORU. Bob went home to be with the Lord at age seventy-eight. I still miss him.

Eventually, over three million families became friends and Partners with me in my ministry, enabling me to build God a university (based on the Holy Spirit and His authority) and a state-of-the-art medical-and-research center, and to introduce the eternal principles of one of the Bible's chief truths: the miracle of seed-faith.

God spontaneously gave me many slogans and expressions that simplified great truths. Here are a few of them:

- Turn Your Faith Loose.
- Get a Point of Contact.
- Sow a Seed of Faith.
- Make God Your Source of Total Supply.
- Expect a Miracle.
- Something Good Is Going to Happen to You.

Before long, these became household faith slogans across the nation. By 1955, my weekly radio program was being carried by eight hundred radio stations and some two hundred television stations. The word of God's saving and healing power was getting out in unprecedented fashion.

God also helped me to write books. In the midst of an extensive schedule, I was able to write some fifty books, from ninety-four pages to six hundred pages each. These have reached a circulation in excess of fifty million copies, almost all of which we've given free and postage paid upon request.

At first, I sold my books at our cost. But as the audiences in my crusades and through television increased dramatically, I offered my books as gifts. We printed more than three million copies each of three of them: *Miracle of Seed-Faith*, *A Daily Guide to Miracles*, and *Three Important Steps to Your Better Health and Miracle Living*. And we distributed a hundred thousand to a million or so of several more of my books.

Our monthly magazine started in November 1947 with no subscriptions. Twenty-five years later, *Abundant Life* magazine passed the one million mark. We have produced several million tracts and pamphlets in eighty-seven different languages. Our quarterly magazine, *Daily Blessing*, which contains a spiritual article a day, 365 days a year, reached four hundred thousand per issue.

The most important thing all this accomplished, and still does, is to do what God said to do, and to do a lasting good work. That was the highest priority.

A sign on my desk reads, MAKE NO LITTLE PLANS HERE. My plan was never to do anything shoddy or just for the sake of doing it. I wanted to meet needs in people—spiritual, physical, and financial, among others—bringing the power of God so close to them they could reach out by faith and receive. If that meant going beyond what was acceptable and favored by others and entering into an area of life that was—and is—not comfortable, so be it!

Giving Back to the Community

I had the best team I ever could have wanted. The Tulsa business community recognized the Oral Roberts team as impeccable in character, excellent in every way, very community minded, taking active roles in the Chamber of Commerce, the United Way drive, and local civic clubs, and in their individual churches. Tulsans had given me more credit than I deserved in saying what a superb businessman I was. The team made me look good in their eyes, although I, too, was involved in the Tulsa community.

In the first three or four years of my ministry, my mind was wholly on it. Before, as the pastor of a small church and a college student, I saw no way to get involved in the life of the cities where I ministered and went to school. In Tulsa, it simply had not occurred to me to get involved in civic and community affairs.

"You're making a big mistake, Oral," Lee Braxton told me. "You're becoming one of the largest employers in Tulsa, and the climate for your ministry here is very good. You owe something back."

He said I should join Tulsa's largest Rotary Club where many of Tulsa's leading business and professional men were members and get to know them and let them get to know me. Next, he urged me to join the Chamber of Commerce and give personal time, as well as that of the leaders of my ministry, to help Tulsa's future growth. He brought up the United Way, the YMCA, the Salvation Army, and other functions in Tulsa where my presence—and contributions—would be helpful.

He said, "Oral, you are a giver. You are a sower of seeds. You are a seed-faith man. God gave you this idea and your giving spirit not just for you and your Partners. He wants you to be a giver and receiver in Tulsa. As you teach everywhere that the seed you sow will be multiplied back to you, that will work locally, also."

I listened. I thought about it and meditated on it. I wasn't sure I would be welcomed. I knew the banks were open to me because cash receipts came in daily and were immediately put in the banks from which we paid our bills. Our credit rating was very good. I was involved, I thought. But I had to admit to myself, I was not involved to give more of myself—and of my office workers—to Tulsa's needs communitywise.

When I knew Lee was right, I promptly began volunteering myself, between crusades, to different groups in Tulsa that had the city's best interest at heart.

I accepted an invitation from the Chamber of Commerce to speak to the group. The news of my upcoming address spread quickly. The place was jammed, and my dear friend, Rev. L. R. Lynch, an Assembly of God pastor, who was a member and also an officer, presented me. I was myself that day, sharing humorous episodes in my life at first, then getting down to the nitty-gritty of who I was, what I was called to do in the world, and how I was eager to help the city I loved so much. I must say, the reception was far beyond my expectations.

Soon I joined Rotary. In Rotary, the local club limits membership to only one person in each category of business or the professions. They opened a new one for me—world evangelism. That made me feel at home because that was my life and ministry. Later, Rotary conferred its highest honor on me by electing me a

Harris Fellow, so named for Paul P. Harris, who founded Rotary in 1905 in Chicago.

I was asked to travel with the executive committee of the Chamber of Commerce to cities like New York to acquaint their leaders with Tulsa. In each city we visited, I was asked to speak, partly, I think, because my name had become quite well known, and partly because I could speak for Tulsa in a different way as a minister of the gospel extolling the great church climate in Tulsa. I knew most businesses considered that before deciding to move to a city or beginning a new enterprise.

I became active in the United Way Committee, the YMCA drives, the Salvation Army (which I loved greatly), Goodwill Industries, Tulsa Boys' Home, and other groups. More important, I asked my top leaders to donate time and money from their incomes to help Tulsa, and I urged our entire number of employees to contribute, no matter how large or small.

Out of that came an invitation to join the Board of Directors of the Bank of Oklahoma, Tulsa's largest bank, and the Board of Oklahoma Natural Gas. My friend, John Williams, the main stockholder in the Bank of Oklahoma, sponsored my membership on that board, and my friend Charley Ingram, the chairman and president of Oklahoma Natural Gas, sponsored me in joining that board.

I served both for some thirteen years until it was no longer possible for me to attend the number of meetings required. I came to know the great men in these banks, and as Lee advised me, they became interested in me as a citizen of the city who cared about its welfare and growth.

PART 4

ORAL ROBERTS UNIVERSITY

CHAPTER 15

MAKE NO LITTLE PLANS HERE!

N O MATTER HOW large the crowds grew or how many thousands were healed or how many souls were saved, I still felt a certain emptiness that would not go away. It was God's way of getting me out of my comfort zone.

To me, comfort borders on the word *impossible*. When I get very comfortable in carrying on my calling, it doesn't take long for God to bring me into a situation where it seems impossible.

Lee Braxton once told me, "Oral, I went through my dictionary and cut the word *impossible* out of it." That stuck with me.

Jesus said to those who have faith, "Nothing shall be impossible unto you" (Matt. 17:20). The sign on my desk, MAKE NO LITTLE PLANS HERE, is a constant reminder to me that after I have thought and prayed over things God has called me to do, I take the "im" off impossible. And then I think and pray in terms that these plans are possible by obedience and by the supernatural power of God.

A restlessness such as I had felt just before I began the healing ministry was growing in me. Despite the enormous success of my crusade ministry in person and also through our filming the crusades for television, I knew the time was approaching when I had to start building God a university. Every year that I grew older, I knew my time was that much shorter.

During the late 1950s, I would stop our car in front of a farm at Eighty-First and Lewis streets in south Tulsa. My wife, four children, and I would get out and join hands in prayer that God would

157

hold the property for building His university. We did that on several occasions.

As strong as God's call was upon me to take His healing power in person to my generation, just as strong was His call to build Him a university on His authority and on the Holy Spirit. Our graduates would provide a successor to my personal healing ministry, and in other fields, while I'm on earth and would continue to after God has called me home.

I knew that His call to build Him a university went beyond me and involved the total ministry of God's delivering power. I'm glad I didn't know how audacious a move it was, especially by a healing evangelist.

From the beginning of God's speaking to me, I understood healing in its larger sense: *wholeness*. I also understood that as I would establish a powerful beachhead for healing, bringing it into the consciousness of people throughout the world, my personal effort would be only a beginning, not an end in itself.

I could not escape the words God had spoken to me in the back of my brother Elmer's car on the way to the service where I received my miraculous healing from tuberculosis:

> *"Son, I am going to heal you and you are to take My healing power to your generation. You are to build Me a university and build it on My authority and the Holy Spirit."*

His words sank deep into my being. I heard what He said, but the urgency I was feeling that night at seventeen years of age was that my healing was near and the primary call on my life was to take His healing power to my generation.

But I never forgot what He said about someday building Him a university. I never lost sight of it, not even when my healing crusades were taking me across America and to many other nations with God's message of deliverance for people in every area of their lives. The command to build the university was in the inner recesses of my soul.

As I look back, I am glad God did not press me to build the university He had in mind early in my ministry. I did do some preliminary exploration during that time. Wherever I traveled, I took time to visit and study colleges and universities. Some of the most prominent ones I visited were Stanford, Harvard, Duke, University of Tennessee, University of Oklahoma, Oklahoma State University, Wheaton College, University of California/Los Angeles, University of Southern California, University of Texas, Emory University, Johns Hopkins University, Vanderbilt (and its seminary where I spoke), University of the Pacific (where I addressed the student body), and several other universities in other nations where I preached. On those visits, I did not merely drive through the campuses. I spent time whenever possible with leaders and professors and students of the schools.

I wrote for information to universities everywhere, and in my spare time I pored over the materials. I talked to architects who built colleges and universities. At every available hour I immersed myself in the history and operations of the schools.

It was no secret that I was to build a university when God's time came for me. I referred to it at times in my crusades, particularly in certain sermons where I dealt with such men of God as Elijah, who passed his mantle to his young prophet, Elisha, following the example of the prophet Samuel. These men carried on the school of the prophets in Bible days (see 2 Kings 6).

Why Build God a University?

I was in Denver for a crusade. I was shaving one morning when I heard the Lord's voice. It indirectly—but positively—dealt with His call to me to build Him a university. His words came in a rush:

> *"There remains a healing for the sick body of My bride. I have raised you up to be the John the Baptist of your time in My healing ministry, and you are to be a forerunner of a mighty healing for My people before My Son returns."*

Then He brought to my mind Isaiah 37:3: "And they said unto him, Thus saith Hezekiah, This day is a day of trouble, and of rebuke, and of blasphemy: for the children are come to the birth, and there is not strength to bring forth."

God showed me in my spirit a vision of a young pregnant woman whose time had come to give birth, but her body was too sick and weak for the final push to bring the baby forth. God was saying that was how He saw His people as they conducted their church services. When it was time to bring souls into the kingdom, often they did not have the inner spiritual strength and faith for miracles or the spiritual power to deliver sons and daughters into His kingdom in the way and numbers God says it must be done.

As I remember it, He went on to say to me,

"My people are sick in their bodies to the extent they are as sick as those who are not serving Me. There remains a healing for them, which they have not seized by their faith. Because of the little emphasis of My ministers on My supernatural power and the reality of miracles and the expectancy for Me to deliver them, it is a time of trouble, a time of My rebuke, a time of blasphemy where many of the leaders not only have ceased to believe that I heal today but are refusing to open their eyes to the sicknesses of My people and to know that My healing power is available in the 'now' of the need of My people."

The other Scripture God gave me concerning His people in the church was Ephesians 5:27: "That he might present it to himself a glorious church, not having spot, or wrinkle, or any such thing; but that it should be holy and without blemish."

God stated that He intends to present to Himself a delivering people, a glorious church of mighty miracles, and that in the final presentation, they would not have spot or wrinkle or any such thing. They would be holy and without blemish. How many of His people would be healed, God did not say, but the emphasis I received revealed that healing would be an integral part of getting His people ready for the end time.

I recall sitting in a state of shock as I listened and grasped at last how deadly serious God is about healing His people, about removing our blemishes from us, and about our having a wholeness in us, particularly of being a holy and whole people.

God let me know in unmistakable terms that a major healing remained untapped by His people, that I, although not some great person, carried His healing call in me, and that I, indeed, was *a* forerunner through my preaching the anointed Word of God and seeing it confirmed with signs and wonders (see Mark 16:20). He was telling me that I was wrong to think my healing ministry was singular. What I was doing in actively pursuing the goal of taking God's healing power to my generation was bigger than myself, bigger than my healing crusades, bigger than my ministry on radio and television and in my publications and books.

In fact, God let me know my efforts were like a pebble thrown into a lake, where circles were being made in the water of life. I was to be aware that much greater outpourings of His Spirit to deliver and cleanse His people were coming. As people heard and saw my healing ministry, they were to see beyond me to what was greater and was on the way.

Through that special message He gave me, I made connection with His words to me:

"You are to build Me a university. Build it on My authority and on the Holy Spirit."

In Denver, two men, Guy Martin and Dr. Charles Blair, a businessman and a pastor, volunteered to give me one thousand dollars each as a small start in beginning the university. I deposited that money and waited on God. That those men of God approached me with such large gifts, based purely on the few words they had heard me say about God's call on me to build Him a university, had a significant effect on my thinking. One of them said, "Oral, your ministry must not die with you. God's idea for you to build a university unlike any other, one that will educate the whole person as you have described, means there's much more of God's healing power to come upon His people through the young men and women coming out of this university."

God spoke to me again in my Norfolk, Virginia, crusade, for which my dear friend and brother, Pat Robertson, served as chairman of the sponsoring pastors. He was eating dinner with Evelyn and me one evening before the service in the big tent. God spoke to me before the meal was finished. The words were so powerful, so dramatic, so far-reaching, that I grabbed a napkin and wrote them down:

*"**R**aise up your students to hear My voice, to go where My light is dim, where My voice is heard small and My healing power is not known. To go even to the uttermost bounds of the earth. Their work will exceed yours, and in this I am well pleased."*

Several years later when Pat gave a commencement address at Oral Roberts University, he reminded me of how I had announced those words to the audience there in the Norfolk crusade, and how the words had made such a deep impression on him. He repeated that happening, and as he flung his arms out toward the campus, he stated that everyone should understand two things: First, Oral Roberts University is a miracle, and second, the healing that remains is soon to come, for God wants a people delivered and ready for the second coming of His Son.

A Healing Evangelist Building God *a University?*

Many critics in public and in private have viciously accused me of usurping God's authority, both in my healing ministry and in my announcement that He had told me to build *Him* a university. There was much laughter and mocking about a simple man like Oral Roberts, a healing evangelist, making such bold pronouncements about being called to build a major university for God.

I couldn't help what they said. It was—and is—my policy never to strike back. God made that very clear to me. I was attempting with all my heart and effort to believe what God told me, obey it, and leave the consequences to Him.

What surprised me most, however, was not the strong negative reaction from the secular media. It was so many of the ministers and churches who held me up to ridicule. Although I was surprised, I understood why that would be their reaction. The evangelical groups knew the Pentecostal groups had not felt educationally moved to build universities as part of their Christian faith and outreach. And there I was, a Pentecostal, actually trying to build a major university.

The evangelicals had watched the first-generation Pentecostals early in this century build little Bible schools and a few small colleges, and by and large, they believed the Pentecostals had lost a major portion of their children to the secular schools and world. I was a second-generation Pentecostal, and I had almost been lost permanently from the upbringing I had received from my parents. The Pentecostals were good people, baptized in the Holy Spirit. They believed in the God of miracles, and they believed God was closer to them than their breath. But they did not have the vision to educate their children. It just didn't seem important to them.

The lives of Pentecostals were built around the church, its services, and the Spirit of God working in their midst. They loved their children, yet the vast majority of their children faded away from the faith of their fathers. The children believed in it to some extent, but they felt it was not relevant to the world they lived in or the challenges they faced with their minds. I believe one of the greatest tragedies of the Full Gospel leaders, and the followers under their ministry care, is the possible loss of most of the second—and now much of the third—generation of their children from the Full Gospel experience.

God's university, the one I was to build with the help of those to whom I was ministering, was to provide a "whole person" education. The education of the person attending Oral Roberts University was to be threefold. First, the *mind* was to be educated with excellence personified. Second, the *body* was to be involved daily in a new aerobics program in order to learn lifelong health habits (designed by the leader in that field, my friend, Dr. Kenneth Cooper of Dallas, Texas). Third, the *spirit* was to be emphasized above both the mind and the body, yet fused into spirit, mind, and body at the same time. Doing all these at the same time was to be the key God had given me for building Him a university.

"It can't be done," they said.

"It's *not* education," many stated emphatically.

"It's a crazy experiment bound to fail," I heard from every side.

The closer the time came to start the university, the hotter the misunderstandings got. My right-hand man in the crusades, Bob

DeWeese, told me, "Oral, I'm not against you building the university. I'm just frightened it will take the place of your healing ministry."

I said, "Bob, I'm glad you are opening up to me with your true feelings. But let me put you straight so you'll never have to be concerned about it again. The university will not stop my healing ministry. God has called me to take His healing power to my generation. That will not change. I believe with all my heart and soul He spoke to me to build Him a university for the very *continuance* of the healing ministry."

Bob said, "How can that be?"

I answered, "We're building the full healing ministry, as God gave it to me, into the very fabric of the university. We will build a Prayer Tower in the exact center of the campus where our Abundant Life Prayer Group will be taking phone calls in eight-hour shifts, twenty-four hours a day, seven days a week. The Prayer Tower will stand two hundred feet tall and tower over the whole campus. Every student and faculty member will have to pass it every day going to and coming from the Learning Resources Center, which will contain the library and most of the classrooms. It will symbolize that healing prayer on this campus permeates everything we are and do.

"We will build into the very heart of all our academic offerings the healing ministry of Jesus Christ of Nazareth. The Bible—God's Word—will be our number one book so that in the undergraduate school of arts and sciences, and in the graduate schools, including our seminary, the delivering power of the Lord will stand out as the very reason for our being.

"The students coming out of ORU will have the opportunity to catch it in the spirit, and regardless of their profession—preachers, doctors, lawyers, businessmen, housewives, or whatever—they will be going into *every man's world* as well as to the uttermost bounds of the earth with the gospel."

I asked Bob what he thought that meant.

He said, "Well, ever since you came to my city of Tacoma, Washington, in 1949 and I was the local chairman of the crusade, I saw your work was the healing ministry."

I said, "But don't you see when God said my students' *work* would exceed mine, He meant the ORU students over the years would go everywhere with the work of healing as God had called me to do, and in their healing works they would exceed mine? Did that not mean ORU would continue my healing ministry but increase it ten thousandfold?"

A light came in his eyes, and he slowly nodded his head. "Yes, I'm finally seeing it. Oral, I'm with you all the way."

That helped a lot, but it did not end the inner turmoil of my other top aides.

The climax came when the twelve top associates who helped me direct my healing ministry worldwide, and who were in charge of our ministry office in Tulsa, rebelled. They called me into the office of Manford Engel.

Manford, speaking for the group, said, "Oral, each of us has left our professions to serve with you in taking God's healing power to your generation. We fear building the university will stop the flow of healing. Also, there will be no place for us. We're here because we feel God has called us to run this office and help extend the ministry with you."

I asked the others to say what was on their hearts. They echoed what Manford said.

Manford ended by saying, "If you persist in building the university, all of us have decided to leave."

In a moment's time I understood that a rebellion within the organization hurts much worse than what any outside group, including the media, could do. I never felt more alone in my life.

It wasn't that my team had not heard me talk about building the university time after time. They had heard me say the words, but their spirits had not absorbed them.

I believe cultural background plays a strong part in shaping God's people, in fact, everyone. The cultural background under which I and my team had been raised was really almost antieducational, as I have mentioned earlier. They simply did not grasp, as I had in my experience, that the total mind is a terrible thing to waste.

I had to make a decision. If I had had any thought that the university was my idea alone, and not wholly God's, I would have had an easy decision to make. But I knew what I knew.

With my heart in my mouth and tears close to the surface, I said, "Men, we've ridden the road together. We've suffered together for this ministry. We've also seen hundreds of thousands of souls saved and great numbers of sick people healed by the power of God. You have been a team with me all the way."

Every eye was on me, and the men were sitting on the edges of their chairs. There was love in that office; there were also tension and fear.

"Despite what anyone may think or believe, God Himself called me to build Him a university, build it on His authority and the Holy Spirit. I am not leaving the healing ministry; it is my life. But God doesn't operate in a vacuum. He is constantly moving forward, and I have learned we must move with God. I have to obey God and start building Him a university, permeating every part of it with the divine principle that God is a healing God. I may fall on my face. I may fail. It may never fly, but I have to do it. If you leave me, it will break my heart. However, if I obey God as I intend to do, I know He will raise up another team to serve with me." I got up and left the room.

A few hours later a secretary was sent to bring me back. As I walked in, they were the happiest group of leaders I had ever seen. Manford said, "Oral, we had to know it was God's call on you to build the university. The only way we could know for sure that it was God was to bring things to a head. We're not leaving. You lead and we'll follow!"

Talk about hugging and crying and rejoicing—it all took place in the minutes that followed. I never lost a member of my team. Instead, they opened their minds and hearts and talents and experiences to help me in ways that excited me to no end. In doing God's work and in employing thousands of team leaders and workers over the years, I have discovered that there can be differences but always within the boundaries of singleness and unity of purpose and with our eyes on God and what He wants rather than our own desires.

That year, 1962, I gathered our eight hundred office workers together and shared the plan God had given me, telling them His time had come. I asked them to continue doing exactly what they had been doing with our publications and books, working with me to produce our radio and television ministry, and assisting in preparing my letters to those thousands of people writing for prayer and seeing they got mailed. But I also asked them to be ready to fit into another dimension of the ministry: building God a university.

From that meeting, the transition went smoothly. We eventually sold our downtown office and rebuilt on the campus of the budding new university. I wanted the true-and-tried members of my office and the on-the-field ministry team to work closely with the new academic team I was assembling.

I was deadly serious when I kept telling all who would listen that ORU was not a university in terms of the sole way the world thought. It was a ministry—a healing ministry—in which there was a university. Little did I know how much I would be challenged on this stand!

CHAPTER 16

YOU CAN TAKE A LITTLE MORE!

M Y CRUSADES were at full strength. All attendance records were being broken. In a single year—1957—a million souls had been won to Christ, and the opposition was at its highest. It was not a bad position to be in if one can stand the heat in the kitchen.

The fight against me and God's call on my life was one-sided. They fought me, but I didn't fight back. It takes two to fight. Someone who observed me closely during the days of opposition that knew no limits said, "Roberts just humps up and takes it."

My friend Rev. Steve Pringle took note of the opposition. He knew even though I did not strike back, it hurt.

He took me aside one day and gave me some great advice. "Oral, I love you," he said. "I have believed in you from the first night you came to us in the tent and started preaching and praying for the sick. I have hurt for you at the misunderstandings both inside the church and out, but let me share something I have experienced on a smaller scale.

"In a particular hard situation I was in, being attacked on all sides, the Lord came to me in the night hours and said, 'Steve, you can take a little more.'

"Oral, I hear God saying in my spirit for you today and in the days to come, 'You can take a little more.'"

I had not thought of it that way. Before Steve spoke to me, I had thought if there ever came a time when I believed I couldn't take any more, I would throw up my hands and walk away. Steve's words resonated in my spirit: *Oral, you can take a little more now and in the days to come.*

My spirit saw that as long as I obeyed God, kept clean in my character and in my efforts—even though Satan would devise ways to have bad and good people oppose me, and some would do it without regard to the truth and without mercy—I could take a little more. And that has been what has happened to this hour: I can take a little more.

My friends, even some who don't agree with my ministry, say to me, "Oral, you never strike back, and that has saved your ministry."

I discovered if I didn't falter in my vow to keep a good spirit toward my adversaries and at the same time to obey my calling, no matter the cost, no power on earth could defeat this ministry, this university, or me.

Today Is the Day to Buy That Land

My spirit was jumping in me that the time was near to build. Despite the fact I had no money, no land, no buildings, no faculty, no students, no curriculum, and very little knowledge of how to build a university as the world saw it, I was under the command of Him who has all authority and all power to bring to pass His will. But God can do this only if He can get servants to obey His call and put their hearts and hands to the call.

The time came to purchase the land on which to build Oral Roberts University. I told my legal counsel, Saul Yager, to approach the owner of the land that I felt God had chosen for His university.

Saul was a former district judge in Tulsa. He was also as good a friend as I ever had during the twenty-five years he served as our general counsel.

When I considered hiring Saul, he opened our first conversation by saying, "I am of the Jewish faith. I am comfortable in my faith. I have had very little experience with a Christian minister who is devoutly Christian and who believes in God as I believe in God."

I understood what he was saying and thanked him for his candor. I said, "As for me, Saul, you're not only older than I am in years, but you're older in your faith than I am in mine. There is no doubt at all in my heart that I am a Christian. But if I understand the Bible, you Jews were the ones with whom God started the Christian faith. I owe a debt to every Jew who ever lived and believed in God." From that day forth, we had a good understanding of each other and a good relationship.

When I told Saul to arrange for us to purchase the acreage where ORU now stands, I didn't even know who owned it, but I knew who its real Owner was. My strong guidance was that it was the exact piece of ground that had been set aside by almighty God on which to build His university. I knew it as much as I know my own name.

Saul reported to me that the owner wasn't interested in selling. The land had been in his family for thirty-five years. I insisted that Saul keep trying to buy it until he got it done. Things dragged on for several weeks. I was growing restless. I felt God's time had come to get that piece of property and to ask the Board of Trustees to break ground for the new university.

Each time Saul went, he was turned down. "The man," Saul finally said, "simply won't sell."

One day I was in California when the Spirit of the Lord came all over me. That piece of land stood out in my mind as if I were standing there looking at it or walking around on it. In my spirit I could see the groundbreaking, the buildings going up, the university opening to hundreds of students. I could see years ahead when major buildings would be there with an enrollment of thousands and with young people going into "every man's world," no matter their own profession, sharing the healing power of Jesus Christ.

I dialed Saul. "Go today and buy that land," I said.

"But, Oral, you're wasting your time. The man won't sell."

"I'm telling you, Saul, I know today is the day. Buy it today."

"If you say so," he said, and we hung up.

Saul was bold in legal things but always cautious in his business dealings. Up to that point, Saul had been cautious in the business end of the deal, but now he put his legal mind to work. He discovered the owner was represented by a man of the Jewish faith, also a high-class lawyer who knew the owner had refused to sell.

Saul told his Jewish lawyer friend my story. He explained how sure I was that regardless of the reluctance of the owner to sell before, today was the day he would sell.

It struck a chord in the brother Jew. He called the owner and recommended he be open to this sale.

"It's strange you would put it that way," the owner replied. "I woke up this morning and decided that if Mr. Roberts's lawyer approached me today, I would sell."

The two attorneys got a kick out of that. They thought it was high drama. I think they felt God was in it. Anyway, when they prepared the contract, the owner suddenly had second thoughts, but both attorneys told him he had given his word and he should honor it. The man said, "I think you're right," and he signed the papers.

Saul later said, "I think it was a deal done in heaven."

We kidded each other a lot. I said, "That's easy for you, a Jew, to say."

He laughed and said, "And that's easy for you, a Christian, to believe."

I said, "Saul, I not only believe it. I know it."

There was only one unexpected change the owner wanted. "I want a small down payment," he said. "I'm also willing for a clause to be included where they can pay it all off at once without penalty."

I really thought that was a heaven-done deal. How did the man know how little I had to pay down? How did he know that we would pay it off soon, and that not having to pay a penalty would ease our burden? How did he know?

I believe the God I know was the One who knew, and somehow, He had the man's attention.

Those were the kinds of deals that we worked out time and again as we proceeded with a growing ministry. An unseen Voice was being heard, an unseen hand was being felt, and unexpected good things were happening.

To a Jewish lawyer who believed in God, and a Christian healing evangelist who believed in God, we both came to the conclusion it was par for the course for God to open doors that had been hitherto closed.

There is so much about Saul Yager that I would like to share in this book, but space forbids. There is one thing I must share, however.

Saul in his later years had cancer of the throat. He flew to New York City to a great Jewish cancer surgeon he knew. The operation was hazardous, but they decided to do it.

I received a call one day: "Oral, this is Saul. My doctor says I should ask you to pray."

I didn't say anything.

"I'm serious. I'm not saying he's a believer. Oh, he believes in God. I'm talking about faith healing."

"He asks me to pray? Why?"

"It's a delicate operation. He knows I'm associated with you. Although he isn't sure about prayer for healing, he says he will feel better in doing the surgery if he knows you are praying."

"Saul, I'll be praying for you anyway. You know that."

"Yes, I know. But would you include my surgeon, too?"

I followed the surgery by phone here in Tulsa several times as it progressed, praying with the full force of my faith for Saul, for the surgeon and his team, remembering in my heart they were blood and spiritual descendants of Abraham, of whom Paul wrote, "That he might be the father of all them that believe" (Rom. 4:11).

Three days after the surgery, which went very well, something went wrong. Saul's voice box was not acting as if it was going to function. They had had to remove so much of it that he was going to have to learn to talk all over again. Saul could barely whisper, and only at intervals. He was able to write down much more quickly than he was able to get out the few whispered words he said to me: "Oral, this time I'm asking you to pray to God to make me able to learn to talk again. I'm asking you."

My heart was thumping in my chest. I was so close to him. We had spent nearly twenty-five years together, closer than blood brothers, and we spiritually understood each other. But for the first time he had phoned to ask me to pray for *him*.

The words coming out of my mouth, winging their way through heaven from Tulsa to that hospital in New York City, were carrying my soul with them. I felt God's presence in my right hand. Oh, how I felt it!

Saul came home in due time, and he learned to talk without any mechanical aid. At age eighty-three, he could carry on a normal conversation. In a sense, I felt it was an example of the merging of medicine and prayer, plus Saul's determination that he would talk again.

At Saul's funeral years later, I was the first Christian minister who ever took the lead in giving the eulogy in a Jewish synagogue in Tulsa. I owe the rabbi of Tulsa's Temple Israel much for that privilege and honor. I owe God, too.

--------- *The Holy Spirit Takes Over!*

There was one thing I knew—and I knew that I knew that I knew it—the secret to the success of building God a university was to build it exactly as He said and operate it on His authority and on the Holy Spirit.

Nobody can defeat the Holy Spirit.

There are times when a man stands mute before the problems and challenges of his life. His heart is hungry for answers, but they seem to be so mysterious and so unreachable as he wrestles with his doubts and inner turmoil. The desire to accomplish his task becomes so big in his mind that it represents everything that he has ever wanted. But when he tries to pray, there's a dark cloud hanging over him, and his human language breaks down in the face of the staggering issues that lie ahead.

I'm not ashamed to tell you that I cried out to God from the depths of my soul during those first few agonizing days and weeks after God told me His time had come for me to build His university. I wanted desperately to obey His voice, but I didn't know how! It was out of my deep anguish and bewilderment that I began walking back and forth across those bare acres we had just paid down on, beseeching the Lord for the knowledge I needed to accomplish the great task.

Oh, I felt like I was carrying such a heavy load! I was literally groaning and praying and crying out, "O God, help me! Show me the way!" Then from the pit of my belly, the Holy Spirit language rose up in me and just rolled out of my mouth. When I stopped praying in tongues, I started praying again, only this time the words that came to me were in English, and they were certainly not words that I had thought of myself. I felt such a tremendous release in my spirit that I said, "Lord, let me do that again!"

I'll tell you, that was one of the most electrifying experiences I had ever had in my life! I was out there all alone, with only the squirrels and rabbits and birds as my audience, walking along praying in the Spirit. When I stopped and listened again inside my spirit, through interpretation words came to me by the Spirit of

God in English, and there was a brilliance to them. Prophetic words were in my mouth—revelational knowledge from the Lord!

In those words, the Lord revealed to me the most astonishing knowledge and showed me the broad outline of how to build Him a university. He didn't give me all the details, but it was a great breakthrough into the knowledge and the ability of how to do what He had commanded me to do.

One thing I've learned over the years is not to jump the first time you feel like you've heard something from the Lord.

What you hear in your spirit from the Lord must be tested by the Word of God and by the Spirit and by practicality. So, as I continued to seek the Lord over the next few weeks and months, the revelation He gave me was confirmed to my heart over and over again. I stepped out in faith with these words from God ringing in my soul: "I want you to build My university out of the same ingredient I used when I formed the world, when I created the earth— nothing."

All at once a Scripture from the book of Job flashed through my mind—"He [God] stretcheth out the north over the empty place, and hangeth the earth upon nothing" (Job 26:7). The Lord hung this earth upon empty space, upon nothing. And God reminded me of another Scripture in Hebrews 11:3, which says God framed the worlds by His word and used the things which we cannot see to make this visible world around us.

That tells me that if you've ever felt like you had so little that you couldn't possibly do God's will, you can stop your worrying! With God, you can do it, because the Bible says He calls the things that are not as though they were! (See Rom. 4:17.)

I'll never forget how I looked out across those empty acres, much as the Lord Himself must have cast His eyes upon the empty spaces when He declared, "I have stretched My hand over the empty spaces and hung the world on nothing." And, in my mind's eye, when I looked at those bare grounds, I caught a glimpse of a university which was nothing yet, *but I could see it by faith*.

I knew this truly was going to be a university, but wholly different in its calling to "educate the whole man!"

But the battle was just begun.

CHAPTER 17

THE BATTLE OF SPIRIT OVER MIND

ONE OF THE universities I had attended as a young man was having a difficult time obtaining and retaining professors with Ph.D.'s who were genuinely Christians and committed to the goals of the university. The chairman of the board of this denomination-owned campus was a warm, personal friend of mine. He took a deep interest in the development of Oral Roberts University.

One day on Tulsa's Southern Hills Golf Course, he said, "Oral, there are times we almost despair of getting committed Christian professors. It's almost to the point where some believe we ought to be happy that if they are not Christians, they at least do not oppose us. Of course, we can't accept that."

Then he said, "Everything you do to build ORU will be tough—raising the money, getting the buildings up, having a great library, recruiting students who believe in what you're doing—nothing will be easy. But I tell you, my brother, getting and keeping a faculty of scholars who are truly Christian and wholly committed to the founding purposes of the university will be your toughest assignment."

"Thank you," I replied. "I needed to hear that."

He was totally correct.

In some ways God helped me to anticipate the faculty recruitment challenge and their continued dedication to our goals and purposes. Earlier I had asked Carl Hamilton, editor of our *Abundant Life* ministry monthly magazine, if he would be interested in taking a leave of absence for the purpose of earning his doctorate; he had already completed his master's degree. I explained that he would also be preparing for a higher role in helping me operate the university.

Carl's grandparents had been among those Pentecostals who were instrumental in leading my parents to Christ. They were strong and reliable people, the kind who could be counted on. Carl's parents had been cut out of the same mold, and so was Carl. An able writer and editor, committed to the Lord and my healing ministry with the whole of his being, reliable in every way, Carl was the one I felt led to for the future task of being the ultimate academic leader of ORU.

We talked a long time. We prayed. We brought up the pros and cons facing us. We both agreed academic excellence with integrity was a must because I always insisted on excellence and integrity in all I undertook. I felt he was that same kind of young man.

He and his wife, Joyce, with whom he shared all his dreams and plans, made the decision to accept my suggestion. Carl enrolled in the University of Arkansas, choosing to major in English literature. But he confided in his Ph.D. counselor that he wanted to learn all he could about university administration. Our ministry funded Carl and his family as they pursued their goal with the spirit of contentment and dedication for which I had hoped.

That was in 1961, four years before ORU was to open officially.

I had a deep knowing that God was directing my every footstep. Although I felt an intensity in my actions, I was not in panic. The Holy Spirit was in charge.

Meanwhile, I sought out an old friend, Dr. John Messick of North Carolina, a Holy Spirit–filled educator, who in one poll was ranked among the ten top educators in America. He had earned his Ph.D. from New York University and had spent nearly forty years in higher education. He knew me and loved my calling. Although a Methodist layman, he was Spirit-filled as I was, and we were compatible.

Dr. Messick was nearing his retiring years when I called him to come to Tulsa and counsel me in building ORU. He had remembered our talks years ago that the time would come for me to build God a university. It didn't take me long to see that I should ask him to pray about becoming the founding dean and chief academic leader of the new school.

I told him about Carl Hamilton, who was only twenty-eight years old, and my plans for him after he received his Ph.D. He was glad to see I was thinking ahead.

The Determining Factor of ORU's Existence

The most significant impact made upon my mind concerning the academic purpose of a university came from the University of Washington in Seattle. I was intrigued by the literature and the view of higher education. The line that struck me with such force was this:

> A university consists of gaining knowledge,
> adding to it, and passing it on.

I disagreed completely. At that point, I finally realized the utter importance of my calling to build God a university. The three things the University of Washington leaders had said composed a university—gaining knowledge, adding to it, and passing it on— were all right as far as they went. But they stopped too soon. God was left out of the picture. I saw it instantly.

I immediately went to Dr. Messick and the task group of Ph.D.'s we had assembled and told them if they were following this prescription in building the curriculum and helping recruit the faculty for ORU, it would not work. God would hold me responsible.

They asked me, "What quarrel do you have with this statement? It represents not only the University of Washington but all secular universities."

My response was as forceful as my feelings about what God had called me to do. As I remember, I said, "But God says, 'My people are destroyed for lack of knowledge' [Hos. 4:6]. Knowledge that is true knowledge has to originate from God, and the principles of all knowledge are in the Bible, the Word of God, and in the power of the Holy Spirit as He brings the Lord Jesus Christ to the center of all things, including our lives, for time and eternity.

"I was told to build God a university, build it on His authority and on the Holy Spirit. That is why every leader and professor must know Christ as personal Savior and be filled with the Holy Spirit in the charismatic dimension of speaking in tongues. The Holy Spirit is to be the common denominator of all of ORU's founding, operation, and future. The reason is that God created man in His own image and not a mere mind or physical being.

"When Adam sinned in the Garden of Eden, rejecting the way God created him, he elevated his mind above his spirit, making his mind take the place of God.

"The result has led all mankind to elevate his mind to the point that he does not put God first in his life. As he has elevated his mind above his spirit, he is out of harmony with his Maker and Savior, and also out of harmony with himself. That is why he thinks knowledge alone is the principal thing in life."

The men of the task force listened to me with respect. They knew that I did not stand in their shadow academically. They also knew they didn't stand in my shadow concerning knowledge of the Word of God or the revelation God has given me on how His university was to be built.

Finally, they said, "Then exactly how do you expect to build a university like that, and yet expect it to become an *accredited* university?"

That was the best question they could have asked me.

"First," I said, "we start with who is in charge of this university —God or man? To me, it is God. Second, who do we believe knows all knowledge from the beginning? I say, God. Third, we view the raising up of this new university as a command from God whose authority is above all authority. He has chosen through His Holy Spirit to make His Son, Jesus Christ of Nazareth, the real Head of what we build."

Then I put out what I believed was the clincher. I said, "This will take faith, not reason. If we try to reason it out, it will fail and leave me in disobedience before my God. I will have let Him down at the very point where the spiritual is to dominate the mental. But if we believe that God is in our hearts as the Lord of our lives, that He is active in the affairs of mankind, and that He still speaks to people today as He has always done, we can build a university where academic standards will meet or exceed whatever accreditation demands.

"I have been led to bring together you top educational leaders, who are first of all committed to God in your personal salvation and relationship with Him, to help me. God gave us the baptism of the Holy Spirit for more than 'edifying or strengthening our inner man.' Through *interpretation*, God will speak back to our minds with *understanding* and illuminate us mentally. In that, we will find our minds able to spiritually gravitate to His thinking and the ways He would have us gain knowledge, add to it, and pass it on" (see Rom. 8:26–27 and 1 Cor. 14:13–15).

One of the team members stated, "Who would have thought that here on this day we would meet and find a way to put a university together from the ground up that is according to *God's* pattern for a private university and still be accredited?"

It was encouraging to me that we were making headway. If we could get this one issue—spirit over mind without reducing the mind from its rightful place—settled in the leaders of the task force, and have it integrated so completely as our founding purpose into the curriculum, the honor code, the academic discipline, the aerobics program, and the moral standard, ORU would have a full opportunity to become God's university in reality.

God honored the days, weeks, and months we spent on integrating spirit over mind. The advisers and the faculty members we hired came to agreement, including our outside consultants, Dr. Robert Frost, Dr. James Scales, Dr. Eugene Scott, and Dr. Richard J. Doney. Dr. Doney had been assigned to us by the North Central accreditors.

I was never a curriculum expert in details, but by the Holy Spirit, I was given an understanding beyond myself that the central core of all we offered at ORU was to be wrapped around the fact that all truth was in Jesus Christ. He was to be the center of the university. I stated we did not have to look outside Him for truth. Therefore, since all truth is vested in Jesus Christ and we look to Him for everything we do at ORU, that is the distinctive.

All that seemed so new back in 1963 when we chartered the university with the state of Oklahoma. To me, we were in a crazy, mixed-up world. Generally speaking, if you were a rational-thinking person, you rejected God and the supernatural. If you were a spiritual person, you rejected natural things that were also put here for our good.

It seemed to me, man was coming apart: the 1960s youth rebellion against authority; the near destruction of the Democratic party's Chicago convention; the burning of university buildings; the rise of rock 'n' roll music; the world impact of the Beatles; the "God is dead" theory coming out of Emory University in Atlanta; the archbishop of Canterbury saying in London, "Better be red than dead"; the civil rights movement getting laws passed for equality, only to see that you can make laws but unless man's heart is changed, law itself is not enough; and seeing a lost second generation of Pentecostals. Those and other things pointed out that the time had come to build God a university because higher education was taking over in America and the world by producing its leaders who led the world to be what it was.

In ancient history, Nero fiddled while Rome burned. In our day, we were seeing the same thing in an almost hands-off policy of educational situations concerning the soul of man.

Jenkin Lloyd Jones, publisher and editor of the *Tulsa Tribune* and a nationally respected syndicated writer, startled the country with his famous editorial, which was later reprinted in *Reader's Digest*: "Someone Is Tampering with the Soul of America."

The time had come. The world needed ORU, whether it realized it or not. God was ready, and so was I.

CHAPTER 18

GET YOUR LEARNIN'
BUT KEEP YOUR BURNIN'

GOD HAD promised me concerning my students,

"Their work will exceed yours, and in this I am well pleased."

I brought the idea of building the university before the seven trustees of the Oral Roberts Evangelistic Association, Inc. (OREA). They voted unanimously to do it, and they delegated me, with Lee Braxton, to form a forty-one-member Board of Regents to govern the new university.

Lee had contacts with the kinds of dedicated and Spirit-filled men and women who had the substance and influence to be Regent prospects. He submitted his list and I submitted my list. The OREA board helped us choose forty-one people, and the ORU Board of Regents was formed in 1962. We elected Lee as the founding chairman. The board elected me as the founding president. Lee served as chairman from 1962 to 1979, when he no longer had the strength to carry on, but he remained a member of the board until his death on November 18, 1982.

Lee's insistence on excellence, I believed, matched mine, and together we presented the ideas God had given me to the new Board of Regents to found the university. Our policy in our board meetings has been to thoroughly discuss a motion until there is unity of thought, then vote yes or no. We've never had a serious disagreement on the board since we began. To us, the unity of the body is all-important. There is plenty of room to discuss, even disagree, before the vote, but like the Quakers, when we get "the sense of something in agreement," the vote is taken and we close ranks.

That is my way of operating. It was Lee's, also, and I owe him much as chairman in skillfully leading the board to its decisions.

The board helped me set up the honor code, which is the heart of the university. It contains what God commanded me to do in building Him a university based on His authority and on the Holy Spirit. Everyone who has attended ORU has signed it. The honor code signing is done each semester with all students, faculty, staff, and the president's team present, and sometimes the chairman of the board. We make no apologies for our rules and regulations, for our discipline, for our beliefs, or for our determination to put God first.

We all want it this way, and we stand up for it. Also, we feel indebted to our Partners who financially and prayerfully helped us build ORU and are still helping us operate it. They have done so on the basis that we operate on the honor code, which is a powerful instrument in making God the real Head of ORU.

The Oral Roberts Evangelistic Association had to amend its Articles of Incorporation to add to its purpose that OREA could be a support agency for a Christian university. The amendments to the charter were made to recognize that OREA was the father of the university. Without my healing crusades touching the lives of millions of people and my individual-person ministry as the central part of it, there would be no university.

I say in behalf of the hundreds of thousands of sacrificing Partners—many of whom didn't get to go to college but who believed God wanted this kind of university raised up—they wanted what my healing ministry offers to suffering mankind to be at the heart of this campus, while student riots were going on in many other college campuses.

In 1965, we opened with a few more than three hundred freshmen. But the plan called for a full university. We started at what appeared to many people to be the worst time in the history of America.

Billy Graham, in dedicating ORU in 1967, said, "If this institution ever moves away from faith in the Bible, and faith in God, and putting God first, then let us this day pronounce a curse on it."

Billy and everyone else can rest assured no curse fell on ORU in its first thirty years when I was president, and I see no way it can change under my able and dedicated son, Richard, its second president and chief executive officer.

As Bishop J. O. Patterson, head of the largest black Pentecostal denomination in America, the Church of God in Christ, said in one of our chapel services, "ORU is a place where you can get your learnin' but keep your burnin'." Bishop Patterson's keenly discerning words became a slogan that still inspires the entire student body every semester. He had caught what ORU as a university is to be.

ORU's Purpose

I asked Ron Smith to have high-level meetings with Dr. Messick and the entire ORU staff on the subject: ORU's purpose for being. He also went to students, since that was five years after the university had opened, and got their input. The students felt healing was the core. They said they had been drawn to ORU to get their education because they wanted what the ministry stood for. Then Ron and I spent many hours together.

This phrase kept coming up: "healing for the totality of human need."

Finally, several faculty and staff were asked to propose their own ideas of our purpose. We felt that Dr. Doney would see their ideas as evidence that even though I was the founder, ORU was not a one-man campus, and that many made contributions.

Ron's report came out of a summary of the ninety committee meetings on the subject, but in the end, the way he put the words together told the real story of our purpose. Here is that report:

> It is the purpose of Oral Roberts University, in its commitment to the historic Christian faith, to assist the student in his quest for knowledge of his relationship to God, man, and the universe. Dedicated to the realization of Truth and the achievement of one's potential life capacity, the University seeks to graduate an integrated person—spiritually alive, intellectually alert, and physically disciplined.

To accomplish this purpose, Oral Roberts University seeks to synthesize by means of interdisciplinary cross-pollination the best traditions in liberal arts, professional, and graduate education with a charismatic concern to enable students to go into every man's world with healing for the totality of human need.

These words have stood the test in every way. I wouldn't change a word. It says exactly what ORU is, and it doesn't take all day to say it.

It was a real test of my thinking when, during the accreditation process, the committee wanted us to back off from some of our positions in spiritual principles and the discipline we had set up for the campus.

———— *Accreditation—Compromise or Stand?*

The North Central accreditors wanted a clear statement of purpose, one coming out of the grass roots of the ministry and the university itself. They understood through my several visits with them in Chicago with Dr. Messick that "ORU was a ministry in which there would be a university." It didn't go over well at first, but when they sent committees to see our facilities and meet our faculty and the students, they saw ORU could actually be a full-blown university and be true to its founding.

How to achieve that was the challenge.

Dr. Richard J. Doney, our main consultant from the North Central Association of Colleges and Secondary Schools, told us that what they wanted most of all was for us to write a succinct statement summing up our complete purpose. Then when they accredited us, they would hold us to it.

"Dr. Doney," I said, "that's music to my ears."

Dr. Doney was a charming man, of high intellect, of rare spiritual understanding, and in deep sympathy with the founding of a university that would be different, yet fundamentally sound academically. His finest conclusion and statement to me came a month before he was to leave and give his report to the North Central Association: "Reverend Roberts, here's how the accrediting people will deal with you and the university. They will set the academic standards but will leave the philosophy and theology of the school to you and your staff."

"As their official representative, would you shake hands on that?" I asked.

"I will, indeed," he replied, "and I assure you I speak for all those who will accredit your university when these standards are met."

It was a warm handshake. I believed him. I felt he believed in my integrity of purpose, in the God-given knowledge I had acquired, and in the people I was surrounding myself with.

Dr. Doney consulted with us several times later. I counted him a true friend.

Dr. Eugene Scott, Dr. Messick told me, had made several incisive contributions to the curriculum and to the spiritual underpinnings of the university. When he left to pursue his own ministry in Los Angeles, I hugged him and told him I wished he could stay with us. "You'll make it, Oral," he said. "As much as God is in this, you'll have to try hard to fail."

"We don't intend to fail," I told him. "We dare not because God is our Source."

When Dean Carl Hamilton and I went to Chicago in 1971 for the final meeting with the North Central Association that would determine whether we would be accredited, I knew in my spirit I would not compromise. We would do without accreditation first. I knew how much we had wanted accreditation and how much we had prepared for it, but as precious as it was to our becoming a full university, I knew where God would have us stand.

I remember when I left the meeting in Chicago with the accrediting body, leaving Dean Hamilton to receive the final verdict. He was to call me so I could share it with the university family (and later the ORU Board of Regents) as we were gathered in the chapel.

When the phone call came through that we had been accredited and would not require a visit of the site team for the next ten years, I announced it, and pandemonium broke out. Several of the young men put me on their shoulders and carried me through the audience.

That accreditation was given exactly as we had laid out the university's founding purpose, and our deepest commitment is never to deviate from it. What few believed could ever happen did happen. The news of our accreditation spread around the world.

No day has passed since that time that the students have not been on my mind and in my heart. All I have attempted to do was with the understanding that "success without a successor is failure!"

I had promised my parents if I ever prospered, I would take care of them; if I had anything, they would have part of it. They had taken care of me while I lay so ill with tuberculosis, and I owed them my life.

After establishing twelve local congregations for the Pentecostal Holiness Church, Papa had virtually no ministry just when my healing ministry began.

My older brother Elmer had sacrificed and built a small house behind his in Ada where Papa and Mama lived a pretty bare life— no car, no pension, no income except what Elmer with his family could contribute.

Jewel and Vaden had their hands full, although they were doing what they could for our parents. I was the only one, if my ministry was received well, who could see they wouldn't be forgotten by the church and all those they had won to Christ.

By 1949, I was able to build them a nice five-room house on a lot near me in Tulsa and move them there, purchase them their first new car, a Ford, and start giving them money each month for living expenses.

I have Evelyn to thank for being willing to share. We were not exactly running over in our own personal income, although our income for 1948 from our ministry was big to us.

During the next ten years, as I became well known, the Lord blessed our crusades. Pastors wanted to know who my preacher father was. Soon invitations came to him and my mother to conduct revivals in many of the churches. They were in their element: Papa was a powerful preacher, and Mama prayed for the sick. They found acceptance and success they had never known before. They would often win two to three hundred souls in each revival. My joy in them was unlimited. At last, I felt, they had a real chance to be appreciated as the able people they were and to have all their needs met.

Ron Smith had built a model retirement and convalescent center in Des Moines. Upon Bob DeWeese's recommendation, who knew Ron and his parents well, I flew up to Des Moines to see

Ron's work firsthand. I saw a facility built for older people. I saw the loving care given there. I saw the happiness many of them thought they might lose in their senior years. I was impressed, and I asked Ron to visit us in Tulsa as a consultant to our plans to build a similar facility.

As usual, I didn't have the money to build with. So far in everything I have built, first, I've had God's clear leading, and second, I've had the privilege of beginning the construction on faith alone.

The great thing about it was I didn't think it was a burden. Others were not so charitable. "Oral just doesn't know any better," they said.

Perhaps I knew something they didn't know. I wasn't operating in the dark. In my study of the Bible, I had seen where God called "those things which be not as though they were" (Rom. 4:17).

I had begun to get the revelation of the miracle of seed-faith to work its three keys, as given in the Word of God. First, God is your Source. Second, sow a seed. Third, expect a miracle!

My father passed away at the age of eighty-seven before we were far along in the building of the facility. As he came to the end, I think he was the happiest he had ever been. He had seen my ministry touching the world, walked on the grounds of ORU, taken part in our seminars for ministers and for laypeople, seen his own ministry flourish as never before, and was looked upon by our faculty and students as a patriarch, which indeed he was.

Mama at eighty-three was strong and vigorous, a power for God. Speaking to a congregation, regardless of whether it was twenty-five people or ten thousand, she could in the first sixty seconds move people's hearts quicker than anyone I had ever known.

Ron and I agreed that there should be a place for senior citizens, a retirement village with medical facilities, a place of dignity and respect. We would call it University Village.

Ron said, "Oral, if we build University Village with your mother in mind, as much as she has labored for the Lord and her family, and considering the deep love you have for her, if the Village is good enough for your mother, it'll be good enough for any mother—or father—or older couple."

"Well, if we build it with my mother in mind as the standard," I said, "it could be the best place any older person could live."

I really meant that.

Again, John Williams came into the picture. He was the main stockholder in the Bank of Oklahoma. I asked him to look over our plans. He brought with him the head of the bank, Dr. Eugene Swearingen, who had been president of the University of Tulsa, and who was one of the most able businessmen in Tulsa. They liked what they saw and loaned us the start-up money, saying, "If you need more, let us know." By that time, our credit rating was A-1.

Ron had a splendid plan ready, full of activities and spiritual enrichment. In a year, the four hundred units were opened as a showplace in Tulsa for senior citizens.

At first, Mama gave me a hard time. She was fiercely independent, and in many ways she was the stronger of the two of my parents. "I don't want to leave my pretty little home," she told me. "I can take care of myself."

I knew her well. I knew I would have to show her University Village—the lovely units, the large dining room, which meant she wouldn't have to cook anymore, and the people, mostly Partners of the ministry from all over the nation, who would be living there.

"You won't be alone, Mama," I said. "If something happened to you where you are now, and we couldn't get to you in time, I would never forgive myself. But make up your own mind."

Claudius Priscilla Roberts had been making up her own mind all my life. Mama looked over University Village. I drove her out there. The new residents warmly greeted her. They would look at her, then at me. "Why, you two favor," they said. "We ought to," Mama said. "He's the one who shows his Indian blood more than any of my children."

She finally gave in. "But, son, there's one thing I want."

"What's that, Mama?"

"My own furniture moved in."

"But, Mama, you have furniture for a five-room house, and you have only a two-room unit here. Besides, the dining hall is only three minutes away. There's a library of books—"

She interrupted me, "Books, you say?"

"Yes, Mama, just because people grow older doesn't mean they stop reading. In fact, the University Village library is an extension of the ORU library. You can check out books exactly like the students of ORU."

"I can?" she said, her eyes shining.

All her life she had never gotten her fill of learning. Hampered by only a third-grade education received on the wild Oklahoma frontier when schools had been few, small, and far between, nevertheless she managed to read every book she could get her hands on, and she passed on her hunger for knowledge to me.

The books sold her.

Mama lived at University Village until her death at age eighty-nine. She loved to be with people. They called her the queen bee.

Although Mama and Papa are in heaven, I feel them with me often. I know that they see me from above and that they talk to Jesus about me. Sounds like a dream only. Maybe it is. But to me, it is a living reality.

My love has been given away on every acre of the university grounds, every piece of material in these buildings, every book and item in the library, every part of the curriculum, every phase of our plans to educate the whole man. Every step has been an uphill step. Nothing has come cheaply. At times, I felt my very blood might be shed.

I started almost every building on the ORU campus the same way. God would give me a picture in my mind and spirit of what it was to look like. I'd call my associates together, and we would pray in the Spirit. Then we would give an offering as a seed of our faith for God to multiply into the millions of dollars that it would take to build Him a university. There were times when we would dig a hole in the ground as a step of faith. God never disappointed us. He always came through with the finances to complete what He had called me to start. I'll admit, however, He sometimes permitted us to come to the very last day before supplying the funds.

The favorite saying of the OREA Board of Trustees and the ORU Board of Regents became, "When Oral dies and is buried, he'll stick one finger up and say, 'Just let me build one more building.'" I laugh, but I don't deny it. Of course, the ORU Board of Regents approved each building before it was begun.

It has been said you can build the finest manufacturing plant in the world, but if you cannot produce a good product, it does not amount to anything. At ORU, the students are the product.

I think, as I am writing this, of the hundreds of ORU students who are on ministry/healing trips to some thirty nations. They come back feeling the burdens of the thousands they prayed for, the large numbers saved, and the dawning of the light from above in the darkened hearts of people who knew not our blessed Savior and Lord, Jesus Christ of Nazareth.

Today, I have finished my presidency during ORU's first thirty years, and I now serve as chancellor. I can go nowhere on this earth without meeting graduates of ORU—and I've ministered in nations in all continents. In 1992, the last time I was invited to the White House, as I was being escorted into the Oval Office to meet the president, I passed a secretary at her desk next to the door. "President Roberts," she said, "I am a graduate of ORU. Everyone going into the Oval Office has to pass my desk. Throughout the White House, there are at least twenty more ORU graduates working, and the White House is asking for more."

In Ghana is Seth Ablorh, a Ghanian graduate of the ORU Medical School; he runs the hospital he built from the ground up. In Norway is Hans Bruterood, founder of one of the largest churches and television networks in Europe. In Russia is John Vande Riet, founder and pastor of the largest charismatic church in Moscow. Terry Law, founder of Living Sound, and the first evangelist to be carried live by the Russian television network; he is thought to be the most responsible for giving Russia the gospel.

Other ORU alumni include the following: Billy Joe Daugherty, founder and pastor of Victory Christian Center, Tulsa's largest charismatic church with over eight thousand members; Carlton Pearson, founder and pastor of the four-thousand-member Higher Dimensions Church in Tulsa, and he is also the national leader of the Azusa Conference, the fastest-growing black movement of the Holy Spirit in America; Jeffrey Wolfe, graduate of the ORU Law School; Richard Lee Roberts, the second president of ORU; and Michael Cardone, Jr., of Philadelphia, owner of the largest remanufacturing plant of used automobile parts in the world.

These are just a few of the nearly fourteen thousand graduates of ORU who have distinguished themselves for the Lord in their careers and work. Some twenty thousand more have attended at least a year or two. They, too, are a part of our growing ORU family.

Today, ORU consists of eighteen buildings on approximately four hundred acres in Tulsa, Oklahoma. We have 4,300 students enrolled with 2,300 in the summer sessions, plus several thousand in ORU's Life Learning Division.

Some things are right to do in this world. We are determined not to lose the cream of the crop of the third generation of the Pentecostal movement and charismatic outpouring. We are also determined to keep ORU open to children of the powerful evangelical movement as well as to young men and women from other churches and all walks of life. ORU is like a little United Nations in its diversity of nationalities, cultures, and backgrounds. Our commonality is an education of the whole man, based on God's authority and on the Holy Spirit.

One morning I awakened with an idea for Christian schools from K through 12, many of them started by local churches, hundreds of them charismatic churches, who feared the accrediting agencies would hamper their spirituality. As a result, they did not seek accreditation.

In seeing that they are based on the Word of God, and that spirituality is not neglected, they sometimes fail to have able designers of their curriculums, they fail to have quality teachers throughout, and they take too big a chance on their graduates being accepted at an academically excellent school, which, like ORU, also builds spirituality into the system and life of the campus.

Those of us at ORU were never afraid of the accreditation agencies. We wanted to exceed what they required, and in many instances, we've done so. As a result, though we're controversial, especially me, the educational world has given ORU high respect, even if sometimes grudgingly.

That morning God gave me the idea to form the Oral Roberts University Educational Fellowship, Inc., our own accrediting agency, to offer these schools that would measure up and not have a reason to be afraid that with a strong curriculum they could keep the spiritual standards foremost. Our academic team went to work on this idea, consulting with both the state of Oklahoma accreditors and the regional accreditors, the North Central under which ORU operated.

Today, nearly one hundred schools that offer kindergarten through twelfth grade have met the ORU standards, and I believe, it has placed them in the highest ranks. Each year the schools have their academic, athletic, and other contests at ORU, our facilities in meeting the North Central and NCAA Division I standards serving them well. This idea came out of my spirit and had to be melded with academic quality. I am proud of it for the kingdom of God and the terrific young people who want a Christian education that stands up academically.

The ORU curriculum, although anchored to its original foundation, is continually revised, sharpened, and adjusted to meeting current needs. It's a continual growth program.

ORU's watchword comes from the Master Himself. "Watch," He said, "and again I say unto you watch." (See Mark 13:37.) In other words, be diligent, be obedient, and hold the call to build God a university sacred.

I believe ORU's last chapter has not been written, and I pray it never will be until Jesus returns!

PART 5

OUR CHILDREN— THEIR TRAGEDIES AND TRIUMPHS

CHAPTER 19

REBECCA—
DEALING WITH LIFE AND DEATH

D R. GIESEN said to me of my darling wife, Evelyn, after Rebecca's birth, which had been perfectly natural, "Young man, that's a great young woman you married. Evelyn is made to have babies."

Evelyn was German and white; I was part Cherokee Indian and dark. Dr. Giesen said, "You two will make beautiful babies."

We did, four of them—two boys and two girls—and the six of us faced the world in togetherness.

Evelyn originally wanted only two children. I was thinking four. She had come from a family of eight children and I, five, so it seemed just right to me for us to have four. I agreed to two, but that was one agreement I was to break. After we had Rebecca and Ronnie, I asked for two more. Evelyn thought about it for four years and finally agreed, and we had Richard and Roberta. Obviously, we decided to begin each child's name with an *R*. After they came, she agreed four were better than two!

Rebecca Ann Roberts, born December 16, 1939, was a robust child. She was dark, showing her Indian features, and carried a heavy mane of black hair, which fell in soft waves over her head and down to her shoulders. She was outgoing in her personality. There was nothing shy about her. But she was definitely a mama's girl. Of course, we introduced her to many people through my ministry.

For three years, she traveled with us as we held our revivals. She said her first word, cut her first teeth, and took her first steps in the houses of pastors who were our sponsors. They all loved Rebecca. Her first day of school was in Toccoa, Georgia.

I wanted the children to learn as much as possible, and Evelyn did, too, so we kept after them. Each Saturday night Evelyn taught them their Sunday school lesson, mainly because she discovered that some of the teachers did not know the lesson.

Once one of our children complained, "Mother, why do we have to teach the Sunday school lesson so often?"

"I didn't know you did," Evelyn answered.

"Well, we do."

Evelyn checked and learned that the Sunday school teachers soon realized that our children knew the lesson so it was easy, if she or he was unprepared, to call on Rebecca, Ronnie, Richard, or Roberta to tell the story in the lesson to the other children in the class. Later, as they grew up, they came to value those extraordinary calls upon them to teach, for they discovered they received more than they gave. They never forgot it.

When the children were school-age, we were living on a farm. My father had urged me to buy a farm for my family to grow up on, if only for a few years. We spent six happy years there, teaching the children the kind of life I had lived on a farm. They were going to school in the little town nearby. Evelyn soon noticed our children were getting all A's. She didn't think the lessons were hard enough, so she switched Rebecca and Ronnie, the two older ones, to Tulsa schools—Ronnie to the new Edison High School and Rebecca to the private school, Holland Hall.

At Holland Hall, which had a superior program, Rebecca graduated with a B average, which was more to her temperament and desire to study. That was before ORU came on the scene, so she went from Holland Hall to the University of Tulsa.

During the growing-up days of my children, I was gone two-thirds of the time in my healing crusades. When I was home, I took special time with them, both as individuals and as a family.

One day after I had come home from an extensive crusade trip, Evelyn asked if I wanted her to bring me up-to-date on all the children. She started with Rebecca and proceeded to tell me that Rebecca had said, "Mother, I'll never make a student. All I really want to do is have a career. I want to work in Dad's office. [By that time, she had attended Tulsa University for two years.] Remember, you promised me I wouldn't have to go to college after I earned a stenographer's certificate."

"What did you tell her?" I asked Evelyn.

"I was waiting to see how you felt about it."

I said, "I think she's described herself very well. She's a strong young woman, she loves the Lord, and she'll make some good young Christian man a great wife."

"Well, you better get ready," Evelyn said. "She's fallen in love with Marshall Nash, the son of Rev. W. J. Nash, whom you know very well and love."

"She has?"

"Yes," she said. "I think they're going to get married. Marshall is waiting to ask you for her hand when you get the time."

The Nash family lived in Georgia. Reverend Nash, as the conference superintendent of the Georgia Conference of the Pentecostal Holiness Church, had befriended me at a very critical time in my life. He and his beautiful wife, Frances, had three sons—Jim, Bill, and Marshall—and all three had come west to Oklahoma to work in my office in Tulsa. I admired the young men very much.

Jim was our photographer for the crusades. Bill managed our radio station. Marshall did much of the mechanical work, especially the printing, and he had a special touch for business.

I freely gave consent for Marshall to marry Rebecca. They had a lovely wedding ceremony in our front yard. She was a beautiful bride, and she became a beautiful wife.

Over the next few years, Marshall became a successful businessman in the Tulsa area, and he and Rebecca had three lovely children. Evelyn and I were thrilled to be grandparents and were happy to see Rebecca so fulfilled in her life. But destiny would soon change all that, ending it in one of the greatest tragedies we have ever experienced.

"God Knows Something About This We Don't Know"

Early on a Friday morning in 1977, our doorbell rang. I got out of bed and went to the kitchen where Evelyn had let in my dear associate, Collins Steele. His face was ashen.

He said, "I have some bad news. Marshall and Rebecca died last night in a plane crash over the Kansas wheat fields on their way to Tulsa. I'm sorry." And he burst into tears.

Evelyn shook as if she had a chill. I felt numb all over. "Oh, the children," Evelyn said. "They'll be up by this time waiting for Mommy and Daddy to come home."

"Yes," I said, "and we've got to go over there and tell them Mommy and Daddy are not coming home."

Evelyn and I threw on some clothes, and we drove to their house. On the way, I couldn't pray except in the Spirit. I felt my insides were being torn out, and no words of my mind were sufficient to pray.

As I prayed quietly in tongues, I asked God for the interpretation. I received it:

"God knows something about this we don't know."

Evelyn took my right hand and held it. "Say it again, Oral."

"God knows something about this we don't know."

I repeated those words all the way over to where the children were waiting: Brenda, thirteen; Marcia, eight; and little Jon Oral, five.

When we rang the doorbell, all three rushed to open the door. They were expecting their parents. Instead, they saw us. We couldn't keep the tears back, and they saw them. Suddenly, they knew something was terribly wrong, and they began to cry.

We took them in our arms. I said, "Children, Mommy and Daddy are not coming home. They were killed a few hours ago when their plane crashed."

Brenda cried harder and picked up one of our plaques sitting on the table, which said, "God is bigger than any problem I have." Marcia grabbed my legs. Little Jon climbed up into Evelyn's lap. We sat there hugging them, crying and trying to emotionally hold on.

Finally, I said, "Brenda, Marcia, and Jon, we prayed as we came over, and the Lord said to me that He knows something about this we do not know."

They couldn't grasp that, only that Mommy and Daddy were gone.

Later, I talked to Marshall's brother, Bill, and his wife, Edna. I said, "Evelyn and I would love to take these children and raise them. But at our age, they need someone younger."

Bill said, "Marshall and Rebecca had made a pact with us and we with them, if anything happened to them, we would take the children. Yes, we will take them. It will be an honor. We'll raise them as if they were our own."

I met with them and the children and officially put them together by prayer. The children's little eyes stared at me with hurt until I thought I could not stand it. But they loved Uncle Bill and Aunt Edna, who were two years older than Marshall and Rebecca.

Then I left to return home to Evelyn. When I walked into the house, I saw she was lying down. "Oral, hold me," she said. "I don't think I can get through the night."

I knew that was right, for I needed something to do at that moment. As I held her, again the only way I could pray was in tongues. Again the words came: "God knows something about this we don't know."

The media picked up those words and carried them nationwide. In his next Sunday sermon on television from the Crystal Cathedral, my friend Dr. Robert Schuller repeated those words as a meaning of God's all-knowing power and His love for His children. Other pastors told those words to their congregations.

Tulsa ministers came to our home and prayed with us. Each one helped us. Among those coming was Dr. Bill Wiseman, pastor of the First Presbyterian Church, who especially ministered to Evelyn in a way that she has not forgotten. Dr. Kenneth Hagin, Sr., came with his wife, Oretha. Dr. Hagin prophesied from the Lord that out of the loss, God was about to bring forth something great for us and the entire body of Christ.

In the aftermath of that awful hurt on our lives, Evelyn and I stood up publicly and appeared together the following Sunday on our national TV program to share with our friends. We had the largest audience we ever had on a Sunday morning—the Nielsen rating put it at over five million. But no matter how strong we were in the Lord, the emotional attachment to our dear ones got the best of us, and I took Evelyn and Richard out of town to try to get over it.

The deaths of Rebecca and Marshall, leaving their little children behind, were beginning to overwhelm us. We had been so close. We loved Marshall as one of our own sons. I could always rely on him. He was a deeply spiritual young man with superior business ability, and he was making his mark on Tulsa. He was gone, and our firstborn was gone.

We got on the plane with tears streaming down our faces. I knew that Evelyn and I sharing our hurt on our television program wasn't enough. I would have to write the whole story. Our Partners were waiting. Also, many other people who were sympathetic to my healing ministry had questions about how such a tragedy could befall a man of God. I would have to depend on God to help me.

In a future chapter, you will see how Kenneth Hagin's prophecy about the loss came to pass.

We are grateful to God that Rebecca and Marshall's children have turned out well. At this writing, Brenda is thirty years old and has her own computer business. Marcia married John Williams of Fort Worth, Texas, in 1993 and is very happy. John is in movie production in Hollywood. Marcia has started a unique company of her own with beads of the nations, which she makes into necklaces with her own hands. They are selling like hot cakes, partly because they are so beautiful with the varied colors of the beads, and each one is an original. She got the idea while majoring in drama at ORU. Jon Oral is twenty-two. He of all the children has seemed to have been hurt most by the loss of his parents. He has had a rough time. Bill and Edna have lavished much love on Jon, and so have Evelyn and I. We have seen him rise above his hurt and come into his own.

Of all the grandchildren, Jon Oral shows his Indian features the most. His grandfather Nash was one-half Cherokee Indian and his grandmother Roberts a quarter blood, and he could pass for a full-blood. He is very proud of his color, and so are we. He and his two sisters are very close, although he lives in Tulsa and Brenda and Marcia in different areas of California. They meet once a year and stay in contact religiously by telephone and by fax. They are committed to the Lord, and I'm happy to say they are close to this ministry. They are a precious legacy from Marshall and Rebecca. As with our other grandchildren, they are very close to Evelyn and me and we to them.

CHAPTER 20

RONNIE— WHAT MIGHT HAVE BEEN

RONALD DAVID, my oldest son, born October 22, 1943, was the intellectual of my children. As someone pointed out, "Ronnie was born smart." Ronnie instinctively knew what to do with books. He loved them, and when he was a child, Evelyn could scarcely keep enough of them in his hands.

Ronnie was a handsome little boy and quick to learn. When he was three years old, he could repeat my sermons almost verbatim.

When we pastored a church in Enid, Oklahoma, I had him come to the stage and sing the action song, "Don't Turn Him Away," and he did it like a grown-up.

When he was in the sixth grade at Bixby, they elected him to be the editor of their little school paper, and in a school play he played the part of a king with appropriate robe and crown. We thought he was every inch a king.

Edison High School was Tulsa's newest and strongest public school in academics. Of course, Ronnie made straight A's there. That was just the way he was constructed. Eventually, his grades and other talents earned him the privilege of being a foreign exchange student in Germany for a summer. Three months later, when he arrived home, he was fluent in the German language. I just shook my head because it was far beyond my language ability.

One day when I returned home from a crusade, Evelyn filled me in on Ronnie's future plans.

"Oral," she said, "Ronnie wants to attend the University of Kansas on an academic scholarship."

Although I had nothing against Kansas University, I knew Ronnie could probably get a scholarship to any university, including Stanford. I decided to talk to him.

Setting him down, I said, "Ronnie, you can go all the way and be the first Roberts to earn a doctorate. You have a thirst for knowledge, you have a natural understanding of the Bible, you know my ministry, you can speak well, and you pick up languages easily. Why not go to Stanford? That's one of the greatest academic institutions in America."

He applied, and to his surprise, a letter soon came from Stanford stating that he was accepted. The admissions people liked that he was an honor student in a good high school, a foreign exchange student, and a member of the orchestra of Edison. It all combined to show his all-around ability and aptitude to learn.

Ronnie took my advice and went to Stanford. I didn't realize it then, but I made one of the most serious mistakes of my life.

After the first semester, he called me in tears. Over the phone he said, "Dad, for the first time in my life, I think I'm in trouble for not knowing any longer what I believe."

I flew to his side, met his professors, and sat in on some of his classes. All was sweetness and light while I was there. I was even asked to speak to some of the clubs on campus and once to more than three hundred students in a large lounge. I received a great reception.

When I called back a month later, I knew in my spirit something was really wrong. I flew out to get to the bottom of it.

I was asked to see his psychiatrist. "Why?" I asked.

"Your son has been placed under her care."

I'll change that, I thought. *Ronnie knows God; he doesn't need a secular psychiatrist fooling with his mind.*

Was I shocked! She wouldn't release him. She gave me some big words about Ronnie's confusion and said it would take her a year to bring him around. I saw that I had to tread softly. Finally, I said, "If you will release my son to me, I'll relieve you and the university of all responsibility."

She reluctantly agreed, and she released him.

My son, in my opinion, was no more confused than the whole of Stanford University and the psychiatrist into whose hands they had placed him. I had asked this lady if she believed in God. "Not anymore," she said. Yet she had, at the moment, the mind of my son in her hands.

It was no accident that I felt my son being sucked into the maelstrom. It was a strike against the Pentecostal outpouring and the new charismatic move, and I felt it was a personal strike against my healing ministry. There was no doubt that much that was happening had a tremendous effect on Ronnie. I knew his life had changed.

I called on many of the men and women who had become charismatic, and we went into agreement in prayer for my son. Also, we went to battle in prayer to stem the tide of the youth rebellion sweeping across America and the serious inroads liberalism was making in our colleges and churches everywhere. We were reaping the bitter harvest of the liberal theology that had come out of the seminaries in Germany during the 1930s—what many call the Hitler era—and that was adopted in many top American seminaries.

Finally, it became a no-win proposition with Ronnie. After he left Stanford, he asked me to let him join the armed services.

"Ronnie, you won't be able to continue your education if you do that. Besides, Vietnam is going to be a horrible war, unlike anything America has ever fought."

"Dad, I feel like I'll die if I stay here. I'm old enough to join without your permission, but I'd like you to agree."

After he volunteered, the military sent two officers from the Security Division to interview me. "The army is considering placing your son in Intelligence because of his linguistic abilities. We have some questions we want to ask you." In answering their questions, I tried to tell about my son in a straightforward manner.

I discussed Ronnie's growing-up years, his tribulations at Stanford, and our times together there to keep his life from falling apart. I told them about the psychiatrist and getting my son out of her hands. I said that at one time I thought Ronnie might be the one who would take up the leadership of my ministry and of ORU, but I could see he was of a different bent in his nature.

As for his joining the army, I believed that was his cry for order and discipline in his life, and his desire to do something for his country. As for the stability of his mind and character, I felt that like most teenagers, he had been through a shaky period. As for using him in Intelligence in the Security Division of the army, I had no doubts as to his trustworthiness.

"Reverend Roberts," one of the officers said, "there is a question I want to ask concerning what you would anticipate your son's reaction would be if we wanted him to learn an entirely new set of languages."

"Like what?" I asked.

"I can't tell you that, sir," he replied.

"Well, I've not seen Ronnie stumped by any language he wanted to learn. I would think since Vietnam is part of the old nation of Indochina, his fluency in French and Chinese would make him useful. In fact, during the time he spent in Formosa, our representative there told me Ronnie's pronunciation was so perfect they couldn't tell he had not been born in China."

"There's a threat from another quarter," he said. And suddenly, I knew they wanted my son to learn a language of one of the Eastern bloc countries. Defectors were coming to the West, and someone had to debrief them as they entered the sanctuary of the United States. Evidently, the officers were satisfied with my answers. They thanked me profusely and left.

Ronnie first went to the Presidio in Monterey, California, to learn Polish. Then they stationed him just outside Washington, D.C., where he served the military as a translator for the duration of his enlistment.

He became proficient in many languages, which he used in his work in the Security Division of the U.S. Army, but he hated being in the army. He wouldn't talk about it, but the frustration was evident.

It took me back to his childhood. He was usually ahead in his classes, and he wanted to go to the top in whatever interested him. I suspected the hierarchy of the military slowed his pace, at least in his eyes, and he didn't like it.

The only time we talked in depth about it ended in my saying, "Ronnie, the translation of intercepted messages in code from the Polish Communists is no little thing. Neither is the debriefing of so many defectors. You could make a contribution through a single translation that could change the course of the cold war." He didn't reply.

I was no different from most fathers who love their children and want to be involved with them if possible. But things were about to take a different shape, and I was caught by surprise. Somehow I had not fully used all the discerning ability God had given me concerning spiritual forces, particularly the unseen demonic spirits under Lucifer, in dealing with my children, especially with Ronnie. I was just a father, and I allowed my mind to rise above my spirit much too often in dealing with them. It was a big mistake.

─────── *A Hard Look at Reality*

Just before Ronnie finished his stint in the army, he married Carol Croskery whom he had known from high school. Then he quickly enrolled in Virginia Commonwealth University. He chose that university because the Philharmonic Orchestra there had a place for Carol, who had played first chair in flute in one of Tulsa's high schools. She was a great young woman and a brilliant flutist. When they added the money she earned to the money from the GI Bill, Ronnie and she could financially make it while he was finishing undergraduate school.

Upon completing his bachelor of arts degree, Ronnie was awarded the Woodrow Wilson Fellowship. It was the first time a student from that great old university had been awarded the prestigious Fellowship in its long history. His Fellowship was for his expertise in French.

By the time Ronnie left the Security Division of the U.S. Army, he knew six languages other than English, including French, Spanish, German, Chinese, Polish, and Russian. And he acquired the first four of them before ever entering the service.

Evelyn and I never knew where Ronnie got such an ear for languages. We didn't have it, although Evelyn had learned quite a bit of Hebrew by studying under a young rabbinical student who would come to our house in Tulsa.

I spoke the English language pretty well. I was good in grammar, but even there, Evelyn, who had taught English, kept me on my toes.

Ronnie decided to pursue advanced degrees in linguistics and become a foreign diplomat. With his Fellowship money, he enrolled at the University of Southern California (USC) in Los Angeles. Because of his advanced skills, he was able to bypass the master's program and go straight to a Ph.D. program.

During that time, the Tulsa school system took Washington High School, a school attended by mostly black students, and turned it into a magnet school. They installed an accelerated curriculum and bused white students there, which was the northern part of our city where most of the black people lived. They were going to teach several foreign languages, including Chinese, French, Spanish, and German, but they didn't have the funds to hire a teacher for each language. One of Ronnie's high school teachers remembered he knew the four languages and felt he could teach all of them and save money for the school.

They telephoned Ronnie in Los Angeles, and although he had nearly finished his doctorate, he set it aside. He and Carol returned to Tulsa where he took the job. Carol enrolled in the University of Tulsa to finish her doctorate in education. By then, he and Carol had adopted two beautiful children, Rachel and Damon.

Soon after he moved back, Evelyn and I went to his home. He was in bed in the middle of the afternoon. "Are you sick, Ronnie?" we asked.

"No," he said, "just drowsy and sleepy. I do this nearly every afternoon."

We didn't catch it. He was on drugs. Because he was to the point in his ability that he could have completed a Ph.D., and he taught four languages to high school students, we never considered Ronnie could be on drugs.

I scolded myself for not being more of a part of the "real world." Our religious beliefs had separated us from drug use and also from the rebellion and violence going on in the nation. We were going about God's business as we saw it. We represented many believers who were doing the same thing.

We knew little or nothing about the drug culture. The young people attending Oral Roberts University were a different breed. Drugs were not on the ORU campus. We had a strong honor code and also a dress code. Along with strong academics, we required participation in an aerobics program and chapel attendance.

We dealt successfully with the few students who were about to get caught up in drug use. It just didn't hit me that Ronnie, my own son, had gotten on drugs and was actually a drug addict. How had it escaped me? Why hadn't I seen it?

When I woke up and let God bring me to reality with my son, I flatly asked Ronnie what was happening in his life. He must have been moved by the tone of my voice, for he blurted out his drug addiction. I took him into my arms and wept and prayed with him.

Ronnie always had a tender heart toward the Lord. He loved the Scriptures. He could talk with me on virtually any subject in the Bible, and sometimes his knowledge of the history of certain parts of God's Word exceeded mine. We had spent many hours on this together, and both of us loved it. That was another reason I was so slow in recognizing that something was drastically wrong.

A month later, we learned he was getting heavily in debt at pharmacies in Tulsa. We also learned how he obtained the drugs. He used some of the doctors' prescription slips he had gotten on his visits to them and made out his own prescriptions for refills without the doctors' knowledge—an unlawful thing to do.

Carol came over one day to show us a statement from the pharmacy. The huge bill was for at least ten times too much of a medication for one month. She said, "Ronnie is evidently addicted to this, and he can't get off it." We asked her to bring Ronnie to our house, and we would pray with him and talk to him about what to do about the problem.

When they came and we prayed and talked, Ronnie made a clean confession. For us, he volunteered to enter a rehabilitation center in Oklahoma City maintained by the Veterans Administration. He stayed there for thirty days and came out believing he was cured.

But soon afterward, Carol talked to us about divorcing Ronnie because she couldn't have him around their two children. Naturally, we hated for the divorce to happen because we knew he needed her support. But we couldn't blame her for her concern for the children.

After the divorce, things came to a head—fast.

I will never forget Ronnie coming to our house, sitting down, and looking at me for some kind of help. In spite of the drug rehabilitation—and our prayers—he was too far gone. I admit, I didn't understand it all.

I learned he never used needles in his arms; he was scared to death of a needle. He took too much of a prescription drug, clinically abusing it, until it got the better of him. Like us, many parents never realize their child can be addicted to drugs by abusing prescription drugs. The devil has his ways of pushing people over the edge when they abuse drugs.

That day, I could tell Ronnie wanted me to lay hands on him and pray. He had grown up under that kind of ministry. He had given his heart to Christ as a young boy, and he knew the supernatural power of God. I assured him that one touch of God upon his addiction could break every bond and set him free.

As I laid hands on him, I felt as much of the presence of God in my right hand—in fact, surging through my whole being—as I ever had. Ronnie broke loose and began to rejoice and praise the Lord. We cried and rejoiced together. From what I felt from God, I was certain the power of God was doing its mighty work. Suddenly, Ronnie stopped.

"What's the matter, Ronnie?" I asked.

"Dad, have you ever known a real drug addict to be delivered?"

"In my crusades, Ronnie, many have testified of being totally delivered. I've heard from several of them that they are still totally free from even the desire for drugs. Don't you believe God is doing this for you right now?"

He didn't reply. He left soon afterward. My heart was breaking. We had come so close to victory. What was holding him back from a final breakthrough?

Three weeks later, I saw Ronnie for the last time on this earth.

He wanted to borrow several hundred dollars. I emptied my wallet and said, "This is the last I'll ever give you, Ronnie. Buying more drugs is self-defeating. What I earn doesn't come easily, and I am responsible to God for how I use it. You've got to make a quality decision to let God break your bondage. I've prayed. I've felt the power of God in me to set you free, but I can't make up your mind for you. You're thirty-eight years old. God has gifted you more than most. A great future lies ahead, but only you can decide. Giving you money will only feed your addiction. Settle it, Ronnie, my dear son, once and for all."

He left.

A few days later, I had just finished playing a few holes of golf and was getting in my car to go home when Richard drove up. He was ashen faced. "What's wrong?" I asked.

"Dad, get in my car and let me drive you home."

I got in. I knew something bad had happened.

"The police have just informed us that Ronnie is dead."

My heart almost burst out of my body. "What happened?" I managed to ask.

Richard explained, "They found him at four o'clock this morning slumped over the steering wheel of his car on a country road. There was a gun on the seat. He had been shot to death. They think it was suicide, but they're not sure. He may have been murdered, but they think he took his own life."

"But Ronnie, in spite of being on drugs, loved the Lord. He wouldn't have taken his own life," I cried out.

"Dad, he wasn't just taking a few drugs; he was taking a handful at a time. The police believe they had chemically eaten up his brain, and he didn't even know what he was doing."

How I hated Satan at that minute and his slimy ways of luring children and young people into drugs. I was able to contain myself until I got home and Richard told Evelyn. We didn't just cry; our bodies shook as we held on to each other and to Richard.

Rebecca was gone, now Ronnie—our two oldest.

Richard and Roberta were left.

I believe God had chosen Ronnie for great things. I had dreamed that when he finished his Ph.D., he would come and teach language at ORU. The call on my life for ORU was for our graduates to "go into every man's world," also to "the uttermost bounds of the earth" with the gospel, and I knew the language department at ORU had to be strong to raise up students to help accomplish this.

John Greenleaf Whittier said,

> For of all sad words of tongue or pen,
> The saddest are these: "It might have been!"

The choice of any individual to go toward God and contribute to His world is always a personal decision of his will. After Ronnie's death, I often thought of King David's words over the tragic death of his oldest son when he cried, "O my son Absalom, my son, my son Absalom! would God I had died for thee" (2 Sam. 18:33).

Not long after Ronnie's death, Dr. Kenneth Hagin, Sr., and his wife, Oretha, phoned that they would like to come by and give us a word from the Lord. Evelyn and I were still grieving over Ronnie when the Hagins arrived at our house.

This prophet of God said, "The Lord has given us a word for you. It's in 1 Corinthians 5:5 and it says, 'To deliver such an one unto Satan for the destruction of the flesh, that the spirit may be saved in the day of the Lord Jesus.'

"Oral and Evelyn, the Lord wants you to know your son has not gone to hell. The Lord gave your son's flesh over to Satan, but because death is the last enemy, He did that so Ronnie's soul would be saved. After Satan kills our bodies, he can do no more."

Then he told Evelyn and me that he had prayed with many people who had a family member commit suicide. He said, "In every case, the person who committed suicide had not known what he was doing, and God took that into consideration."

Dr. Hagin gave us the answer that we needed. We knew that at the last, Ronnie had no control over his mind. We knew Ronnie was saved because of the powerful prayers we had prayed together weeks before his death. We accepted the prophecy as coming straight from God for our encouragement.

Later, God sent two other friends in the ministry, Velmer Gardner and his wife, Wilma, to us with another Scripture. It was 1 Corinthians 4:5: "Therefore judge nothing before the time, until the Lord come, who both will bring to light the hidden things of darkness, and will make manifest the counsels of the hearts: and then shall every man have praise of God."

That meant God was saying to us we were not to trouble our minds about where Ronnie's soul went when he died, for he was in God's hands and God would take care of him. We gained a sense of peace, which we have had since these precious friends came to us in our need with the Word of God.

A few nights later, the Lord gave me a dream about Ronnie, which I told to Evelyn at breakfast the next morning. In the dream, Ronnie was standing there talking to Jesus, his sister Rebecca, and his grandmother Roberts. (Mama had passed away in 1974.)

Evelyn asked me if I could hear what he was saying. I said "Yes, he was talking to Jesus, and I heard him say, 'I'm so glad to be free from a body out of control.'" Evelyn and I both rejoiced because we knew God had used the dream to further confirm what we already felt.

Heaven was growing closer to us all the time. If Satan thought he had defeated us, he was 100 percent wrong. In all of our hurting, God was never more real to us. And we felt the strength to get on with our lives and God's call upon us.

My two younger children would figure prominently in the journey forward, Roberta in her way in becoming a lawyer, and Richard in the special calling into the ministry that God had put in his heart.

CHAPTER 21

RICHARD— GOD'S CHOICE

RICHARD LEE, our third child, was born November 12, 1948. I would have to say that out of my four children, he and I had the most in common. That mainly came about through our activities together on our farm. Papa would try to come to the farm three or four times a week.

Sometimes when Evelyn would promise Richard a quarter to sweep off the breezeway, he would look and look, and sure enough here would come Papa. "Papa, would you like to make fifteen cents?" he would ask. "I sure would," Papa would reply, knowing what was coming. "Well, I'll give you fifteen cents if you'll do this job."

Papa would do it, then Richard would give him fifteen cents. He would still have a dime left and not do any of the work. Then Papa would go in the house chuckling, telling Evelyn, "That boy is smart. You just watch him. He'll be the president someday when he gets grown."

We never once thought Richard would be either a preacher or a president. We thought he would be a solid citizen, who would get along with everybody. A scholar he wasn't, at least not at that time.

Every school day, Evelyn would have him dressed spic-and-span. With his lunch bucket, he'd climb on the school bus, wave, and off to school he'd go in nearby Bixby.

Many days when he got off the bus and came walking down the road to our house, Evelyn would throw up her hands. His shirt-tail would be out, his belt lost, one shoe off, and his face scratched.

Grinning, he'd walk up to Evelyn. Each time the conversation would go something like this.

"What's wrong with your face? And your clothes are just barely hanging on you! What happened?" she'd ask.

"I got in a fight."

"You got in a fight?"

"He hit me first."

His lips would start trembling. He was wondering if she was going to give him a licking. He knew his mother was still a school-teacher at heart. Fighting among the kids was not something she liked. But the way he looked, like something had run over him, broke her up, and she couldn't keep from laughing.

She'd say, "Well, come in here and wash up and change your clothes. I can't stand to see you look like that."

The children loved summer's arrival. Then Evelyn could bring them to my crusades. They all liked to see me pray for the healing of the sick.

Richard would wiggle and twist a lot as I preached. But when the healing line formed, he would sit as still as a mouse, his eyes glued to every move I made as I laid hands on each one and prayed, "Jesus! Heal in Your name!"

When someone received healing and it was apparent, Richard would jump off his chair and clap his hands. He of all the children seemed to love the healings the most.

One sport Richard and I especially loved to play together, and still do, is golf. I tried to get all my children at young ages to take up the game, but only Richard wanted to. I put a club in his hand at age five, teed up the ball in our yard, and told him to swing the club and hit the ball. He was born left-handed, but I made him swing right-handed so he'd be swinging against his strong left side and he'd be a better player.

I remembered my first swing at age thirty-five. I missed the ball completely. But that day, Richard swung for the first time as perfectly as he did years later when he was a "scratch" player and thought about joining the professional golf tour.

The only trouble was when he hit the ball, it sailed right through the picture window of our front room and landed at his mother's feet. The window was cracked wide open.

Evelyn came rushing out. She was furious.

Richard's chin was trembling, and a tear ran down his cheek. I tried to hold back from laughing but couldn't. When Richard saw me laughing, he burst out laughing.

"Oh, you two," Evelyn said, "do you know how much it will cost to replace this window in our living room?"

"No, darling," I said, "but I take responsibility since I told Richard to hit the ball. I'll get it fixed."

Over the years as I learned to become a low handicapper, I taught everything I knew to Richard. I can remember the day when he hit his drive on a 380-yard, four-par hole, just 50 or so yards in front of the hole and I hit mine something like 80 or 100 yards shorter. From that day, his golfing ability passed mine like a freight train passes a hobo.

It is a paradox that the very place where we enjoyed being together the most—the golf course—would be the same place where we would separate, seemingly permanently.

——— *The Rebellion*

Many years after my rebellion at sixteen years of age, I learned a vital lesson: You reap what you sow, and I was about to see my harvest (see Gal. 6:7–8).

In 1965, when the time came to open Oral Roberts University academically for our first freshman class, Richard was seventeen and finishing his senior year in high school. He had been accepted at three universities outside Oklahoma. Of course, Evelyn and I wanted him to attend ORU. But he flatly refused to attend his father's university.

Right under my nose he had developed musical gifts and goals of which I was unaware. In fact, I learned he was the lead singer in one of Tulsa's most popular rock bands. With his exceptional singing talent, he wanted to study at a university known for its music department. So he chose the University of Kansas, renowned for the great musicians and singers who had graduated from there.

At ORU, we were developing the genesis of a music department that, by the time Richard graduated, would have begun to attract the attention of the music world, including famous people on nationwide television. I needed and wanted his singing voice for my ministry. Nothing could convince him, though, so off he went to Lawrence, Kansas, and enrolled at the university with a major in music.

During the summer after his freshman year, Richard sang with Shirley Jones and many others in the Starlight Theater in Kansas City. Unknown to us, he had also been doing some nightclub singing. We learned that a singing contract offer had come from Las Vegas, and that scared the daylights out of his mother and me.

About that time, Kenneth Copeland, one of our older students who was also our copilot, asked to see me in my office. He said, "It's about Richard. The Spirit of the Lord spoke to me that you and Evelyn should stop worrying over him. God has His hand on him, and He's already working things out. I feel this so strongly I had to tell you." And he left.

I had confidence in Ken. I knew in my spirit that he and his wife, Gloria, were gaining tremendously in their education and in their move toward the calling of God on their lives. I paid attention and told Evelyn what he told me. Both of us felt a witness in our spirits that Ken had indeed received a word from the Lord.

But first things turned sour.

One weekend when Richard came home, we went out to play a round of golf. During the game, he tried to stay away from the subject that was sore with him: God. By the sixth hole, I couldn't hold back any longer. His face aflame, he said, "Dad, get off my back about God!"

Well, as a true Roberts, I let his reaction fly all over me. I promised I wouldn't speak of God to him again unless he asked me to. Then I picked up my golf bag, and he picked up his. We walked to the car and drove off without another word.

While we were driving home, my memory was superactive. I heard a Voice inside me say,

"You remember telling Me to get out of your life when you were about Richard's age? And you remember I did it?"

Oh, how I remembered. My memory took me back to the time when I sowed the seed that was giving me such a bad harvest with my own precious son.

Only God in His mercy can undo what the devil tries to do to our children. No matter how much we hurt inside and want so much to control their lives, only God can right the wrong and give us a wonderful harvest in our children, by His grace and mercy. Richard's change was to come about later, but without any further intervention on my part.

Shortly after Richard returned to Kansas University, he became ill with a serious colon problem and was taken to the hospital. All types of tests were done, and the doctors recommended surgery. While he lay in that hospital room, he had time to think about God. All that Evelyn and I had put in him as a child about God and His ways was coming up in his spirit. He began to pray. Then he told God, "If You'll heal me, I'll serve You." The next morning when he was examined again by the doctor, the surgery was canceled.

Richard was released, and he immediately returned to his dormitory room. One day while he was alone, he heard a Voice. But it was not the voice of his dad. The Voice said, "You're in the wrong place." He looked around the room to see who was there. He couldn't find anybody. The Voice said to him again, "You're in the wrong place."

So Richard said, "If I'm not supposed to be here, where am I supposed to be?"

"You're supposed to be at Oral Roberts University," the Voice said. He knew it was God's voice.

Richard phoned his mother and asked if she thought ORU would accept him for the next school year.

Evelyn said, "I don't know, Richard. You'll sure have to change some of your habits." She knew he had begun to smoke and drink, and he was into other things or was near it. We had been very distressed over him.

He said, "Well, Mother, I could change."

We learned that he called the ORU admissions office, and the officers told him they had room for him the next semester. Our son was coming home. And although Evelyn and I were ecstatic, we knew he would still need some space. We didn't press him about anything.

Soon after he enrolled, he got in trouble and found himself in the Dean of Men's office. Then the Dean of Women called him in.

He had arrived at ORU, but he had brought all his habits with him. He discovered that being my son didn't help him. He had to learn that there was a time at ORU when he would have to learn to submit.

It was the fall semester of Richard's junior year at ORU before he yielded to God. One day while I was in a crusade in California, I received a phone call from Evelyn. She said, "Richard wants to say something to you," and she handed him the phone. Richard was crying and praising God. "What's happened, Richard?" I asked.

"Dad, I came up from my dorm to see Mother today. I wanted God to come into my life. I remembered how I as a little boy had laid my head on her lap and Mother would pray with me. Well, I knelt down and put my head in her lap again, and I asked Mother to pray for me. She did, and I accepted Jesus Christ as Savior right there. He forgave me of my sins, and I feel clean all over."

We had a praise-the-Lord time together over the phone. Richard said, "Dad, you're not on my back any longer. I want to be at your side. I want to sing in your crusades and be involved in your ministry." My heart leaped for joy, and I couldn't wait to get home.

Later that night as Richard returned to the dormitory, he heard a noise in a room across the hall. He knocked on the door and asked them what they were doing. They said, "We're praying. Come in and join us."

It was the room of one of his closest friends, Paul Craig Paino, from Fort Wayne, Indiana. Richard went in and sat down. The Spirit of the Lord was all over the room. Several of the young men were praying in tongues. Soon Richard felt the Holy Spirit coming up from his belly, as Jesus had said in John 7:37–38: "If any man thirst, let him come unto me, and drink. He that believeth on me, as the scripture hath said, out of his belly shall flow rivers of living water." As he opened his mouth to praise the Lord, there was a flow of heavenly language coming up from his inner being—his belly area—over his tongue. God was baptizing him with the Holy Spirit, and he was unleashing the power of praying in the Spirit.

Soon afterward, Richard was surrendering his singing gift to the Lord, working by my side, and feeling inwardly a strong tug toward preaching and entering the healing ministry.

Like anyone who earns a leadership position, Richard had to go through his own time of testing. It seems to me, God has no other way of getting people into their proper position for His plan for their lives, and to live by faith, without permitting them to go through trials and tribulations.

For some reason, in this life we just can't develop when everything goes our way. We have to be hit, not once, not twice, but many times, and make up our minds and set our faith to survive. We must stay the course. Then we must hope someone following us can do the job better than we did.

As I have said to Richard many times, "Who said life was fair and easy?" His first time of testing came after the break in his marriage in 1979.

A Devastating Divorce

For many people, divorce is hard to handle. It haunts them and causes great pain. But with God there is forgiveness, and we have a right to claim that forgiveness through Christ and His atoning work.

As I understand the Scriptures, the Bible permits divorce only in certain circumstances. I sincerely feel that Richard had a biblical basis for divorce. If divorce is granted, remarriage is permitted. Richard voluntarily submitted himself to the elders, and they led him in this decision.

In my ministry, the fact that Evelyn and I had a loving, stable marriage was known everywhere. It positively affected the members of my team with me on our healing mission. It also had a powerful effect on the hundreds employed in our Tulsa office.

More than that, I believe it gave me and my ministry a wider acceptance by the thousands who attended each of my crusades. I never forgot that some one-half of the American people were or had been divorced. My audiences were made up of both church people and unchurched people, with the larger part being unchurched, many of whom didn't profess to be Christians at all.

I tried to set a standard in the whole of my life, in our team, and in my efforts to present a united front of integrity in our personal and our public lives. One of the results was that I had been able to help many thousands of couples to build stable marriages. I vividly recall the many letters I received from both younger and older couples who said their marriages had been healed. In addition, there were many who learned the biblical way of dealing with divorce. I counted that one of the greatest miracles that God did through my ministry.

I'll never forget when Richard came into my office to tell me of the divorce initiated against him. Dr. Carl Hamilton, the provost of the university, was with me at the time. Richard sat down and said, "Dad, where does this leave me with you and this ministry?" He began to weep. Through his tears, Richard looked back at me. The strain was on his countenance.

"You want to know where it leaves you with me and this ministry?" I asked.

"Yes," he said. "I've poured my life into it. It's where I feel called. But I don't know how you'll feel about me being a divorced man. I know your stand on divorce."

"Richard," I said, "I know more about what's happening than you may realize. Now it's over. I'll say this to you as I would to any other person in this ministry. If you stay clean morally after this divorce and continue to do your job, I'll stick with you with all the love and strength I possess."

"What about Mother?"

"You'll have to ask her yourself. I have a feeling she'll give you the same answer." (Later that day, Evelyn confirmed to Richard that she felt the same way.)

He slipped to his knees, placed his hands in mine, and said, "Will you pray for me?"

I laid my hands on my son's head, unable to restrain my tears, and committed him to God. I told God that at age thirty, my son, soon to be single, would face many temptations.

I told Richard what I understood about divorce, and that it was not blasphemy against the Holy Spirit, which is the only unforgivable sin Jesus spoke of. I opened my Bible and read him Matthew 12:31–32:

> Wherefore I say unto you, All manner of sin and blasphemy shall be forgiven unto men: but the blasphemy against the Holy Ghost shall not be forgiven unto men. And whosoever speaketh a word against the Son of man, it shall be forgiven him: but whosoever speaketh against the Holy Ghost, it shall not be forgiven him, neither in this world, neither in the world to come.

Next I told him to remember these words of Jesus, not man's, and get on with his life. I said, "God has a Spirit-filled young woman who will be a real wife and helpmeet to you, who will love you as you love her. In the meantime keep yourself morally clean, and obey your calling of the Lord. If you do this, God will work things out to His glory."

I felt in my spirit the words were not coming merely out of me. They were by the grace of God and were a prayer in themselves. I realized there would be some tough times ahead, but I believed "with God all things are possible."

Privately, some of my minister friends suggested I send Richard away from my side and out of the country for several years until it all blew over. Others said to place him on a five-year trial to prove he would continue to live clean, then allow him to minister beside me again.

I listened. I prayed. I thanked my friends and asked them to trust me as they had in the past. They were emphatic in saying they would do that. The key issue was how would God have us respond or react. As I was quiet before the Lord, I was letting His Word flow through me and listening for revelational knowledge by the Holy Spirit according to God's Word.

These serious questions came up from my spirit: What are we as Christian leaders and believers to do about all the divorced and remarried people in our world? Are we going to shut out the one-half of Americans in this condition, saying to them, "You have no right to a second chance through the gospel"? Aren't they subjects of God's love, too? Having faced these questions many times as I dealt with such individuals and couples, both in the healing line and in my replies to their letters to me, I was grateful that I had felt the Lord Himself causing these questions to come up out of my spirit.

I realized again, this time with my own flesh and blood, that God's grace extends to all, except those who have blasphemed the Holy Spirit. He is concerned with precious divorced people in a far more merciful way than many are who are in the body of Christ.

I was grateful to all my associates closing ranks with me on the stand I had taken in the situation with my son. I allowed Richard to fulfill the call of God to work with me in this ministry, providing he heeded the conditions God had led me to lay down for him to follow in the days to come.

There were tears and careful examination according to the Word of God, but what I most appreciated was that there was no bitterness, which is self-destructive. And there continued to be no stain on this ministry. I could not be more grateful that I serve a Savior and Lord who, when we put things in His hands, takes things beyond our control and by His grace brings the answer that gives us peace. Then those who are called of Him can continue to be His obedient and anointed servants.

My heart is overwhelmed that a good God offers hope to divorced people and that "His grace is sufficient." I say this when divorce was heartbreaking for me and my family for a son called of the Lord. But in going through its devastation, we learned a most important lesson. God forgives when forgiveness is earnestly sought and comes forth as the God of a second chance.

CHAPTER 22

GOD IS THE GOD OF A SECOND CHANCE

I WAS AMAZED at how things began to change positively in the next few months.

The quiet way Richard went about his life and ministry, keeping himself clean and pure before the Lord, was making a solid imprint on a great many people, including those in high places. He was maturing in every way. Even when some people were critical and said unfair things against him in judgment, he refused to strike back at them.

As the months passed, a profound change began to emerge from Richard's spirit. God was obviously dealing with him as he continued with me on television and in ORU. Soon he began receiving calls from pastors saying, "God is leading me to ask you to come to my church to preach." The calls were from small and large churches, from both white and black pastors. In fact, scores of black pastors threw their doors wide open to him. The love we'd had for black people was coming back in bushels. I recall weeks later Richard's saying, "Dad, everywhere I've gone, the pastors and people are receiving me just like they do you."

Those who tend to throw a divorced person on the ash pile don't really understand that God has a second chance for every human being. We humans stare at the other person's mistakes and shortcomings, sometimes saying, "Well, it's over for him." That's only true, I've discovered, if the person gives up. God's love for each of us is the strongest bonding we will ever know. He simply does not throw a person away.

"It's got to be God," I said. The pastors knew there had never been a stain on my life or ministry. For them to receive my son, Richard, as they did me was a preview of "great events casting their shadows before them."

Something good was about to happen.

The media had trumpeted the divorce, especially quoting those who predicted Richard would vanish from the scene of the gospel. But God was sending a different message. It was Spirit talking to spirit, and it was like Richard was being hurled by heavenly forces into the hot fires of healing evangelism. The results were nothing short of miraculous.

While all that was going on in Richard's life, God began sovereignly dealing with a young woman far away in Florida. Her name was Lindsay Salem.

Lindsay's family had lived in Flint, Michigan, until she was a teenager. Her father, Harry Salem, was the Lincoln-Mercury dealer, and he had been very successful until he became ill with cancer. The family turned to my television ministry for help, learning all they could about healing.

One of Mr. Salem's employees was related to Bob Goodwin, one of the ORU students whose family in Tulsa had been our friends for years. They in turn arranged for me to call Mr. Salem in the Ann Arbor hospital for prayer.

The family was so grateful that I called to pray. Others said, "Why don't you just let Mr. Salem die in dignity?" But the family's faith was very strong. Even the children were believing for a miracle.

Lindsay later told me that she believed her father made a real commitment to Christ during the prayer. And although sometime later Mr. Salem died, his family never forgot our time on the phone.

Lindsay, with her family, continued to watch us regularly on TV, and her mother, Patricia, began writing to us, becoming a Partner of my ministry.

Several years after the father's death, the Salem family moved to Florida where Lindsay completed high school and entered Rollins College. She graduated in 1978 with very good grades and a desire to go to law school. From the time she was a little girl, Lindsay had dreamed of becoming a lawyer. But she wanted to attend a law school that wouldn't conflict with her faith in Jesus Christ. She heard that the O. W. Coburn School of Law of Oral Roberts University was to open in 1979—one year later—and she decided that was where the Lord was leading her.

After working full-time for a year, she applied to ORU's Law School and was accepted. On her way to Tulsa, the Lord began speaking in her heart about a young man named Richard Roberts. She was completely taken by surprise when the Lord kept bringing Richard's name and face before her during the long drive to Tulsa. She was aware that nearly a year earlier Richard had been divorced.

She said to herself, "This is why God has been bringing Richard before me in prayer. He needs help!" But she remembered her own dream of becoming a lawyer, and any relationship with Richard Roberts would get in the way. Also, she did not want to become involved with a divorced man. Meanwhile, God kept dealing with her.

On the first weekend of that school year we conducted an ORU family seminar. It was to be a special time of preaching, singing, personal ministry, and getting to know everyone as we started the new semester.

On Saturday night Richard preached a powerful message titled "What Is Your Biggest Giant?" It was a message taken from the Bible story of David and Goliath and their great battle.

At the close of his message Richard asked all the students to think of the biggest giants that stood in their way of being successful at ORU. A strong time of prayer followed.

Backstage, a friend of Richard's, a student who had also just enrolled in our law school, introduced Richard to Lindsay. Lindsay told him she enjoyed his sermon. And like I do so many times when people say that to me, Richard said, "What did you enjoy the most?"

"I liked the part about your biggest giant," she replied.

Richard said, "Well, what's your biggest giant?"

She looked him straight in the eyes and said, "*You* are."

He felt like saying to his friend, "Thanks a lot for introducing me to this nut." They laughed about it, and Richard thought that was the end of it.

But as the days passed, Richard couldn't stand the suspense any longer. He *had* to know just what that beautiful girl meant by saying he was her biggest giant. Reaching her by telephone, he said, "Will you please explain to me your remark about my being your biggest giant?"

She said, "I came here to go to law school, but God simply will not stop bringing your face before me and telling me that I'm to meet you and that you are hurting and there will be some kind of relationship with you. If that happens, it's going to throw all my plans clear off."

Richard blurted out, "I'm not so sure you really want a relationship with me." A two-hour phone conversation ensued in which Richard told her his story and Lindsay told her story to him. Afterward Richard began to list all of his hurts and problems, telling her he didn't believe in secrets and if that drove her away, they would both save time. But when he finished, she was still there on the line. He invited her out to dinner several nights later.

After they returned that night, Lindsay called her mother. "Mom," she said, "guess who I went out with tonight?"

Her mother very calmly said, "You went out with Richard Roberts."

Lindsay was shocked. "How in the world did you know that?"

"Well, the same God who speaks to you speaks to me, Lindsay. And He spoke in my heart that's what you'd be doing tonight."

The conversation with her mother, who knew nothing of her dating Richard, but who had received a word of knowledge from the Lord about it, eased Lindsay's mind that that was indeed God.

I learned later that as they began to date, Richard came right to the point: "Lindsay, I want a *Bible wife* in every sense of the word—one who won't try to control me, one who will be faithful and stand beside me as a wife, the mother of my children, and who will understand and support God's calling on my life as an evangelist in the healing ministry as well as my work here at ORU. Someday soon God is going to give me a mighty healing ministry, a word of knowledge ministry. Whoever my wife is will be a great part of it and must understand what I am to do with my life and not have any ambition to be a star. I will not even consider dating a person who wants to be famous. I'm not looking for a business partner. I need a wife."

They decided to pray about it and take their time in waiting upon the Lord. They began dating regularly, and their relationship seemed to flourish from the beginning.

During Richard's divorce and the months afterward, he developed an ulcer. He received medical treatment and healing prayers, but it stubbornly held on. Within the first two weeks of his and Lindsay's dating, their earnest and down-to-earth talks, and their utter dependence on God, the ulcer completely disappeared.

He believed that his being healed in the midst of their courtship was one of the most remarkable evidences that perhaps at last he was on the right track for his future and Lindsay for hers.

Three weeks later, both realized they were falling deeply in love with each other. It was not a mere infatuation. It was a love born of God and birthed in their hearts by the Holy Spirit.

Richard saw Lindsay as a woman different from any he had ever met before. She genuinely cared for him. Not because he was Oral Roberts's son, but because, as he said later, "I was me."

He sometimes encountered people who wanted something from him or thought he could do something for them because he was my son. He was always concerned about the people who wanted to be close to him for that reason, and he became somewhat skeptical because of certain people who were trying to use him in relationships. Lindsay understood that. By loving him just for himself, she helped break down those walls of skepticism in him.

Something else even more serious concerned him during that period. He was worried about the hard road of criticism that would face them if they married. That became his chief topic of prayer.

His mother and I committed him to God in our prayers and left him, in a sense, to work it out by himself. Although he was our son, it was his life, and over time he would have to find his own way with God's purpose.

Richard and Lindsay began to talk seriously about marriage. He asked her if she thought she was prepared for the onslaught of criticism—the backlash she would receive as his wife—from people who might misunderstand his remarriage, maybe from people who were close to them.

Lindsay said, "Since I was twelve, I've grown up under this ministry. I've heard it and read it until I feel like it's part of my very being. I have the support of my family, and if I have the support of yours, that will make a tremendous difference in coping with the criticism."

Richard told his mother that he and Lindsay were planning to get married, that they cared for each other very deeply. He asked if Lindsay could come up to the house and talk to her.

Evelyn said, "Sure."

So Lindsay told Evelyn some things about herself and her family and said she was really in love with Richard and wanted to marry him.

In relating the conversation to me, Evelyn told me she said, "Lindsay, Richard has been married, as you know. You've never been, have you?"

"No, I haven't," Lindsay replied.

"Lindsay, if you were my daughter, I would tell you to find a man who has never been married and not to be marrying a divorced man."

"But, Mrs. Roberts," she said, "I love Richard."

"Well, you think you do now!"

"No! Not only do I love him, but it is God's will that I marry him. The Lord spoke to me even before I came to Tulsa."

"Lindsay, Richard has been beaten down hard from his first marriage. He is not fully recovered. If you marry Richard, your first years together will be hard ones financially, too! Are you sure you are ready for that?"

"Oh, yes," Lindsay said. "The Lord has prepared my heart. I not only want to marry your son, but I want to be a Bible wife to him and help meet his needs. Mrs. Roberts, I'm not in this for money. [And she meant it.] We also plan to have children."

Evelyn told me there were several moments of stillness as both women were weighing the situation. Then Lindsay looked straight at her. "We'll make it just fine with the Lord's help."

"Lindsay, there's something else," Evelyn said. "You've never been criticized, and you will be if you marry Richard."

"Yes, I know," Lindsay replied, "but I have assurance from the Holy Spirit that everything will be all right."

The Spirit of God began to move in Evelyn as she listened intently to Lindsay's words. So she said, "Well, Lindsay, you're a lovely girl, and it's evident you and Richard know the mind of God in this decision. I'm proud to have my son marry you. Oral and I will help you all we can."

Richard felt led to bring Lindsay to talk to me. The Spirit of the Lord had already revealed the rightness of Richard and Lindsay's relationship. So when she walked into the room, I said to Lindsay, "So this is Richard's bride!" Somehow I knew, as Evelyn did, that the coming marriage was of God. After that, I reinforced what Evelyn had told her, telling her there had been nothing easy about our lives.

"Mine hasn't been exactly easy, either," she said, mentioning losing her father from cancer at twelve and growing up without a dad. Shortly after that, her mother had become ill with cancer but was miraculously healed. "I withstood every criticism of coming to attend the ORU law school. I've spent a lot of time with Richard, and I think I know pretty well what you're saying. One thing we both have is peace about this marriage. The Lord is very close to us, and we are not acting hastily. We both need and want your blessing."

Taking the hand of the lovely dark-skinned Lebanese girl in mine, I prayed with her. A great sense of peace filled my heart, and I *knew* that they were entering the marriage with the greatest care and dependence upon God. I gave her my blessing, also my promise that as a member of our family, she would be our daughter as Richard was our son.

A remarkable thing happened. One particular week, our chapel speaker was Dr. Kenneth Hagin. He certainly was not one of the people who knew anything about Richard and Lindsay's situation. After he preached and while the faculty, the administrators, and the entire student body were still present, the Spirit of prophecy came upon him.

We had known Dr. Hagin for many years. Our whole family loved him and knew he was a prophet of God. We'd seen him prophesy many times, and not one of the prophecies had failed to come to pass.

He turned toward Richard, and although he didn't speak in specifics, Richard knew in his spirit exactly what Dr. Hagin was talking about. He said, "Richard, the thing that you have been praying about, and you've been concerned about what people are going to think and say and do, it is of God. Do it, and don't worry about what they think or say or do."

Richard looked out over the audience at Lindsay's reaction and saw her. She looked like she was going to slide under her seat! They were probably the only two people in the building, except

Evelyn and me, who knew what Brother Hagin was talking about. Lindsay knew *exactly* what he meant and she knew that he knew.

Richard and Lindsay didn't feel led to go up to Dr. Hagin to talk to him about the prophetic message he had given. They just accepted it as being another confirmation from the Lord. However, after they were married, Richard had an occasion to talk to him about it. He said, "Dr. Hagin, that day in chapel when you gave the word of prophecy to me, did you know the implications of what the Lord was having you say?"

A big grin came across his face and he said, "Well, Richard, I'll tell you this. I could have told you her name, but I didn't think it was appropriate right then."

After finishing the fall semester in law school, Lindsay returned to her mother and family in Florida. She and Richard were keeping their wedding plans very quiet. From Florida, she called the Director of Admissions at ORU and said, "I'm officially withdrawing from ORU. Law school is just not for me." But she didn't tell the other reason—the fact that she and Richard would be getting married in a few weeks.

What she didn't know was that she and Richard might not marry at all. After she had gone, Richard asked the leadership of Oral Roberts Evangelistic Association and Oral Roberts University to permit him to sit before them that they might judge his decision as the elders of the ministry. They included ordained ministers of our graduate school of theology, Rev. Bob DeWeese, my associate evangelist in the crusades, other leaders of the crusades, and deans and other leaders throughout the university—fifteen in all.

Richard submitted his case of his desire to remarry. It was one of the hardest things he ever did. I deliberately refrained from being present. Both Richard and I wanted them to know that we were willing to submit to spiritual authority, although I was the leader of the ministry and Richard held a position at my side.

Richard asked them to hear him out, to freely share their leading from the Lord and His Word, then to lay hands on him in unity for what they believed was God's final word on his decision. His submission was so definite that had they not felt his decision was of the Lord, he would have reconsidered the whole thing, called Lindsay, and canceled the marriage.

"I'm asking for your blessing if I remarry," he said, "but I will abide by your decision." ·

That was the last confirmation for the peace he needed for Lindsay and him before they got married.

I learned that, to Richard's joy, the leaders weighed the matter, brought it unitedly before the Lord in prayer, and then threw their arms around Richard and applauded him for his submissive spirit and for living clean before God in the year that he had been single. In essence, they said, "We've seen you and Lindsay together, your lives blending together in God's love, and we have a good feeling in our hearts about this marriage. We support you 100 percent, and you have our blessing."

In Richard's eyes and in mine, there were no more hurdles to their being married as soon as possible. He boarded an airplane and flew to Florida. He married Lindsay on January 11, 1980.

God had given him not only a second chance at living but also a second chance at love. Enough years have passed to see this new step in the light of God's Word and His blessing.

God has truly given Richard a Bible wife in Lindsay. I've seen her stand in the midst of the fires, her spirit strong, the anointed words flowing beautifully out of her mouth, and her can-do spirit going into Richard, telling him, "Richard, you can do it!" The effect has been miraculous.

They have proven that they are one of God's anointed and trusted couples who, with their children, have helped set a new standard of Spirit-led living and doing.

My Indian forebears said, "You've got to walk in the other fellow's moccasins before you can understand what he has been through." I thank God for the hundreds of thousands of people, married and single, who have caught the vision through Richard and Lindsay that God is the God of a second chance.

Richard was a late bloomer, but when he began to bloom, it seemed God sent the rain and put the bloom on the sage. It was beautiful to watch. In his healing ministry, he was having huge crusades overseas, was frequently ministering in churches and conferences in America, and was on live daily television nationwide. He served as executive vice president next to me on all ORU responsibilities, presided over the ORU chapel services, preached, and taught. He was becoming his own man and was being seen as God's man.

In the face of tremendous hardship, he was becoming fear-less and capable. He and Lindsay lost their first child, Richard Oral, within thirty-six hours of his birth, but I saw him deter-mined to obey God, no matter the cost. Prior to little Richard Oral's death, Lindsay had two miscarriages. And then an ovarian tumor required surgery that could very well have led to a total hysterectomy.

But Evelyn and I watched this young woman of God stand up tall in her faith and believe God would save the ovary. Just before the scheduled surgery the doctor came into Lindsay's hospital room to explain the procedure and what the tumor was like. He said, "Lindsay, it's like a mountain in you."

Lindsay said, "Doctor, did you say mountain? Jesus said I can speak to my mountain, and it will obey me!"

When the surgery was performed, the tumor that had been seen on ultrasound, X ray, and B-scan had totally vanished, and Lindsay was healed.

Three precious daughters have now come along, Jordan Lindsay, Catherine Olivia, and Chloe Elisabeth. They are truly blessings from heaven. Added to that, when Christi and Juli, Richard's two oldest daughters, reached age eighteen, they chose to live with their daddy and attend ORU. They didn't stop loving their mother, but their unceasing love for their daddy drew them to him. Lindsay received them with open arms.

The maturity in Richard was continuing at a very fast pace, es-pecially as he continued to take a stronger role on television and in Oral Roberts University. He was also being hit by the media almost as much as his dad was, yet I felt he had a gift from God to deal with it. I saw his humanness, his mistakes, and his shortcomings, but I knew God had no perfect ones to work with, only those who would be "willing and obedient" (Isa. 1:19).

God spoke in Richard's spirit that he is to minister in forty dif-ferent nations, always at the request of the leader of that country, such as a president or a king. He knew his dad in the fifties and sixties had suffered severe persecution, sometimes because I had to go in the back door with either no sponsors or sponsors who had no clout with the government. In those days, the Full Gospel people overseas often had little or no influence with the govern-ments where they served as missionaries. Therefore I had no covering, except the faith of myself, my associates, and the Partners. I had paid the price, and it didn't often need to be paid again.

In almost every nation he has gone to so far, an invitation from the leader has first come to him, sometimes through a letter, at other times through a top aide arriving in Tulsa to invite him. I think that is no small thing as a confirmation that he heard God speak to him. Richard has also been invited to minister God's healing power personally to these leaders or their relatives in their government chambers or homes. In one nation, he led fourteen members of the ruling family to Christ.

Richard, through my example and through a special leading he felt from God, began to preach to many black congregations in churches and in ministers' conferences, mainly through personal invitation of the bishops. He has probably preached in more black churches and conferences than any other white man of this generation. He greatly loves them, and he feels their love in return. His ministry is chiefly responsible for the 20 percent of black students we average each year at ORU, which has added a richness in spirit we didn't have before. Many of ORU's black graduates are heads of businesses, members of the White House staff, pastors of thriving churches they started from scratch, officials in their denominations, professors in universities, including ORU, and leaders in many other fields.

Richard is due a lot of credit for that much progress. He has always known his dad's heart about black people, as I knew the heart of my own dad as a preacher for this great race of God's people. This feeling has extended beyond black people. The minority students of different races constitute one-third of the ORU student body. According to the percentages of these races in America, that is a high percentage—the highest, we've been told, of any private school other than a school built for one minority race.

I can remember a special moment in 1977. In the ORU cafeteria the Spirit of prophecy came upon me. I leaned over to one of our finest black students, a rising young star for the Lord, Carlton Pearson, and said, "Listen carefully, Carlton. Hear this in your soul. Carry it with you. The next great outpouring of the Holy Spirit, and the mighty healing power of God, is to be upon black people, and you're to be one of the major leaders in it. It's the black race's hour to look up to their true Source—God—and expect an outpouring of His grace and gifts as they've never known before as a race of people."

Recently, Carlton reminded me of those words as he shared with me his soul in the great Azusa conference he holds annually in the Mabee Center on the ORU campus and in some ten major cities across America. Up to ten thousand people throng the meetings in every service, believing the hour of the great black race is coming into fulfillment of this prophecy. Carlton, who is like a son to me, said, "There have been other prophecies of the same thing happening, but it never struck fire in me until that moment in the cafeteria when you held both of my hands and said those words to me."

Today, Carlton Pearson sees the Azusa move ultimately sweeping across America as an answer to some of the most serious problems of a people who are seeing fathers and sons going to prison in an unprecedented way. He believes it will also help bring the Holy Spirit into black churches in the measure Reverend Seymour first led the Azusa Street Holy Spirit outpouring in Los Angeles at the beginning of the century.

ORU is an ecumenical campus, it is a Holy Spirit–led campus, and the racial diversity—in its unity—is the way it should be. It pleases God and benefits everybody and everything.

———— *Papa Was Right*

At age seventy-two, I announced to the ORU Board of Regents that I would not serve as president of Oral Roberts University past my seventy-fifth birthday. I told them that after watching Richard work his way up for twenty years in everything I had required of him in my ministry and at ORU, and seeing him stay the course against all odds, I was recommending that he succeed me as president and chief executive officer.

"However," I told the Regents, "my recommendation, as you know, is not binding on the Board. You are legally free to elect whoever you feel God wants you to. My announcement is to help set your spirit into seeking God for His choice as the second president of Oral Roberts University. I will have served the first thirty years of its chartering as your president. I hope the second president can serve as long and be as much in God's will."

The one thing I did not want to do was to fall into the trap that as I grew older, a spirit of possessiveness would grip me, causing me to hang on long after I had given my greater usefulness. I think nothing can be worse than that.

When I was a young pastor and left pastoring a church, I told the people not to write to me except in a matter of life or death, or I wouldn't answer them. I set the line so the new pastor could have his best opportunity to be the pastor. I felt that way as my time as head of ORU was drawing to a close.

The Board took me seriously, as I prayed they would. They knew we were dealing with the most sensitive, the most spiritual, and the most recognized academic university existing in the charismatic world. The election was set for January 27, 1993, three days after my seventy-fifth birthday.

Then the Enemy struck!

On October 6, 1992, I suffered a massive heart attack. I saw Satan trying to take me out before my time, knowing those next few months would be the most crucial. But then I saw that God stretched out His mighty hands (and with the doctors working over me) to take hold of my heart and do something so miraculous that less than a year later, the doctors could not find any sign I had ever had a heart attack. The merging of God's healing streams of medicine and prayer had worked for me again, something I wished for every sick person on earth.

Of the people who are stricken as I was, I'm told that 80 percent die; another 16 percent carry dangerous scars on their hearts; only 4 percent do not. I'm in the 4 percent who survived to complete health again.

As I recall this remarkable deliverance of God giving me back my health from a disease that is the number one killer in the United States, I think of the wee hours of that first night after the angioplasty. It was four o'clock in the morning. The doctors had left. My nurses were busy with others. Dr. Ralph Wilkerson, pastor of Melodyland Christian Center in Anaheim and my faithful friend for over thirty-five years, had spent the night there and slipped in several times to pray for my restoration. Of course, I was not aware of Ralph's presence because I was not yet fully awake from the emergency surgical procedure.

I came awake in the dark room and took several moments to orient myself. When I grasped the fact of what had happened and where I was, I wanted to pray. I couldn't get the words up from my throat, which was really hurting because of the tubes the surgeon had to place there. When I can't pray, I'm devastated in any circumstance. That was the worst of all.

Then it dawned on me I *could* pray. I had the baptism of the Holy Spirit. I could pray in tongues at will—even under my breath. I had done it many times before with my prayer language of the Spirit when I was in a crowd, with a small group, or with two or three other persons. I could feel the Holy Spirit coming up in my belly area, words given by the Holy Spirit Himself, words that were not created by my mind but by the Holy Spirit and my spirit together.

As the tears rolled down my cheeks, my mind struggling with the thought I might die in that room, I can't tell you of the joy I felt as by my will and faith I was able to bring up the words from my inner man. Although the words were under my breath, they were clear and distinct, and I knew I was talking to my heavenly Father.

As is my custom, according to the apostle Paul's direction in 1 Corinthians 14:13, "Wherefore let him that speaketh in an unknown tongue pray that he may interpret," when I had prayed in the Spirit, I asked God to let me interpret His response to my mind. The interpretation came in six words:

"You shall live and not die."

Instantly, I fell asleep and didn't awaken until the next morning. Richard had arrived from Tulsa and was standing there praying for me. I was so glad to see him, not only because he was my son, but because he was now operating in a powerful healing ministry. If there's anyone I want to see when I'm seriously ill or something else is going wrong, it's a believer exercising the healing power of Jesus.

I heard Richard praying in the Spirit, and then I heard his words as he took me in his arms: "Dad, the Holy Spirit has just told me, 'You shall not die but live.'"

The sun was shining into my room, but there was another shining. The prophet Malachi speaks of it: "But unto you that fear my name shall the Sun of righteousness arise with healing in his wings" (Mal. 4:2). The pain that had been excruciating was gone. I felt light all over. I was going to live. And the way the interpretation came to me, then was confirmed to Richard by the Spirit, it meant I would live and "be in health."

I knew that because 3 John 2 had flooded my spirit: "Beloved, I wish above all things that thou mayest prosper and be in health, even as thy soul prospereth." The words that stood out were "and *be* in health."

By that time, Dr. John Hagee, of the Cornerstone Church of San Antonio, who had flown in with Richard on the same plane from Dallas on their way to Orange County, California, was there. As he prayed, he looked at me and said, "Brother Oral, God has said this is not unto death. You shall live and not die."

He had no more than gotten the words out of his mouth before Dr. Tommy Barnett, pastor of the large First Assembly of God Church in Phoenix, flew in. Without knowing what the Spirit had said, he got the same words as he prayed for me.

Then my longtime friend, Bill Swad, of Columbus, Ohio—the Chevrolet dealer there and also a minister of the gospel—flew two thousand miles to reach me after he heard on the nation's news that I had been stricken. He got the same interpretation.

Ralph Wilkerson was standing nearby, smiling, nodding his head in agreement, and it came to me what a good God I served, what an awesome God we have. I had been alone in the room praying in tongues under my breath and getting the word direct by interpretation from the Father that the massive heart attack would not take me out or leave me incapacitated. And the Scripture came to me, "That in the mouth of two or three witnesses every word may be established" (Matt. 18:16).

There were more than two or three witnesses to confirm the revelation, "You shall live and not die." There was also a preciousness engulfing me of such men of God, all with charismatic gifts of the Spirit, getting up in the night, flying for hours, converging in my room. And dear Ralph Wilkerson was already in the area. Without knowing what God had said to me or to each other, the men received the same words of life for a servant of the Lord.

More than two years have passed since that night. No happier man is there over this than Dr. Myla, along with his team at Hoag Hospital in Newport Beach. He humbly refused to take the credit, saying, "It was God and us together who did this."

As for me, everything I've ever done in the healing ministry, in seeking to merge God's healing streams of prayer and medicine together, has given me an inner vindication of my call and of my healing ministry that Jesus is a healing Christ and He is in the "now" of every one of our lives!

My strength has returned. I rejoice because there are no scars on my heart, and at age seventy-seven, I'm still praying for people and turning out prodigious amounts of work, including writing this autobiography by hand and getting it published so that many will know how God can take even the smallest and most unworthy life and raise it up to glorify His name.

God almighty allowed me to be at ORU's annual Board meeting on my seventy-fifth birthday as, one by one, the Regents spoke their feelings about Richard. Just before the vote, Richard asked our able chairlady Marilyn Hickey if he could say a word.

"If you are voting for me because I'm my father's son, then I don't want to be elected. However, if you believe in your hearts that I am God's man for this job, then I want it," he said.

There was a brief moment of silence, then the vote was called for. Richard was elected unanimously on the first ballot to be ORU's second president and chief executive officer and I was to be chancellor.

I knew it was right; so did my darling wife, Evelyn. She and I had helped grow a president. We both felt his grandfather Roberts, who was up in heaven, was saying, "See, I told you Richard would be president someday." Papa was right. He was not president of a nation; he was president of God's university.

I had believed my strength was in building, but Richard's would be in managing. That has proven to be an accurate assessment. God had said to me, "*Build* Me a university," but God was saying to Richard, "*Run* Me a university."

The university had been built debt free and had continued that way until 1987 when the so-called televangelist scandals struck along with the recession in America. My ministry and I had not been involved, but we took some, what I believed to be, satanic hits financially. Nevertheless, we continued to grow in ORU's enrollment and our ministry outreach. Many people who had been blessed through the ministry and who had been among its chief supporters seemed to believe everything the out-of-control news media paraded before the nation. The whole inference was that because two or three highly visible ministers "fell," the rest were not trustworthy. Whatever the reason, income went down, and we entered a struggle to keep the ministry and ORU alive and on a sound financial base.

When Richard received the mantle on January 27, 1993, he faced all the bills and the seemingly impossible task of getting everything financially back on track. Well, he has been a pleasant surprise. In spite of being handed the leadership of the university when it was in debt, Richard's spirit was up. He rolled up his sleeves and told the devil to get out of the way! His management style is quite different from mine. However, it works, and works well, even beyond our expectations. The finances have slowly improved, and the endowment fund is once again beginning to get some help. We are not where we need to be yet in our finances, but the dawn is breaking. I'm convinced God will get His university out of debt and see it through. It may be out of debt by the time this book is published. It is His property, not ours.

When I look at Richard, as he has assumed the full duties of president and chief executive officer of Oral Roberts University and president of Oral Roberts Evangelistic Association (I remain chairman and chief executive officer of Oral Roberts Evangelistic Association) and also the worldwide healing ministry, I shake my head. I've often said, "He's the most improbable choice of anyone I would ever have thought of."

I'm reminded of what the Lord told Samuel the prophet when he was choosing someone to anoint as the next king of Israel. As the father, Jesse, paraded all of his older, seemingly more capable sons, the Lord spoke to Samuel and said, "Man looketh on the outward appearance, but the Lord looketh on the heart." Finally, Jesse brought in David, the youngest son who was just a shepherd boy. When the great prophet approached David, the Lord said, "Anoint him: for this is he." He was God's choice. And the Bible says that the Spirit of the Lord came on him from that moment (1 Sam. 16:7, 12).

Richard is fulfilling Papa's prophecy, and God's, too. He truly *is* God's choice!

The best thing of all to me is that Richard's healing ministry is exploding. The same powerful anointing and healing spirit that permeated ORU from its founding is there, except I honestly believe it's stronger than it's ever been as President Richard Roberts, the administration and faculty, the student body, and the Board of Regents have closed ranks in an openness to the Holy Spirit and in a unity that is truly a gift of God.

That doesn't keep me as the founder and the first president from praying every day that what God began in ORU will continue to thrive. I'm not alone in those prayers. Friends and Partners, pastors and others across this nation and many other nations, are praying, also. They feel ORU is their university because God led them to help build it and to keep it going until Jesus returns. This is a strength that doesn't always meet the eye. As the original leader of such a university, with its size and scope and audacity, I was catapulted into the limelight far beyond the ordinary, and it also bears my name. But God knows, I know, my family knows, and our Partners and friends know it's not just a Roberts's university; it is God's, and it is to continue being His.

Now let me tell you about a very special young woman.

CHAPTER 23

ROBERTA—
A VERY SPECIAL DAUGHTER

R OBERTA WAS born December 14, 1950. She was a beautiful child with blue eyes, heavy black hair, and a winning smile. She was not very outgoing, unless she was alone with her mother or with girlfriends her age. She was the shyest of our four children, an eager learner, and a lover of the Bible and her dad's healing ministry and all things of the Lord.

Roberta, from a child, saw things through the lens of all we taught the children about Jesus. All the "little Jesus" books would end up with her, and she memorized much of the content.

Of the four children, Roberta seemed to have the least fun, liking the times she could be alone with her books and her dreams. She often seemed insecure, and she had to be assured over and over again that we loved her. While I was in the crusades and often overseas, Roberta would often say to Evelyn, "Nobody loves me."

Each time I phoned home, I made it a point to talk not only to Evelyn but also to each child. Rebecca was always grown-up in her talk, and she felt self-reliant. Ronnie would have a story to tell me or a question to ask about what he had run across in school or about the Bible. Richard just had a good time talking to his dad. Roberta was more withdrawn; I had to keep talking until she opened up. Each time that I would say, "Roberta, I love you," she would say, "I love you, too, Daddy."

When Evelyn would ask her what her daddy said to her, she would reply, "Oh, he loves me."

Roberta made straight A's at Memorial High School. She was a student like Ronnie. I've never seen a girl apply herself better to her studies. We were proud of her.

When Roberta began to attend ORU, she loved everything about it. She absorbed its spirit into her being. She took part in its main areas—academics, aerobics, and spiritual life—with quiet determination. She was also at the top of her classes.

She and her father were much alike in the things we dreamed for God's purpose for ORU. During her four years in the undergraduate school and her three in the law school, she saw God was plowing new ground with ORU as one of His sharpest plows. At last, He found a man who would obey Him in building Him a university, while keeping the healing ministry at its heart, and He found an administration, faculty, students, and Partners who would be sensitive to His every move and respond to His will.

As I watched her study and grow and dream my dreams with me, Roberta caught the vision early, just as she had done when she grew up in the healing crusades. Believing and seeing the supernatural were as natural to her as eating and drinking.

Dr. Howard Ervin, a professor in the seminary and one of our ablest charismatic speakers, saw the soul hunger of my daughter. She was in every service of a seminar where he was a leader, and she had her hands outstretched to God, seeking to be baptized with the Holy Spirit.

Howard is one of the most learned and articulate men on our faculty. He carries himself in the Spirit like a prince and talks like a king. You notice him and you listen to him when he is merely being himself. He earned his doctorate at Princeton's theology seminary and received the baptism of the Holy Spirit at the International Conference of the Full Gospel Business Men's Convention under its founder, Demos Shakarian, held that year at Miami Beach, Florida. The Holy Spirit was as real to him as to any man I'd ever known. When he saw Roberta so hungry for God and learned she wanted to be filled with the Holy Spirit and be able to release her prayer language, he turned aside to help her.

Among Dr. Ervin's many gifts is his extraordinary gift to sense when a person is ready to receive the baptism of the Holy Spirit and to pray a quick but powerful prayer for her. Almost as soon as he touched Roberta, the power of the Holy Spirit flowed up within her, and she began to speak in a most beautiful language in the Holy Spirit.

One of the most satisfying and closest times we ever had together came later after she was satisfied God had baptized her with His Holy Spirit. We sat down and prayed in tongues together, effortlessly, with "joy unspeakable and full of glory." The timidity with which she had grown up had given way to a boldness I had not seen in her before.

Roberta had always been a serious girl. She saw life in terms of black and white with hardly any shades between. God was good, the devil was bad, the Bible was the Word of God, there was a plan for her life, and her steps would be ordered of the Lord. Not many girls at her early age were so affirmative in their views and convictions.

She had no doubt that there was a young man waiting to be her husband who came from her same background, who loved God first and foremost, and who would love her as she loved him. Ron Potts, son of an Assembly of God pastor in Iowa and of a beautiful mother who was sold out to God, fit the bill. They met at ORU and fell in love. After some very cautious checking of her spirit and Ron's, Roberta knew he was for her. Ron loved her the same way, although he was not like her in temperament.

Ron had been an athlete at junior college, but since his parents wanted him to come to ORU, he gave up athletics and secured three jobs to support himself toward his graduation. He understood things of the Spirit, he loved the healing ministry, and he loved ORU.

Their marriage was a highlight for both families.

After her graduation, Roberta and Ron moved to Colorado where he became a coach, and she took a job as a paralegal secretary for a lawyer in Denver. She loved it. Her boss loaded her with work but couldn't work her down. When the law school opened at ORU, Roberta got her lifelong wish. Like her great-grandfather Roberts, like me with my early desire for my life, Roberta wanted to be a lawyer. When she moved back to Tulsa to help me at ORU, then to enter our law school, the lawyer in Denver who was head of his firm said, "I'm only willing to give Roberta up because I know she will make a fine lawyer."

I wanted Roberta to learn everything about ORU from the ground up, starting at the mailing and shipping department. I

wanted her to work her way through every department until she
knew firsthand how it related to the other departments in the university and to the ministry as a whole.

Right in the midst of Roberta's working her way through every
department, she entered the law school. By that time, she had two
major responsibilities in addition to being a wife—two fine little
sons—Randy and Stephen.

It fell on Ron to assume the responsibility of keeping the house
going and raising the sons. Ron saw it all in the light of this question: What does God want? Ron was the kind of young man of God
who rolled with the punches and had an easygoing manner. He
was bright and supportive.

Roberta fell in love with the administrative side of ORU in
which I was training Richard, under the direction of Provost
Hamilton and other leaders on campus. Richard was also with
me in all my major decisions. He was being tested "as by fire"
(1 Cor. 3:15).

In effect, Roberta had come right behind Richard in learning
from the ground up until she was placed under the guidance of the
highest academic area. She was to work there until she had a good
understanding of academic leadership under Provost Hamilton.

Richard had done it; now Roberta was doing it. The difference
was, Richard, upon spending sufficient time there, moved on with
me in being my right hand in all phases of both ORU and the ministry. That would be his supreme test. He knew I was giving him
an opportunity and not a guaranteed position. In the final analysis,
he would have to pay the piper and earn it.

Roberta, as I saw it, fell in love with helping to run the school
academically and helping us make sure we were putting the Lord
first. Her keen eyes saw things that needed correction, and she
went at them with a vengeance. Anything that would threaten the
balance of ORU academically, aerobically, and/or spiritually was to
be corrected or moved out of the way. At that point, she was worth
her weight in gold.

By that time, two forces began fighting inside her: to be an academic leader and to become a lawyer. The wellsprings of her heart
were fed with a fierce determination to find her place and fill it.

Since childhood, Roberta and Richard, while having a love for
each other, seemed to be on different wavelengths. I suppose

because Richard loved all the things I did, including farm life with horses and cows, and golf, and the ministry, it appeared I spent more time with him as the children grew up.

I don't think it bothered Rebecca and Ronnie, for they were our first set of children. There was a difference of five years between the time when Ronnie was born and when Richard was born, with Roberta coming along two years later. The two older children were born *before* the healing ministry began, the last two *after* it started. It seemed they were two different sets of children.

The major difference between Richard and Roberta was that Richard was a happy-go-lucky boy and Roberta was a serious girl. They clashed at an early age, yet if one of them was challenged by someone else, they would fight for each other. As children, Richard was especially protective of his little sister, although he loved to tantalize her, which she hated with a passion.

For whatever reason, by the time Richard began to fit in with me at the university, Roberta seemed to feel left out. At least that's the way it appeared to her mother and me.

Roberta wanted to feel equal to Richard. By the time Richard had gone through the process of getting his education at ORU, then marrying, and working with me, starting at point zero, I was putting Roberta through the same duties as far as fitting into my ministry and ORU were concerned. As a man who considered excellence a priority, I thought it was not *who* is right but *what* is right.

Richard knew that. I'm not sure Roberta did. That was normal because children, who want to fit in with their parents' work or call, take for granted more or less they will have a top position in it.

My associates closest to me knew that however much I loved my family, the bottom line was, Who could help carry on the work best, family or nonfamily? They also knew I felt the Roberts name was both a help and a hindrance. That is why I told all my children they had to do better than others in order to be recognized for themselves or to be appreciated as standing on their own faith and two feet.

Whether Roberta intended it or not, it appeared her love for the academic leadership meant someday she wanted that job to be hers and that I would give it to her. It became evident to me she felt she had a long way to go to catch up with her brother in her dad's eyes.

One day, when I was talking out loud to myself with some of my associates, I said I hoped Richard could be "Mr. Outside," and Roberta, "Mrs. Inside," at ORU, speaking of the years down the road. Roberta picked up on that while Richard simply put it in the back of his mind. He knew there would be no free lunches, even for him as my son or for Roberta as my daughter.

In the midst of going to ORU's Law School, Roberta came to me to ask my advice on dropping out.

"Didn't you feel God wants you to be a lawyer someday?" I asked.

"Yes."

"Aren't you making good grades?"

"Yes."

"Don't you love it?"

"Yes, but. . . ."

"But what, Roberta?"

"How can I ever be 'Mrs. Inside' if I'm a lawyer?" she asked.

I saw where she was going. "Roberta, honey, if God really wants you to work inside ORU with your having another degree, don't you think He knows how to work that out?"

"But wouldn't a Ph.D. be better?"

"In your case, maybe so, maybe not."

"What do you mean?" she asked.

"You've always wanted to be a lawyer. Changing now, in your second year of law school, is a serious move. You could get off God's track for you."

"Well, I'm not happy in law school."

"Is someone mistreating you?" I asked.

"Oh, no, I was never treated better. Dean Charles Kothe is excited that I'll be a lawyer. He believes I'll be a good one. I'm excited about it, too."

I said, "Roberta, do you remember as a twelve-year-old girl, you were taking both piano and organ lessons? You remember the day you came to me much like you have today and said you weren't happy, especially on learning to play the organ, and you asked if you could give it up?"

"I remember."

"Do you remember what I advised you?"

"Yes, you said if down deep in my heart the organ was not for me, I should give it up. If I wasn't sure, I should stay with it."

"Well, you stayed with it. Now you are excellent on both piano and organ. Are you sorry?"

"Oh, no."

"Then isn't there a moral here similar to that?" I asked.

"I hadn't thought of it like that."

"Why don't you make it a matter of supreme prayer? Really get serious with God. He knows your heart, He knows His plan for you, and I'll be praying, too, that you make the right decision."

As I've said, Roberta is a serious person. About two weeks later she saw me and said, "Dad, I'm staying in law school."

"You're clear on it now."

"Very clear."

"What about your feelings on academic leadership now?"

"God can make that clear, too."

Roberta wasn't over her academic yearnings, not by a long shot. She was staying in law school, determined to get her degree and pass the bar, but the future wasn't clear to her.

Meanwhile, she and her mother had brought pressure to bear on me to hire Ron at ORU. When I had asked Roberta to come into administration, I had made it clear I didn't think it wise to hire both her and Ron. I had hired him earlier in their marriage, but it hadn't worked out and I knew Ron would have no difficulty finding a job elsewhere. After all, he had worked his way through ORU holding down three jobs at the same time.

Meanwhile, Roberta had worked through the different areas, and she was in an office next door to Dr. Hamilton. She loved every part of the ways and means of carrying on the academic responsibilities of ORU while keeping it in harmony with my call.

I had cautioned Dr. Hamilton to work with Roberta in the same way he had with Richard, giving her every opportunity but not abrogating any part of the responsibility I had placed upon his shoulders. He assured me he would do that.

But there were mitigating circumstances. Roberta saw that working directly under the chief academic officer gave her instant access to every department. With her sharp mind, she found herself unconsciously going around Dr. Hamilton. I didn't feel it was intentional. It was just her burning desire to fulfill her potential. The way Roberta carried herself, and said so well what she wanted to say, appealed to the academic people of ORU and to the student body.

Dr. Hamilton never let me know, but one day I discovered Roberta had moved from her office area to admissions. I called her.

"Dad, I'm not getting anywhere in Dr. Hamilton's office. He's running the academics of the school."

"Sure he is. That's his responsibility."

"But I thought. . . ."

"Roberta, Richard learned everything he could from Carl, who's a top professional, and you remember that's all I wanted you to do."

"Well, they needed me in admissions."

"Roberta, there's no question with your analytical mind you can find something wrong in every department. But that's not your assignment right now. Just report any findings to Dean Hamilton, and he'll fix them or bring them to my attention. You see, one of the difficulties is that as my daughter, you feel you can bypass everybody and come straight to me, the president. Maybe you should do that in extreme cases, but it won't work all the time."

My comments hurt her deeply. I could tell I had made a serious mistake by opening my mouth when I mentioned her being "Mrs. Inside." What *I meant* by it was one thing; what *it meant to her* was another thing.

I berated myself for not watching more closely and for not being sensitive to my deeper feelings. I could have saved embarrassing her had I been more diligent.

Roberta had her law degree by then, and the academic community called her Dr. Potts. Dean Hamilton had assured me he had called the North Central accrediting body and discovered those with law degrees acting in an academic capacity were called Doctor. It was perfectly proper to call Roberta Dr. Potts. She had, indeed, earned the doctor of jurisprudence.

Things came to a head quickly. I believe she sensed in her spirit that her immediate future didn't lie high up with ORU. I could be wrong in this. However, she came into my office with Ron one day and said she was leaving.

Ron told her he thought she was making a mistake.

I expressed my feelings: "Don't leave now, Roberta. Things will work out, but you'll have to understand your dad is not just your dad but the president of ORU and subject to the Board of

Regents. I'm doing the best I know how, and I don't feel you can, by being my daughter, appear to move from one place to another without my express permission. Richard didn't and you shouldn't."

As she was leaving, I asked Ron to intervene. He said, "No, she's my wife. I'm sticking with her."

I admired him for that.

Suddenly, it hit me. She had passed the bar. She was ready for her law practice. God was "stirring her nest" to leave what seemed so attractive and get on with the career God had in mind all the time. She had gained so many important things by learning ORU from the ground up, by getting her law degree as part of her working contract. Her world was waiting—a world that would inevitably have to do with Oral Roberts University and her favorite ministry, the healing ministry of the Lord Jesus Christ.

Roberta formed her own firm, and her work has flourished. She appears regularly on radio talk programs. Her legal services are sought after by several ORU people, church people, and many outsiders. She appears very happy in her career.

There is a great new world out there for my daughter, and I have never been more proud of her, of Ron, and of my two fine grandsons, who are both over six feet tall, dedicated to the Lord as they pursue their schoolwork. Stephen is a freshman at the Air Force Academy, and Randy is a senior at Oklahoma University. Ron manages the business end of the law firm and also works in stocks and bonds. What could have been a break in the family has turned out better than we could have expected at the time.

As head of her own law firm, Roberta is carrying out the purpose that was the slogan of the ORU Law School: "Lawyers should be healers"—not only trial lawyers but *mediators* according to the biblical meaning of that term. Since much of the original foundation of the system of American law came out of the Bible, especially the Law of Moses, the Ten Commandments, and the Sermon on the Mount by Jesus, it makes me proud to know my daughter is making that live. Our very special daughter is even more special to Evelyn and me and our family, and to the world at large, because she is following God's plan for her life.

Had we not raised two more children, having lost Rebecca and Ronnie in tragic deaths, we would have had none left. As I look at Richard with his tremendous healing ministry and presidency of

Oral Roberts University, and at Roberta with her law practice in which there is a healing aspect to her skills, I'm convinced it was more than my personal desire for two more children. God wanted it and in His own way convinced Evelyn who, when she felt it was the Lord's planning, entered joyously into their births. I owe so much to her for their attitude, and so do all those who are blessed by Richard's and Roberta's strong witnesses for the Lord.

It's not going to be easy to take you into the next phase of my life, but I guarantee it will be fascinating. I've never known greater joy or deeper pain.

PART 6

NOT SO WILD A DREAM

CHAPTER 24

MERGING PRAYER AND MEDICINE— THE LONG, HARD BATTLE BEGINS

A LL THE BATTLES that raged against God's command to me to take His healing power to my generation came to a climax in 1977, exactly thirty years after I began my healing ministry, which is the surprising story I am about to reveal in detail. I carry many scars and feel I know intimately what the apostle Paul felt when he said, "I bear in my body the marks of the Lord Jesus" (Gal. 6:17).

In 1975, ORU was fully accredited and growing at a rapid rate of success. The Spirit of the Lord came upon me and said to me that His timing had come to add seven graduate schools to the mission of ORU.

I believe that four inescapables deal with life: theology, law, medicine, and business. And we were going to establish graduate schools relating to all those areas. It was like the four corners of the earth coming together at the same point. One of the first of the graduate schools was to be a school of medicine where doctors would be trained to merge prayer and medicine in an unprecedented effort to bring what I call God's healing to the whole person.

As I was seeking God in 1947 when He said my time had come to take His healing power to my generation, and someday to merge His healing streams of prayer and medicine, He showed me very clearly that all true healing power is His. He then led me directly to the New Testament, where I saw the two coming together.

I read where Jesus said, "They that are whole need not a physician: but they that are sick" (Luke 5:31). The need is there,

He said, for physicians. When I studied Paul's life as the greatest apostle of all, I saw that he took Dr. Luke on his team. Paul called Luke "the beloved physician" (Col. 4:14), and on another occasion said, "Only Luke is with me" (2 Tim. 4:11).

God made it unmistakably clear to me that He wanted the minister of the soul and the physician of the body side by side, taking the good news of the gospel to the world. I believe that is because health (wholeness) itself is at the very heart of God's plan for mankind.

And God does not separate the natural and supernatural methods of His healing power. "I am the LORD that healeth thee," He said (Exod. 15:26). Many were the ways He did it.

One of the first recorded acts of combining the natural with the supernatural occurred when the people of Israel were confronted with bitter waters on their way to the Promised Land. The prophet, Moses, took a certain kind of small tree, "which when he had cast into the waters, the waters were made sweet" (Exod. 15:25). The doctors I have talked to, who have studied this kind of tree, state it had an ingredient that caused bitterness to be drawn out of water.

That was clearly an act whereby Moses used the word of knowledge (the supernatural), combined with the natural, to heal the waters so the people could drink and not die. Their survival prevented Satan from frustrating God's plan to have a people, the Israelites, who would bring forth the Messiah.

Another example is Isaiah's account of the death sentence on King Hezekiah. On his deathbed, the king cried out to Isaiah, a prophet of God, to call upon Him to stay the hand of death.

We read,

> And it came to pass, afore Isaiah was gone out into the middle court, that the word of the LORD came to him, saying, Turn again, and tell Hezekiah the captain of my people, Thus saith the LORD, the God of David thy father, I have heard thy prayer, I have seen thy tears: behold, I will heal thee: on the third day thou shalt go up unto the house of the LORD. And I will add unto thy days fifteen years; and I will deliver thee and this city out of the hand of the king of Assyria; and I will defend this city for mine own sake, and for my servant David's sake. And Isaiah said, Take a lump of figs. And they took and laid it on the boil, and he recovered (2 Kings 20:4–7).

Notice first, it was a tremendous prayer from the king and a promise that God would add years to his life. But even so, Isaiah had to combine it with nature.

I may not be a Bible scholar as polished as some others; however, I am bold to say I have studied diligently and long. I have gained knowledge of the sweep of the Bible's teaching and events, so that I have been able to put them in proper context as God was dealing with me to merge the natural and the supernatural in a way soundly based on His Word.

In 1975, I was clear in my call from God that the time was rapidly approaching to build the School of Medicine as part of ORU's mission and His purpose to put the natural healing branch of medicine together with the supernatural power of God to heal.

When God told me that I, with a spiritual healing team, was to take His healing power to my generation and to bring healing to the sick bodies of those in the body of Christ, He gave me the call, with the principle and the general outline, but not the fine details. The working out of the human part had yet to be done.

I had immersed myself in what the Bible taught concerning the way God works. I needed to work with top medical people, who also knew Christ as their personal Savior, were Spirit-filled, and were willing to risk their medical reputations with me, a healing evangelist.

It didn't matter that I was the founder of an accredited institution of higher learning. I was still a healing evangelist and always would be. That fact was to become the stumbling block with many of the "powers that be" in the medical community.

The reaction was to be the same with a great many Pentecostal and charismatic leaders in this particular area. They had apparently never seen the correlation of the two systems in the Bible or as part of the Last Day move of God. I had very little encouragement. Some of the Spirit-filled spiritual leaders ignored what I stated was God's call on me; others shook their heads; still others outright opposed me. Although I understood where they were coming from, I had a larger obligation: to obey God rather than man. And God clearly indicated that all systems were go.

A very well-known and influential physician, an orthopedic surgeon, was soon to cross my path at precisely the right time.

When he joined my efforts, shock waves went across the Tulsa medical community and hospital owners.

——— *A Physician Joins a Healing Evangelist*

After graduating from the University of Tennessee College of Medicine and practicing general medicine in private practice, Dr. James E. Winslow was trained to be an orthopedic surgeon with the famous Campbell Clinic in Memphis, which specialized in turning out topflight surgeons in orthopedics. There he first heard of Oral Roberts—and not in a positive way!

At that time, cortisone was a relatively new drug. The clinic had as a patient a little girl with a rare disease. One of Jim's supervising physicians wanted to give her the new drug in the hope it might help her. Giving the drug could be dangerous, but it appeared the child was going to die if she did not get it. So it was a question of choosing the lesser of the two evils: almost certain death without it or some risk with it.

The mother, a widow, was unable to make the decision, so the grandfather had to make it. He refused on the grounds that he didn't wholly trust the "impetuous young physicians who could not come up with anything else but the new drug."

The doctors felt he was withholding from his grandchild her only possible chance to get better. The more they persisted, the more he resisted. Finally, the grandfather told them that he called Oral Roberts to pray and Oral said the girl was going to get well and did not need the medicine.

A short time later, the doctors, after failing to change the grandfather's mind, got together. They were really mad, Jim said, because they assumed the man was telling the truth, and a big argument ensued as to whether somebody representing Oral Roberts, or even Oral himself, would in fact say to withhold the drug that might save the girl's life. They finally decided that although they did not know the man, Oral Roberts, it was unlikely he would have said what the grandfather reported.

Jim said, "Back in the corner of my mind was the question: Is this man Oral Roberts on the level?" He did not know whether I was or not. A few years later, he would discover a great precaution in my ministry in encouraging people to see their doctors and follow their instructions.

Upon completing his orthopedic residency, Jim went into the air force and served as a surgeon. Later he decided to establish his orthopedic practice in Tulsa. He began performing surgery at St. John's Medical Center, then ended up at St. Francis Hospital.

Just after he and his family had settled in, he ran into a friend who asked why he had decided to come to Tulsa. "I really don't know," Jim told him. "But my wife, Sue, and I just felt it is the right place, and we're supposed to be here."

He said his friend jokingly told him, "Well, you can always send your failures to Oral Roberts" (meaning he could send his medically hopeless cases to me as a healing evangelist).

Time passed until 1969, when Jim's wife was diagnosed with ovarian cancer. Although the cancer specialists did not say it with words, Jim knew from the tone of their conversations that Sue was going to die.

Sue's dad, a manufacturer in Mississippi, came to Tulsa, and he and Jim discussed what they were going to do. Between them, they had the money to get the best medical care in the world.

Jim told me later they both believed that a person has some control over her illness by the approach she takes to it. Jim's mother thought a person could either fight the disease or lie around until it killed her—one or the other.

His father-in-law's mother was once a temporary devotee of Mary Baker Eddy, and she read all of her works and believed much of them. She taught her son that a person could influence her state of health by her state of mind and beliefs.

He and his father-in-law discussed that and decided they would try to set in motion a circumstance that would cause everyone who came in contact with Sue to be positive, not negative.

Sue was a Methodist layperson. She began attending a prayer group and received the charismatic experience of speaking in tongues. She told Jim about it, who felt he needed to do a lot of reading and studying on it. He wasn't for it or against it; he was just unschooled about it.

During that time, strange things began happening. Sue did not get terribly sick with radiation therapy, and the chemotherapy did not bother her much. She did not even lose her hair. Jim accused the medical oncologist of not giving her any chemotherapy. But her doctor said that he was giving Sue about twice the usual dose.

Sue told us later that as she lay on the table taking chemotherapy she was saying, "Lord, let Your healing power go into every cell of my body." Soon she recovered.

Jim and Sue have been married many years, and she has not had a problem with cancer since then. This incident would play an extremely important part in what God was about to do in helping Jim understand God's call on my life to merge prayer and medicine.

One night Jim brought Sue and their three children to a basketball game at ORU. Our team had a player from Chattanooga, Tennessee, the state where Jim came from. His name was Richard Fuqua, and he was averaging thirty-six points a game. The ORU basketball team was leading the NCAA Division I in points made and in rebounds.

That night our leading rebounder, Eddie Woods, fell and hit his head on the floor and was carried off. Jim got up and went to see about Eddie. Soon Eddie recovered and went back in the game. Coach Ken Trickey asked if Jim could provide medical care for the ORU basketball team, and Jim told him he would do it.

Two years later, in 1972, I injured one of my knees playing golf, and Coach Trickey said I ought to go see Jim Winslow, an orthopedic surgeon.

After Jim examined my knee, I asked him if he ever prayed *with* any of his patients. Jim thought I said *for* the patients, so he told me that sometimes he did. I asked if he would pray for my knee.

Jim told me later that the thought went through his mind: *If I can't pray for Oral Roberts, I can't pray for anybody.* So he said, "Yes, I guess I can pray for you." And he did.

After he finished, we got into an argument as to how much I owed him because he said his office didn't charge ministers. Finally, I said, "If you won't take my money, will you play golf with me at Southern Hills?" He said yes. That summer as we played several times late into the evening, important things began to happen.

I remember most that Jim and I became friends, and soon we were talking at great length about healing—what it really meant to come at healing from an alternative perspective, which was the one I believed God had given me. Jim and I stimulated each other's thinking, probing healing from what he thought of it from his background and his medical practice, and what I thought of it from my healing ministry.

I asked Jim to tell me how medicine operated. Right away he saw that in my father's family and in mine there was no barrier to medicine and the hopes of what it could do. My family and I had been under doctors' care before any healing ministry and all during it up to that hour. So he didn't have to waste time on trying to knock down any defenses I had built up.

I was always intrigued with medicine from the standpoint that I had not studied to be a doctor and did not know the inner workings of the system. How does the system work? How are medical students chosen—prepared—trained—and how do they finally become practicing physicians and surgeons?

Jim's answer was enlightening. He said, "Oral, the first thing is that medicine is committed to leaving very little to error in the training of its physicians. By and large, this country does not turn out any bad doctors. It turns out some great ones, but not any bad ones."

I said, "How does the system do that?"

He replied, "Well, you cannot get through the filter. There are too many places to get filtered out. If you cannot meet the standards in your training, you are dropped from the system. At least I think this is true in the last fifteen to twenty years of medical training, say, from about 1955 on. The system is tight and getting tighter."

That interested me because I know of little or no such filtering system in the ministry. Almost anybody can decide to preach, whether called of God and well prepared, poorly prepared, or not prepared at all. Jim's perception was that something was to be said for the tightness of the system with which medicine tried to guarantee its product. And he thought something probably could be done—but he did not profess to know the answer or to know how to do it—to tighten up the way the ministry turns out a superior product, so that the quality of what people heard about the gospel would be the best.

He said, "If you stop to think about it, there is only one American Medical Association."

I said, "I notice that physicians share their knowledge, their expertise, and their research efforts. Is that part of the system?"

"Yes, it is," he answered. "The American Medical Association and its member doctors share this practice in common. I don't mean to indicate they do it perfectly, for they are only human beings. But they know medicine can advance only as they gain new ways of helping the sick and sharing that to the extent any other doctor has access to it. That is why there are years when suddenly a new miracle drug or surgical procedure comes on the scene. Sickness and disease resistant to past medical methods can be treated more successfully. The system is constantly seeking to improve itself, to advance medical breakthroughs."

I remember as we discussed this point, Jim laughed and said good-naturedly, "There are almost as many different religious denominations as there are people to invent them."

I didn't take offense at his words. I recalled a fellow minister commenting on the practice of doctors "referring" beyond their expertise to specialists. He said, "Many ministers would fight to keep their own patients, whether they could help them or not, because of their ties to their denomination."

I said to Jim, "You're not far wrong on the number of denominations. In my opinion, because of these rigid differences and the belief that they are right or more nearly right than any other, they are virtually closed organizations, especially as far as sharing information and proven breakthroughs in getting unsaved and sick people delivered."

I added, "I don't know how the American Medical Association elects its leaders, but to me, the tragedy in most denominations I know is that they seek out good administrators rather than their most spiritual people and those who have the most proven results of helping people come to know and serve God and also to expect His supernatural intervention in their lives."

Jim said, "There is some of that in the way medicine chooses its leaders. One of the chief weaknesses is that the mind is so finely trained, there is little emphasis placed on how physicians can encourage their patients, talk with them, and cause the patients to be comfortable in their spirits in getting their medical care."

I said, "This is the first time I've heard you mention the spirit of a person. Doctors do believe people are more than minds and bodies, don't they? That they have souls?"

He said, "I can't say I have thought very much about the spiritual overtones of the way doctors help people get well. I know it is not in our training in medical school or in our residencies. I suppose it depends on the individual doctor and whether or not he or she is a spiritually minded person."

I said, "And if he or she is not?"

He said, "That's one I hadn't thought about, either. I can only say that when doctors don't have some belief in God, and in involving the spirit of a person with the treatment, it could leave a void."

I explained to Jim that probably as much or more than most people, I've had to fight for my health and continue fighting for it. It's the reason I want the best of medical care and the most anointed people of God praying for me. What had been the most defeating to me is that doctors seem to see me as a physical and mental being only, and praying people see me as a spiritual being only. Yet they are both in the process of bringing healing to me. It was very frustrating, and God had been dealing with me about it. "In fact," I told Jim, "He has spoken to me that He wants His healing streams of prayer and medicine merged and that His time has come for me to be a forerunner in getting it done."

I told him how I had been near death's door with tuberculosis, and God had spoken audibly to me that He was going to heal me, that I was to take His healing power to my generation, that someday I was to build Him a university based on His authority and the Holy Spirit, and that I was also to build a medical school for the combining of medicine and prayer.

That almost stopped the golf game. Jim grew very quiet. We played several holes without any more conversation on the subject of medicine as he practiced it or prayer for the sick as I had been doing it.

Finally, Jim said, "Now I know why we met. I know why we've been having these talks. And I think I understand that my wife's recovering from cancer, with all due respect to my medical colleagues, was also due to her faith and a divine intervention from God. I've never put all this together before. I hadn't even thought about it.

"She first received everything we could get done for her by the oncologist, by radiation, chemotherapy, and so on. We left no stone unturned. She had received what you call the charismatic experience, the baptism of the Holy Spirit with tongues, and she was receiving direct healing prayers from her prayer group. One day I woke up and saw my wife was healed. The cancer was gone. She glowed with health. As I said, she's not had a sick day since. Sue's combining medicine with prayer was better than either one of them alone."

That was a powerful moment!

Right here is the rub, as I see it. Who do you trust as your Source? Who, indeed, is the Source of all healing?

I believe the Bible, in which God teaches He alone is the Source of our total supply: "But my God shall supply all your need according to his riches in glory by Christ Jesus" (Phil. 4:19); and "I am the LORD that healeth thee" (Exod. 15:26). Our total supply most certainly includes our deliverance from sickness and disease. Therefore, both healing coming through supernatural intervention, through believing the gospel and the prayer of faith, and healing coming through medicine or surgery really come through God our Source.

As far as supernatural intervention is concerned, it can come—as I know it—in two different ways. One, God acts sovereignly; that is, God is entirely on His own without anybody doing anything. This is really under God's control, and although it happens, it doesn't occur often. Two, a believer or a group of believers pray and agree in prayer for supernatural intervention to heal a sick person or destroy a disease. That is the way supernatural healing most often happens as I know it.

After forty-eight years of continuous healing ministry, I am familiar with both ways. But I am also familiar with receiving healing through the principle and process of medicine. When I have been under medical care by a doctor, or in a hospital as a patient, I have come with faith in God, basing my hope of a cure on God as my Source working through the physician, the nurses, the medicine, and medical equipment. Never once have I looked to any man, however skilled, or medical facility, whatever the state of the art, as the Source of my recovery or health. I have trusted God as my Source, whether in medicine or in prayer, or in both together.

That is the way I have been trained through my parents, through the study of the Bible, through the Holy Spirit indwelling me, and through the personal presence of Jesus of Nazareth in my life. God is my Source. I see everything through Him.

Many doctors and ministers of the gospel have told me when they were in medical school or in seminary or Bible school, they were not taught to look only to God (either through medicine or through prayer) to heal them both naturally and supernaturally.

I have personally seen, as I have laid my hands on more than 1.5 million sick persons, that as a result of this lack of right teaching, uncounted numbers of desperate people have become cynical, fearful, and frustrated. They have simply given up because they no longer believe there is a God who loves them or who cares whether they are sick or well. They know very little about God as their Source.

I had been one of those people before I got it straight in my mind that God cared about me in my terminal illness and was working through both the doctor and a healing evangelist. Before then, I simply did not know. Knowing made all the difference about whether I got well or just lay there and died before I had a chance to live my life.

God spoke to me, and He gave me a mandate to help merge the natural processes of medical care with the supernatural intervention by His grace through prayer and faith. He brought a prominent physician/surgeon, Dr. James E. Winslow, and Oral Roberts, a well-known healing evangelist, together in the same city, Tulsa. We both were aware of the presence of God at work with us. We may have had different names for it, but we knew we meant the same thing. I believed I had found my medical leader at last.

God gave me the mandate, but I had to learn the details. It became both an exhilarating and a painful experience.

CHAPTER 25

MY RUDE AWAKENING
TO THE MEDICAL WORLD

WHEN DR. Jim Winslow and I first began talking about his helping me build the ORU School of Medicine, he asked me, "Do you have a timetable to open the medical school?"

I said, "I don't, but God does. He has impressed upon me very clearly we are to open in the fall of 1978."

Jim nearly exploded. "You don't even have the facilities designed, let alone built. What are you going to do?"

"Jim," I said, "this whole ministry of healing, including ORU, is a faith outreach. God said I was to build it out of the same ingredient He used to create the earth—'nothing' (Job 26:7). God spoke and called the earth into existence. We get His directions and His words. We speak, by our faith, 'and calleth those things which be not as though they were'" (Rom. 4:17).

Jim said, "That's the exact opposite of the way medicine operates. If you tell that to those who have the power to grant you a license to open a new school of medicine, you won't get anywhere."

"Maybe so, Jim, but that's exactly the way I'm going to approach them when you and I apply to them."

He replied, "All I can say is this: It will take God to go with us. They could throw us out of their offices."

"Jim, as much as you believe in your practice of medicine, I believe that much in obeying God's call on my life. Nobody believed I could have a healing ministry or build ORU, and now I face seeming impossibilities in merging medicine and prayer. No way have I been able to do anything by myself. I've had to believe God and obey Him when I didn't know anything else to do.

"So let's get on with building the medical school, getting the American Medical Association to work with us, finding a dean, getting the right students—and the rest of the know-how—and the money! I hadn't told you, but we don't have the money, either. We never have had any when we started something God told us to build. All I know to do, Jim, is to use the three keys of the miracle of seed-faith: First, trust God as our Source, second, put our own seed in, and third, expect a miracle."

I know it all sounds crazy. I knew because many told me it did. But I had found God's man in Dr. James E. Winslow. All he wanted before joining me was to know more about the charismatic experience that his wife, Sue, had had and for me to share with him my experience and knowledge of the Holy Spirit. That turned out to be an exciting project.

Meanwhile, Jim had had an accident while mowing his lawn. He had caught the fingers of his right hand somewhere in the mower. At first, he didn't think it was serious, but his colleagues worked on his hand and said that was all that could be done. He had lost the feeling in his fingers. His surgery days seemed to be over.

I received a phone call on Saturday morning from Jim. "Oral, I need some help. Can I come over?"

"Sure," I said. "Come now!" I could tell by the tone of his voice it was something serious.

As we sat down, he laid his hand in mine, and choking back his emotions, he said, "If God doesn't heal my hand, my surgical career will be over."

We sat there a moment, both of us realizing that something like this, an injury or a sickness or a disease or some other hit, usually comes to each of us sooner or later. Ultimately, we will have to turn to our faith and trust God for a miracle. If we don't look to God, chances are, the consequences will become disastrous or at least a great hindrance.

Holding those quivering fingers of a surgeon who had brought God's medical healing to thousands and was now dependent in a different way on God as his Source, I thought of the hundreds of healing lines. I had never been able to bring God's healing to all sick or injured persons I prayed for, but I had been able to help many with what He said, "I give you power to heal all manner of sickness and disease" (see Matt. 10:1).

I had seen all manner of human sickness and hurt healed among people of virtually all walks of life. I had prayed for several doctors before in my ministry, but none about whom I felt as I did Dr. James E. Winslow. He was hovering between two worlds: one in which he was an orthopedic surgeon, and one in which he was no longer a surgeon. I could feel in my spirit what he was going through inside himself.

The presence of God moved immediately through my right hand as I held his hand and prayed to God to restore feeling to his fingers. I released his hand and told him to get his mind off it, and we would talk about the blessed Holy Spirit.

For five hours I shared with him, both of us with a Bible in our hands, what God said about the work of the Holy Spirit, the third person of the Holy Trinity, and the personal way He infills our lives with the unlimited, unmeasurable power of Jesus Christ of Nazareth.

I told him how the tongue is connected to the spirit, just as it is to the brain or mind. I said I had discovered, upon being baptized in the Holy Spirit as a born-again believer, that I could will my spirit to use my speech organs easier than I could will my mind to use them. All speech is under the will, and the will governs whether we speak by our minds (our intellect, our brains) or by the spirit under the power of the Holy Spirit.

I said speaking in tongues comes out of the spirit and is a language of the Holy Spirit given to us with which to express our deepest thoughts and needs to God. Then after we've spoken in tongues to God, He tells us to pray that we will be able to interpret His response to us through the mind. This interpretation is not a translation of what we've said in tongues. It is an interpretation of God saying back to the mind what we said to Him by the spirit, or it is a word of knowledge, or a word of wisdom, or a discernment. In all cases it is an enlightening of the mind, illuminating it so it's more on God's thought level.

Jim was intently listening. "How do you do it?" he asked.

"First," I said, "you start in John 7:37–39 where we're told, 'In the last day, that great day of the feast, Jesus stood and cried, saying, If any man thirst, let him come unto me, and drink. He that believeth on me, as the scripture hath said, out of his belly shall flow rivers of living water. (But this spake he of the Spirit, which they that believe on him should receive: for the Holy Ghost was not yet given; because that Jesus was not yet glorified.)' This means you recognize as a human being that you have a *thirst for God*. He made you that way. It also means, Jesus said, you start by believing in Him. Believing in Him as our Savior and with your mouth confessing that God has raised Him from the dead—and that as you believe saves you, giving you a new birth inwardly, making you a new creation as He says in 2 Corinthians 5:17, 'Therefore if any man be in Christ, he is a new creature: old things are passed away; behold, all things are become new.'

"Next, Jesus says, 'When you believe, out of your belly area—your inner man—shall flow "rivers of living water"'—life from God in the deepest levels of your being. It will flow up and over your tongue. It is then up to your *will* to choose to say whatever the Holy Spirit gives you to say in a language that bypasses your mind—for the moment—and gives you special words to express your deepest self to God."

Jim said, "I'm not really sure I am saved in the way you are talking about from what Jesus said. I grew up in the church and felt close to God at times. And I believe in Him. But this is a deeper experience, isn't it?"

I said, "It is to me. Why don't we just start over as if you knew nothing of Jesus and pray together the prayer of repentance, then confess with our mouths that God raised Jesus from the dead?"

A holy hush came over us while I led Jim in this prayer. As I felt, then saw, how he was responding to God so completely, I asked if he felt the Spirit flowing up and up out of his belly area, his inner man.

"Yes," he said, "I feel it right here." And he placed his hand over the solar plexus area of his body.

"Do you feel the assurance of your salvation now?"

"I do, Oral." And he could no longer hold back the tears. We were praying together as brothers in His love.

"Jim," I said, "Jesus Himself said when you believe, rivers of living water of His Spirit will flow up out of your belly. You said it was happening. Is that right?"

"It is!"

"Then by your *will*, will your spirit to bring up from your inner self what is there. Bring it up over your tongue to God."

"What words will I be using?"

"The Spirit will decide that. Just start speaking any words He gives you. That will be the beginning of speaking or praying in tongues."

Jim, being a doctor, knew how important cooperation is to get a good result. Words came up, and by his will, he spoke them. I joined in with my own prayer language of the Spirit. This went on, off and on, for several minutes as he became accustomed to submitting his mind to the Holy Spirit for purposes of speaking to God from his spirit. He discovered that opportunity resides in the belly area, as Jesus said.

It was a start. It was enough for Jim to take with him and to join with Sue in praying in the Spirit together until Jim was fully comfortable using his new prayer language of the Spirit. Then he could pray as his mind chose the words, learn to praise God after praying in tongues, and ask God to give the interpretation or the meaning back to his mind. I cautioned him to understand that speaking to God in tongues—the prayer language of the Spirit—is not a one-way street. After praying in tongues *to* God, we are to pray He will give us the ability to interpret what He says back to our minds. After we do both, we can do as Paul did: "Pray with the spirit, *and* with the understanding" (see 1 Cor. 14:15). I told Jim I had learned that praying in the Spirit, then asking God to let me interpret His response back to my mind, I was able to get the understanding of how I was to pray. Really, I was then able to pray the understanding I had received.

Jim was to see over the next several years the exquisite blessing and the practical value of tongues and interpretation as we worked in an area unknown to both of us in bringing forth a school of medicine and later a medical center of exceptional quality. It was the beginning of merging God's healing streams of prayer and medicine. It was a daring experiment, or rather a daring experience, and I wouldn't take anything for the years we had our hands on the most inspiring promise I had ever seen for the total healing of human beings.

Jim's fingers were healed sufficiently for him to continue his surgical practice, then to be put to the practical building of the medical school.

─────── *The Awakening Comes!*

It didn't take me long to learn that the most powerful people in the world system are not politicians, lawyers, or preachers. They are doctors with control of the science of healing through a system of medical schools, clinics, and hospitals; with control over people's lives when they are the sickest; and with the power vested in the medical associations of this world.

I was in for the shock of my life. I was glad I didn't know that when I began to build the ORU School of Medicine. The driving force I felt was to obey God, whether I fully understood everything or not. In looking back on my undertaking to incorporate medicine with the prayer ministry of healing, I often wonder how I was able even to *begin.*

Jim explained to me that a medical school would turn out only young men and women with M.D. degrees who could not become practicing doctors until they had, upon graduation, completed a three- to seven-year residency in an accredited hospital. They have to prove they are qualified by working with practicing physicians and surgeons before they can become practicing doctors on their own.

Jim said the medical school would need an affiliation with one or more Tulsa hospitals in which our ORU medical students could do their residencies. He didn't know if that would be possible. The community owned one, Catholic orders owned two, and the fourth was an osteopathic hospital, which the American Medical Association hadn't accepted at that time.

I could feel the hackles coming on my neck. Hospital affiliation had never occurred to me. Inwardly, I was raising questions with God that He had chosen the wrong man for the task—me.

I said, "Do you expect any trouble?"

Jim said, "Each hospital has its ownership. Each is a competitor of the others. And . . . ," he stopped.

"And I am a healing evangelist," I added.

He didn't say anything. We both knew that could be a stumbling block to them.

"But," I said to Jim, "I have felt no leading to build a hospital. I see now the necessity of a hospital affiliation in the educating process. But I do not know what to do when I've not been given any instruction to build a hospital. You'll just have to call on the hospitals in Tulsa."

He went to see an oil man of great means and influence, who was the founder and benefactor of St. Francis Hospital, known as the finest in Oklahoma. Jim did his surgical practice there.

He told Mr. Warren about Oral Roberts building a medical school. Mr. Warren said he had already heard about it.

Jim said, "Mr. Warren, I've heard you say that if you ever affiliated St. Francis with a medical school, you preferred that it be with a private rather than a state-run medical school. Therefore, you must have some interest in medical education. If so, here is an opportunity to affiliate with a private medical school. President Roberts is going to put up the money for the basic science program and support the medical faculty and help the medical students beyond what they can pay. What he needs you to do is to make the hospital available. You're both here in the same town, it looks like a pretty fair match, but you are the man who has to make that decision. Apparently, it is all right with Oral Roberts because I told him I was going to talk to you about it."

Mr. Warren said, "I will have to think about that."

A month later, Jim met with him again. Mr. Warren sent his aides out of the room, and when they were alone, he said, "Dr. Winslow, I am not going to affiliate St. Francis Hospital with Oral's medical school."

Jim asked Mr. Warren if there was room for them to have more discussions.

Mr. Warren said a single word: "No."

Jim told me that meant that was the end of that.

Next, Jim went to St. John's and Hillcrest to negotiate an affiliate agreement. The fact that Jim had practiced in both hospitals led to their putting together a negotiating group. They said they would not negotiate as individual hospitals, but each would participate if the other one would.

By that time, Dr. Charles B. McCall, dean of Jim's old school—University of Tennessee College of Medicine—agreed to be dean of the ORU Medical School and help with the negotiations for affiliating with a Tulsa hospital.

They would make progress and then, as Jim said, "backslide." Finally, it became like trying to fit a square peg into a round hole.

"Somebody's nose was always out of joint over something," Jim said.

They could not reach the point of making an affiliate agreement.

In February of 1977, Jim sat down with me, and we talked about where we were. I asked Jim what he thought was going to happen on hospital affiliation in Tulsa. "I really don't know," he replied. "I've never been in as many political situations as exist in these hospitals. There are some who like you and some who dislike you. Some like what you have done; others don't understand the charismatic experience and doctrine. There is a big mix of factions in hospitals, and there are no exceptions. My opinion is that if they feel it is to their benefit, both privately and publicly, they will probably end up doing it. If they think it's just for our benefit, they won't do it. It's got to be mutually beneficial."

He said, "Oral, we have a chance, but we're running out of time. We're getting everything ready in ORU's science facilities and in the medical faculty, but if you had the affiliation agreement in hand today with these hospitals, we *might* be able to open on the timetable you believe God has given you. Without it, I just don't know."

Jim was being honest with me. But I was still under God's mandate. The next Sunday, Jim went to see my son-in-law, Marshall Nash. Marshall had grown quite prominent in real estate in Tulsa by then, and Jim valued his opinion and advice. All the possibilities of the medical school came up.

They talked of all the blockades and problems that lay before us. As Jim was going out the door, the last thing Marshall ever said to Jim on this earth was, "Oral will figure out a way to resolve this. Just stick with him. I don't know the solution, but Oral will find it."

The next Friday night, Marshall and Rebecca were killed in the tragic air crash.

When Evelyn and Richard and I decided that we must get away, after we had planted a seed to the world by sharing our grief and our faith on national television, Jim was in full agreement. He knew it was a tremendous blow to take on top of the extreme pressure we were under concerning the medical school.

Before I left, I told Dr. Winslow he'd better be thinking of some options. "Suppose these hospitals never agree? What are the options?"

Jim said, "The option is to find hospitals outside Tulsa. Texas Tech University is affiliating with hospitals outside Lubbock where their medical school is located. It may not be a very good idea for us to go to other major cities for hospital affiliation, but it may be doable."

I'll never forget our standing there before Evelyn, Richard, and I got on the plane to go to California. I felt Jim was moving in the Spirit, and I loved him for it. He said, "Oral, if we are going to obey God's order to get this open in the fall of 1978, then somewhere along the line He is going to have to step in and do some things supernaturally."

God's supernatural move was just around the corner!

CHAPTER 26

"I Will Rain Upon Your Desert!"

A
S WE FLEW west to work through our sudden grief of losing Rebecca and Marshall, the devil was mocking me: "You have said God is a good God. You even told the people there is going to be a breakthrough from heaven in 1977. Now where is the breakthrough for you, for the people?" The devil was trying to intimidate me to get me to quit, so people would lose hope of any healing they would gain through my ministry.

I had told Evelyn and Richard that I felt when we reached California, we should go to the desert. Down through the years, the desert was one of the places I had gone at times of special need for God to reveal Himself to me. In the vast quietness of the desert, I had been able to reach out to God, to listen in my heart to what He wanted to say to me.

That first evening, after we had checked into the hotel, we went to the dining room and were eating. Suddenly, I heard God's voice inside me, coming up like a roaring in my head:

I will rain upon your desert!

I asked Evelyn if she had some paper for me to write on. She handed me a little notebook with several blank pages. As the words came, I began writing them down. Soon, however, I knew I had to get back to our room. I asked them to excuse me. Seeing that God was dealing with me, Evelyn and Richard said, "Go ahead. We'll join you later."

In the room, I heard God say again,

"I will rain upon your desert!"

In my heart, I knew this was a powerful thing God had spoken to me—something very special. He would rain upon my desert.

On the way to the hotel, as we had driven into the desert, I had seen the stark, barren land, the shifting sands, the gullies, and the scars on the environment. I saw the trackless miles beneath the burning sun and felt the land crying for rain from beneath . . . crying . . . crying.

I remembered a previous time I was there. A great cloudburst had poured down on the parched land, and almost instantly, I had seen a miracle. Everywhere it was like an explosion of life bursting forth. The long-dried-up vegetation leaped into newness of life. Soon, all over the desert the rain had brought to pass the prophecy of the Bible: "The desert shall rejoice, and blossom as the rose" (Isa. 35:1). My eyes saw the rain as a breakthrough from heaven for the desert, which had been denied it so long.

As I sat there in my room, it was like that again. I felt God's words deeply that He would rain on my desert, and He was about to show me something I had not seen before. I continued writing as He said these words:

"Son, you cannot put the vision I have given you into a place where My full healing power is not freely accepted. . . . You must build a new and different medical center for Me. The healing streams of prayer and medicine must merge through what I will have you build. The physicians, nurses, and Partners chosen to pray must be in harmony with My calling to merge prayer and medicine.

"All medical and surgical staff, all research for a cure for cancer and other diseases destroying man, must be carried on in an atmosphere of dependence upon Me as the Source of healing and life.

"You build it exactly as I will show you.

"As people come from throughout the world to this new health-care center to receive the best of medical science and the most anointed of healing prayers, they will come to know: 'I am the LORD that healeth thee'" (Exod. 15:26).

The Lord led me to open my Bible to Revelation 21 and 22. There I saw portrayed the holy city, the New Jerusalem, with its river of life and its broad avenues. I saw the tree of life, whose leaves are for the "healing of the nations."

I saw the holy city as a reflection of God Himself bringing medical cures and health to those who entered there. Suddenly, God gave me a new name for the health-care and research center I was to build in His name.

"You shall call it THE CITY OF FAITH."

I thought my heart would burst as an overwhelming sense of the "joy of the LORD" filled me (Neh. 8:10). THE CITY OF FAITH. What a name! I knew it was not Oral Roberts talking or dreaming up something. I knew only God could give a name like that. FAITH! THE CITY OF FAITH!

My whole life in this ministry has been built on faith. Everything I have tried to do has been an act of my faith, as a seed of my faith. And ultimately, much of medicine is built on the faith of the sick person.

I continued to write as God said,

"In the new City of Faith, I want My resources used, medicine, but more than medicine; prayer, but more than prayer. I want the thinking and the atmosphere charged with faith and hope, where My healing love permeates the entire place. I want the people who come for medical care to feel this atmosphere in their minds, in their spirits, for it will open them up to having a greater opportunity for a cure. Inspire everyone to have faith and hope in Me as the Source of healing.

"You will pray for the healing of the sick all your life. The City of Faith will enlarge the borders of My healing power throughout the world. The idea will go into all nations as a result of the City of Faith. It will be a seed, which I will multiply to reach millions who have not known before that I am the Source of their healing and their health, spiritually, mentally, and physically."

As clearly as I saw the walls of that room, God let my inner eyes see the details of the buildings. They were to be towering buildings. From a single base, three tall towers were rising—a 600-foot tower, a 300-foot tower, and a 200-foot tower. The towers were connected on a four-story base. Everything was gold in color, a crown jewel rising in the sky, pointing upward as a symbol to people to praise God and trust in Him.

He showed me that the 60-story tower would house the doctors and prayer partners and also be a clinic and diagnostic center. The 30-story tower would be the hospital. The 20-story tower would be the research center where dedicated scientists would work to find a cure for different types of cancer and other dread diseases.

As for the hospital itself, He showed me that because it would be interconnected to the other two towers from the single base, the physicians and their teams and the prayer partners shouldn't have to come from their offices in different parts of town. All of them would be under one continuous roof.

I knew from personal experience that having to drive from one medical office, laboratory, or clinic to another was a great hindrance and drag on me. I felt I needed the doctors to be closer together and their equipment only several feet or yards away. I wanted a whole-person approach to the sick person. I had felt that was a serious missing link in the healing success of any hospital in which I was a patient, especially in all the medical facilities I had to go to in preparation of being admitted. I felt everything medically should be designed and located with the patient in mind, giving him the feeling he was what all medical (or prayer) efforts were about, and having him in the calmest possible condition so his faith and hope could work at the maximum level.

God was revealing this to me in greater detail than I had seen it before. My experience of laying hands on so many sick people and praying for them had given me a sense of person-centeredness. I found no two sick persons alike, but I discovered faith is always the same, and so is hope. The principles of the ministry were to do everything possible to help a sick person get into faith and hope.

I saw so plainly and unmistakably that the City of Faith had to function with all the necessary medical personnel and equipment, and all the prayer partners' help, in close proximity at the same time—and in the same place! To me, that would be a miracle in itself. It would create a family atmosphere instead of a sterile environment where the patient so often feels detached from human contact and comfort. I am sure that you, the reader, know what I'm talking about.

I had never thought of building a hospital. Now, just as God had told me earlier about the deaths of Marshall and Rebecca—"I know something about this that you do not know"—I realized the same was true concerning the ORU Medical School and my call to attempt to merge His healing streams of prayer and medicine.

I didn't know, but God knew from the first we would never get Tulsa hospital affiliation that would satisfy our needs. At best, we would have to use hospitals in other cities, as far as three hundred miles away.

Before the City of Faith revelation, I was operating by faith concerning obtaining affiliation—that's all I could do—step by step. It was a new world for me. I felt God had, doubtless, asked others to merge prayer and medicine, but for whatever reason, they had declined or had refused to run the gauntlet. God had fused in me a listening heart for His voice and an obedient spirit. He knew if He commanded me in no uncertain terms to undertake this seemingly impossible task, I would go at it with everything in me—no matter the cost. To me, the single most important thing, as my mother had told me over and over, is to obey God.

The apostle Peter said to the religious leaders opposing the gospel in Jerusalem, "We ought to obey God rather than men" (Acts 5:29). I knew there were many ways I could be faulted. I had failed many times. But ingrained in my very soul was obedience to God.

After showing Evelyn and Richard all I had written, and sharing what God had shown me, I could feel they were with me, but they had much wonderment and many questions. Like the original

Roberts clan coming to America from Wales some two hundred years ago, we were very closely knit, and we had a deep desire to obey God.

As we came to a place of feeling rested and at peace in ourselves, we flew home to Tulsa. On arriving, I called Dr. Winslow and laid my writings in his hands. I tried to explain what I had been shown concerning the shape and position of the three massive towers on their single base.

Over the next few weeks, Jim and I did a lot of sharing on the plan—how it could be brought into practical reality. One day I asked Jim to get chalk and start drawing on a blackboard what God had shown me as to the shape and position the buildings were to be. As I talked, he would draw until he had the three tall towers rising from their single base.

"That will put everything under one continuous roof, Oral," Jim said. "Now, if we could pull this off, it could revolutionize the way sick people are cared for in a medical center and by individual doctors."

"Jim," I said, "read that part in the writing where God said not to put His program in a *defeated* place. Maybe that's what's been holding things up. Maybe we've been expecting something out of them that they do not believe is possible."

Jim's medical pride rose. "What do you mean about not putting it in a defeated place? How can these hospitals be defeated places when they're doing so much good?"

I said, "Jim, I know these hospitals are doing a lot of good. I'm not underestimating that. I and thousands of others have been helped by them, and I deeply appreciate them. I believe God is talking about His plan of the merging of prayer and medicine, and it will never be allowed to happen in those places because they are defeated in the one way God is sick and tired of."

"What's that?"

"Defeated in the sense they are walking by sight and not by faith."

"You mean, then, God wants us to keep our spiritual eyes open and walk by faith, but not shut our physical eyes?"

"That's saying it a different way, and maybe it's what He means. But let me ask you a question: Are you game for the battle if they don't affiliate or if we have to build the City of Faith?"

Jim smiled, "I got on this boat for the long haul. I'm not leaving now if they affiliate or if they don't. We'd better get our architect to make an artist's rendering of the building so we can announce it if we have to."

Announcing the City of Faith

On September 9, 1977, the announcement was made, with banner headlines in Tulsa, and the news media picked it up and spread it across the nation. The announcement had several effects. It forced the Tulsa hospitals to do something. As it turned out, they had made up their minds in the beginning to oppose the City of Faith.

The next thing that was required to build and open the City of Faith was what was called a certificate of need. (A certificate of need is a document the federal government requires the state to make in an effort to control the possible duplication and maldistribution of health-care facilities and services.) Jim hired Bill Luttrell, an expert who had helped get certificates of need for the huge Hospital Corporation of America, headquartered in Nashville.

Almost immediately, it became one of the biggest political battles that had ever been in the state of Oklahoma. And we were in significant danger of being denied the certificate of need.

Mr. Lloyd Rader, who directed Oklahoma's Department of Human Services, called Dr. Winslow and said he needed to come over and talk with him and the parson (which is what he called me). Jim and Mr. Rader knew each other from the time when Jim was chief of staff of Children's Medical Center in Tulsa.

When Mr. Rader came to see us, the gist of what he said was, "You fellows have quit preaching and gone to meddling. You cannot imagine how big this hassle is going to be. The Tulsa hospitals have not only refused to affiliate with you, but they are going to fight tooth and nail to keep you from getting the certificate of need and building your own medical center."

He said the Health Planning Commission, of which he was chairman, might turn out to be on their side. He did not know. Personally, he didn't care whether we built our own hospital or not. But he warned us that it could be the biggest flap we've ever seen. We might win, or we might lose. He said, "But I believe you have a *right* in America to do whatever you are able to do." That was a statement we often referred to later.

He advised us that the Health Planning Commission must give us an opportunity to have our petition heard. "You will get that opportunity; the law requires it. But your evidence will have to be convincing."

The media took it up from there, and almost daily the struggle was played out on the front pages of the newspapers and on radio and television.

Personally, I was tired of reading or hearing what the media were saying. But that was not the first battle I had been in. The important thing to me was what God wanted. I hadn't wanted to build a hospital. I had thought Jim's idea of affiliation with local hospitals would have been the way to go. I had no idea at the time that God had already seen the refusal coming and that He had something bigger in mind. Once again I learned that faith isn't always fully revealed the first time you are given a project.

We went about our business preparing the application for the certificate of need. The opposition was using money to stop us. We also tried to influence people to help us. Wherever Dr. Winslow went in Oklahoma City, our state capital, he said he met several legislators and other people who had a hand out for money. Jim told each one, "If we cannot get your vote fair and square, we won't have it."

I sent out a letter to my Partners. More than four hundred thousand letters in favor of the City of Faith poured into the state capital, so many that they had to put them in boxes for storage.

I believed I had the most loyal Partners. People didn't usually become Partners unless they or their families had been definitely blessed by the supernatural power of God through my preaching and praying for the sick. They felt my heart. They had watched everything I attempted—the crusades, the way I answered their letters, the Abundant Life Prayer Group, the building of ORU, and a life without a touch of immorality, dishonesty, or lack of love for them.

But never in my wildest dreams had I thought that my Partners would send so many letters into the legislative and executive branches of Oklahoma government. I remember reading the headlines: "400,000 Letters from Oral's Partners Pour into the Capital." That had never happened before in my home state of Oklahoma.

Oral at his desk with the sign bearing his life's motto

Oral's father and mother, Rev. and Mrs. E. M. Roberts

Oral, Evelyn, and their children at a crusade

Rebecca and Marshall (just before their tragic deaths in 1977) with their children, Brenda, Marcia, and Jon Oral

Brenda, Marcia, and Jon Oral at Marcia's wedding in 1993

Richard and the World Action Singers on a primetime TV special in 1978

Annual meeting of the International Charismatic Bible Ministries Fellowship, which Oral founded in 1986

Oral preaching at a crusade in Ghana in 1988

Oral preaching at a crusade at Olympic Stadium in Seoul, South Korea in 1989

A crusade in Philadelphia, Pennsylvania

Packing Madison Square Garden with an overflow crowd in 1982

Oral preaching at a crusade in San Diego, California in 1980

I couldn't hold back the tears. I knelt down to thank God and to ask Him to especially bless everyone who had written to stand with us.

It all boiled down to one thing: There ought to be one place on earth where prayer and medicine could be put together in a major hospital. It had not been tried. It ought to be tried. If we had the calling, and we could raise the money, we ought to be allowed to do it.

Soon the governor of Oklahoma announced he was for the City of Faith, and the Oklahoma state Senate voted 35 to 0 and the House voted 74 to 15 in favor of supporting the resolution. I had known Governor David Boren since he was a little boy, and also his dad, Lyle Boren, who had been a well-known congressman for Oklahoma. David Boren recently left his third term as a U.S. senator from Oklahoma to become the new president of the University of Oklahoma. He has been our speaker at an ORU commencement and also a chapel speaker. David is a born-again believer. I love and respect him very much.

We were able to meet the Tulsa zoning laws, so if we got the certificate of need, no one could stop us from building the City of Faith. Next, we came before the first committee, the Health Services Agency, that would or would not recommend our plan to the Oklahoma Health Planning Commission. They voted no.

The petition denied by the HSA went before Mr. Rader and the other two members of the Oklahoma Health Planning Commission. The place was packed, with people standing. The media were everywhere. They escorted Dr. Winslow, Dean McCall, Richard, and me to front-row seats. The lawyer for the Tulsa Hospital Council's side argued against; our lawyer, Jack Santee (who is still with us), presented a passionate case for us.

Then it was time for the final vote, and the whole place grew quiet.

Mr. Rader stated the conditions of the laws of Oklahoma, then asked the other two committee members if they were ready to vote. They were.

"Dr. J. Frank James, do you vote yes, or do you vote no?"

"I vote yes."

Nobody stirred. That was one out of three votes.

"Dr. Joan Leavitt, how do you vote?"

"I vote yes."

Every eye was on Mr. Lloyd Rader, the chairman. Many regarded him as one of the most powerful men in Oklahoma. If he voted no, then in spite of the yes from the other two, the opposition would, in effect, feel they could ultimately win.

Mr. Rader took his time. He whispered something to the other two members, and he rearranged some things on the table in front of him. In a firm voice, he said, "I vote yes!"

Pandemonium broke out. People stomped and shouted, and several burst into tears. I cried.

We Meant Business with God

We had already dug the hole for the first of the huge pilings that had to go down fifty feet into the water table because ORU was near the Arkansas River, and we had purchased several of the huge pilings to have them in readiness. Our plan was that if the vote was positive, we would drive the first piling as soon as we could phone our construction leader. Bill Roberts, my nephew, got Jim's call at approximately three o'clock in the afternoon. He started driving the piling, and by nightfall it was in. The City of Faith construction had begun!

The Tulsa Hospital Council appealed the grant of the Certificate of Need to the district court in Tulsa and tried to get an injunction to stop us, but the judge ruled we could continue building. The district court ruled against the Certificate of Need, but we appealed to the Oklahoma Supreme Court. Meanwhile, we continued putting the pilings down to bedrock, and soon the building began to rise. By the time the Supreme Court ruled, more than a year later, the building was already taking shape. The court held that we had demonstrated a health care need and affirmed the Certificate of Need.

After that, the Secretary of Health in Washington, D.C., issued a statement against the construction of the City of Faith, which was carried by the media. I thought, *When it rains, it pours.*

We tried to reach her in Washington, but she did not return our calls.

We just kept building.

Next we heard that the opposition was thinking of appealing to the U.S. Supreme Court.

I remembered my mother telling me how God spoke to her about her unborn child, and the vow that she would give me to Him to preach the gospel. I also thought of that little stuttering boy and the mockings he endured, and the faith Mama had that some-day God would heal me and through me bless the world.

"But why, God," I asked, "do I have to be opposed in every-thing I undertake to obey You?" That was a big question to me.

The weeks passed while members of the opposition made up their minds on whether or not to appeal to the highest court in the land. They finally came to the point that they did not think they could win in a free society. They did not appeal.

"He Is Going to Get the Money from God"

Soon after, when Saul Yager, our former general attorney for twenty-five years, was in New York City, he met the attorney for Mt. Sinai Hospital. The man couldn't understand how one man could build the City of Faith, costing $100 million or more. He said it was a mighty big undertaking for one man. Then he asked Saul, "Can Oral Roberts do it?"

Saul replied, "If he says God said for him to do it, then he will do it."

"But where is all the money coming from?"

Saul smiled and said, "He is going to get it from God." Saul, a Jew, believed that God owned all the money in the world. And he knew I, as a Christian, believed that, too.

I continued holding the City of Faith project before our televi-sion viewers and Partners for months, telling them the cost of each part of the construction and equipment, and of the recruiting of highly qualified doctors and staff.

Some months the money rolled in; other months we ran out. When it came in, we built; when it stopped, we stopped and told the people. Time after time, we would come right up to the dead-line, and that day checks would arrive.

I held nothing back from my Partners. In my monthly letters, I kept them up-to-date on our income for our ministry, including ORU, and the progress of constructing the City of Faith. My Partners and I have always felt a closeness. I dealt with each as an individual, and that brought us into a relationship that was very personal. Every need they had and wrote down on their return prayer sheets was brought to me, and I faithfully prayed over them, as I still do today.

Checks from many of my Partners usually averaged around $25 a month. However, as the construction bills and the cost of bringing in doctors and staff people increased, some Partners made special pledges over and above their regular monthly giving.

Even many people who were not Partners sent their checks, large and small. Every dollar counted. As for those who had never written to me before, a few times we would open an envelope, and there would be no message, just a check for $25 or $50 or $100 and more.

I felt the Lord dealing with me on the number seven, the perfect number as used in the Bible. The figure came before me like a great moving light:

$77.77.

$777.77.

$7,777.77.

I wrote and shared this with my Partners, and thousands of them sent $77.77, many sent $777.77, and several sent $7,777.77 because they had felt it in their spirits.

I wrote each one that Evelyn, Richard, and I were giving our seed-faith in sevens, and I believed God was going to bless each of us. I urged them in their giving to look to God as their Source, then start expecting to receive. I said, "God is going to multiply the seed each of us sows. The miracle will be coming toward us or past us. If we're not expecting when the miracle comes, we won't know it has arrived, and it will pass us by. If we are expecting it, we'll recognize it and reach out and receive it. It will bring blessings financially but also blessings in other areas of our lives."

One day an envelope came in with nothing but a check for $1 million. When I finally met the man who sent it, he seemed rather aloof. "Why did you give, sir?" I asked. "How could you have known we were facing a $1 million bill on one of the final phases of the City of Faith's construction?"

He said just a few words: "I felt God wanted me to. That was it: God wanted me to."

As I left, the presence of God ran through me something like electricity. It just stayed with me. "Lord," I asked, "I never knew of this man. I've had no contact with him, and I probably will never hear from him again. Does this mean You are speaking inside people to give different amounts solely on the basis that they feel You want them to do it?"

One day, Kay Lambeth, a member of the Board of Regents from North Carolina, brought a woman from Florida to visit me. "Oral," she said, "my friend here has heard God speak in her spirit that she is to sponsor the healing hands you've said God is leading you to place in front of the City of Faith."

The woman had no outward appearance of above-average wealth, of being able to sponsor the sixty-foot-high sculptured hands made of bronze, which would be very costly.

I said to the woman, "Do you have any idea how much these hands will cost?"

She said, "No, but God spoke to me, and He knows."

The sculpture was so large, only two nations had experts who could form them—Italy and Mexico. Those in Italy could not deliver them in time, and the company in Mexico, which I had flown down to negotiate with, said the cost would be in the neighborhood of $800,000.

When I told her this figure, she said, "I'll sponsor them."

"My sister," I said, "do you realize I'll have to pay this company so much down, then pay them as the work progresses, and make the final payment when they ship them to Tulsa and put them in place?"

"I can do it," she said, "over three years."

"I'm sorry, but in the contract we signed we have only twelve months for all the money to be paid."

Tears came to her eyes. She told me the story of how one of her sons had been in a car accident and was thrown out of the car into a river. One of his arms was severed. As the doctors were working to reattach the arm and hand, she sent a call for us to pray, and the prayer partners in the Prayer Tower prayed over the phone with her. Her son's arm and hand had been saved. She said the doctors called it a miracle.

"Now do you see why hands mean so much to me, and why God spoke to me that I was to give the healing hands for the City of Faith? I'll do it in twelve months. My husband and I have just sold our company, and I can use the part of the stock that is mine as I am led of the Lord. You'll have the money on time"—and we did!

I met her husband, a man high up in Rotary International, a civic club operating throughout the world. His support of his wife was crucial. He and their children, including the son whose arm and hand were saved, decided they were all for what she wanted to do.

But some of the biggest obstacles to building the City of Faith lay ahead. I could feel it in my spirit. I remembered back in 1947 how I had fasted and prayed so often in Enid as I was trying to obey God's healing call on my life and to get the healing ministry going that He gave me. It was a gift of God, but as with all gifts, the way has to be made to receive them and to use them properly.

My Gethsemane

Every day I was in a wrestling match with Satan, who I felt was the one clouding the issue and would do everything possible to destroy the very idea of the City of Faith.

Over and over as I read my Bible, God would focus my reading on places where Satan knew God was going to do certain things for the salvation of mankind, and he would step in to try to steal it away, kill it, or destroy it from the face of the earth.

John 10:10 stayed in my mind and spirit: "The thief cometh not, but for to steal, and to kill, and to destroy: I am come that they might have life, and that they might have it more abundantly."

I could see Satan trying to kill the baby Jesus there in Bethlehem before He had a chance to grow up as the Son of man and also the Son of God.

I saw how Satan stirred up the people against Jesus during His ministry to stop Him from preaching and teaching, and from healing the people, to stop Christianity before it was birthed.

In the book of Acts, I saw the opposition coming at the Spirit-filled believers in everything they attempted for God. Stephen, James, and many others were martyred.

The main thing I saw was that they were not quitters. They never gave up!

Burning in my spirit was my determination that I would never, never, never give up. I did everything in my power to look to God as my Source. I gave of my own means, sometimes taking the last amount I had to sow as a seed of my faith, so I could get into a greater expectancy to receive from God.

Expecting a miracle became the key to building the City of Faith while at the same time meeting our weekly television bills; operating our ministry office and answering the letters of my Partners and others who wrote for prayer; maintaining the Prayer Tower and the forty or fifty prayer partners on duty; and keeping ORU going by supplying the difference between what the students paid for tuition, board, and room and what it costs to operate month by month.

Those were scary times. I would cry out to God, feeling like an arrow was piercing my heart—like Jesus in Gethsemane crying, "Father, if thou be willing, remove this cup from me" (Luke 22:42). Then after an agony of soul that made His sweat like drops of blood, He said, "Nevertheless not my will, but thine, be done" (Luke 22:42).

At this time, I came to understand—really for the first time— what I believe is the real meaning of each of us having a Gethsemane. Mine was to obey God at all costs. Never give up, never turn back, and never strike back at anybody, including leaders in the Tulsa hospitals. I was to submit my will to God's higher calling without allowing bitterness to enter my spirit.

I knew something had to break above all that had happened up to that point. We were trying to get the medical school opened on schedule in the fall of 1978, and the time was upon us. Other major breakthroughs had to happen—and soon.

CHAPTER 27

My Determination Grows

I CONTINUED TO feel the Lord pressing me that the medical school had to open by late 1978. He would not let me off that date.

The City of Faith would be able to handle residencies for all of the ORU medical students, plus others, after it was built and operating at sufficient capacity, but we weren't going to have it open and operational until 1981. Because of that, we needed an interim affiliation with a Tulsa hospital at which ORU medical graduates could begin their residencies. We were able to work that out with St. John's.

In the background of helping our affiliation with St. John's Hospital was the work of Joseph L. Parker, a businessman who was the board chairman of St. John's, and of his close friend and mine, John Williams—head of Tulsa's largest corporation, the Williams Companies. They, as business leaders, wanted the affiliation during the interim because they believed the medical school and the City of Faith would be good for Tulsa.

In the power structure of Tulsa or of any city, there are always ins and outs that the leaders must work out together. It seemed a blessing that both of the men were my personal friends and friends of ORU. I deeply appreciated their efforts, and I told them so.

I had not forgotten what John Williams had done for us only a few years earlier. He, along with another prominent Tulsan, both personal friends, headed our drive when we were building Mabee Center, our athletic facility. It was designed for many other uses for the university and certain types of public events. It seated up to 12,000 for public events or 10,500 for basketball games. John Williams and Frank G. McClintock, head of Tulsa's First National Bank, led that drive. Their names and contacts were potent in gaining support for building Mabee Center. Since its opening in November 1972, more than 15 million people have attended athletic events, religious meetings, certain types of entertainment concerts, and several charity events in Tulsa. Many people have said, "Mabee Center is the most useful public facility not only in Tulsa but in Oklahoma."

I must also mention that behind the scenes of the Tulsa fund drive for Mabee Center was our dear friend and tax attorney, Don Moyers, whose influence with foundations caused several million dollars to be given to build the university.

The Medical School Opens!

The new relationship with St. John's went extremely well. The medical school started with twenty in its first class before it went on up to its larger size granted by the accrediting committee of the American Medical Association (AMA). St. John's would be able to take care of their needs through the third and fourth years of medical school, but it was not large enough to handle all the students when we were full-sized.

The City of Faith was under construction, and if all went well, it could handle all of our students and students from several other medical schools.

An interesting sidelight is that several years later, the American Medical Association tightened up immeasurably on admitting new medical schools. Jim said later, "Oral, only God could have known in advance that if we hadn't opened the medical school on His timetable, it probably would never have opened."

The most difficult thing of all was to bring all phases of my healing ministry along at the same time. It took faith, a hands-on kind of work every moment of every day, and the finances to operate out of debt. But the medical school did open on time, with some of the finest science facilities in any medical school according to the accreditation team who evaluated us. "You've done your homework," they told us. But more battles were coming.

The concept of health care putting the patient first may not have originated with me, but founding ORU out of the hot fires of healing evangelism with its entire focus on the healing of the individual awakened the entire AMA. In 1981, the City of Faith Medical and Research Center opened its doors in the midst of a worldwide hailstorm of criticism. The sheer size of the City of Faith—2,200,000 square feet—and the fact that everything was centered on the sick individual's needs appeared to the critics, whose comments were carried by the media, to be too good to be true.

As I mentioned earlier, I had learned and disciplined myself to think not in parts but in wholes. All of the ORU graduate schools—the medical school, the law school, the dental school, the nursing school, the business school, the theology school, the school of education—along with the college of arts and sciences, were given a mandate to interrelate. Everyone in each school had to interact with those in the other disciplines. I saw Spirit-filled professors in each school meeting together to harmonize their disciplines and goals to meet the needs of the individual, and I saw the students making special efforts to regard all these disciplines as existing to educate the whole man.

In my earlier study of the four Gospels—Matthew, Mark, Luke, and John—and the book of Acts, in addition to the rest of the Word of God, I saw that Jesus' favorite word seemed to be *whole*. It appeared to me over and over that His favorite expression in saving or healing a person was "Be thou made whole," or "Thy faith hath made thee whole."

Jesus had been sent by the Father into a world where every person was "unwhole"; indeed, the world at large was unwhole. So He said, "I am the way . . . I am the truth . . . I am the life—I AM ALL OF IT!" (See John 14:6.) He dealt in wholes, not in parts.

So putting medicine and healing prayers together, combining these streams of God's healing power, was like an invisible drive in my spirit. I was totally restless until I saw we were bringing it forth. Not perfect, not as well as I conceived it, but enough of it was taking shape that it captured the attention and admiration and opposition of a number of those in the professions and of the man on the street.

At first, I was hurt deeply by the failure of people to understand what the Bible word *whole* could mean for their lives. In

Tulsa, when the controversy was unceasing, the front pages of the press and television and radio reports only mirrored what seemed to be the almost total opposing forces of the medical profession—really nearly all the professions, churches included. I began to understand what not understanding can do to an enterprise or a new idea. Each time, when given the means to strike back, I did not find striking back in me. I simply said of the leaders, who I thought for the most part were really sincere and good people, "They simply don't understand." I never lost my love for my favorite city—Tulsa.

"Oral Roberts Says God Is Going to Kill Him!"

By 1986, five years after the City of Faith had opened, we had dropped behind $8 million in carrying on all our medical enterprises, including medical missions. The Lord had spoken to me to present the shortfall to the Partners and my television audience, which I had done.

Eight months had passed since I had mentioned it first on our television program and had written about it to my Partners. The media had said nothing about this, which was most unusual. Before, it seemed every time I breathed, there were headlines about me.

The Lord spoke to me near the end of 1986 and said,

> *"I told you to raise $8 million to carry on My medical work. You have from January 1 to March 31 to get it done. If you don't, then your work is finished, and I am going to call you home."*

At first, I was glad He might be calling me home, for I thought of shedding the burdens, laying down my armor, going home, and being at rest. Why God had selected me from all of His more able servants to do seemingly impossible tasks was beyond me. I had simply obeyed, which meant my life was on the line at all times in the healing ministry.

I announced the following Sunday—January 4, 1987—on our television program about the $8 million deficiency. I said if it didn't come in to carry on this special work of God, my work was finished, and God was going to call me home. It seemed everybody was listening.

The media went into action. "Oral Roberts Says God Is Going to Kill Him if He Doesn't Raise $8 Million!" was front-page news and was the main story with TV news anchors in the United States and throughout the world.

I went up into my prayer room in the Prayer Tower and vowed to the Lord I would stay there until the deadline. If the money came, I would continue with the medical school and the City of Faith. If not, I would be ready for Him to call me home.

It made perfectly good sense to me. It meant God was not playing around with His call on my life. It meant there was something very special yet to be done through us to heal the sick, to help change the way medicine and prayer are usually carried on. I knew and felt it in every bone of my body, in all my senses, and in the core of my inner being: my real self.

I believe the devil knew it, too. That's why he, as "prince of the power of the air" (Eph. 2:2), went to work in the most vicious and untruthful way against my life and ministry and God's higher purpose in blatantly misstating what I said God told me.

The media sent their helicopters flying over the Prayer Tower where they knew I was in prayer and where we were making Richard's daily live TV program. Many charismatic ministers flew in daily to stand with me in prayer. They knew I would never falsely report words from God. But some ministers taught that God does not perform miracles or heal the sick anymore, and they were the ones who raised their influence and voices against us. It was the opportunity they had been waiting for. They believed what the media said I said—when I hadn't said that at all.

I stood as firmly as I've ever done in this ministry because no matter what anybody said or did, I knew God had spoken to me, and I was dedicated to living out His words.

God said, "I'm going to call you home." The media said, "Oral Roberts says God is going to kill him." Quite a difference in the two statements, isn't there?

The very false way they put it only strengthened my resolve to obey God. At no time in all my years in the healing ministry had I felt Satan had loosed so many of his forces against me, nor had so many human leaders and opinion makers made me the topic of their conversations—and mostly in a mocking way. While I was in the Prayer Tower, Richard appeared on many national talk shows, such as "Larry King Live" and "Good Morning America," at their requests to explain what God actually said, but it couldn't stop the tide of criticism from rushing in.

In my spirit, I reached the place where I felt the old faithfuls of God's people were praying for me. I mean, I could feel it! It was like meat and drink to me, for I fasted "oft" during those three months.

The Dog Track Man

As the time God had set was coming to a close, each day I was able to supernaturally know the amount of donations that came in before anyone told me. Each day, when our chief financial officer came over to the Prayer Tower or phoned to give me the amount that arrived, I would stop him and say, "Let me tell *you* the amount." He told me he was dumbfounded that the Holy Spirit revealed to me the amount. I told him, "The word of knowledge works today the same way it did in the day of the first Christians. We must never forget God is concerned with every detail going on in His gospel today."

As we approached the absolute deadline of whether God would complete what He planned for the City of Faith and the medical school, a most unusual thing happened to a man in Florida.

One day Evelyn and I were on Richard's daily TV program, and Evelyn corrected me on an error I made in giving the difference between the total donations we had and the amount we lacked.

The ORU students have always loved it when Evelyn corrects me in public. She loves me, she knows I desire to do the right thing, and as my devoted wife, she has the right to speak up when I need correction.

Right on the air, Evelyn said, "Wait a minute, Oral. You're wrong."

"Darling, how am I wrong?"

"You're wrong on how much of the $8 million we lack."

"Well, I've had it right every day. How am I missing it today?"

"I don't know how you're missing it, honey," she said, "but we lack only $1.3 million."

A man in Florida, who owned dog racing tracks, turned to an associate and said, "You know those are honest people. Evelyn has the nerve to correct her husband even if he is Oral Roberts . . . and on live TV."

He was so impressed he got up and phoned us that he was sending the entire $1.3 million. The next day he flew to Tulsa with the check. I asked him if the Lord had told him to do this.

"I don't know," he said, "but I know it wasn't the devil."

Everybody in my special room up in the Prayer Tower whooped and yelled and praised God.

"You're a dog man?" I asked.

"Well, I own dog racing tracks."

"Are you a saved man?"

"I don't know."

I took him by the hand and asked him to repeat after me the sinner's prayer. Tears came in his eyes as he prayed with me. His countenance changed, and we all felt the presence of God filling the room. He and I hugged each other. I thought, *They're shouting in heaven right now.*

The next thing that happened, the media and some leaders in religious circles jumped on me for taking money from a dog track man. I quoted to them where God said, "The silver is mine, and the gold is mine, saith the LORD of hosts" (Hag. 2:8).

I said, "All money belongs to God. There is nothing wrong with money; something is wrong only with some people who have it. As for this man, we did our best to lead him to Christ. He felt Christ had come into his heart as we prayed with him up in the Prayer Tower, and he believed he was to give that $1.3 million to the Lord's work."

When that response failed to satisfy the worst critics, including some preachers who had lambasted us from their pulpits and written articles against us, I asked different pastors: "Would you have turned the money down?"

Every one of them said no.

The strangest thing of all is that when Evelyn and I went to the man's home later to thank him and his wife personally, he said he had received more than four thousand requests for money since he had given us the $1.3 million. "I read every one of them," he said, "from churches and individuals and different types of organizations."

"Did you send them any money?"

"Not a one!"

The one-time command from God to raise a certain amount of money to complete His mission, the one-time major gift in addition to the thousands of smaller ones, and the one-time focus of the attention of the whole world meant to me: God intends to merge His healing forces.

God didn't want to call me home. Above all, He wanted what we had built to go on. We felt we had built it under nearly as much opposition as Nehemiah felt when God told him to "rebuild the broken down walls of Jerusalem" (see Neh. 2:5). While his enemies laughed at him, mocked him, then turned to destroy him, Nehemiah, with a trowel in one hand and a sword in the other, alongside his men, restored the walls of God's holy city.

God has not stopped having those who hear and obey Him do mighty exploits in His name.

I was alive and a witness to that! But I was soon to realize anew how human I am.

CHAPTER 28

GOD'S IDEA TAKES WINGS!

G OD'S COMMAND to merge prayer and medicine was so much a part of my being that I felt
I agonized as Jesus had when He looked over His beloved city of
Jerusalem and said, "O Jerusalem, Jerusalem, thou that killest
the prophets, and stonest them which are sent unto thee, how
often would I have gathered thy children together, even as a hen
gathereth her chickens under her wings, and ye would not!"
(Matt. 23:37).

What I was facing showed me how human I am. I admit it took
many days of trying to get myself ready to face the pain of writing
what I am about to share with you.

We had already experienced a steady financial decline that
would threaten to have devastating results. Then we began to have
other problems besides financial ones.

The ORU medical students were required by the American
Medical Association to have a hands-on type of training in a particular variety of illnesses. As the medical students began fulfilling
their residencies at the City of Faith, we were having great difficulty in meeting those requirements. The number of patients in
the City of Faith was not yet large enough to handle all the clinical
needs of our medical students.

In conjunction with the medical school, we had opened and
were operating the dental school. After years of preparing the dental students to serve as missionary dentists for the first few years of
their practice, we were not succeeding in sending them out. I

concluded that some of them were not mature enough to know the mind of God concerning their avowed commitment to become dental missionaries, or they just didn't have a full awareness of what they were saying when they steadfastly refused to volunteer to go. It was a crushing blow to me and to those who had specifically helped to finance the School of Dentistry. I knew something would have to change and soon because of the enormous cost of dental education, especially since it had not fulfilled its founding purpose.

But the greatest and most far-reaching blow came when the news broke about "scandals" involving two ministers. The fact that the media played up what they called the fall of the two men— keeping it before the nation every day, month after month— caused the public to question other ministries. The consequence was that the income of thousands of churches decreased, and ministries like mine were hit as well. Although there never had been a stain morally, financially, or any other way on the Oral Roberts Ministries, we experienced a tremendous drop-off in donations.

As the donations fell off quickly and without warning, and the bills kept coming each week for our contractual obligations, we were all shook up. To our good people who had sold us supplies and services with the understanding they would be paid on time, it was heartbreaking, at least for a man like me, to be unable to pay. Not once in the years going back to our beginning in 1947 had we failed to pay any bill and on time. Our credit rating was A+.

Almost everybody else in business, church work, and government services was in the same boat. The government went on borrowing and getting the nation deeper in debt. Many churches and ministries, seeing income fall as ours had, found themselves with their backs to the wall. At about the same time, the recession hit America. People began losing their jobs as businesses failed or filed for bankruptcy. *But God's work had to go on.* Faith had to work as never before, but faith worked only as people worked it.

Evelyn was a bulwark of stability. Her faith in God, and in me, never wavered. Many were the tears we shed when we went for months without paying honest vendors and the TV stations who trusted us, but we just couldn't catch up.

Standing before our 4,500-plus student body and our dedicated faculty and staff without blinking, letting our inner faith in God our Source come through in spite of the doubts Satan tried his best to shackle us with, was an accomplishment.

My son, Richard, and his lovely wife, Lindsay, stayed in there with us. He and I, as president and executive vice president, took cut after cut in income, and we gave and planted seeds of our faith as never before.

When people wrote of their needs, we kept answering them with first-class letters as before. There were some days we had no money even to buy stamps. But somehow we would get through the week, paying as much as we could to each vendor and supplier. We told them that if they would be patient, we would eventually come out of the setback and try to pay them all. However, we made it clear we would pay our coworkers first. We had to reduce staff, cut down on departments, and do double duty, but we met our payroll.

I discovered early in my healing ministry that however much I committed my life to Christ, however I sought to be honest and aboveboard in all my dealings, however large were the positive results of my ministry, or however much I could show what the money raised had been used for, there is a spirit of this age, of Satan himself, that is diametrically opposed to any church or ministry with large results for the Lord in the realm of supernatural signs and wonders.

I felt it was a trick of the devil he had been waiting to spring on the body of Christ and on the secular world. Another thing I felt was that the devil knew the message of deliverance had reached into the very citadels of power in America and the world in an understandable way that God still heals today, that He is still the God of miracles. The secular world used the tragic happenings surrounding those two brothers in the Lord to strike at the very root system of the great Pentecostal-charismatic outpourings of this century.

In the midst of all that, God had called our Spirit-filled ministry to invade the world of medicine, perhaps the most powerful system in the world today. Who was I, a healing evangelist, to tell medical people in all their greatness that many of them were missing the boat, that there was power in prayer, that they were falling short to practice medicine alone when people's spirits were crying out for medicine *and* prayer?

I remember a visit of a medical site team, which came every year to look things over and talk with our medical leaders, our medical students, and me as president. Their purpose was to find any weakness, bring it to our attention, and give us a deadline for fixing it. They did that with all new medical schools. But I felt this particular site team was dealing with us differently.

At the end of the visit, the chairman of the team cut the two-day meeting short, folded his papers, and refused to let me reply as other site teams had done on previous visits.

One thing I admired about the AMA was that the group sent site teams to help with continuous corrections and healthy growth, which keep all medical schools on their toes. Up until this team's visit, I had been delighted to get the final report and go to work to improve the school. We had had good success, and we believed we were in the best position of our existence at the time.

Yet as I stood before the members of this particular site team, I realized the chairman's abrupt behavior was a signal of a change of some kind that was not in our favor. Our doctors knew it, too. They told me later, "We felt a tension we hadn't felt before."

Dr. James Winslow had been promoted to head Worldwide Medical Missions, and he was vice provost of Medical Affairs. With my concurrence he appointed our very able Dr. Larry D. Edwards, chairman of the Internal Medicine Department, to the deanship. The members of the previous site teams couldn't say enough good things about our two leaders. And they were especially impressed by our medical students. Some of the members even said they wished they personally had that caliber of medical students to teach.

I phoned the head of the liaison committee who had sent the latest team. From the beginning of our application, this great man had received me cordially. He was so much in favor of our trying to merge prayer and medicine that he had personally interceded with the larger committee to authorize the opening of the ORU School of Medicine.

When I reached him by phone and told him of the events, I requested he send the same site team back or send another and have the members give us a full hearing. It was evident he knew what had happened. His whole demeanor seemed changed toward me, and he would not accept my request.

"But, [I called him by name], this kind of treatment has never happened before. We fully recognize the power of the AMA. All I'm asking is to be given the same kind of site team visits we've had each year."

I hurt. Oh, I hurt!

I prayed nearly the whole night.

The Prophecies

A year prior to that site team visit, David Wilkerson, a minister who has spent much of his life dealing with drug addicts in New York City (his story is told in the best-selling book, *The Cross and the Switchblade*), had come to Tulsa to speak to the student body of ORU and to give me a prophetic word.

Dave had preached to our students with a strong judgmental emphasis. Quite literally, Dave is a man of God highly respected and revered by great numbers of people, including me.

After Dave's sermon in chapel, he asked to talk with me privately. His prophetic word went something like this. "Oral," he said, "God had you raise up the medical and dental schools and the City of Faith. He wanted prayer and medicine merged, and He wanted your medical and dental graduates to become missionaries as you were advocating. But I have a word from the Lord. You have made the point He wanted made. The world knows it, the church knows it, and you are to close these institutions."

He just about shocked me out of my shoes.

"Are you sure God gave you this as a prophetic message to me?"

"I am."

As a Bible-based man, I felt I was instantly in Gethsemane with Jesus where many of the things He wanted for Jerusalem and for all people were coming to an end at the time. Jesus had to close down His physical time on earth and return to the Father.

I felt smitten in my being as if lightning struck me. I didn't tremble or fall to the floor, but it was like a knife ripping through my stomach. I felt sorely distressed.

David never batted an eye.

"Is there anything else you feel you must tell me?"

"Yes, don't be concerned about what the church will think of you. They know and feel your heart and know that you have obeyed God. They will understand. But God is saying to close them down. You've made the point He wanted made."

I asked if he would go with me and take a tour of the City of Faith. "Sure," he said, "I'd love to."

It took us two hours, for it is a huge place, the largest medical complex on one base in the world.

David said, "I feel the presence of God in this place."

I said, "It's been here from day one."

He talked with some of the doctors, nurses, and patients. I asked him to pray for some of the patients so that he could see how the Spirit of God was working through prayer and medical care, and how well they fit together as none of us had ever seen before.

"This place is different. It's exactly like you have told the world it is," Dave said.

"But you gave me the prophetic word I was to close all the medical facilities. God's point has been made."

He didn't answer. He sat down and was quiet for a long time.

I sat down beside him and waited.

Finally, as I remember it, he said, "Oral, my first word to close it down still holds. You've done what God wanted you to do. It's over as far as this place is concerned, but the concept is released, and you can add no more to it."

We parted on that note. I've not seen or heard from David Wilkerson since then.

Something in me just couldn't close down the medical and dental schools and the City of Faith. I had heard the prophetic word of a man I knew was as true a man of God as I had ever known. He stated it compassionately but clearly.

More than once I've looked back to that time, listened in my spirit to those words, remembering how I felt, but not being able to put Dave's words all together. Yet two years later, the message from God came directly to me that we couldn't go on.

Bill Swad, a former Regent of ORU and a good friend, prophetically confirmed to me—and to Richard—that it was God's time to close the City of Faith and medical and dental schools. He said it when we had not said a word to him about closing them. I had known Bill Swad for several years, and I had not known one of his prophecies to fail.

I know the Lord's voice better than I know any other voice. How much influence David Wilkerson's and Bill Swad's prophetic words had on me I do not know. I know one thing: We were dealing in big, big issues in the kingdom of God.

In 1987, we officially closed the ORU School of Dentistry. Then in 1989, we closed the ORU School of Medicine and the City of Faith.

Few people have had their losses and failures trumpeted by the media and other people as happened to us. It seemed to me they brought mine to the whole world. I stopped reading the ridicule after I saw there was no end to it. I hurt so bad I sometimes felt as King David did: "Oh that I had wings like a dove! for then would I fly away, and be at rest" (Ps. 55:6).

Merging Prayer and Medicine Impacts the World!

Even though we could not stem the overwhelming tide of opposition and misunderstanding and therefore had to close those parts of ORU's mission, it was not before God's idea had been hurled around the world by the media, by the professions, and by the man on the street. Invisibly, it began to take shape and form in doctors, hospitals, and other health professionals everywhere.

Since the closing of the City of Faith, which to me seemed to be a disaster and to take away part of my very soul, I have discovered that what appears to be a failure is not always a failure at all.

Everything moving forward operates on ideas. Because the City of Faith and the ORU School of Medicine were so large, so newsworthy, and so opposed, the most powerful idea for *wholeness* had pervaded medicine as I never dreamed it would.

As Dr. Harry Jonas, the secretary of the Liaison Committee on Medical Education of the American Medical Association, said to me personally and to our medical staff when he came down to Tulsa to assist us in relocating our medical students, "Reverend Roberts, do not think you have failed. You have forever changed medicine and the way the medical world looks at it."

"How could that be, Dr. Jonas?" I asked.

He replied, "This idea with a focus on combining medicine with prayer, with a view toward wholeness, is an idea whose time has come. This idea has reached into virtually every doctor's office, clinic, hospital, nursing school, and nursing practice in the whole world."

I was taken aback. He saw my reaction and said, "Oh, I know what it appears like. To be fought as you were, to be misunderstood on such a scale, may have left you thinking everyone in medicine was against you—not so. *The fact is, the idea is bigger than you are.*"

As I tried to absorb what he said, failing completely to block out of my mind the scars I bore over the battle to bring God's call into the medical world, he added, "Before you die, you will see that the changes have begun to take place everywhere."

Today, I can say I'm grateful I got to help initiate it. A lot of it is happening. I've not been in a single doctor's office or clinic or research center or hospital since then without finding that some of the medical professionals are using prayer in their work and with their patients far beyond anything before. Even in Tulsa hospitals, that began to happen. Some have even run ads in the newspapers that prayer is part of the healing process.

No, prayer and medicine are not fully merged yet; only a beginning has been made. It will come! As a result, millions more will have a far greater chance to get well and be in health, which is part of God's overall wish (see 3 John 2).

I am not ashamed of anything I have done to obey God. I am not sorry I tried to put the City of Faith and the medical and dental schools together for that one purpose. I'm humbled to have been tapped on the shoulder by the Lord, and to have felt my heart "strangely warmed" to try to obey God's command to me to merge His healing streams of prayer and medicine. Regardless of what anyone says, I believe to a great extent they are now being merged, and it's time to give them to God for greater results in healing suffering people. The bottom line is that people get well and serve God.

As I continue to preach the full gospel and pray for the healing and wholeness of sick people while I yet have time, I hold before them the real possibility that they can be made whole. I never tire of quoting my favorite Scripture for wholeness: "Beloved, I wish above all things that thou mayest prosper and be in health, even as thy soul prospereth" (3 John 2).

The medical world was not the only place where healing and wholeness were needed. The call also came to take God's power into the world of law. The ORU Law School had a spiritual founding purpose that had to fight for our religious freedom! I was determined not to lose that battle.

CHAPTER 29

FIGHTING FOR RELIGIOUS FREEDOM

I HAVE ALWAYS believed somebody has to *start* or nothing gets done. God says, "Faith without works is dead" (James 2:26).

A year after the medical school opened, and the same year it was accredited—1979—we were opening the ORU School of Law. Some people thought that because it had been my boyhood dream someday to become a lawyer, I wanted to add a law school to ORU. I can't argue the point. What I know in my heart is that there was a powerful leading in my spirit to do it.

Through the exceptionally able Christian lawyer, the Honorable Charles A. Kothe of Tulsa, a man of national reputation and a warm personal friend, we began to move toward opening the ORU School of Law. He had arranged a meeting with me and one of his closest friends, O. W. Coburn, a successful Oklahoma businessman and a committed Christian. Mr. Coburn had wanted to donate $100,000 to the law school. As I so often do when people want to donate to ORU, I asked him why he wanted to do it. His reply was, "Because I have it."

Based on my revelation of God's way of giving and receiving, I explained to Mr. Coburn that his reason was a poor one, that giving should be out of his need and as a seed for a harvest.

After that day, O. W. Coburn eventually donated $1 million to the law school, and the Board of Regents named the school the O. W. Coburn School of Law of Oral Roberts University.

Things looked promising. Our first class of fifty-four was excited to learn the Honorable Byron White, associate justice of the

United States Supreme Court, was our dedicatory speaker. Tulsa's legal profession turned out for the event. Enrollment went up. And good, sound, Christian lawyers were added to the faculty under Dean Kothe.

The Learning Resources Center, the academic hub of the university, had been enlarged from 230,000 square feet to more than 675,000 square feet. It housed the law school and most of the other schools. This seven-story building has enough space to cover sixteen acres if it were on one floor.

We set ourselves to establish a strong law library, and soon many in the legal community believed it to be equal to any law library in Oklahoma. I knew that although a law school must have a strong faculty, the heart of a law school is its library. We originally invested some $12 million in the library, and we kept adding to it as the need arose each year.

We had unusual success with our graduates passing the bar, the highest percentage of any other law school in Oklahoma. It became evident that the law school was following in the path of excellence we set for the entire university when we opened in 1965.

From the first, we made our goals as follows:

Our first goal at the O. W. Coburn School of Law is to equip our students with the ability to bring God's healing power to reconcile individuals and to help restore community wholeness. That goal requires students not only to become technically competent lawyers with high ethical values but to learn how to integrate their Christian faith into their chosen profession. . . . Our second goal is to restore law to its historic roots in the Bible.

We unashamedly stated we wanted our law graduates to be healers, and we stated that over and over. I saw that we could strike a blow for the healing ministry through the law school by having a healing emphasis in the way we taught law, which would cause our graduates to have a spirit of healing and reconciliation in their practices.

Everything was going almost too well when we were unexpectedly struck a blow from the American Bar Association's

Committee of Admissions. I still feel the pain of that episode in 1981.

In 1978, we had been given authorization to begin the law school by the North Central Association of Colleges and Secondary Schools. There was a feeling that gaining accreditation from the American Bar Association (ABA) would be far more difficult.

We applied to the ABA in 1980, and the group sent a site team in October. The report praised the school's financial strength and the academic program, but expressed displeasure with the stated purpose for its founding. (You may want to reread our founding goals a few paragraphs back.)

Dean Kothe and Provost Carl Hamilton appeared before the site team, which would eventually make a recommendation at the ABA's meeting in August 1981. Dean Kothe felt immediately that the team members were hostile. He well remembered the first question he was asked: "Dean, if one of the male members of your faculty wanted to marry another male member of your faculty, what would you do?"

At first, Dean Kothe thought they were kidding, but he soon learned they were deadly serious. "Why, I'd fire him," he answered.

That was only the first stumbling block.

Another concern of the team was what they termed the "religious discrimination implicit in the written purpose of the O. W. Coburn School of Law of ORU, and specifically the requirement that *all* students sign the code of honor, affirming a belief in Jesus Christ as Lord and Savior." They said that was a violation of the ABA's Standard 211, which prohibited accredited schools from discrimination on the basis of religion.

Dean Kothe replied that ORU was in compliance if Brigham Young University's School of Law was, and he boldly stood up for our constitutional right to freedom of our religious beliefs. He stated he and his aides of the university had personally visited over thirty law schools in preparation to apply for accreditation and had formed their religious freedom closest to Baylor University, owned by the Southern Baptists; Mississippi College, also a Baptist school; and Pepperdine University, owned by the Church of Christ. But they believed that Brigham Young's position, which posed the most flagrant challenge to Standard 211, was the strongest of all. "In any case, I believe that the regulation barring our religious freedom is unconstitutional," he finally stated to the team.

When the team left, Dean Kothe informed me that ORU might have to contest Standard 211 in court.

My reaction was instant: "We're going to go all the way."

Securing the services of the eighth largest law firm in the United States, a Chicago firm, ORU filed suit in the federal district court in Chicago. On July 17, 1981, the court ruled that the ABA could not deny accreditation to the university solely on religious grounds. It was a great day for us, but we learned it was only a beginning of the ABA's determination to discriminate against our religious freedom. They summoned us to be present at the ABA's House of Delegates meeting in New Orleans.

At that August meeting of the ABA in 1981, the most controversial item on the agenda was the ORU Law School. Though overwhelmingly opposed to the administrative standards set by ORU, the House ultimately decided that the O. W. Coburn School of Law was qualified as a law school and that it had a right to require "the oath"—the honor code.

The House vote was 147 to 127 to amend Standard 211 to allow schools to have "religious affiliation and purpose."

The decision cut across the grain of the ABA leaders. During the mid-year meeting of the ABA, there was a stormy two-hour debate on the issue, but the ORU accreditation was sustained by a 176 to 138 vote.

Never to give up, the House of Delegates once again had us in the frying pan at their annual meeting in 1982 as they tried to reverse the previous votes in our favor on the thorny issue of constitutionality. The new wording they handed us allowed "religious policies as to admission and employment only to the extent that they are protected by the United States Constitution." It was evident the highest law body in the land was drifting farther and farther from religious freedom.

Yet we had our defenders. A prominent Jewish attorney, in response to the opposition of several other Jewish lawyers present, stood up and said, "You're telling me I couldn't have a school for Jewish people. I think that's wrong."

The continuing efforts to find ways to deny our law school its rightful accreditation stirred my soul. Every one of us felt one reason we were being attacked was that the ABA thought I was just one man and therefore vulnerable, while the Mormon political clout made Brigham Young University's Law School exempt from similar pressure.

Dean Kothe believed the ABA and the media simply didn't want a healing evangelist starting a law school.

In spite of all opposition, in 1982 the accredited ORU Law School graduated its first class, having successfully challenged the most powerful legal association in the nation on the constitutionality of its own rules.

But we discovered the battle wasn't over. In fact, I was afraid that the ABA would never relent, that it would keep us in court over the next ten years at a cost to us of $1 million a year in legal fees. I knew that would wear us down, not in our right or our determination, but in our willingness to pay that outrageous amount of money for the legal defense of our position.

Also, in different ways, it seemed to me that the ABA was undermining our recruiting efforts for qualified law students. At the end of our third year, it appeared we would soon reach our desired enrollment goal of three hundred in the law school. There was great excitement among us. Then the enrollment began to plummet.

More than that, it seemed to me there was a plan to ensnare me as the founder.

The dean and I were summoned to a meeting of the Deans Council, which met at Vanderbilt University in Nashville, where I had spoken once several years before. Some eighty law school deans were present. The dean and I were seated on the platform, and the floor was opened for questions. One question kept coming at us: "Will you permit homosexuality in your student body and faculty? Will you allow homosexual marriages?"

The dean handled the answer with graciousness and firmness. I remained quiet. It seemed I could feel it when they turned their attention on me. The same question, stated in different ways, was asked of us again and again.

I leaned over to our dean and asked what power this group of law school deans had. "The full power of the ABA," he whispered back. *Then this is it*, I thought, *no more appearances before the House of Delegates*. Their answer would determine a yes or no, not only that day but for years to come, and we might spend ourselves broke in constant court challenges.

I knew it was time to stop being nice. I told the dean I would answer. I stood up and faced them. I felt like Stephen before the Sanhedrin in Jerusalem when they were challenging his faith in the Lord Jesus Christ. And when he stood firm, giving the greatest Christian oration in the New Testament, they were "cut to the heart." They stoned him to death, making him the first Christian martyr. (See Acts 6:9—7:60.)

The Spirit of the Lord rose up out of my belly like "rivers of living water" (John 7:38). I told them my testimony of how Jesus saved and healed me, how the Lord called me to take healing to my generation and to build Him a university based on His authority and on the Holy Spirit.

Then I said, "There's no need to carry this sordid charade any farther. Here's your answer. You can do what you will, but as for the ORU Law School, I will not permit it to be homosexual. I am committed absolutely to obeying God and making it the same as all of ORU's schools, and that is to operate under God's authority and on the Holy Spirit."

With that I sat down.

You could have cut the atmosphere with a knife. They weren't openly gnashing their teeth, as the group of elders did at Stephen, but, I believed they were doing it in their spirits.

The chairman asked whether there were any more questions. There were none. He dismissed the meeting.

On our way out, several of the deans intercepted me. "Can't you give a little bit on homosexuality, Dr. Roberts?"

"You know the answer to that," I said.

"But we want to help you," they said.

"You have a strange way of doing it," I replied.

We returned to Tulsa.

I felt they had singled me out because I was a preacher and especially because I was a healing evangelist. It seemed to me they didn't want me and my stand for God's authority and the Holy Spirit to be an embarrassment to them.

I believed I had sensed the presence of Satan in the final meeting. Not one dean had stood up for a law school that wouldn't tolerate sodomy and that wouldn't compromise our constitutional guarantee of religious freedom. Not one.

God brought to my mind our slogan. At the entrance to the beautiful facilities of the law school, the words were imprinted on the wall: "Lawyers Can Be Healers."

The ABA members never brought up our concept that lawyers should be healers—because they didn't want to tackle us on that issue. I believe the number one need in the legal profession today is healing—to bring mediation and healing instead of a constant over-crowded docket of court trials, which has made ours a litigious society, costing billions of dollars, hurting tens of thousands of lives, and creating terrible discriminatory treatment of people on the basis of race, religion, and economic status.

I knew God wanted the ORU School of Law. Our graduates were passing the bar with the largest percentage of any law school in Oklahoma and in several other states. We had a top-quality law school faculty, some formerly supreme court justices in their states. We had both white and black faculty members and a great unity of purpose. The Holy Spirit was working among the faculty and students, and I was thrilled at what God was doing. I felt I was fully obeying Him, but I knew we couldn't go on.

We had lost the battle but not the war. I knew in my spirit that God would show us the way, even as we knew the ORU Law School would close rather than compromise and spend astronomical legal fees by being constantly in court against the ABA, with its huge financial resources and endless numbers of lawyers.

I began to feel that God had a plan to continue the law school, but in the hands of a Spirit-filled man who had been my dear friend for more than thirty years: Pat Robertson.

Seed-Faithing the Law School

Before Evelyn and I ever met Pat and Dede, his dedicated wife, they had received Christ and the baptism of the Holy Spirit. And because of that, they underwent some severe sufferings. In New York, they lived on practically nothing in a tiny apartment with their four little children, but they dreamed big dreams for the Lord in the area of Christian television.

When I took the big tent to Norfolk in 1966, Pat had moved there and was ceaselessly working to get his first TV station going. He was elected chairman of my crusade by the sponsoring pastors, and we grew to know and love each other. One day, he took Evelyn and me to his house on a rented farm where Dede served us lunch, and we met the children.

After lunch, he asked me to go to his new TV studio and lay hands on it and the TV equipment and pray for God's anointing on it to open and for everything to glorify God in the future. It had rained, and he and I walked through the mud from the car to the studio. We prayed and wept and rejoiced all at the same time; we both knew we were touching destiny in the kingdom of God.

Meanwhile, I had asked about thirty young men like Pat and some young women to serve on the president's cabinet at ORU as an advisory group, and Pat was elected president of that group. The young men and women from across America really contributed to the building of ORU, and I felt their enthusiasm, faith, and commitment.

Pat remembers he had very little money at the time. He was anxious, however, for the group to sponsor needed projects of the university. When he saw the need of six tennis courts, he pledged one thousand dollars when he had only five hundred dollars of his own.

He paid it out. From that seed he told how God supplied money from unexpected sources and gave him ideas, some of which I understand were used to build a Christian network, which eventually became a very large cable network, CBN (Christian Broadcasting Network) in Virginia Beach, Virginia. Out of that has come the remarkable "700 Club."

Pat also felt the leading of the Lord to raise up a Christian university consisting of graduate schools only. There was not to be an undergraduate college of arts and sciences such as was the underpinning of ORU.

One day Pat felt God speak to him out of the blue for his ministry to send fifty thousand dollars to Oral Roberts University and our ministry. At the same time, God dealt with me to send a seed of ten thousand dollars to be used for Pat's ministry and to help with his new university for the Lord.

Neither of us knew that God had spoken to both of us. Our checks crossed in the mail. The fact was, both of us were planting seeds out of our need. As we talked about it over the phone, we were blessed that neither knew that the other felt God speaking at the same time, but that we both had obeyed.

My hope from the beginning of my healing ministry was to help bring about the unity of the body of Christ, as Paul states, "endeavouring to keep the unity of the Spirit in the bond of peace" (Eph. 4:3). I had refused to take my healing crusades to a city if the Full Gospel pastors didn't come together in unity. My position became known throughout the nation, and later other nations, and it was a thrilling sight to see the platform filled with pastors, some of whom hadn't ever spoken to one another. They certainly helped give me strength to boldly preach the whole gospel and see the Word confirmed by signs and wonders (see Mark 16:20). I owe them much for their cooperation, as does the body of Christ. Later—in 1986—I, with twenty-seven other well-known ministers, founded International Charismatic Bible Ministries (ICBM), which is an organization of ministers whose slogan is "Love and Unity Through Signs and Wonders."

It was the hour of the supreme test of whether I really believed in helping bring about the unity of the body. I can remember the very time and place that the Holy Spirit began dealing with me about the law school library and about how it could save the law school God had commanded me to raise up. The vision came very, very clear: Pat Robertson had a powerful position in government circles. He had built a Christian TV network and a Christian graduate university. He was located close to the nation's capital, was close to the president, had many loyal friends in Congress, had been trained as a lawyer, and was fearless for the Lord.

He was preparing to start a Christian school of law. Pat's great concern, I think, grew out of his legal background. He was a graduate of the Yale Law School and the son of a powerful member of the United States Senate.

The main building of CBN's law school was to open a year after we were going to close. We had almost everything he needed. If only he could speed up construction, we could offer him a great nucleus for his faculty, students to be transferred, and one of the finest law libraries in the country.

Offers were coming in from other universities trying to buy that library, to hire our faculty members, and to enroll our law students. The excellence of the school was on a par with that of the total university—and that could not be hidden.

The Lord spoke in my heart to go before the ORU Board of Regents and propose to seed-faith the ORU Law School with its top library, its accreditation, and as many faculty members and students as possible to CBN University (now named Regent University).

First, I called Pat and could hardly talk for weeping. I knew that the ORU Law School must not perish from the earth. I wanted it so much to be at ORU. But I wanted more for it to be a law school belonging to God that would graduate its students to become healers rather than divisive in nature as I had just seen in the ABA.

Pat said, "Oral, this is of the Lord. I believe God has me in position with CBN to preserve the law school under our banner, and it will still be the Lord's law school. What do you want me to do?"

"Pray," I said. "I'm going before our board, which is coming in to its annual fall meetings this week. The members must feel it, too, or it won't be done."

We prayed together over the phone, and I went before the forty-one-member ORU Board of Regents to tell them what I felt in my heart.

I didn't have to do much convincing. Without them, there would not have been a law school at ORU. The control of ORU is vested in its Board of Regents and, of the forty-one members, only four are Robertses. They are solid, Spirit-filled, faithful stewards over God's university.

Everybody on the board who was present expressed feelings on the issue. Then it was put to a vote. There was not a dissenting vote, and there was only one abstention. It was like a miracle, the unity of purpose was so strong.

I called Pat and asked if he could come the next day, meet the board, and officially accept the precious gift of the law school library. I invited him to bring his staff and meet with any faculty and students he wished. Despite his heavy schedule, he flew in the following evening to a great ovation.

The Tulsa media were present for the most unusual occasion. They reported that "Roberts called the transfer 'an opportunity for two ministries in the body of Christ to work together and to show to the world the unity of the body of Christ.' Robertson called the decision 'a historic moment in American Christianity.'"

Pat said to me, "I can't think of any instance in our history when one ministry has made a gift of this magnitude to another."

I responded, "We're not rivals. We're friends, we're brothers, and we're colaborers for Jesus Christ."

Pat told us how by working with the contractor on the building for the law school at CBN University, he believed they could open the law school the following fall. Since it was then November, the opening would occur in slightly less than a year.

The media asked if I was disappointed. I said, "Yes, because I wanted the law school to be part of ORU. But I was unable to take on the whole American Bar Association and continue to spend millions of dollars of the Lord's money uselessly. I believe with Pat Robertson's clout with Congress and with other leaders, this law school will be preserved according to its founding purpose. Besides, we are brothers in the Lord, and the unity of the body of Christ comes first!"

I didn't know at the time the full scope of Pat Robertson's plans. Through the law school, he has challenged those who have taken prayer and Bible reading out of our schools and removed symbols of the Christian faith from parks and other public places. Within five years he had a Christian lawyer, Jay Sekulow, on the law school staff. Eventually, with the very special help of Paul and Jan Crouch, the very able founders of Trinity Broadcasting Network, the first worldwide all-Christian network in history, he was instrumental in having Jay go before the U.S. Supreme Court. There Jay was the first lawyer in these times to prevail with the Supreme Court to win back some of the precious religious freedom for our public schools that had been guaranteed in our Constitution.

I didn't know that the gift of our library would speed up Pat Robertson's overall plan to become such a mighty force in the land for freedom of religion, and that through the staff of the law school, including Jay Sekulow, the nation would soon feel the might of this new instrument of God to help turn this nation, at least partway, back to God. Today this effort, in my opinion, is the single most effective effort to change things back to being more nearly like our public schools used to be.

I visited our library after it was installed in the great new building of CBN. I walked through it, laying my hands on the legal books and other items we had given as a seed of our faith. I prayed with the dean, and we had lunch with several of ORU's former faculty and students. It was a time of great peace and rejoicing in my spirit.

I continue to hear how the influence of being lawyers who are healers is strong in those we graduated over the seven-year period that the ORU Law School was in operation on our campus in Tulsa. Several have become judges, heads of law firms, and partners of others, and they are doing a new work for God in the legal profession. Indeed, they are "going into every man's world"—in their case the world of law with the love of God in their hearts and actions.

I also believe ORU has a great harvest coming to us, for the Word says, "And let us not be weary in well doing: for in due season we shall reap, if we faint not" (Gal. 6:9). I have learned to live out that Scripture every day of my life: "We shall reap, if we faint not." Many times, the adversaries of my life have tempted me to grow weary in well doing. But here I am . . . still obeying God the best way I know how. And the adversaries? Well, wherever there is an open door, there will always be adversaries as you will see in the story I relate next!

CHAPTER 30

THE OPEN DOOR AND THE ADVERSARIES

AS IMPORTANT as the schools of medicine and dentistry and law were, neither they nor the graduate schools of education, business, and nursing have been able to exceed the graduate School of Theology. The very life of the university is in what we believe in terms of God, His Son Jesus Christ, and the Holy Spirit—the Holy Trinity—and we give that belief system top place in all our academic offerings.

I had known God wanted a new kind of theological seminary, one that was solidly anchored in His Word, and that would give the theology students a strong understanding of the baptism of the Holy Spirit and the value of speaking in tongues and praying for the sick, and would give them a worldview.

Little did I realize that building such a seminary would cut across the established lines of the powers at the top of many denominations. The ORU Seminary would not open until 1976, but years before that, a ministry-shaking event would take place that would influence its founding.

Prior to 1968, many old-time Pentecostal preachers and leaders, and especially of the Pentecostal Holiness Church, the one I was ordained with, had grown uncomfortable with me—and I with them.

Dr. Vinson Synan, my lifelong friend in the Pentecostal Holiness Church, once said, "Oral, the leaders of the Pentecostal church did not know how to handle you because your ministry was so large. They weren't against you as much as they couldn't control you."

In 1968, I received a telephone call from Bishop Angie Smith, who was over the Oklahoma Conference of the United Methodist Church, and Dr. Finis Crutchfield, pastor of Boston Avenue Methodist Church (Tulsa's largest), to invite me to meet with them on a matter of importance. The meeting resulted in the bishop's invitation to transfer my ordination to the Methodist church.

I said, "Bishop Smith, do you understand I am Pentecostal and charismatic in experience, that I speak in tongues daily and pray for the sick as a healing evangelist?"

He said, "Yes, I do. That's the reason I am inviting you."

I replied, "If the Lord leads me to do this, you must understand I must be free to be myself and true to my calling and way of worshiping God."

The bishop replied, "Dr. Roberts, if you change, we don't want you."

Dr. Crutchfield added, "Oral, during the past several months, Bishop Smith has received dozens of letters and phone calls from Methodist pastors and laypeople to ask you to join us. We need you."

"Will I be totally free to preach and pray for people as I'm led of God?" I asked.

"In the Methodist church, we have a free pulpit," the bishop said. "While you're in the pulpit, no man can stop you."

I really responded to that. I said, "Bishop Smith, let me lay before you a revelation I believe I have received from God. I believe the structure of the Methodist church and the hunger I've seen among the people to become as spiritual as the church was in the beginning when John Wesley founded it make it one of the only historical denominations where *a renewing of the Holy Spirit can happen*. The Spirit has spoken to me about this. If you really want me, and you give me my freedom, I'll consult with my leaders at ORU and the Oral Roberts Evangelistic Association and let you know as soon as possible."

With that, we joined hands and prayed.

I consulted first with Bob DeWeese, with whom I was very close in my ministry and whose spiritual judgment I admired the most.

Bob, as crusade director and my coevangelist, had borne the brunt of the criticism of pastors in the cities where we went for crusades. He was wise enough to keep all but the constructive part from me, leaving my mind free to stay with my preaching instead of being tempted to strike back at the critics. Only God knows what Bob endured—and without developing a bad attitude in return. Not once had he ever drawn me into one of those controversies. His help was priceless to me.

Bob, however, was stinging from what he felt was the mistreatment, some of it deliberate, over the years. He just had grace to bear it. In my conferring with him on a step I was seriously considering taking, which would have ramifications nationwide, he looked straight at me for several moments.

"Oral," he said, "I don't know how you've survived these twenty-one years under the most intense pressures I've ever known against a man of God, but you have. While many of our Pentecostal brethren have cooperated and benefited, many, especially some leaders, have been unrelenting in their opposition. And the sad thing is that in their hearts, they believe in healing and the miraculous. But because they seek to control, they have, in effect, joined those who fight God's healing power being poured out upon the people through your ministry."

"Bob, I know. But if I take this step, it won't be because of the stand of some of those leaders and their uncomfortableness with me."

"What else could it be?" he asked.

"You've known me and worked closely with me from 1951 to 1968. I ask you, have you ever seen me take a major step unless I felt in my spirit God had spoken to me?"

"No, I haven't. And I believe that's the main reason I've stayed with you. Are you saying God has spoken to you about this move?"

"Yes, I am. And you know that my main thrust is to get people saved, healed, and filled with the Holy Spirit. I believe without the miraculous and the baptism of the Holy Spirit, the denominations as we know them will get colder and colder and less and less effective—and all in the face of Jesus' soon coming."

"Yes, I know that. You've even established ORU on God's authority and the Holy Spirit."

"I ask you, Bob, in the fear of God, how do you feel about my accepting the bishop's invitation to bring my ministry into the Methodist church?"

Bob's countenance brightened, and he said, "I think you should do it. God raised you up to take His healing power to your generation, and this will give you a new and larger platform on which to do it. I only wish I were coming into the Methodist church with you."

Soon the Lord gave me a Scripture for guidance:

> "*For* a great door and effectual is opened unto me, and there are many adversaries" (1 Cor. 16:9).

I caught on immediately. He was giving me an open door through the Methodist church, but there would be many adversaries.

So when the bishop presented me at the 1968 annual conference in Oklahoma City, I was very aware of the open door and the adversaries. But I was obeying God, and obedience has always been essential to my walk with God.

The bishop kindly stated he was not requiring me to be reordained; he was accepting my ordination coming to me by the good man who had ordained me in the beginning, Bishop Dan T. Muse.

Earlier that day I had met with the fourteen-member examining committee for new ministers coming into the conference. I got off to a bad start on the first question: "Dr. Roberts, why do you want to be a Methodist?"

"I don't," I said.

"Would you care to explain?" the chairman asked.

"I desire to be a Christian, and by coming into the Methodist church at this stage in my ministry, I believe God will use me more to win people to Christ, to bring His healing power to the sick, and to be part of a renewing of the Holy Spirit in the Methodist church."

They asked other questions, which I answered to the best of my judgment and ability. I let them know of my love and respect for them, for the grand old Methodist church, which I had first joined as a young boy in Stratford, Oklahoma. I said that I meant no offense by saying my highest desire was above being a Methodist, which was being a Christian.

I could see, however, what God meant about an open door being accompanied by adversaries, some of which were in that room. Despite that, the vote on the conference floor to receive my ordination was unanimous.

Immediately, the open door opened wide . . . wide . . . wide.

———— *God Working Through Me in the Methodist Church*

As I look back to 1968 through 1987 as a member of the United Methodist Church's ministry, I can describe it only as a miracle beyond my own doing. For several months, God dealt with me about a renewing of the Holy Spirit in the great old historic church, and I was to have a large part in it. Like Mary of old when the angel visited her about giving birth to God's Son, I "pondered" this in my heart.

My father—and his forebears all the way back in Wales—had been Methodist until he received the baptism of the Holy Spirit through the Pentecostal outpouring in 1910. Despite becoming an ordained minister in the Pentecostal Holiness Church, he still loved the Methodist church. Grandfather Roberts, a frontier judge in Pontotoc County, had been both a lay preacher and a steward (a deacon) in the Methodist church in Ada.

I joined the Methodist church at age ten and remained until my conversion and healing at age seventeen when I joined the Pentecostal Holiness Church. But I, too, never lost my love for the Methodists. Great numbers of them had attended the churches I pastored before my healing ministry began. Many Methodist pastors were friendly and open to my healing ministry, and I appreciated them.

I was absolutely delighted that my first invitation was to a black Methodist church. The pastor and the people seemed to be "dancing in their spirits" as I entered the pulpit and later prayed for the healing of their sick. I felt totally at home.

Soon invitations began to arrive from bishops from New York State, North Carolina, Georgia, Iowa, Minnesota, Arkansas, Kentucky, and all over to speak at their annual conferences. The subject each of them asked me to cover was the Holy Spirit and speaking in tongues and healing.

I discovered I really had a free pulpit as I preached exactly as I had in the crusades. I soon learned, however, I couldn't meet all of the demands and run ORU, my TV ministry, and my ministry to my

Pentecostal brethren and all others. During those first several years, the door was wide open to me and my call throughout the Methodist church, and it seemed to me the renewing of the Holy Spirit was meeting a genuine hunger.

Yet some writers in some Methodist publications raised questions concerning whether or not I fit into the denomination, and whether they were a people who wanted a renewal of the Holy Spirit or should embrace healing by faith. The most critical comment came, however, from three or four Methodist seminaries. My message cut right across the German theology that came to America in the early thirties, and that had been embraced by many Methodist theology leaders and professors. There was no room in their theology for a renewal of the Holy Spirit. I felt deeply for the young preachers studying their theology, for I personally knew how easily they could miss out on the work of the Holy Spirit in their ministries.

A Seminary with Theology and *God's Power*

Dr. Jimmy Buskirk, a Spirit-filled Methodist professor at Emory University Seminary in Atlanta, had caught the Holy Spirit's move and God's healing power. He attended the Sunday evening services of Mt. Paron Church of God in Atlanta, pastored by my dear friend Dr. Paul Walker, who was the chairman of two of my Atlanta crusades.

Jimmy received the baptism of the Holy Spirit and spoke in tongues. In many respects, he became the most popular professor in the Emory Seminary, which was thought to be the most spiritual and conservative of the Methodist seminaries. As professor of evangelism, he taught overflowing classes, and his name was moving swiftly through charismatic circles.

Jimmy attended my last Memphis crusade, bringing a member of his church with breathing problems with him. He took home a healed man. The next Sunday morning, he had the man give his testimony at his church.

Jimmy was typical of a small but powerful move of the Holy Spirit in the Methodist church. When we met while I was at Emory Seminary to give a speech, we hit it off instantly.

Later, following an invitation to minister to the faculty and students of ORU, Jimmy's anointed ministry touched us deeply in the

Spirit—and perhaps me the most. I saw him as the founding dean of ORU's new seminary. We had a meeting to discuss the possibility and to make sure he knew where I was coming from.

I began by saying, "Let me put it to you straight whether you feel led to be the founding dean of our graduate School of Theology."

"Please do," he said.

"I believe that the charismatic movement has the power *without the theology* and that the church at large has a very critical theology *without the power*. I want the new ORU graduate School of Theology to put the two together, and I want to see the church become the church and therefore become the instrument of the Holy Spirit it is intended to be."

We went back to the day of Pentecost as described in Acts 2 when the Christian church was born. Jimmy said all that happened in the church's beginning—and was to be happening today—was his theology. He stated that through most of his ministry, he preached things I believed. We may have said them differently, but they meant the same thing.

He said, "Oral, I see now that you come at theology in a systematic way, not on who is right but on what is right, and that is systematic with you. You are a systematic theologian in your thought processes and preaching processes. You lay the whole groundwork from the Bible view. You don't take bits and pieces, but from a historical view from Genesis to Revelation, you fit everything into a whole. You're like few people I've ever heard or talked to."

After much deliberation and prayer, Jimmy accepted. Soon the seminary was all I had dreamed about, and it grew rapidly.

From the beginning, Jimmy said it would take some doing to staff the seminary with the best people available: "We have to pick believers out of the cesspools. We don't want to spend the majority of our time defending what we believe. We want to spend our time building on what we believe."

I spent many hours with members of the faculty in both individual and group discussions as we sought the mind of God to be the seminary He wanted us to be. Soon we were accredited, and not long after, the Methodist church put its stamp of accreditation on us for the Methodist young men and women who wanted to graduate from a charismatic seminary.

I did my graduate theology work with the Methodists by corre-
spondence, since they required a master of divinity degree or its
equivalent. However, I decided to finish my theological assignments with the ORU Seminary. Dr. Buskirk asked me to do a special dissertation so that if outsiders doubted the authenticity of my
theological scholarship, the dissertation alone would convince
anyone that I had more than successfully completed the requirements. The ORU Board of Regents asked Dean Buskirk to confer
my master of divinity degree on me in their presence. It was a
great moment for me.

During Dr. Buskirk's time as dean from 1975 to 1984, I named
him vice provost of Spiritual Affairs, as I had named Dr. Winslow
as vice provost for Medical Affairs. Under Jimmy's spiritual leadership, ORU reached a new high in diversity of student backgrounds
and in a bond of unity that was precious to me.

I was a classical Pentecostal and charismatic before I transferred to the Methodist church. I was the same during the nineteen years I was in the Methodist church. I am the same now.

In Jimmy Buskirk, I had found a man of God who, as far as I
could discern, walked the same path with me, although he was
faithful to his Methodist heritage and loved the church. He hurt for
it, he dreamed great dreams for it, and he tried to build a seminary
that would be like a beacon to his Methodist brothers and sisters in
their seminaries. He longed to see them come out from their growing stance of liberalism and return to the simple roots of John
Wesley, whose ministry was the most supernatural in the Holy
Spirit the world had seen since the days of the apostles up to his
time.

Some 50 percent of ORU's seminary graduates had been appointed to Methodist churches in Oklahoma, some 20 percent of
all pastors in the Oklahoma Conference. The other graduates
began pastoring in Pentecostal, charismatic, and other churches,
including many who built independent churches or ministries.

I urged them, and all other seminary graduates, to ask to go to
the smallest or hardest places and then allow the Holy Spirit to
empower and lead them in bringing those churches out of the doldrums. They were to pray in the Holy Spirit and strive to become
great churches for the Lord and the church. And that's what they
have pretty well done.

The bishops and leaders of other churches asked for more and more of our graduates to become pastors. "We have no trouble with them or their egos; they are happy to go anywhere just so they can let the Holy Spirit work through them," they told me.

I knew the lay Methodists were happy to have young pastors like the ORU seminary-trained ones to be assigned to lead their churches. They told me that time and again.

There was definitely a move of the Holy Spirit on. It was part of the "open door" God had promised me through His Word when I entered the Methodist church. But as such inroads were being made in the great old historic church, there were, as God had said, "many adversaries."

Typical pastors and laypeople were as open to my ministry as I could have asked for in Tulsa, and across America, and as far away as England. Lord J. Arthur Rank, the leading Methodist layman in England, received the baptism of the Holy Spirit with speaking in tongues in a meeting he sponsored, "A Day with Oral Roberts," for other Methodist laymen in London. Later, he brought me to England for a crusade, and even the archbishop of Canterbury attended.

Lord Rank was the first to sponsor a chair at ORU, and to my joy, it was a chair on the Holy Spirit with me as the first to occupy it. Today, every entering ORU student is required to take those foundation classes based on what I taught on the Holy Spirit. It's another way God proved that He meant what He said when He told me to build His university on His authority and on the Holy Spirit.

Meanwhile, the graduate School of Theology, under Dean Jimmy Buskirk, continued to prosper. It received early accreditation from the American Theological Association, which included the United States and Canada. Not long after, through Dean Buskirk's influence, the school was accredited by the theological division of the Methodist church, which meant young men and women studying at the ORU Seminary could receive the same financial assistance as at other Methodist or Methodist-approved seminaries.

Those attending the seminary came from more than thirty denominations and several independent groups. The Holy Spirit pervaded the seminary and gave a strong spiritual boost to the entire university.

Two major happenings brought about a dramatic change.

The First United Methodist Church in Tulsa was rapidly leaning toward the Holy Spirit renewal. Dr. L. D. Thomas, the pastor, had received the Holy Spirit in my living room. He was anointed before, but after he was Spirit filled, a boldness came upon him concerning the full gospel. Soon the formerly staid First United Methodist Church began to come alive, and it attracted overflow crowds.

Near the close of 1983, Dr. Thomas died suddenly.

I knew Dr. Buskirk ached to get back into the full-time pastoral ministry. He did not tell me at first he was seriously contemplating the call of the First United Methodist Church in Tulsa to be its pastor.

Jimmy had a pastor's heart, and I think because he felt he had the seminary solidly based on the Holy Spirit and growing, he could safely leave. The call of First United Methodist for Jimmy to be pastor was unanimous.

I do know how proud I am of the way he has taken hold of that great church Dr. Thomas left, and he has built it into an even stronger charismatic United Methodist church. I know how spiritual the sermons are, how unashamed of the Holy Spirit Jimmy is, how he is unintimidated by any to tone down. In fact, they have just commenced building a new addition to the sanctuary beside the old building, which has been Methodism's cathedral in Tulsa for over one hundred years.

Jimmy is very happy there. He still speaks at our chapels, he continues to advise and boost and assist the seminary, and our friendship has never been closer.

I suspect it was God's time for the move, for God had a very special man to be the second dean, Dr. Larry Lea.

The New Dean—A Man of Prayer

Dr. Larry Lea, a graduate of the Southwestern Baptist Seminary, served under Dr. Howard Conatser, pastor of the Beverly Hills Baptist Church in Dallas. The church had entered into the baptism of the Holy Spirit and the gifts of the Spirit. Larry had been right in the middle of this sensational happening in a strong Southern Baptist church.

Upon the death of Pastor Conatser, Larry was asked to succeed him, but he felt led to enter his own calling. That calling in a few short years led him to build from scratch the ten-thousand-member Church on the Rock in Rockwall, Texas. He became nationally known not only for building the great charismatic church but also for having a powerful prayer ministry.

I met Larry Lea first on a Sunday evening when he preached for Victory Christian Center in Mabee Center on the ORU campus. Pastor Billy Joe Daugherty had asked Larry to lead a large prayer gathering.

He was a scholar in his own right and full of the Holy Spirit, and I listened with an open heart to him that evening. In the midst of his sermon on prayer, Dr. Lea suddenly stopped and asked me to come forward. As I stood near him at the pulpit, he began to weep, asking me to lay hands on him for a greater anointing of the Spirit upon his life and ministry, especially his prayer ministry.

As I did so, the Spirit ran all through me, and prophetic words flowed from my lips: "This is a young apostle of prayer. I knew it not until I touched him. He will lead thousands into the deepest prayer ministry they have ever known."

The place exploded. Hundreds stood, clapped, rejoiced, and affirmed the prophecy. It was an unforgettable moment.

I felt in my spirit Dr. Lea would soon be connected with ORU. When the assistant dean, Dr. Paul Chappell, one of ORU's graduates, brought Larry to my office, he told me that he and the entire faculty, and many of the students, were praying I would consider Larry as the new dean. The witness of it flowed through me like quiet but deep waters.

Depending on Dr. Paul Chappell for most of the administrative work so he could continue pastoring Church on the Rock, Larry hit the seminary on his knees. Soon a spirit of prayer engulfed the faculty and students and those of us in the leadership of the university. Larry did three most important things from the very beginning, in addition to his prayer leadership.

First, he spent time with the faculty and with the students in groups and as individuals.

Second, he knew my calling by observing me for many years before I met him and by receiving revelation from the Holy Spirit. He also knew how I had an overview of the entire Word of God and showed how everything pointed toward Jesus: His preaching, His teaching, and His healing. Larry reemphasized that by his own superb knowledge of the Word and his close relationship with the healing Christ.

Third, Larry made contact concerning the seminary with spiritual leaders with whom he had a working prayer relationship in the U.S. and other nations. Soon the enrollment began to swell, and by the end of the two years he was dean, we had some five hundred enrolled from the master's to the doctoral level, making us the fifteenth largest seminary in the country out of two hundred accredited seminaries in the U.S. and Canada. We received much favorable attention, including our black constituency. Talk about integration—not only the seminary but the whole university was rich with the diversity and race of its student body. Larry Lea is partly responsible for that.

I must say that those two short years catapulted the seminary into another dimension: in prayerfulness, in scholarship accomplishments, in theological breakthroughs in the Bible, the church, and the Holy Spirit. Not only did the seminary attract a larger number of students, it took on a definite spirit of prayer, with an emphasis on the supernatural that I had longed for. I don't know where Christian people, including Christian educators, got the idea the scholar had to steer as far away as possible from the teaching of Jesus that He confirms His word by signs and wonders. Jesus' confirmation of the preaching of His word supernaturally is totally and absolutely essential *if* we are to call ourselves His followers.

When the call rose in him to take his prayer ministry to the nation, Larry announced he had to obey God to do it, a language I understood.

We moved Dr. Paul Chappell into the deanship, partly because of Dr. Lea's and Dr. Buskirk's strong recommendation, but primarily because we felt in our spirits his hour had come to lead the seminary. During the years since then, that feeling has been more than justified in Dean Paul Chappell, one of our very own. There is no doubt God is in charge of the ORU graduate School of Theology, and it is on the right track. We are graduating approximately one hundred seminary students each year, and they are filling important posts all over the world.

I'm also happy to report the graduate School of Theology is now having a higher graduation rate than any other graduate school of the university. Dr. Chappell has also established a branch of our seminary in the Church on the Way in Van Nuys, California, with my dear friend, Pastor Jack Hayford, as the deputy dean. The branch is under the umbrella of our accreditation. I see good things ahead for our first branch of the ORU Seminary.

──────── *Head-On with the Adversaries*

Meanwhile, in 1987, I was to face head-on the clever work of the adversaries whom I had largely ignored. But they had not ignored me.

Vinson Synan once told me that while he lived in Oklahoma City, he had come to know the Oklahoma United Methodist bishop, Dr. Hardt. One day he asked Vinson how to handle me. Vinson said he told him, "You don't handle Oral Roberts. He is his own man. He will respect you, but he will do what God tells him to do, no matter the cost to himself. If you understand that one thing, he will continue to be a great blessing to the Methodist movement." Bishop Hardt thanked him and said, "You have helped me."

I well remembered Bishop Hardt's kindness to me and the powerful message he delivered at one of the ORU chapels, one that our students received enthusiastically. I admired him greatly. However, not all of the hierarchy of the Methodist church shared Bishop Hardt's acceptance of me.

One day I learned the Methodists had withdrawn their accreditation. That loss meant young men and women studying from that church who were in the ORU Seminary lost their financial subsidies, which was a serious concern to many of them.

Next, six professors of the Methodist church resigned. It was an amicable parting. I loved them and they felt my love. It was true, United Methodist churches and seminaries had been trying to hire some of our professors. Two of the six seemed glad to leave, but four were extremely reluctant. I could not help thinking that their leaving was in part due to the time I spent in seeing to it the seminary stayed with its founding purpose: operating under God's authority and on the Holy Spirit. One of the professors later told me he had received an implied threat that he might lose his ordination credentials if he stayed at ORU.

My response was, God had sent them there and He was leading them away. A far larger number of theological professors
who had an earned doctorate and who believed in ORU's position
were anxious and ready to come. That proved to be a great blessing. However, I want to state unequivocally that the number of
highly qualified and Spirit-filled theologians from the Methodist
church was one of the keys to getting the accreditation the seminary received from the American Association of Theological
Seminaries. We owe them a great debt not only for their Spirit-
filled lives but also for their scholarship they brought to the seminary.

The move of the hierarchy, the ones who head the Methodist
church, had been in action concerning my ministry for at least the
last six of the nineteen years I was ordained as a preacher in the
Methodist church. I was blocked here and blocked there, but my
Tulsa Methodist brethren decided to overlook it. They said they
didn't feel it represented the feelings of Methodist pastors and people or most of the bishops.

It made no matter with me because God kept that steady hand
on me to stay where I was. He was doing a mighty renewing of the
Holy Spirit in the Methodist church.

Reliable leaders gave me an estimate that a million Methodists
—pastors and laypeople—had received the infilling of the Holy
Spirit during the nineteen years I was ministering among them. In
no way do I say this to infer this happened only because of my
ministry. Many other anointed ones within the church, such as
those in the Lay Witness Movement, had a hand in the moving of
God to bring a renewal of this dimension.

All I know is, one morning I woke up and a headline in the
Tulsa World stated that Oral Roberts had been cast out of the
Methodist church by a special committee of leaders. The news was
carried nationwide. No one knew what to think. When a reporter
from the Tulsa paper called me to respond, I stated,

> I knew nothing of the revocation of my ordination until I read
> it in the newspaper, as nothing was communicated to me
> orally or in writing.

> But I will always carry the deepest love and appreciation for
> the United Methodist Church and its people. I am profoundly

grateful that I had at least a small part in the charismatic renewal in the Methodist church, and pray that it increases.

I will continue to exercise my ministry as I have for forty
years as one called of God to teach, preach, and have a healing ministry.

Bishop Solomon, the current Oklahoma bishop, and dear
Jimmy Buskirk met with me and tried to help me believe it was
not true. That was because it had come down from a high-up
group whose names and positions were not named. No one
seemed to know who they were.

I couldn't help thinking somebody in the hierarchy of the
Methodist church had grown too uncomfortable with Oral Roberts,
and the group had a way of acting that couldn't be countered by
my bishop.

Evelyn's reaction was entirely different from what I was feeling. She told me, "Oral, it was God's time for you to come out of
that denomination, and God just used that unknown group to put
you out." She's a pretty wise woman, and after more than forty
years of being married to her and seeing her wisdom at work, I
didn't dismiss what she said. God has His ways and they supersede
any human action.

Today, ORU seminary-trained preachers are everywhere in
the United Methodist Church. I have not heard of one of them becoming noncharismatic. I believe that is because God is true to His
word to me in 1968 that He was sending a renewing of the Holy
Spirit in the Methodist church and that I was to be a part of it.
Although I became a stumbling block to many of the leaders, that
was nothing new to me.

I'm thankful that I've kept many friends among this powerful
denomination. I love them dearly and keep them in my prayers always, the same as I do for those in the Pentecostal Holiness
Church.

A New Fellowship

I'm relating this because I feel believers should know there
are powers at the top of many denominations who can't deal with
people they can't control, regardless of how God is using them,

preachers or laypeople. Therefore, it should strengthen our determination to keep God as our Source, and not man or any institution.

I'm convinced when you obey God, regardless of whether it's easy or tough, when one door closes, He has another door open for you to enter. For me, it was the voice of God speaking in my spirit to form a fellowship that would have no one at the top with power so secretive or so absolute as I'd just experienced: the International Charismatic Bible Ministries Fellowship.

Just one year earlier—1986—I had felt an irresistible urge in my spirit to call twenty-seven top charismatic leaders to meet with me in a Dallas hotel. Each one responded. We discussed that through this fellowship, those who felt led could remain in their denominations, and those who were independent could come together in nothing but love. This fellowship would not be a denomination. We would meet each June in a major conference where anybody in ministry or church work could come and feel at home. We elected seventy-seven trustees, including the founding twenty-seven, who would receive no pay, and who would pay their own way to this annual conference to meet with the thousands of ministers and others attending with one agenda: to give them what we had in our callings in a nonjudgmental way and just love them without reservation.

Our theme would be:

Love and Unity Through Signs and Wonders

In June 1986, ICBM took off at its first conference with more than four thousand ministerial and church leaders attending. It was like a fresh breath of the Holy Spirit. I don't think the trustees had ever felt such love in our entire ministries coming from ourselves as we, as trustees, ministered and as we received in return.

ICBM has met annually each June for three days, and many say it is the most Holy Spirit–anointed and –led conference they've ever attended. I know that's true in my experience.

Meanwhile, my life and ministry have gone on with integrity of heart and purpose. That's one of the secrets of my ministry. Later, I will be sharing the ten greatest secrets of my life and ministry, but first, let me give you my impressions of the presidents.

CHAPTER 31

THE PRESIDENTS

NEVER IN my wildest dreams did I think I would ever be invited to meet a president of the United States. As a young man, I was very politically minded, and as I've already indicated, my goal in life was to become a lawyer, then governor of Oklahoma. They were high dreams for a stuttering youth from a preacher's family living in poverty.

The hook of my own ambition was deep inside me, but when the final moment came to choose, God's call was compelling, and soon it was like I never had the old dreams. All that mattered was to obey God, no matter the cost.

John F. Kennedy

It never entered my mind that I would be invited by President John F. Kennedy to visit with him in the White House. The invitation came straight from the White House, but I was to learn later that forces behind the scenes had precipitated my meeting President Kennedy.

We had the big tent cathedral stretched in Cumberland, Maryland, with capacity crowds. On Saturday morning, the day before we were to close the ten-day crusade, Bob DeWeese, my crusade manager, rushed to my room with the message that President Kennedy wanted me to meet him at 11:00 A.M. in the White House.

"Bob, you've got to be kidding," I said.

"No, Oral, I'm not kidding. This is the second call we received this morning. It's really the president."

I had always felt great about Billy Graham's open door to the presidents from Truman on. I felt he represented a larger following than mine, was born more to having that kind of influence, and would be a force for good with our nation's highest leaders.

So I was surprised and really didn't believe the call was genuine. I asked Bob to call the White House and be absolutely certain President Kennedy was calling for me. Returning soon, Bob said, "It's on the level, Oral, and I've got a plane ready to fly you there during the next forty minutes."

"But what about my 2:00 P.M. service when I preach to the Partners of my ministry? You know this has been announced all week. How do you know I can get back in time?"

Bob, rather exasperated, said, "Oral, the president of the United States wants to see you at eleven o'clock this morning. Now come on, you can't keep a president waiting."

It was so hard to believe. But what a morning! When the special assistant, Mr. Kenneth O'Donnell, met me near the Oval Office, he greeted me and said, "The president has had to summon the Cabinet, which meets next to the Oval Office, but there's a little room between. He's waiting for you there. Follow me."

Mr. O'Donnell opened the door, and I walked in alone. Standing there in the middle of the room was one of the most striking men I'd ever seen. He was taller than I expected, seemingly an inch or two more than my six one, very trim, and dressed impeccably in a dark suit. He wore a smile that covered his whole face.

As I walked up to shake his hand, his physical presence was so strong it almost knocked me down. The magnetism of the man was more powerful than any I'd ever encountered.

His grip was steel. His eyes flashed, and he looked straight into my eyes. "Thank you, Reverend Roberts, for coming on such a short notice. How is your healing crusade in Cumberland?"

I started to say, "How did you know about my crusade?" Instead, I began to tell him.

"And the healings? The miracles?" he asked.

"The Lord Jesus is healing many, Mr. President," I answered.

"Great," he replied.

Never taking his eyes from my face, he said, "Reverend Roberts, what is your feeling about our country right now? Do you see your religious revivals and the work of the churches rising in influence to inspire our people?"

Before I could answer, he said, "Oh, yes, I want you to know I've enjoyed your television programs."

"You watch my crusades here in the White House?"

"Yes. That's how I know about the healings and the miracles."

I'm not usually at a loss for words, but all I could reply was, "Thank you."

Lining the little room between the Oval Office and the Cabinet room were several full-sized windows. To my right, I noticed one was being opened from the outside and a man was stepping through. The president turned and said, "Reverend Roberts, I want you to meet my younger brother, Robert."

I knew Robert was the attorney general, but that was about all I knew of him.

He stepped forward and laid the coldest hand in mine I'd ever felt. It was not a handshake like the firm grip of the president. He said in a low voice, "Glad to meet you."

I looked into the coldest eyes I'd ever remembered seeing.

The president smiled. "Robert usually comes in that window when he gets a quick summons to a Cabinet meeting."

I thought it was time for me to leave, for the moment had turned awkward for me. The president hadn't moved, his eyes still pleasantly on me. Almost impulsively, I reached for both his hands and said, "President Kennedy, may I pray for you?"

"I'd be honored," he replied.

I don't remember what I said to God in my prayer. But I do remember pressing my right hand against his and feeling the presence of God shooting through it into this man of such striking personality and friendliness.

With that, I told him good-bye and Godspeed and left.

Bob DeWeese had me back in Cumberland shortly after 2:00 P.M., and I went on with the crusade service. I didn't mention to the crowd where I had been. But inside I think I glowed a little bit.

President Kennedy was tragically killed a few weeks later in Dallas. Like most everyone else, I recall where I was when the news flashed over television. I felt a physical shock to my system that such a promising leader had been cut down at age forty-six, and I felt the tears, not only for his death and our country, but also for the chance I'd had to pray a prayer for him, however brief, such a short time before.

It kept coming into my mind how wide a difference, at least outwardly, between John and Robert Kennedy. One day I was relating this to my friend, Rosey Grier, who had become a member of the Board of Regents of Oral Roberts University. He told me how wrongly I had judged Robert.

Rosey was the man, you may recall, who held Robert Kennedy's head on his lap in the kitchen of the Ambassador Hotel in Los Angeles. Robert had just made a speech for his candidacy for president, and the assassin, Sirhan Sirhan, shot and mortally wounded him.

I had seen the scene on TV as Rosey held the dying Robert and wept over him, and I was deeply moved by this gentle giant. Rosey Grier was one of the "Fearsome Foursome" in the awesome defensive line of the Los Angeles Rams' professional football team.

Rosey said to me, "Oral, you're completely wrong about Robert Kennedy. He was one of the kindest, ablest, and most compassionate men I ever knew. I traveled with him in his campaign tours and was very close to him, and I saw him in every kind of situation. America lost a great man when Robert Kennedy was killed."

I felt much better about my brief encounter with Robert.

I previously mentioned forces behind my meeting President Kennedy. Robert Kerr, who had served as governor of Oklahoma and was then a member of the U.S. Senate, was widely reported to be one of the most powerful people in the Senate. From those early years, I had loved and admired Robert Kerr. We didn't see each other often, but we kept in touch. He was always very supportive of my healing ministry. A well-known Baptist layman, he believed in miracles; in fact, his whole family did. His nephew, Bill, later attended ORU.

Senator Kerr and Senator McClellan of our neighboring state, Arkansas, had used their powerful influence to get legislation passed for the Arkansas River, the main river in both states, to become navigable from north of Tulsa to the mighty Mississippi River. It was a billion-dollar project back in 1960, and it has been hugely successful.

Senator Kerr had a large cattle ranch near Poteau, in the mountains of eastern Oklahoma, where the new river channel would flow through. He asked President Kennedy to dedicate the lock of the new Arkansas River project and to spend the night in his new home he had built on the ranch.

I later learned that when the president agreed to come to Oklahoma for that purpose, he asked Senator Kerr if there was anything of a personal nature he might do for him. "See my young friend, Oral Roberts, in the White House," the senator replied. "Done," said the president.

It reminded me that things don't just happen; more often they're made to happen by forces behind the scenes.

The President's Daughter, Caroline

Before I relate my visits with four other U.S. presidents, I think it might be interesting to describe the visit of the president's daughter, Caroline Kennedy, to Oral Roberts University in 1978.

Caroline was visiting a girlfriend in Tulsa when she asked her if she would take her out to ORU. Her friend called my secretary, Mrs. Ruth Rooks, and arranged the visit.

When I met her, I was in Dean Jimmy Buskirk's office on the sixth floor of the Learning Resources Center. Caroline was in her twenties, a fine-looking young woman, very bright and friendly. After we were introduced, she told me that she had toured the campus and had gone up in the Prayer Tower, which is the centerpiece of the campus. She said that the university had exceeded her expectations.

I thanked her and we talked awhile.

Somehow we got around to discussing the charismatic movement. She said she had heard about it and had a few friends who spoke in tongues. She asked me to explain just what it means for a Christian to speak in tongues, which I did.

I was quite surprised at the depth of her interest.

After I had explained in detail, Caroline stood up, and I offered a prayer for her. She thanked me. I told her good-bye and said I hoped someday she would have the Holy Spirit's infilling and the prayer language of the Spirit for herself.

Bringing Salvation and Healing to a Few in Vietnam

I believe President Lyndon Johnson probably changed the nation more than any president since Franklin D. Roosevelt. Although I never personally met him, I was told much about him by two personal friends, Calvin Thielman, an aide to Billy Graham, and Jim Jones, later a congressman from Tulsa. Both of them worked closely with President Johnson during his time in the White House.

President Johnson was a big man physically and big in his grasp of the problems of America, especially concerning giving our black people their rights, instigating programs for the poor and, through Congress, making such powerful changes that there is much second-guessing over them today. His fatal flaws were underestimating the will of the North Vietnamese people to fight, not assessing the impossibility of fighting an unpopular war on the land mass of Asia, and above all miscalculating the deep feelings of the American people concerning the Vietnam War.

When I was invited to make a tour of South Vietnam, the U.S. Chief of Chaplains took me to many places where I ministered. I traveled up and down that bloody land with him by plane, by helicopter, by Jeep, and by foot power. I preached to troops and prayed for the injured in makeshift jungle hospitals as well as in the largest hospital in the world at the time, which was located in Saigon. It was literally overflowing with both American and Vietnamese soldiers injured in the war. I also preached to more than a thousand captured Vietcong in a large barbed wire enclosure, led over three hundred to Christ, and followed that by laying hands on each of them in prayer for healing. I had been warned not to touch the officers among the Vietcong as I prayed. But they seemed to welcome the laying on of hands as I prayed for the healing of their bodies.

Traveling from Saigon in the south to Da Nang near the DMZ line, I was torn with compassion at what I saw, yet another side of me felt like every hour there was a week. I saw inevitable defeat for our young men and women, many of whom were giving their lives. I felt we would be fighting there for years to come.

Looking back, I realize that being in low-flying army helicopters was one of the most dangerous things I have ever done.

Just after I left, I read that American helicopters were shot down in most of the areas where I had flown. There's nothing glamorous about war.

I well recall that every media person or group I met was against the war.

I also recall my first crusade upon returning home, in Cobo Convention Center Arena in Detroit. I told the ten-thousand-member audience, "This is a war America cannot win but cannot afford to lose." Whether I was right or not, it expressed my feelings after seeing, touching, smelling, and feeling the devastating effects of the war.

Later on in the Vietnam War, as Calvin Thielman and Jim Jones described it to me, there was a brooding presence in the White House. President Lyndon B. Johnson, a man of immense ability and a burning desire to right long-standing wrongs in America, finally came to the conclusion not to run for another term because he saw no way out.

President Johnson was followed by President Nixon, who brought an end to the war, with the nation still divided over whether we should have been in Vietnam or not.

President Richard Nixon

Meeting President Richard Nixon is another story. I was not an admirer of the man from his days as vice president under President Eisenhower. Blame it on my being a Democrat (raised in Little Dixie, the heart of which is Pontotoc County where I mostly grew up) and Nixon being a Republican. Maybe it wasn't that—I simply didn't admire him. However, after he fought his way up to being president—almost against all odds—I felt he had some inner force driving him that might be good for the country.

I had had a strange experience concerning my feelings toward Nixon. Martha Roundtree, the founder of "Meet the Press" and a powerful woman in Washington at the time, was the wife of Oliver Presbrey, who was part of the New York City advertising agency Geyer, Morey, Madden & Ballard, Inc. My television ministry was really taking off nationwide, and it needed to be in strong hands in dealing with the TV stations. Geyer, Morey, Madden & Ballard, Inc., was our choice. They assigned Oliver Presbrey to head up the account. Ollie asked Evelyn and me to come to Washington and spend a few days with him and Martha in their Georgetown home.

On our last night there, Martha had arranged a private party in their home in my honor with such leaders as Senator Talmadge from Georgia, Senator Anderson from New Mexico, Senator Bricker from Ohio, and an ambassador or two, along with their spouses. Just before dinner, and after these leaders and I had engaged in what I felt was fascinating and enlightening conversation, the subject came around to Richard Nixon. Most of them were for him. I was silent until they drew me out. I said my piece, which was mostly negative.

Martha took that moment to say she had a friend who was a seer, and she had great confidence in her. Upon learning I was to be a guest in Martha's home, this friend had asked to meet me. That left me pretty cold.

About that time, the doorbell rang. "It's my friend," Martha said. "Oral, you've just got to meet this woman."

Martha went to the door and brought the lady in. She was a well-dressed, very nice-looking person. Well, she walked straight over to where I was sitting between Senator Talmadge and Senator Bricker.

I stood up to meet her, and she immediately said, "Oral Roberts, you've been sitting here tonight talking about Richard Nixon and you're wrong."

Everyone gasped. How could she have known?

"You don't like him. You think because he was defeated by President John F. Kennedy, his political life is over. You're wrong."

Something began to tingle in my spirit. In a clear voice she said, "Richard Nixon is going to be president of the United States. It's in his lines, and you'll see it happen!"

With that she said she was glad to meet me and believed God had called me to heal the sick. Then she left. Believe me, her brief visit dominated the dinner conversation that evening. Of course, they asked me if I believed in seers, and I said she was the first one I'd ever met. And it remained to be seen if her prophecy (if that's what it was) came to pass. I said I didn't know her life of walking with God or anything about her, but as a general rule, I did not believe that the Bible, especially the New Testament, taught there are seers operating in God's kingdom today. I said I believed in the revelational knowledge of the Holy Spirit above all, and I left it at that.

Several years passed. The year Richard Nixon was nominated as the Republican candidate, I was asked to pray at the Democratic Convention in Miami Beach—my one and only time. I accepted because I felt the need was such I could really pray.

Nixon won.

I believe it was in the beginning of his second term that Nixon went to China and opened relations between China and the United States. It was a coup of world implications. Still, I hadn't thawed toward the man, although I kept my thoughts private.

We had a very outstanding man in Oklahoma who would be instrumental in bringing President Nixon and me together. I had met Dewey Bartlett when he was state senator of our district in Tulsa. Later, he was elected governor and asked for my book *The Miracle of Seed-Faith*. It was my first big-time circulated book. Through his reading of my book, he became quite interested in me and my ministry. After his first term of governor, he was elected U.S. senator from Oklahoma. Soon thereafter, he began calling me to see if I was interested in meeting President Nixon. I politely turned him down.

"He needs to meet you," he said.

"I can't remotely understand why," I replied.

Six or eight times Senator Bartlett called me. *What's going on?* I asked myself. The next time the senator phoned me, he sort of keyed me to the reason. "You know how stiff the president is on TV?" I told him I was well aware of that.

"He's a brilliant man, especially in foreign relations, but on television he just can't talk relaxed to the American people. His gestures are mechanical. He doesn't project much warmth."

"Isn't that why he lost the debate with John F. Kennedy?" I asked.

"Exactly," he replied. "Won't you come to see him?"

To my own surprise, I said, "Yes, if you can work out a suitable date."

Weeks passed, and I thought the visit would not occur. One day the phone rang and my secretary said, "It's Senator Bartlett."

The date had been set, and he asked if I would come to Washington, D.C. I agreed.

President Nixon was waiting for me in the Oval Office. When I was ushered in, he rose and stuck out his hand, saying, "At last we meet. I'm so glad you could come."

He was taller than I expected, very slim, and almost fragile looking. There was no charismatic presence or power of physical presence coming at me as I had so forcefully felt in President Kennedy. They were two different men.

I soon realized, however, there was steel in him. It was more in the whole office than in just the man himself. His aura and demeanor were quiet, sedate, but friendly nevertheless.

Immediately, President Nixon reached in his desk for a Bible, which he autographed for me, taking his time. Handing me the Bible, he said, "I know you have lots of personal Bibles, but I wanted you to have this one from me."

I had a small New Testament and Psalms, which I always carried on my person. I took it out of my shirt pocket and autographed it for him. He seemed genuinely pleased.

As we sat down, I congratulated him on his China trip, stating my feeling that it was a historical move for him to take the initiative, and that it portended something great in the future for that vast country and ours as well as for the entire world, including the kingdom of God.

His countenance lightened up and for about ten minutes he gave me the step-by-step of how it happened, of Kissinger's secret trip that had not been discovered by the media, and of the genuine good feeling he received from Mao Tse-tung. He said there was no strain on either side; it seemed that it was an event whose time had come.

I realized he was in his element, feeling deeply as he relived this unprecedented world experience that in the long run would quite possibly change the world. He was relaxed, he looked straight at me, and I felt we were truly one-on-one.

I thought, *This is a side of the president that is not known. The stiffness, the seeming aloofness, and the reaching for ways to get his ideas across, which are so apparent in his talks to the nation on television, simply are not here. I feel a warmth from this man.*

As if reading my mind, he said, "I need your help."

"My help? What could I possibly do for a president of the United States?"

"I don't know about other presidents, but you can help me."

Although Senator Bartlett had partially let me know a possible reason for Mr. Nixon's wanting to see me, I was impressed with his openness to someone outside the political arena in asking for help.

I blush now as I recall how bold I was the next few minutes. "It's about your comfort zone on television, isn't it?"

"Frankly, it is."

"Mr. President, why did you think someone on television who is in the ministry could help you?"

He stood up from behind his desk, reached for a chair, pulled it near me, and sat down. "Reverend Roberts, as I and my family have watched you on television over the years, two things have become evident. You come across totally sincere in what you believe, and you talk right to me, the viewer. In fact, it's like we're sitting face-to-face, like we are now."

He paused. A faraway look came over his face. "God knows that I'm sincere and that I believe in what I'm trying to do for our nation as president. But. . . ."

"Would you like for me to describe the way I see you when you address us on television?" I thought, *Sometimes I tread where angels fear to go*.

"Why, yes, I would."

"Is it all right for me to be perfectly frank?"

"Please do."

This is how I recall what I told him: "President Nixon, as you sit here with me, you are perfectly relaxed, yet animated. You've made me feel at ease to be here with you. I want you to know when I first started on television, the camera scared me to death. Not only was I bothered by the camera, but the whole affair got to me. First, everything was laid out for television. They made me up and brought me into the taping area that was lighted so brightly I could barely see the camera, at least six or seven technical people were scurrying around, the floor manager had me sit or stand in a certain spot so I'd be well lighted, my associates were hovering near, I was trying to remember what I was going to say, especially the opening and closing, and . . ."

"How well I know," he said.

"That wasn't all. Someone was counting time for me to start, in minutes, then in seconds. Another was whispering in my ear to look right into the camera. Worst of all, there were no people to talk to, at least that I could see with those lights in my eyes. I could hear people clearing their throats, so I started clearing mine."

He was smiling and nodding his head.

"In spite of my preparation and my prayers, a knot was forming in my stomach. Yet I was hearing a voice saying, '10, 9, 8, 7, 6, 5, 4, 3, 2, 1.' And then a finger pointed at me and a person mouthed, 'Go!' In all of my work in preaching and dealing with people, I found myself in the worst position I'd ever been in."

Then I asked, "May I tell you a story to illustrate what I mean?"

"Please do."

"Well, this little boy was to be in a church play. He had only one line to say from the Bible where Jesus said, 'It is I, be not afraid.' They rehearsed him until he was letter perfect. On the opening night, his time came to walk out on the stage and deliver his line. He walked from behind the curtain, he felt those bright lights shining in his eyes, and suddenly, he knew the house was full of people.

"He stood there, shifting from one foot to the other. His teacher kept whispering his line to him: 'It is I, be not afraid.' Finally, he blurted out, 'Folks, it's only me, and I'm scared to death!'

"Mr. President, that describes exactly how I felt when I first went on nationwide television, prime time, back in the early fifties."

Quickly, he interjected, "But you come across so relaxed, like you're talking directly to me as a friend."

"I hope so," I said. "But after all these years, the scene hasn't changed much technically. My associates are near to remind me what not to forget. The camera crew are doing their thing—adjusting the lights and sound level as I stand there during the countdown. They are all concerned with their particular things they must do for me to be rightly in position to speak into the camera and be at my best. I'm the main character, but it seems to me, by the very nature of their jobs technically, they are the main characters. I was like the little boy, feeling, 'It's only me, and I'm scared to death.'"

"But you did something to overcome that."

"It was when I finally woke up and understood that when they finished the countdown, and the light near the top of the camera flashed on, the camera was not a camera but a person, one who had voluntarily invited me into his or her home. And that person and I were just talking to each other. I knew I could talk to one person, no matter what age, who was friendly enough to invite me to talk through the TV screen."

"Then you talk not to a group but to one person?"

"Well, back in my subconscious I realize I am talking to a large number of people—TV viewers—perhaps hundreds of thousands at the same time. But I've learned in preaching to crowds of ten thousand or more in my crusades, the bigger the crowd, the more they become one person. Usually, they react as one individual. On the other hand, I learned if I'm talking to a very small crowd, say, twenty-five or fifty, each of them has a presence, a personality, and each of them is coming at me separately but at the same time. It's much easier for me to talk to a big crowd than to a handful."

The president was following me. "Then when I speak to the nation and open with, 'My fellow Americans,' the fact that there are millions watching should be in the back of my mind only. The camera is to be a friend who has invited me into his home, and I can talk to him as if we're alone. Is this what you are saying?"

"Exactly. I'm not saying it's always easy to do that among the technical surroundings required to put you on television, but when that light comes on just above the lens of the camera, then I know that's Mr. Jones or Mrs. Jones or a little boy or a little girl or a young couple, really just one or two, perhaps three or four at the most, to whom I'm preaching or talking. Now after all these years when I finally get through everything to the moment the camera comes on, I feel as much at home as anywhere else, including my pulpit."

President Nixon was a good listener, and in a sense, I felt presumptuous in saying all those things to one of his stature. I knew if my trip was to be worth anything, I had to treat him as a close personal friend who was asking my advice based on my personal experience.

An aide opened the door, which caused the president to stand. I knew it was time to leave. I asked him if I could pray a brief prayer for him, to which he graciously agreed, then I asked him to pray for me.

"I'm a Quaker, you know. We don't say our prayers out loud very often. They're more thoughts of our inner selves. But, yes, I will pray for you."

And he did.

Later, each time he addressed the nation, I watched with a close eye to the way he looked at me (through the camera and, in effect, at the camera), and I liked to think he was freer than before. I may have been wishing the best for him, but I thought I felt more warmth coming through my TV screen.

After he was forced from office, and a few years passed, I bought the book he had just written concerning war and peace. I thought it was well done and reflected knowledge and wisdom that the tragedy of the Watergate affair couldn't obscure. I wrote and told him that I enjoyed the book and learned a lot about our nation dealing with other nations, both friend and foe. I received a nice letter and an invitation that if I were ever in New Jersey, where he was living at the time, to drop by for a chat.

I was saddened to learn of the death of President Nixon on April 22, 1994. I thought his funeral was the most powerful one I had ever witnessed. It was carried on worldwide television, and it seemed the world stopped. I think many were surprised at the force of this former president on the average man and the nations of the earth. I was impressed by the many speeches of powerful American leaders, but I was more impressed by Billy Graham's sermon that closed out the ceremonies. When that prophet of God neared the close of his message, he came down on personal salvation through repentance and faith in Jesus Christ the strongest I had ever heard him.

Talk about courage, about faithfulness, about being true to his convictions over a half century—Billy's message seemed to me to stop the world for a pivotal moment as possibly three billion people heard the gospel from the life and lips of a man they knew was speaking truth as they had not heard it. That moment, in my opinion, will never die.

So in the end, President Nixon's death precipitated a platform for the world to encounter the only One who can change us all: Jesus Christ of Nazareth.

President Ford took President Nixon's place after his resignation (before he could be impeached) and was later defeated by Governor Jimmy Carter of Georgia after fulfilling Nixon's second term.

───── *President Jimmy Carter*

I met Jimmy Carter when Evelyn and I took a trip to Atlanta where I was invited to preach in the historic Grace Methodist Church. A couple of weeks before our scheduled trip, we received a phone call from the Georgia governor's mansion. Governor and Mrs. Carter were inviting us to spend Saturday night with them before I was to preach Sunday morning at Grace Methodist.

We were given southern hospitality at its best. In the evening, the whole family took us into the large kitchen for cereal before going to bed. We were served by maids from a nearby Georgia prison, all of whom knew Evelyn and me from television and were delightful to us.

Gradually, our talk got around to the Lord and the new birth. Jack, their oldest, asked me to explain being born again, showing an eagerness that went beyond mere asking.

I told how through the fall of man in the Garden of Eden, sin had entered man's heart, and since that time, every person born had this seed of sin in him, and from a spiritual standpoint was "dead in trespasses and sins" (Eph. 2:1). For us to pass from death unto life with God, we had to be born again. To become alive to God, we had to realize we were sinners and, under the conviction of the Holy Spirit, repent and believe that God raised Jesus from the dead. (See John 3:4–5; Rom. 10:9–10.)

Jack's eyes were shining. Obviously, he was eager to be born again right there at the kitchen table. When I offered to pray with him, he said, "I'd like to know how Dad feels."

"It's okay, son," Governor Carter said.

"But, Dad, have you been born again?"

The governor sat silent for several seconds while we all waited for his answer. Looking at Jack, he said, "Yes, I have been and, Jack, I think you should be, too."

That broke the ice. Taking Jack by the hand, I asked him to repeat the sinner's prayer after me: "God, be merciful to me, a sinner, and come into my heart and give me a new birth."

Tears flowed down Jack's cheeks. Obviously, he was earnest about his soul. Great joy erupted from inside him, and he leaped up to hug his mother and dad. Soon we were all praising the Lord. One of the young black women who had been serving us started a powerful old spiritual, and we all joined in.

Rosalynn took us to our room, where the covers of the bed were already turned down and our luggage was opened. She told us she hoped we slept well and they were looking forward to hearing me preach the next morning.

We were very taken by her gracious manner.

Sunday morning the governor had to teach his Sunday school class at the Baptist church they attended, but he urged the whole family to go with Evelyn and me to Grace Methodist. He would join us later.

I preached with great liberty to a packed house. My subject was the miracle of seed-faith, and when I gave the invitation, several came forward to receive Christ as their personal Savior. Afterward, Pastor Sam Coker and his lovely wife, Jean, joined the Carters and us for Sunday dinner.

The next day, Governor Carter had me address the Georgia state legislature, the very first time I'd ever done a thing like that. It almost turned into a praise service as the legislators responded with amens to my talk.

When all that was taking place, I was given no indication Governor Carter was planning to run for president. Later, when he appeared on a national panel carried live by television, he was the hit of the speakers. His upbeat spirit and contagious smile, his grasp of facts, and his ability to articulate his views impressed many, including me, as I watched.

Still, he hadn't announced his candidacy.

Sunday, August 24, 1975, Jimmy Carter flew into Tulsa in a light plane at Riverside Airport near Oral Roberts University. He was so little known in Tulsa that Edna Earl, the wife of Marshall Nash's brother, Bill Nash, drove out to pick him up and take him to their bank. There Bill had the top one hundred Democrats in Tulsa gathered to meet him.

A couple of hours later, I entered into the picture in a most unusual manner. After the governor spoke, answered questions, and shook hands with everyone, he called Bill aside: "Can you get me in to see Oral Roberts?"

"Easy," Bill replied. "We're just a half mile from the campus and the president's home." Bill called me, then secured a state trooper as a driver and told them how to get there. Soon there was a knock on our door.

"Governor Carter!" I exclaimed. "This is a surprise. Please come in."

I led him into the living room. Evelyn walked in to greet him, asking all about Rosalynn and the children. He was very friendly, but I quickly saw there was something on his mind.

Without another word, he knelt and said, "Oral, I came to ask you to pray for me. I'm going to be elected president of the United States, and I need guidance and wisdom to fulfill my responsibility."

Saying I was astonished is putting it mildly. For a moment I didn't know how to respond. I didn't know for sure he was even running for president, although the news media had conjectured that he would. Also, the thought struck me: *Was he the one to be president? How was I to know? How was I to pray?*

I didn't wait any longer. The man who had received Evelyn and me in the governor's mansion in Atlanta was now in my home kneeling and asking for prayer. He seemed to know in advance he would soon assume the awesome task of being president of the United States of America.

With Evelyn standing by, I laid my hands on the head of Jimmy Carter and prayed as best I knew how. He rose and said, "Thank you, Oral, and God bless you." He went immediately to the car, and they drove off.

Jimmy Carter was elected president. Nearly all the political pundits seemed surprised. I admit I was somewhat surprised. I didn't credit my prayers for much that day since I was caught by surprise. I concluded it was meant to be.

I felt one thing very strongly: He was a very able and good man, one open to God and not ashamed of being born again.

I didn't meet him as president until the late 1970s when he and Rosalynn invited us to a private luncheon in the White House. It was during the fight to build the City of Faith. Strategically placed medical people in Tulsa, for the most part, were lined up solidly against it. Then we learned from her statements to the media that Secretary of Health Patricia Harris had come out against the City of Faith.

Our efforts to build the City of Faith had challenged the power structure in our city and the high medical authorities and then someone high up in Washington. The battle was fierce. In the midst of the struggle, a call came from the Carters in the White House, as the previous call had to visit the Carters while he was governor of Georgia.

We took Richard and Dr. James Winslow, the medical leader of the ORU School of Medicine and the City of Faith. I think Jim wanted to test the waters in Washington since the secretary of health had made her position known.

I had never been in the family quarters of the White House. Rosalynn led us into a private dining room, all laid out with a beautiful tablecloth, magnificent china, and heavy silverware.

Delicious food was brought piping hot from the kitchen, and the server was immaculate. We had never experienced such service. I had never seen so much silverware to the right and left of my plate, and I watched Rosalynn to see which piece she picked up first.

The nice thing was, President and Mrs. Carter were totally relaxed and down to earth—the same as they were in the kitchen of the governor's mansion where we had eaten cereal together and where Jack was born again. Soon we were relaxed, too, and after the president had said the blessing, we had a good time just talking as people do every day at mealtime.

After lunch, Dr. Winslow was told one of the president's key aides was waiting to see him. The president asked me to go into another room with him while Evelyn and Richard remained to visit with Rosalynn.

I spent a whole hour with the president, his sharp mind probing mine on almost every conceivable subject, including many things about the Lord. We prayed together and returned to the dining room. Soon Dr. Winslow appeared, and we took our departure to the airport.

Many thoughts were swirling through my mind on the way back to Tulsa. Once again I had been invited to the White House without asking or expecting to be. Richard reminded us, "God works in mysterious ways His wonders to perform." The visit was certainly a wonder to me.

We were all deeply impressed with Rosalynn. If it were possible, we concluded, she was more brilliant than her husband.

There was no question about the president being in charge, but there was a quality of charm and leadership about the First Lady that was inescapable. Evelyn and Richard said while I was with the president, she had exuded warmth, attentiveness, and a knowledge of what the presidency was all about. She was most interested in our ministry and everything we were attempting to do, and she seldom talked about herself.

Afterward, while the fierce opposition to our efforts to build the City of Faith continued unabated, a subtle change became apparent. The right vibes were coming out of Washington and the office of the secretary of health. I didn't know it at the time, but it seemed that something had happened high up in the power structure of this nation that smoothed our path enough to finish and open the City of Faith against all odds.

Since the subject never came up during my visit with the president, I cannot attribute our success in any way to our trip there. Wherever it came from, something had changed the course of events.

Presidents Ford and Bush

My meetings with President Ford and President Bush, the only other two presidents I have met, were not on such a personal basis, but I appreciated the opportunities.

After President Ford left office, he built a home on the twelfth hole of Thunderbird Golf Course in Rancho Mirage, California. Since I was a member of Thunderbird at the time, I was invited to play golf with him and his close friend, Leonard Firestone, a few times, and I got to know him in that way.

I was impressed with him. There were no put-on airs, no sense of arrogance or of being overbearing. He was a typical American, a good man, and a far deeper thinker than met the eye while he was in office. He loved golf. Between speaking engagements and other matters, he spent as much time as possible either practicing his game or playing Thunderbird Golf Course.

The news media have made much of his physical awkwardness. I didn't sense that at all. A former athlete, big and strong, he could hit the golf ball a country mile. He had an infectious laugh and was a delight to play with.

As for President Bush, I met him briefly in the Oval Office of the White House on November 21, 1989, along with several nationally known ministers who had been invited for a special briefing.

I didn't know George Bush. But Billy Graham told me they had been friends for twenty years and Mr. Bush was a good man, a deeply religious man.

At the briefing of the ministers by President Bush, each of us was called into the Oval Office from the small auditorium where the president addressed us and was given a personal moment with the president. I'll never forget mine. Although I had never met him, when my turn came to shake his hand behind his desk, he said, "Reverend Roberts, keep your prayers going for me." Richard had also been invited, and the president knew him on sight and asked for his prayers, too.

President Bush is over six feet tall, rangy and exceptionally friendly and personable. Richard and I felt he was a man of genuine Christian faith, and a man of strength and ability.

Praying for Our President

President Clinton, formerly governor of Arkansas, a neighboring state to Oklahoma, is a man I heard much about before he ran for president. I have never met him. I know what an almost impossible task he faces to lead our country. Every day I pray that he and his wife will seek and follow the mind of God, and that somehow the blessings of God will give him that something extra to help make the light shine again upon our beloved nation.

I feel my place as a minister of the gospel of Christ's healing power, as the founder of Oral Roberts University and the City of Faith, and as an author of many books is not in the political arena. I do, however, take my citizenship role seriously. Evelyn and I and our children are faithful in voting our convictions and standing up for what is right as we feel led by the Master's guidance. And I pray all citizens will do the same.

Now, as I promised earlier, here are the ten secrets to success of my life and ministry.

CHAPTER 32

THE TEN SECRETS OF SUCCESS OF MY LIFE AND MINISTRY

EARLY IN my healing crusades, I started having breakfast meetings with the sponsoring pastors. In the beginning, only eight or ten attended, but later, the number increased to fifty or more, and a few times we had one hundred.

I shared the same secrets with them that I am sharing in this chapter—secrets that I was proving in my life and ministry—in the hope that someone would pick up an idea that would help or change him. Most of the sponsoring pastors had small congregations. I knew when they saw the huge crowds and the amazing results in our crusades that they might be thinking I had something beyond them, and they would get very little for themselves unless I shared the things I felt God was using to make my ministry possible.

My respect for ministers of the gospel, beginning with my minister father, Rev. E. M. Roberts, has never wavered. We've had differences, some of them very hurtful, but there has never been a time I wanted to throw up my hands and say, "Oh, what's the use? Let them go their way, and I will go mine." I've wanted none of that. No other group, as a whole, means as much to me as do God-called and dedicated ministers of the good news of the gospel.

1. I Discovered the Message Is Greater Than the Messenger.

No matter how important we sometimes think we are as the messengers of the Lord, we are never as important as what He wants to do and say through us to the people. That takes care of having personal pride, of getting a big head, and of believing all the compliments we may receive for doing what God has called us to do: to follow Jesus' example of preaching, teaching, and healing (see Matt. 4:23–24).

Sometimes when people hear a strong message, they praise the minister rather than thank God for the minister's delivering the message. They can remember the preacher, but they often forget the message.

Every minister appreciates a compliment, but compliments help very little to one who knows God's message has been delivered under the anointing of the Holy Spirit. I tell ministers I'd rather have people strike at me than overcompliment me, for then at least I know the message touched a nerve in their being.

—— 2. I Tried Each Time to Be Absolutely Certain I Was Anointed by the Holy Spirit.

We must give the message and stay anointed while we give it. I discovered that secret the hard way. There were times when I felt my message so strongly in me that I got cocky and didn't spend enough time seeking God to anoint me as the messenger to help deliver those who were suffering.

God's Word is already anointed. Preachers or teachers must also be anointed. *We are handling divine material*, not just a secular message or some argumentative theory. *We are to deliver the Word as an oracle of God*, knowing God personally and intimately, feeling the needs of the people to the extent we feel what they feel, and knowing that as mortal beings, we cannot of our own knowledge and ability do anything in the spiritual realm by ourselves. "And the Lord *went with them*, confirming his word with signs following" (see Mark 16:20).

I soon knew when I was anointed and when I was not. It is awesome to face a group of people, few or many, knowing that they have mortal bodies but immortal souls, that some are terminally ill, that all are sick in some way, and understanding they came not only to hear me but also to hear God's voice speaking inside them through the Word preached. Not feeling that awesomeness leads to tickling their fancy with a message that has no heart or soul in it, or lulling the people to believe God is *not* all-powerful and able to do "exceeding abundantly above all that we ask or think" (Eph. 3:20).

That is the reason many who are called do not enter the ministry; the awesomeness of it intimidates them. That is also why some feel they must preach the gospel, but they seek an easy way out by preaching surface-type talks, without the Holy Spirit's powerful anointing to prick the hearts of their hearers.

One day as I was studying Jesus' words in Luke 4:18 on the anointing, the Lord spoke these words to me:

> *"The anointing is that divine energy that separates you from yourself and fills you with the glory of God so that when you act, it is like God acting, and when you speak, it is like God speaking."*

I knew it was God speaking because it lined up with His Word and with what happened in Jesus Himself when He had *preached* and *taught* and *healed*—the three things He did during His earthly ministry. Those three things He did have burned in my spirit, and I have risked everything to understand how to apply them to myself and to my preaching, teaching, and healing in Jesus' name.

The anointing separates you from yourself so that God is in charge of you. The anointing fills you with divine energy so that you are not limited to preaching or doing God's work solely in your own strength or reason.

That is one reason the prophet said, "The anointing breaks the yoke." (See Isa. 10:27.) There is a yoke on people, and it's not Jesus' yoke, which is "easy," as He says in Matthew 11:30. It is the yoke of bondage to sin, fear, hate, vengeance, jealousy, ego, lying, stealing, murder, sickness, disease, lack, and demon possession—in fact, to everything that destroys human beings and their dreams and hopes.

The anointed preacher, who has spent hours preparing himself *and* his message, sends the hot fires of the Holy Spirit to burn the yoke off people who believe, and supernaturally brings them into totally new attitudes, new purposes, new commitments, and new expectations. There is simply no other way to do this through ministry for people.

Jesus explains it in Luke 4:18:

> The Spirit of the Lord is upon me,
> because he hath anointed me to preach the gospel to the poor;
> he hath sent me to heal the brokenhearted,
> to preach deliverance to the captives,
> and recovering of sight to the blind,
> to set at liberty them that are bruised.

The mortal person doing the preaching can prepare until he or she memorizes every word of the message and delivers it flawlessly, but unless he or she is anointed, the message will not cut through Satan's wall of bondage, it will not open the eyes of the understanding of people to their possibilities in God, it will not activate the listener's faith, and it will not heal, deliver, recover, set free, or bind up the wounded!

I discovered that the difference in being anointed and not being anointed is monumental. Without it, you're on your own. With it, all your senses come alive, your mind blossoms, your body feels light and graceful in its moves, your spirit is in control, and you realize what you're doing is God inspired beyond any measure you know. People hearing or dealing with you know all this, too. That is, they feel something powerful and wonderful that they can't always understand or explain. But it reaches inside them for a decision to be made one way or the other toward the Lord.

——— 3. *I Learned to Reinforce My Preaching of the Word of God by My Personal Testimony.*

There is nothing harder to understand—or duller—than a sermon in which the preacher has no personal testimony of what he is preaching about and how it has affected his life or the life of someone else. A preacher trying to sell his message of the gospel without living it himself is like a salesman trying to sell something without knowing and showing the product personally.

One of the best examples of using testimonies is the Full Gospel Business Men's Fellowship International. Demos Shakarian, a thirty-eight-year-old Armenian and California dairyman, along with his wife, Rose, began the organization in 1951. Demos, with his dad, Isaac, owned the world's largest private dairy in the world—four thousand producing holstein cows in Los Angeles, California. They began sponsoring youth meetings, then large rallies, and they always had at the center of their meetings testimonies of the power of the Holy Spirit in their lives.

When I took the big tent to Los Angeles in 1951, Demos served as chairman of the crusade, and we became acquainted. I heard and loved his testimony. As a businessman, he was not a smooth speaker, but he was sincere. You could feel what he had experienced, and it was real.

He carried a growing conviction that the Lord wanted him to organize businessmen and professional people, who were believers and baptized with the Holy Spirit, into local meeting chapters. They would also hold an annual convention where the men would give their testimonies.

Demos hadn't found a way to start it when he shared the call with me. I liked the idea instantly. Business and professional men with the Holy Spirit would be dynamite if they could be brought together at Saturday morning breakfasts across the land as Demos had envisioned.

I said, "Demos, now is the time while it's burning on your heart to begin. I'll present you tonight in our crusade service to announce a breakfast for next Saturday morning and to invite business and professional men to come."

He asked me if I would come and speak to the men. I said I would on the grounds that after I spoke, the men would give their testimonies.

That Saturday morning made history. At the next one, I helped install Demos as the president. Right after that, whenever Demos could be present, announcements were made to have the same kind of breakfast meeting in the cities where we held my crusades.

The idea took off like a rocket. The secret was that Demos had the call, and he was anointed. He took my advice not to let any of us preachers dominate the breakfasts when we were asked to speak but to put the men's *testimonies* for the Lord in first place.

In the first five years, hundreds of local chapters sprang up; in ten years, thousands; in thirty years, the group went worldwide in 120 nations, with a million men meeting each Saturday morning— giving their testimonies.

The meetings attracted business and professional men, whether believers or not but for the most part, they knew nothing about being baptized with the Holy Spirit and praying in tongues. These men are pragmatic; they want something that works. They saw it working in the lives of men giving their testimonies, and soon they were eagerly coming forward to receive.

Demos passed on to be with the Lord on July 23, 1993, two days after his eightieth birthday. I preached his funeral, and as I had installed Demos as the first president of Full Gospel Business Men's Fellowship International, I helped install his older son, Richard, as the second president.

Many of the men thought at first they couldn't share their testimonies. Some thought they were not important. Others were shy. But seeing others give a testimony inspired them to try. Whether eloquent or hesitatingly spoken, the testimonies did the job. All of us wish to know something of others, their experiences, their ups and downs, their failures and triumphs. That's what a testimony is, with the glory being given to God, and God working His wonders through it.

Some people feel unworthy to give a testimony or feel no one will desire to hear it. I say let go and let God. You'll learn to love it, for it is an extension of what God has done in you. You'll multiply yourself over and over for the Lord.

If you're a minister, as you preach or teach, continually include some part of what God has personally done in you or through you, or something you have had a part in doing. The people may forget what you preached about, but they will remember your testimony. I don't mean your testimony is taking the place of your message, but it's like wings to a bird—*your sermon flies better.*

--------- *4. I Tried Always to Dedicate Myself to Having Integrity of Heart and Purpose.*

A young preacher asked me, "How did you decide to enter the ministry?"

I said, "I didn't."

He said, "Did someone decide for you?"

I said, "Yes, the Lord Jesus Christ."

We talked about that a minute, but he still hadn't gotten the answer he expected. "Well, I decided for myself that the ministry was something I wanted to do," he told me.

"Then I feel sorry for the people you preach to. I also hurt for you when you face God at the Judgment."

He looked at me and said, "That's not a nice thing to say to me. I think I give some pretty good talks."

"Yes, I'm sure you do. There are thousands of churches where the people hear pretty good talks but not anointed, compelling messages to convict them of their sins, to reveal that God is a good God, and to build their faith to believe that God raised Jesus from the dead, and that He has sent His Holy Spirit to reveal His risen Son to us at the point of our needs and to point the way to deliverance."

"I don't know what you're talking about."

"I'm sorry you don't. Probably the people you give these nice talks to don't know what I'm talking about, either."

I realized I had offended him. I hoped it kept him from becoming a minister *if* God had not called him—for his sake and others.

I for one had no desire to decide I would be a minister, then be one who gave some pretty good talks. In the first place, I hadn't even considered entering the ministry. I had another dream and goal for my life. Only when God had worked His wonders to bring me to personal salvation and the healing of my terribly ill body did He confront me with the understanding that He had called me to preach His Word and bring His healing power to my generation.

During these forty-eight years of being called of God to preach, teach, and heal, and to build a university, thousands of whose graduates will help carry on the ministry of healing after I am gone and do other exploits for Jesus, I have seen that without integrity of my heart and of myself as a man of God, that having done all these things to the best of my ability, I would have failed.

I've often suggested to ministers that they take a Bible concordance and turn to the section on *integrity* and see how many times and ways it is referred to in the Bible. I've seen the value of doing this, for I believe integrity must be at the heart of the outflow of a minister's calling from God.

I'm not talking about honest mistakes and shortcomings that are in all of us, and failures that we all suffer at one time or another.

I know in spite of integrity of heart and calling, these things happen. We can minimize the number by constantly working at it in the most conscientious way, but we will make mistakes, suffer shortcomings, and do things that turn out to be mistakes.

However, I never remember waking up any morning and saying, "God, today I'm going to see how many mistakes I can make or how many failures I can have." I never know I have made a mistake until it's done and I look back on it. In integrity, all I can do is attempt to rectify it as much as possible and ask God to help me not to repeat it.

The critics have helped me, whether they intended to or not, by holding up my mistakes. My mother always told me in receiving criticism to ask myself questions along these lines: "Did I do right? Is the criticism true? Can I do anything about it within the sphere of my integrity?"

My father was a man of God whose strongest point to me was his integrity. If he learned he had done something that reflected badly on his integrity, he couldn't wait to try to make it right with the person or group, or if it was something only he knew about, to try to make adjustment in himself. That was a powerful example for me.

5. My Best Work Was Done When I Worked with Believing Believers.

I concentrated on doing my work with *believing believers*. I mean by that, if people believe God through my calling and my efforts, they are believers in what God called me to do, not ones who have chosen to live in unbelief, regardless of the faith and results God gives me.

When I began the healing ministry in 1947 with such anointing and compassion, I was terribly idealistic. I actually thought that since I was coming only to do good for people, everybody who knew about me, heard me preach, or saw me pray for the sick would receive me—and all the sick I prayed for would be healed.

Was I in for a shock! I hadn't recognized the nature of man as Jesus had done in Matthew 10:1: "And when he had called unto him his twelve disciples, he gave them power against unclean spirits, to cast them out, and to heal all manner of sickness and all manner of disease."

I misunderstood Jesus' words. I thought He said He had given them power to heal *all sick people*. He didn't say that. He said, "I gave you power to heal *all manner* of sickness and *all manner* of disease." That was 100 percent different. Jesus was saying He gave those who believed in Him the power to heal all types of sickness or disease, but *not all people* who are sick or diseased—those who received the Word and believed!

The big *IF* divided them into two groups: believers and non-believers.

The eternal fact is that God has put in the heart of man, when he hears the Word of God preached, it brings him inevitably to an *IF*.

That *IF* is the most important jumping-off place in anyone's life. If during those times he confesses with his mouth the Lord Jesus Christ, and believes in his heart that God has raised Him from the dead (the most incredible fact of all history), he shall be saved.

But God's wise decision was to make man a free moral agent, giving him the power of choice, *to believe God or not to believe God.*

The number one Scripture to me for this secret is Romans 10:8–9: "But what saith it? The word is nigh thee, even in thy mouth, and in thy heart: that is, the word of faith, which we preach; that if thou shalt confess with thy mouth the Lord Jesus, and shalt believe in thine heart that God hath raised him from the dead, thou shalt be saved."

I can remember following my preaching one evening in a crusade by praying for a little blind child. I was so moved when God actually restored the little girl's sight that I cried out to the people: "Don't wait! Come to Christ now. Believe God now. Turn your faith loose."

A longtime personal friend, Bob McLaughlin, happened to be sitting near the parents who had brought their little blind daughter forward. When they returned to their seats, he saw that the little one could see. How thrilled her parents were! Bob began to weep silently. To my knowledge, he had never confessed Christ with his mouth or believed in his heart God had raised Him from the dead. Bob's wife was a member of the little church I had once pastored while I attended the university in that same city, and I had gotten to know him.

As he watched the people around the child praising God, he heard a new voice. It was a minister of a denomination that didn't believe God still heals. He asked the parents, "How long has your daughter been blind?"

"Since she was born," they said.

"I don't believe it," he replied.

"Sir, here she is and she's seeing."

"I don't believe she was born blind."

"We're her parents. We know she was."

"I still don't believe it."

Then the minister announced to those around him, "I don't believe Jesus Christ heals today. This is a put-up job. I don't believe Oral Roberts's preaching or his praying for sick people. It's a scam. I don't believe it."

Bob McLaughlin, who had left the believing in his home to his wife, spoke up to this minister: "All my life I've wanted to believe in God. I've wanted to see a miracle. Now I've seen this child go up blind and come back seeing. For the first time, I believe." And instantly, Jesus came into his heart as his personal Savior.

Later, when I saw Bob and he told me about that, he threw his arms around my neck and cried like a baby.

The little girl's family were *believing believers*, and they saw the child healed. The preacher had let the big *IF* turn him to unbelief. Yet he kept on preaching, and those poor people listening to him were not brought to face the big *IF* in their lives to become believing believers in God's healing power for today. Instead, that minister's church became an open critic of all we were doing in the crusade, and the news media played on that until others joined in and made it appear no one was getting healed.

But you can't rob a miracle of its incredible effectiveness. A miracle settles the issue.

People who knew the family, and knew the child had been blind, saw she could see. That news spread, and soon the crusades were packed. I had thousands of believing believers to work with.

Jesus said, "Neither cast ye your pearls before swine" (Matt. 7:6).

Jesus also said,

And into whatsoever city or town ye shall enter, inquire who in it is worthy; and there abide till ye go thence. And when ye come into an house, salute it. And if the house be worthy, let your peace come upon it: but if it be not worthy, let your peace return to you. And whosoever shall not receive you, nor hear your words, when ye depart out of that house or city, shake off the dust of your feet. Verily I say unto you, It shall be more tolerable for the land of Sodom and Gomorrah in the day of judgment, than for that city (Matt. 10:11–15).

Jesus taught that when believing believers receive you, work with them. When they're committed to being unbelievers, go to the next place or to people who want to believe.

After my father became a minister, he did much of his preaching among the Indian people of Pontotoc and other counties. He established twelve local churches, and quite a number of Indians joined them. I loved going with my father as he lived with and preached to the Indians.

I never came across any unbelief among Indian people, and I've preached to many tribes in many states. Their belief in the Great Spirit is not quite like our belief in Jesus Christ, but their belief in the Great Spirit as God, and in the supernatural, is very real to them. In fact, it remains the most important part of their lives.

In 1963, I was named the Outstanding American Indian of the Year by the American Indian Exposition, with its headquarters in Anadarko, Oklahoma. It represents the more than 150 Indian tribes in the United States. I believe that was because of my father's love for the Indians while I was growing up, and because of the many revivals he conducted among different tribes. Also, I think it had to do with their pride in my mother's Indian heritage and later my ministry of healing to them.

Few know it, but most Indian leaders are orators. I've never heard more eloquent speeches than at the banquet held in honor of my being named the Outstanding American Indian of the Year.

Soon tribal chiefs from one end of the nation to the other gave me open invitations to preach on their reservations. The chiefs of the Navajo in Arizona and New Mexico, with headquarters in Window Rock, Arizona, chose me as the first preacher to conduct a major crusade among them. In their five-thousand-seat amphitheater at Window Rock, I ministered for ten days, praying for their sick. We taped it to be shown on my regular Sunday morning television program, and large numbers of people got a glimpse of that reservation and of the many miracles the Lord performed among them.

My most profound experience at Window Rock was to pray for the healing of a one-hundred-year-old Indian chief at his request to help him receive Jesus Christ as his personal Savior. I had to do it through an interpreter. I believe his conversion to Christ was genuine because the change that came over his leathery countenance shone on his face and reminded me of Saul of Tarsus when the light from above shone on his face (see Acts 9:1–3).

That was the first time he really understood the Great Spirit in terms of our Savior, Jesus Christ, and knew that salvation had come to him before he was to die. There was a sixty-two-year difference in our ages. Our tears mingled as we hugged each other, an embrace that I can feel even as I write.

Another experience there that greatly affected me involved a disabled Indian child. His whole family brought him from their hogan, deep in the huge land area of the Navajo, and he was healed by the power of God. Suddenly, the stoic Navajo were stoic no longer. Shouts rose from them as the little boy ran and leaped among them. We were fortunate to capture it on tape and show it on our next television program.

It is almost unbelievable that some thirty miles east of Tulsa there are Cherokee Indians who cannot speak English, who live isolated from the white man, wanting nothing to do with him or the government. They are almost the same as when they first migrated to what later became Oklahoma, more than 150 years ago.

Many students of Oral Roberts University have spent their weekends teaching them English, building them churches and schools, and helping to bring them into the life of our country and into a personal knowledge of Jesus Christ as Savior and Lord. I am immensely proud of this volunteer student activity. I love it when some of the Indian families see me and tell me of their "new young friends from ORU."

I carry in my heart love and caring for Indian people that I am unable to put into words. Their expressed love for me is one of the most precious things in my life.

6. I Learned to Find the Key Issue.

Soon after I met Lee Braxton in 1949, he gave me Frank Bettger's book *How I Raised Myself from Failure to Success in*

Selling. The point Frank Bettger made that helped me most was about the key issue. He said if you find the key issue and work from there, you will have a solid base on which to build to reach your life's goals.

The key issue—what is it? The key issue is discovering what is at the bottom of what you are reaching for. It's the heart of the issue. It's the guts of the whole. It's the real purpose.

I went to work in my Bible with the key issue in mind. I studied the events of the Bible to discover the number one thing that caused those events to happen. And I looked for the central issue of what is going to happen in the drama of the end time.

The word *deliverance* stood out to me as all-inclusive of what God had done in the past and what the Bible events pointed to that He would do in the "now" and in the future. I began using that word *deliverance* as the key issue of everything I was attempting. My mission is to heal the sick. It took me a long time to understand why I couldn't always bring God's healing to deliver the person from sickness when I felt the healing power of God flowing through my right hand. There were times when something stopped the healing from happening to a person I had prayed for.

Jesus never tells me everything at one time or gives me all His power in an instant. He lets me grow . . . grope . . . seek . . . read . . . pray . . . cry out . . . experiment . . . fail . . . falter . . . stumble . . . get up and try again . . . and always I press on to learn, to receive from God and give what I receive to the sick person.

Never could I forget His command to me:

"You are to take My healing power to your generation."

I knew I had God's command, His call. I saw it work time after time. Disease was a terrible problem but not the main problem; it was helping to bring the people with the disease into position for God's healing power to deliver them.

Slowly, it began to dawn on me: Jesus was born a whole man, but we are not. We are born unwhole. We have to be *made* whole.

Perhaps Jesus' favorite expressions in healing were, "Be thou made whole," and "Thy faith hath made thee whole." Jesus had the power and the know-how to *make* people whole. He knew how to help them activate their faith and to release it to God the moment He touched them, or they touched Him, or He spoke the word of healing to them, or He told them *to do something*. When they did something, their faith went up to God and they were healed—actually delivered to the extent that they were made a whole person at that time.

I was fascinated. I felt I was living it with Jesus, living it with the person being made whole, and living it with people I was praying for to be delivered.

As I prayed for people, I began to see that there was a man inside each one of them. I saw this inner man as a host, that his house is the house where he resides, the temple where he lives and where all ceremonies and functions are, that the host determines *much* of what *goes in*.

The key issue is dealing with what makes the healing or deliverance happen, not with some peripheral thing.

I am always studying what the key issue is. What makes the miracle happen? What causes the light from above to come on? I share this the best way I know how.

7. I Found How to Use a Point of Contact.

When I sought God for the answer to the term point of contact, I received these words:

"A point of contact is something you do and when you do it, you release your faith to God and expect to receive your miracle."

In my estimation, more sick people have received their healing through using a point of contact than by any other means through my ministry.

I believe the reason is that God revealed the use of the point of contact to me early in my healing ministry as I studied His Word. I kept wondering why He had people *do* something when He was about to bring deliverance to them or through them.

Jesus touched sick people when He healed them. Why?

He let sick people touch Him. Why?

He spoke the word of faith to some who were sick. Why?

He told a blind man to go wash in a pool of water. Why?

He spit on some clay and put it on the blind eyes of a man. Why?

He told lepers to go show themselves to the priest for their healing. Why?

In Old Testament times, God healed people in different ways. He had the prophet Elisha tell Naaman, the leper, to go to the river Jordan and dip seven times and his flesh would be clean. Why?

The prophet Elijah stretched his body upon the body of a mother's little dead son and he revived. Why?

He told Samson to let his hair grow uncut in locks, and it became the secret of his great strength for the deliverance of the people. Why?

So many times God instructed people to do things and then the miracle of deliverance would happen. Why?

The answer came to me through the Word of God by the Holy Spirit's revelation: *God was giving them a point of contact.*

There flashed before me what happens when we flip on a light switch—light comes on. When we turn on the water faucet, water comes out. When we turn the key in the car, the motor turns over and starts.

I saw the reason. The light switch is connected to the electric power plant, the faucet is connected to the water supply, and the key is connected to the car motor. It dawned on me that all sources of power have a point at which you make contact with them.

I began to understand that Jesus, in recognizing our humanness, knew we would often need to use a point of contact to turn our faith loose to make connection with His power of deliverance.

I read in the Bible where Jairus, the ruler of the synagogue, came to Jesus to ask Him to heal his little girl who lay at the point of death: "Come and lay thy hands on her . . . and she shall live." When Jesus did as Jairus asked, the child was restored to life (see Mark 5:22–43).

A woman sick with an issue of blood for twelve years had spent all of her money on doctors to cure her but found no cure. She said within herself concerning Jesus, "If I may touch but his clothes, I shall be whole" (Mark 5:28). And when she did, she was healed. Jesus said to her, "Daughter, thy faith hath made thee whole" (v. 34).

In each case, faith brought the deliverance, but a point of contact got Jesus' attention and caused the faith of those involved to be released to God.

I have personally touched more than 1.5 million sick people as a point of contact, having carefully told them that a point of contact was something we did, and the very moment we did it, both of us should at that moment release our faith to God. Wherever there was a deliverance, faith was released, and a point of contact helped release it to God.

Often when the twelve thousand chairs were filled, and I was sitting on the stage with a sick person before me, I would ask the persons in the audience to help me pray for healing by touching the back of the chair in front of them, understanding it was a point of contact, something they did, and when they did it, they were to turn their faith loose and believe for a healing. It would be like they were touching the sick person the moment I did. When that happened, I felt such a wave of faith going up to God that it was far easier for me as I touched the sick person and prayed and released my faith. It became a faith atmosphere like the sun rising in its fullness.

One result of this faith action by the audience was that many were healed who never came in the healing line. Later, many wrote and told me of the healing they received when they joined my healing prayers by touching the chair in front of them.

I still teach people who write to me, "The moment you mail your letter, as it leaves your hand, make it a point of contact and release your faith to God." Time after time, people have told me later their healing or the answer to their prayers began when they mailed their letter as a point of contact. I have learned there is much going on in the heavenlies we're just now learning about with our spiritual senses.

I knew I was not the healer, the deliverer; only God could do that. But as is the case in all of life, instruments are used to help us, and I saw myself as an instrument through whom God could work as I obeyed Him and gave Him and the people my best.

I'm not saying God does His mighty works through a point of contact every time. He is sovereign. He healed people at times (although it seemed to be rare) by just doing it—when they apparently had done nothing. He acted on His own. He still does at times.

Having said that, I feel obligated to act on my faith in God. I don't believe it is wise for any of us to sit around or lie around waiting for God to act sovereignly on our behalf.

In my youth, I lay in bed for 163 days hovering between life and death, and God did not act sovereignly on my behalf to heal me. Only when I did something did God act. My family did something. The man of God who laid hands on me and prayed for me did something. And when we both did something, we released our faith, and my deliverance from the terminal illness of tuberculosis began.

I use a point of contact personally in all that I do in approaching God. Helping someone is a point of contact to me. Giving money as a seed of my faith is a point of contact, saying a good word is a point of contact, writing a faith letter to someone is a point of contact, and on and on. I use every one of these to turn my faith loose to God, then I begin that minute to expect a miracle. I find when I don't key myself to expectancy for something good to happen, I begin to deteriorate—and that's not something I can allow to happen! I try to remain in a miracle mood, a frame of mind in which, as I release my faith through points of contacts, I am in a constant state of expectancy.

The answer doesn't always happen instantly. More often than not, when it does happen, it happens over a period of time. Paul said it succinctly: "And let us not be weary in well doing: for in due season we shall reap, if we faint not," if we don't give up (Gal. 6:9).

I find that to be even a small part of a miracle happening is a humbling—yet exhilarating—experience. I've never grown tired of seeing God continue to do His miracles. And I'm looking to Him as the Source of greater and more miracles while I live and after I've gone to heaven. All the glory to God!

At one time in my life, I never would have dreamed such things could happen. The secret had not been revealed to me. Knowing now such things have happened through my ministry for all these years is like receiving a new slice of life for me and thousands of others. To me, there's no doubt it can happen to anyone who goes for it with faith!

8. I Have Changed Methods, but Principles Have Stayed the Same.

Being married to a method has gotten me into difficulty many times. Thinking that a *method* works continually, because it worked for a while, can be deceiving. But changing a *principle* of the Word of God can be fatal. Above all, I try to hang on to the principle—the principle of preaching the Word first and foremost so that as people hear the Word, their faith comes up and out of them. It is an eternal principle that never changes: "So then faith cometh by hearing, and hearing by the word of God" (Rom. 10:17).

The principle Jesus followed was preaching, teaching, and healing. (See Matt. 4:23–24.) The whole of His ministry developed around that one principle. He never varied that principle from the beginning to the end of His earthly ministry. And He commanded His disciples to follow the same principle. But when I studied the methods of Jesus, I noticed again and again He never hesitated to change a method in presenting that principle.

One of the methods I changed was the length of time of my sermons. In the early years of my healing ministry, most people apparently didn't know that the Bible teaches Jesus can heal and still heals. He had called me to preach to build their faith and then to pray for them. Because of the lack of knowledge existing at that time, I had to preach long sermons, an average of an hour and a half a service. When I preached less than that, I couldn't get the truth across. When I prepared a sermon that built to a climax, even if it took over an hour or up to two hours, the large audience hung on every word and indicated they would have sat there longer, if necessary, to learn the truth of God's healing power.

Preaching sermons that long was my method through the 1950s and 1960s. In the seventies, it changed. People had a greater knowledge of healing due to several factors: Millions had seen me in person or on television; many had gotten interested enough to read the Bible and books on healing and miracles for themselves; thousands of pastors and teachers and evangelists had awakened to their responsibility to bring healing to the sick, in addition to those few who had already been preaching it. All that meant people could now get the truths of the message in shorter sermons. I changed the length of my sermons to twenty-five to fifty minutes, depending upon when I sensed in my spirit people were grasping the truth of healing for themselves.

Another method I changed was *how* I got the message to the people. I began with public healing crusades in the big tents. We also used auditoriums and stadiums. Then in 1954, as I mentioned earlier in the book, we achieved what some said was an impossibility by filming the tent crusades and airing them on prime-time television each week.

One year we were trying to win one million souls in the crusades. But when we went on television, the number of testimonies of conversions far exceeded that number each year thereafter. I learned the value of communication.

In 1968, I again changed our method but stayed with the principle. Television professionals from NBC helped me work out one-hour prime-time specials to be shown on national television each quarter. Al Bush and later Ron Smith helped me make the transition from filming the crusade services to going to NBC studios in Hollywood. Al and Ron were my top aides, with Richard, to help me come up with our new TV format of prime-time specials.

During Billy Graham's 1966 Berlin Congress on Evangelism, in which I was a delegate, Billy learned of my new plan for TV, and he recommended his old film director, Dick Ross, in Hollywood to me. Richard recommended Ralph Carmichael, the noted Christian songwriter and arranger, to work with us in developing a new kind of singing group out of the ORU student body. We put together sixteen young men and women from ORU to sing a new type of gospel song written not only to be sung but also to have programmed movements in harmony with the songs.

Some religious people had a hissy fit, for they called it dancing. The songs had choreographed steps for the singers, which appeared to be dancing, but they helped get the attention of non-churchgoers, non–Full Gospel people, by the millions.

Prior to that time, singing in religious services was confined to choirs, to special solos or quartets and so on. People knew what to expect. That method had its place then and now. The presentation and movements by our ORU singers, though widely received and just as widely criticized, were so daring that other ministries and many churches, primarily those that were charismatic and independent, developed a praise-and-worship type of singing the gospel.

I fell in love with praise and worship. We introduced it in our ORU chapels, and the students and faculty joined in as the small group on stage led us in singing both old songs and new choruses—mostly right out of the psalms of David and other parts of the Bible.

Soon it caught on in some old-line churches. Other ministries on television went heavy into praise and worship, both on TV and in their independent congregations. By 1976, we were no longer choreographing our singers, but we entered into what it helped birth: praise-and-worship-type songs and singers, which I think came to be far more effective.

On the TV specials, our invited guests were well-known show personalities, principally famous singers, who would sing a popular song, then an old gospel hymn, usually backed up by our ORU choral group who were choreographed by a professional to fit in with each particular performer.

I presented Richard, who was backed by a great orchestra, to belt out a great hymn of the church. I followed with sermons in the language of the "now," which were approximately fourteen minutes long and into which I had condensed the heart of my ministry of God's healing power. I would also offer to the viewers one of my books or another gift without charge or obligation.

At the end, I would stretch forth my hands to pray for God to save souls and heal sick people. The specials produced by Dick Ross and his son, Dick, Jr., along with the talented NBC crew at their Burbank studios, took off like lightning. Our ratings soared, and we were soon reaching tens of millions with the message of God's healing power with a different method.

God used this method so powerfully that even we were surprised at the response—and also at the criticism. The news media wrote big stories about this "phenomenon" on TV, yet took powerful shots at us.

At first, most of the Full Gospel ministries and churches felt I was leaving my original ministry. To them, the change was so abrupt, and the presentation so much of the "show type," that they didn't know what to make of it.

For the first time, many Jewish people responded to what I was doing through the TV specials, although my short message was fully Christ-centered, followed by a healing prayer as anointed as I had ever given in praying for hurting people in the crusade healing lines.

There was a method in our madness, as many churches and ministers finally came to understand. Perhaps for the first time in the life of the nation, there was a religious program coming on at prime time that could compete with the highest-rated secular programs. One year our ratings hit the fifty million mark, second only to Elvis Presley's special.

I remember driving from Tulsa to Oklahoma City one night to hear Billy Graham. Afterward, he asked if he could ride back to Tulsa with me to catch an early-morning flight to New York, since the flight originated in Tulsa. We had just aired a special with Anita Bryant as the guest star. I had preached a Christian message that included Jesus' being born to deliver the people in spirit, mind, and body and make them whole.

Billy complimented me by saying, "Oral, that's the best Christian program I've ever seen on television. I admire your willingness to change your methods when it will get your message across better."

I thanked him, knowing he didn't give compliments carelessly.

In 1975, Ron Smith worked out the details with the NBC production studio in Burbank, California, to move all TV taping to the ORU campus in the ORU Mabee Center. We asked Partners to come to seminars to be blessed and also to help us with purchasing several million dollars' worth of new TV production equipment, including RCA cameras.

We stopped the prime-time specials in 1980. To this day, we are still on a weekly half-hour Sunday program, and Richard and Lindsay have a new "now" type of daily program. The testimonies of salvations, healings, and needs being met flood our office each week. The Trinity Broadcasting Network, led by our dear friends and Partners, Paul and Jan Crouch, is carrying our weekly program and Richard and Lindsay's daily program.

The Example of Paul and Jan Crouch

One of the best examples of holding to principle but changing methods as need arises is Trinity Broadcasting Network. TBN is the largest Christian network, spreading throughout the world with the gospel twenty-four hours a day on more than four hundred stations, and it is carried by cable into millions of other homes. TBN was founded by two of my closest friends, Paul and Jan Crouch, who have played a major part in my life and ministry and whom I love dearly.

I met Paul around 1960 in Rapid City, South Dakota, where I went to preach to the Sioux and Cheyenne Indians. They had invited me because of my Indian heritage and because I was the best-known preacher to them. Paul and Jan were ministering in Rapid City at the time. He was the main newscaster of the local TV station but also a young minister of the Lord. He met me at the airport and drove me directly to the TV station. He personally interviewed me concerning why I was there and what I hoped to accomplish with my ministry to the American Indians, and also concerning my healing crusades.

I noticed he was one sharp and able young man, a newsman who was objective but got the best out of me. I've told Paul many times, "You're the best interviewer I've ever encountered." Afterward, he drove me to the auditorium where it was packed with my Indian brothers, quietly awaiting me to preach to them, then pray for their healing. I enlisted Paul's help in the healing part of the service.

Jan, his wife, is the daughter of Rev. Edgar Bethany, the Assembly of God pastor in Columbus, Georgia, who was the chairman of the local pastors sponsoring my crusade there. I remember Jan was a strikingly beautiful teenager who was just finding herself in the Lord. Now each time I see Jan in person or on TBN, I'm amazed not only by her spiritual gifts but also by her inner and outer beauty, which she possesses after more than thirty years since the Columbus crusade.

I encountered this couple again around 1975, just as they were getting their network started. At that time, VHF broadcast stations had become more popular than those in the UHF band. NBC, CBS, and ABC had cornered the market on "V" stations, and the rest were independent. My weekly TV program was on approximately two hundred "V" stations and maintained the number one weekly audience year after year. The "U" stations that had been built were languishing or had gone out of business; also, most of those channels had not been allotted. Cable hadn't come on the market yet as a viable entity.

By the Holy Spirit, Paul and Jan Crouch had a far-seeing vision of building an all-Christian network starting with channel 40 in the Los Angeles/Orange County area of California, which was in the doldrums. Somehow, some way, they got the down payment for channel 40 and began the network on a faith shoestring.

None of us took but scant notice of two visionaries daring to believe they could take the unpopular "U" channel and literally build a world network solely for the gospel. They saw this other method as no one else of whom I knew. It was just lying there, waiting for the right leaders and the right time.

Soon Paul and Jan were covering the Full Gospel Business Men's conventions and interviewing many of us who were the invited speakers. My admiration for those two unusual believers caused me to be willing to be interviewed in the conventions, and that was true for other ministers and businessmen who spoke on their struggling little network.

Paul and Jan believed in the principle of the Great Commission, to go into all the world and preach the gospel to every creature. Seeing that all the other methods were not reaching enough people, they found a new method to use, scorned by many, that they committed their lives to bring into a successful existence. They stayed with the principle of the gospel, but they changed the method of getting it to the people.

I will never forget when a light shone in my spirit, and the Holy Spirit said,

---

"Tell Paul he'll soon be on one hundred stations, then one thousand!"

It almost took my breath away—and Paul's. The fact was, I was not the only one who was speaking prophetically to him about seemingly impossible numbers.

Paul and Jan had the independence to lead with the new method. They had integrity with God; they had a direct vision from God; they were gifted in operating such a network and in personal charisma and sincerity. They were also careful with the money sent in by grateful people who were getting the gospel through TBN.

There were glitches in the equipment, setbacks in getting stations on the air, shortfalls in financial gifts, and tiredness of working virtually day and night. But as the song says, "We're working on a building and we won't come down."

Before long, Ted Turner and others believed in cable enough to invest in it and get it going, an amazing feat in its own right. When that happened, Paul was ready to lease great transponders that hooked up with the new satellites RCA and others were putting over 22,000 miles up in the mid-heavens. From there the signal could be beamed to a whole nation, as long as enough people had signed up with cable companies.

Paul simply saw it as another method never before used on VHF on this scale for the gospel, and soon with his growing number of full-power UHF stations—medium and low power—he began leasing SATCOM 3R Transponder 3 and hooking everything up with cable. Now to make things even better, Congress has passed a law that cable has to carry the local TV stations, and it includes those of Trinity.

They say, "Where there's a will, there's a way." In Paul and Jan's vision it was, "Where there is God's will, there is God's way"—and they are pouring their lives into using every kind of station they can get their hands on, along with cable. The body of Christ had scarcely even thought anything of such magnitude could be used for the gospel twenty years ago. I'm proud of my dear friends and fellow workers, Paul and Jan Crouch, in the kingdom of God who are unashamedly sending the whole gospel to the ends of the earth, with much more on the way.

The main thing concerning this eighth secret is that we didn't change methods for method's sake. We waited on the Lord to impress us until we knew we were to launch out, however imperfect it was at first. We refined any new method and used it until God had fulfilled His purpose with it or decided we were to discontinue it.

I think another change in method is Oral Roberts University. God made it abundantly clear to me: Success without a successor is failure. I had known of several powerful ministries that virtually ceased at the death of the founder. I can think of only a few who have left something behind.

Few people understood why I founded ORU, and because of that, I had to begin alone again and bring forth the concept of its being more than a Bible school. It was to be a full-fledged academic university, accredited from the bachelor's to the doctorate level in degrees, yet centered in God's authority and on the Holy Spirit. It was and still is a totally new method.

Building the two-hundred-foot-high Prayer Tower in the middle of the academic campus only proved our commitment to obey God when He said to me,

"Build Me a university."

ORU was the first charismatic full-scale university ever built, and it came directly out of the principle of the healing ministry God called me to bring to this generation. I cannot thank God enough for revealing to me to stay with the principle but not to be married to methods.

9. I Learned That Faith Is Where You Find It.

This was a true secret revealed to me. Maybe others knew it, but I had not known it. I had become a spoon-fed denominational preacher. I had accepted about 95 percent of everything the denomination taught and did, without ever questioning why or studying the Word of God for myself "to see if these things were true." (See Acts 17:11.) I had become an echo, not a "voice of one crying in the wilderness" (Matt. 3:3).

I cannot blame the Pentecostal Holiness Church, the denomination I belonged to for the first years of my ministry. The people of that denomination were there long before I was converted and healed and given the call of the healing ministry. They had paid the price to form their own beliefs and denomination and worked hard for it. In many ways, they were a blessing to me. They helped form the early patterns of my life in learning the value of being baptized with the Holy Spirit, of living a holy life, of learning loyalty and developing integrity. I also made lasting friendships among the people.

The very first words God had spoken to me on the afternoon of the evening I was healed were,

"Son, I'm going to heal you and you are to take My healing power to your generation, and to build Me a university on My authority and on the Holy Spirit."

Whether by divine design or by my belonging to that denomination and submitting wholly to it, that calling of taking God's healing power to my generation became submerged. For my twelve years as a young minister, I went without ever making even a small start in doing what God had said. I freely admit they could have been twelve formation years—from seventeen to twenty-nine years of age—during which I studied the Bible and hundreds of other books, conducted revivals, pastored four small churches, and attended two universities.

That denomination had a little book called *The Discipline*, and in it were printed the fundamental doctrines and practices of that church. It included a strong section on the healing of the sick being in the atonement of Christ on the cross. That was a powerful doctrine and statement of purpose. There was, however, no major emphasis on healing as being a practice of the church that I could observe, other than a belief that if you got sick, you were to have faith, *and* if you could hold out, you were not to go to a doctor.

I do know one thing: I became intensely loyal to believing in the exclusiveness of that denomination, although I differed with it on medical science as a viable part of what God has placed on earth for our better health, and on the smallness of its vision.

In 1947, the second time God spoke to me, He said these words:

"Son, don't be like any denomination, don't be like other men; you be like Jesus and heal the people as He did."

That was the first time I understood from God's point of view that I had allowed myself to become an echo of other men, and particularly of a denomination, instead of a voice for Jesus Christ with a total commitment to be like Him. In addition to the preaching and teaching I was doing, I was not doing the third part of His ministry —I was not healing the sick in His name.

I didn't find faith for healing where I expected it to be—in the ministries I knew, or in the denomination I was ordained in. I found it by revelational knowledge directly from the Holy Spirit to me through the Word of God.

Among the common people, many of them unchurched, I found faith. To stand on the platform of the big tent and look over the thousands filling it, most of them drawn by my preaching on deliverance for all, and the hope of seeing a miracle or getting healed themselves, you would have been struck by the absence of all but a handful of upper-class people. Of course, I was one of those common people. I felt right at home.

I can remember a few instances when I found faith in influential or wealthy or famous persons. One was a maharajah when I was conducting a crusade in Trivandrum, India. The crowds were averaging seventy thousand people a day. A runner came for me one afternoon from the maharajah of that region. He wanted me to pray for his wife and his mother in his home. He, as a Hindu, and I, as a Christian, were worlds apart in theology.

I talked it over with Bob DeWeese and Tommy Tyson, my co-evangelists at the time. "Do you suppose such a great man in the eyes of the world with all of his wealth and position could have faith?" I asked them. We all felt a compelling influence for me to go. Tommy went with me while Bob preached the afternoon service.

The young maharajah, thirty-seven years old, met us at the door and ushered us in.

I never saw a greater palace. Entering it was like entering a kingdom. Lavishness was everywhere. Sickness, however, is no respecter of persons. The best doctors had tried to bring a cure. The famous and rich maharajah found himself at a point where only a miracle could save his wife and his mother. He had found out a healing evangelist from America was nearby, and he sent for me.

He wished to talk of the faith he had in nirvana, in which he was striving to be one with God. Feeling for the sick women, I asked, "Your Highness, is that greater than demonstrating the compassion of God to heal sick people?"

That had never entered his mind, he said, so intent was he on gaining nirvana in this life. The question was like a rope jerking at him. "Come," he said. "I have heard from my servants attending your crusades of your God healing my people. Please have compassion on my poor wife and mother and heal them."

"Your Highness, I cannot heal. There must be faith present."

"But I have faith. That is why I sent for you."

We walked into the large area where the two women were. Both were very sick. I walked right to them, saying, "Tommy, let's pray for them."

The moment we touched them, we knew they had faith to be healed. His Highness watched open-eyed as his wife and mother rose up, like any common folk experiencing a miraculous healing, and began clapping their hands and praising Jesus.

I told the man Jesus could do for his soul what nirvana could never do, and I asked if he would allow me to lead him in the sinner's prayer. With graciousness he agreed, and Tommy and I felt free to pray for him to receive Jesus of Nazareth as his personal Savior. He thanked us and we left.

A message was sent to me later that week that a change had come in that palace. How much I never learned. One thing is for sure, I found faith in those people. I hadn't expected to find it there, never being in a place like that. I learned a new respect for God's uncanny ability to have faith placed in the hearts of those in whom we sometimes least expect to find it.

_____ *10.* *I Have Practiced, and Do Practice, the Eternal Truth of Sowing and Reaping.*

Bob DeWeese often told me my discovering the principle of sowing and reaping would be the most lasting thing of my ministry. It is the Bible principle of giving and receiving—which I was led by the Lord to call the miracle of seed-faith.

All I knew was that this revelation changed my life once and for all, to first sow a seed of my faith and then to expect to receive a miracle harvest in return from the Lord.

I had been a strict tither. I was taught that if I didn't tithe, I was robbing God, but it was not taught or emphasized by the church leaders that when I stopped robbing Him and started tithing, I could expect Him to give back to me more than I tithed. Also, He would literally rebuke the devourer (Satan) from trying to diminish and destroy my life. (See Mal. 3:10–11.) I didn't grasp God's promise that I was to receive a miracle harvest from my giving to Him. Neither did I grasp the Bible principle that my financial giving or seeding was the giving and seeding of myself to God.

Later in my crusades, when on a given night ten thousand would be present, and an offering was received for the expenses of the crusade, the people averaged giving eight cents apiece. We were continually struggling to meet the budget needs of the crusades, and I had to find a way from the Word of God to change this or my crusades were going to be over for lack of money to pay the bills. I knew the poverty syndrome had to be broken off the people, especially church people.

I can remember going back to my Bible and discovering that Jesus said, "If ye have faith as a grain of mustard seed [as small as a mustard seed], ye shall say unto this mountain, Remove hence to yonder place; and it shall remove; and nothing shall be impossible unto you" (Matt. 17:20). How it struck home to my heart!

Faith has to be like a seed, even if it's only a small seed. A seed is something you sow to reap a harvest, to receive a return. That's its purpose set in motion by the Creator. (See Gen. 8:22 for God's word on seedtime and harvest.) When that seed is sown to God as an act of our faith, it opens the way for us to speak to our mountain of need and command it to be removed, and it will obey us. Jesus added that when we do this, "Nothing shall be impossible unto you." Jesus' incredible teaching on the seed and wrapping our faith around it opened my heart and eyes—wide!

During the next weeks, I sought God to reveal a practical meaning of this to me in ways I could make it simple—and desirable—to His people. Seed-faith had blessed me in that first little "happening" in Enid in which my giving for a new parsonage was returned sevenfold from a totally unexpected source (Art Newfield), and this principle blessed me much more as I gave my tithes to God with a new and clearer understanding that He would give back to me. And if I was expecting it, a miracle harvest from my seed sown, instead of letting it pass me by, I would receive it and have God's supply for myself and my family, plus more from which to seed to God again. I saw that living Christianity is not a system of diminishing return. It is a life of multiplication and the "more abundant life." (See John 10:10.) I can't tell you the awesome effect it had on my believing system as it dawned on me from God Himself.

It was changing things for me personally, but I had not begun to preach it yet. That's when the Lord gave me revelation of the three steps of seed-faith giving: One, *make God your Source.* Two, *sow your seed as an act of your faith in God.* Three, *expect a miracle harvest to follow in due season.* These three keys were entirely new to me from the standpoint of following them step by step.

As to making God my Source, I had been making some serious mistakes by looking to the people in the church I served as my source rather than instruments. Also, I was making them my only source instead of looking to God to open up totally unexpected ways of giving me miracle harvests following my seed sowing as acts of my faith in Him.

I had been getting disappointed too often and having some bitterness in my heart at God (as many people do) for not supplying my needs as He had promised in Malachi 3:10–11 and in Philippians 4:19 and in Scriptures throughout His Word. I saw clearly that I must focus my expectancy solely on God as my Source, as the only One who would cause people and things to be instruments of His supply for me. I was to look to God as my Source of total supply. This really inspired me and gave me new confidence in God.

I remember as a farm boy that when I helped my father put out our crops, we sowed seed first. We never thought of expecting a harvest if we didn't put good seed in good ground first, then cultivate it, and look forward to the time the harvest would grow for reaping. We went into the fields with great expectancy and brought it in to our barn.

I changed my entire attitude toward the spirit of my giving: I became as the farmer who sowed seed out of his need for a harvest. I would give to God what was already His as an act of my faith and my expectation for a miracle return.

I had always been strict in my giving, but I changed from giving as a debt I owed to a seed I sowed, and I sowed it with joy. I saw as God received my seed first, I had given Him something to work with in growing it into harvest for His gospel and to return it to me multiplied in a miracle harvest for the needs of my family—

and for those needs to be more than met so I would have more to give to Him.

Luke 6:38 became very real and personal to me: "Give, and it shall be given unto you; good measure, pressed down, and shaken together, and running over, shall men give into your bosom. For with the same measure that ye mete withal it shall be measured to you again."

It was exhilarating to my whole being and outlook on my future. I saw that expectancy was the final key to receiving what God would return to me in bountiful harvest in every area of my life.

In other words, as I looked to God as my Source, when I made my tithes and offerings as a seed, an act of my faith in Him, He would not fail to send the miracle harvest in both expected ways and unexpected ways, and I was to live in a continual state of expecting to receive!

I saw that since God would be true to these principles by causing reaping to follow sowing, receiving to follow giving, if I sowed, if I gave, He would send the miracle harvest whether I was expecting it or not. If I didn't expect it, when He sent it, I would fail to recognize it, and it would pass me by. That would leave me doubting God and wondering why He didn't care about supplying my needs. The words *Expect a miracle!* became a powerful force in my life, and I shared them with multitudes of people in person and in our television ministry.

The three keys of seed-faith began to work for me as I worked them. The results were miraculous.

First, I continually taught it to myself: *My giving to God is not a debt I owe but a seed I sow*. If it was a debt, I could never pay it. But since "Jesus paid it all" on Calvary, then I, like Him as the seed of David, could make my giving a seed of my faith in God who owns it all, and He said He would multiply our seed sown and increase the fruits of our righteousness. (See 2 Cor. 9:10.) He also said, "Whatsoever a man soweth, that shall he also reap" (Gal. 6:7).

As I began to preach on the miracle of seed-faith, I met stiff resistance from a great number of church leaders and Christian laypeople.

"Why, that's giving to get," they would declare.

"That's demanding God to give back to you."

"There's heresy."

And many other not-so-nice statements.

I wrote a little book in 1970 called *Miracle of Seed-Faith.* Instead of selling it, I gave it as a seed to anyone who asked for it. Soon I was deluged with requests. That little book enabled me to give example after example of how the three keys work for anybody who sows a seed, then trusts God as the Source of supply and starts expecting to receive if he will recognize it when it comes and receive it with a thankful heart.

That little book is available to any who ask for it. It's a joy to give it, for it means I've sown another seed of my faith. And there's always a miracle harvest on the other end of a seed sown to God.

I'm sure there are other secrets that I could mention, but none have been a greater guiding force in my life and ministry than the ten I've just discussed. I thank God for every one of them and especially for *Him.*

CHAPTER 33

PUSH! PUSH! PUSH! ONE MORE TIME!

A S I CLOSE the final pages of my autobiography, I say with great fervency, I'm glad I serve a God who is in the "now." HE *IS*. His stream is always flowing. And every so often He says, "It's time for another level of My move." Then He lays His hand on someone that usually nobody has thought about to bring the move forth. But the King of kings and Lord of lords knows something that we don't know about each of us.

Before I was born, when I was only a thought in the mind of God, I know now He set me aside and breathed His Holy Spirit upon me, so that when I came forth from my mother's womb, the hands of the Holy Spirit pulled me out and put me on new ground. He put a stirring in my heart that was stronger than my rebellion against Him. The day came when I looked up and saw the Daystar, the shining of a new Son, sensed the moving of a new stream, heard the sound of a new Voice, and felt a new presence— the Lord.

I cannot—and will not—deny that God's dream overshadowed my own in a totally different way. His love for me as one of His creation dramatically got my attention and made it unmistakably clear to me that I had come to a fork in the road. I had to choose to obey God or disobey Him.

I knew the disastrous results of disobedience. I remembered my father reading to me the Bible account of Saul, Israel's first king, who had been called to do a great thing but had finally disobeyed God. I remembered God's words to him in his disobedience: "To obey is better than sacrifice" (1 Sam. 15:22). Saul had been trying to substitute sacrifice for simply obeying the Power that was higher than he. The terrifying account of his premature and untimely death stayed with me. (See 1 Sam. 31.)

But I remembered something else: the call of God to unite all Israel and stop the mouths of their adversaries and the onslaughts of their enemies. He raised up another to do this—David, the unknown shepherd boy from the hills of Bethlehem; then later his son, Solomon—and through his obedience the job began to get done and God got the glory and the praise.

Standing at the fork in the road, I chose to obey. I chose to take up the battle against Satan to bring healing and health and the more spiritual abundant life to people on the planet, which is so important.

God once spoke to me and said I was to be

"a forerunner of a mighty healing" that was coming.

I believed God then; I believe Him now that there is much more of the abundant life He is going to reveal. He will speak to many, many more to catch the vision and take it to suffering people everywhere. As one of the forerunners, I believe God cannot be God and do any less.

When there is a great idea of history whose time has come, no matter how much it is misunderstood by people, opposed by those with axes to grind, and held back after repeated attempts to succeed with great outlays of money and faith and effort, it will finally become like waters bursting through a dam, and it will change man's life forever. You can depend on it. God is Life with a constant—and unstoppable—upward swing in His dreams and purpose for mankind.

I have more than forty-eight years invested in taking God's healing power to my generation; in building Him a university based on His authority and the Holy Spirit; and in establishing the largest medical building on one base ever built for the sole purpose of merging God's healing streams of medicine and prayer. However, I never thought of myself as one individual. I was more like a composite of all my staff, all my Partners, all the people I led to Christ, all for whom I prayed to be healed, and all who have prayed for me. I am an individual, and yet I'm not. Each time I attempted to carry out His mandate, I couldn't do it alone.

I am the man God spoke to some twenty-three times. In this book, if you read carefully what I stated God said to me, I believe you will agree that I, a mere man, could never have said the words He used as well as He used a tiny bit. When God speaks audibly to me, His words are distinct, orderly, and perfectly put together as no man can do, and they are completely original and outside my own ability to create. The words are always different as they come forth in their original form.

The fact that I have told others what God has spoken to me has made mine a very controversial calling. The criticism has been steady from the very beginning, increasing all the time, until I had to seek God specifically for ways not to lose my mind, not to strike back and feel bitter, which would have made me useless, and not to quit.

The Lord has been very direct with me, yet oh, so tender, in His replies and in His revelations from His Word to me concerning the controversies that became the rule and not the exception in anything I have undertaken or done. God showed me how the controversies that have swirled around me without any abatement are but a smattering of the violent controversies and attempts on the life of His very own Son, Jesus, that beset Him at all times.

Shortly after Jesus was born, King Herod sent soldiers to Bethlehem to find and kill Him. From that act on, the controversies intensified until the people killed Him at the early age of thirty-three. God told me when the going got too rough I was to stop and read again the four Gospels and Acts. There I would see what controversy really is. When it struck me, I was not to be blindsided by it or let go of God's call on my life. Reading and studying God's Word, particularly anything about Jesus, gave me a solid foundation that nothing of a negative nature has been able to shake.

I must admit that this saved my sanity over and over. Being accused by powerful leaders and groups of things you never even thought of can wear on every nerve in your body. Setting the record straight has its own point in time, and that time is now.

Although I believe my critics have been mostly wrong according to the Scriptures and according to the integrity of my life and ministry, I believe it's a proven fact they have been of enormous benefit in helping me grow, in my becoming tougher and stronger, in my learning how to maintain sweetness of soul, in my not striking back, and in my being able to pray for them with the deepest sincerity of my soul.

Criticism is a fact of life. It isn't going away. Leaders and every child of God must face it according to God's Word.

I've never claimed to be perfect, but I must look not only to my failures, I must look to the successes of what God did in healing so many people through me as His instrument. I live with both failures and successes. That is one way that I believe God builds character in me.

To those people who say they have no ego, I say, Bosh! God made every one of us to be somebody, to act like it, no matter how humble He wants us to be. The important thing is to control the ego and not let it control us.

My sincere efforts have been my best, and I believe that better things are casting their shadows before them.

I have a sermon titled "PUSH! PUSH! PUSH! One More Time!" That's the story of my life. God is still speaking, and I'm still pushing with my shoulders squared back, with my head held high, and with undaunted faith in my heart in God, my Source!

Jesus said, "Out of his belly shall flow rivers of living water" (John 7:38). And those rivers have been moving in me all these years. I'm three-score and seventeen years old, and I know that there is at least one other powerful thing for good I have to do before my angel comes for me. Recently, a man of God I trust gave me a word from God concerning my future. Here it is:

The end is not yet. The end is not yet, for that which I shall do even in these latter days in your life, in your ministry, shall be a new and a fresh thing. Yes, for I've spoken it to thee in the night hours and you've seen it in your spirit. And it's time for it to come forth now.

But My hand is upon you and shall be in even a greater measure. And this shall come, even the fruition of that which I showed you many years ago shall begin to be birthed forth in this day, in this hour. For there's much to be done and the end is not yet. And He shall renew your youth like the eagle.

For that which you have shall be imparted unto many, for a mighty wave of evangelists are being raised up, even in this day and this hour, with a fresh anointing. They shall not be an echo, but they shall be a voice. They shall speak as an oracle of God. They shall go forth. They will not be the same. They are a new breed. Yes, they've broken the mold and things shall be done differently.

And many shall be looking unto the men—the fathers of the faith—who have gone before. And they shall be looking for help and encouragement and for inspiration, and many, saith the Lord, I shall give you and you shall speak a word unto them and their lives shall be touched. For this is the day that I shall visit you in even a new way, saith the Lord.

I have poured out my life with an unquenchable thirst to obey God and not man in every area. My life and my ministry are not over yet. I am healthy, enthusiastic, energetic, still believing, still working, and I won't give up—never, never, never with everything that's in me. I believe that the best is yet to come!

When I say the best is yet to come, I see it in the awesome miracle ministry of my dear young friend, Pastor/Evangelist Benny Hinn, whose crusades are unprecedented in our time, particularly concerning the anointing. There is no auditorium or stadium that holds his crowds. When I'm there with him, I cannot help rejoicing, also weeping for joy that God's signs and miracles do not diminish but keep on increasing.

Benny's bold, uncompromising ministry says "the best is yet to come."

I see it in my own son, Richard, not only as president of Oral Roberts University but a mightily anointed healing evangelist in his own right. The Holy Spirit's working of the gift of the Word of Knowledge (see 1 Cor. 12:8) through him, along with the holy laughter of the Holy Spirit flowing through him, shows me that while my years of ministry and building for God are bringing me closer and closer to my homecoming, Richard's ministry has just begun on a worldwide scale. As I see the miracles, often exceeding what God has done through me, I see the best is yet to come.

I see it in Kenneth and Gloria Copeland, that stalwart, Word-centered, Holy Spirit-anointed couple who flow together as one on television and in crusades across the earth, bringing new hope and deliverance to multimillions. Their lives and ministry say the best is yet to come.

I see it in many others, not the least of which is Rodney Howard-Browne, South Africa's gift to America whose anointing surpasses any I've seen in bringing the "joy of the Lord" to the body of Christ. Like a breath of fresh air, Rodney's ever-increasing faith and ministry are a revelation that the "joy of the Lord is your strength" (Neh. 8:10).

Finally, I'm not worried about God or His eternal purpose being fulfilled in the time we have left. I know if we obey God "we can't go under for going over."